W0036417

THE
TORAH

CLASSICS

First Published 2024

FiNGERPRINT! CLASSICS
Prakash Books

Fingerprint Publishing
@FingerprintP
@fingerprintpublishingbooks
www.fingerprintpublishing.com

ISBN: 978 93 6214 237 5

CONTENTS

GENESIS

בראשית

GENESIS

בְּרֵאשִׁית

CHAPTER 1

¹In the beginning God created the heavens and the earth.

²And the earth was without form, and void; and darkness was upon the face of the deep. And the Spirit of God moved upon the face of the waters.

³And God said, Let there be light: and there was light.

⁴And God saw the light, that it was good: and God divided the light from the darkness.

⁵And God called the light Day, and the darkness he called Night. And the evening and the morning were the first day.

⁶And God said, Let there be a firmament in the midst of the waters, and let it divide the waters from the waters.

⁷And God made the firmament, and divided the waters which were under the firmament from the waters which were above the firmament: and it was so.

⁸And God called the firmament Heaven. And the evening and the morning were the second day.

⁹And God said, Let the waters under the heaven be gathered together unto one place, and let the dry land appear: and it was so.

¹⁰And God called the dry land Earth; and the gathering together of the waters called he Seas: and God saw that it was good.

¹¹And God said, Let the earth bring forth grass, the herb yielding seed, and the fruit tree yielding fruit after his kind, whose seed is in itself, upon the earth: and it was so.

¹²And the earth brought forth grass, and herb yielding seed after his kind, and the tree yielding fruit, whose seed was in itself, after his kind: and God saw that it was good.

¹³And the evening and the morning were the third day.

¹⁴And God said, Let there be lights in the firmament of the heaven to divide the day from the night; and let them be for signs, and for seasons, and for days, and years:

¹⁵And let them be for lights in the firmament of the heaven to give light upon the earth: and it was so.

¹⁶And God made two great lights; the greater light to rule the day, and the lesser light to rule the night: he made the stars also.

17And God set them in the firmament of the heaven to give light upon the earth,

18And to rule over the day and over the night, and to divide the light from the darkness: and God saw that it was good.

19And the evening and the morning were the fourth day.

20And God said, Let the waters bring forth abundantly the moving creature that hath life, and fowl that may fly above the earth in the open firmament of heaven.

21And God created great whales, and every living creature that moveth, which the waters brought forth abundantly, after their kind, and every winged fowl after his kind: and God saw that it was good.

22And God blessed them, saying, Be fruitful, and multiply, and fill the waters in the seas, and let fowl multiply in the earth.

23And the evening and the morning were the fifth day.

24And God said, Let the earth bring forth the living creature after his kind, cattle, and creeping thing, and beast of the earth after his kind: and it was so.

25And God made the beast of the earth after his kind, and cattle after their kind, and every thing that creepeth upon the earth after his kind: and God saw that it was good.

26And God said, Let us make man in our image, after our likeness: and let them have dominion over the fish of the sea, and over the fowl of the air, and over the cattle, and over all the earth, and over every creeping thing that creepeth upon the earth.

27So God created man in his own image, in the image of God created he him; male and female created he them.

28And God blessed them, and God said unto them, Be fruitful, and multiply, and replenish the earth, and subdue it: and have dominion over the fish of the sea, and over the fowl of the air, and over every living thing that moveth upon the earth.

29And God said, Behold, I have given you every herb bearing seed, which is upon the face of all the earth, and every tree, in the which is the fruit of a tree yielding seed; to you it shall be for meat.

30And to every beast of the earth, and to every fowl of the air, and to every thing that creepeth upon the earth, wherein there is life, I have given every green herb for meat: and it was so.

31And God saw every thing that he had made, and, behold, it was very good. And the evening and the morning were the sixth day.

CHAPTER 2

[1]Thus the heavens and the earth were finished, and all the host of them.

[2]And on the seventh day God ended his work which he had made; and he rested on the seventh day from all his work which he had made.

[3]And God blessed the seventh day, and sanctified it: because that in it he had rested from all his work which God created and made.

[4]These are the generations of the heavens and of the earth when they were created, in the day that the LORD God made the earth and the heavens,

[5]And every plant of the field before it was in the earth, and every herb of the field before it grew: for the LORD God had not caused it to rain upon the earth, and there was not a man to till the ground.

[6]But there went up a mist from the earth, and watered the whole face of the ground.

[7]And the LORD God formed man of the dust of the ground, and breathed into his nostrils the breath of life; and man became a living soul.

[8]And the LORD God planted a garden eastward in Eden; and there he put the man whom he had formed.

[9]And out of the ground made the LORD God to grow every tree that is pleasant to the sight, and good for food; the tree of life also in the midst of the garden, and the tree of knowledge of good and evil.

[10]And a river went out of Eden to water the garden; and from thence it was parted, and became into four heads.

[11]The name of the first is Pison: that is it which compasseth the whole land of Havilah, where there is gold;

[12]And the gold of that land is good: there is bdellium and the onyx stone.

[13]And the name of the second river is Gihon: the same is it that compasseth the whole land of Ethiopia.

[14]And the name of the third river is Hiddekel: that is it which goeth toward the east of Assyria. And the fourth river is Euphrates.

[15]And the LORD God took the man, and put him into the garden of Eden to dress it and to keep it.

[16]And the LORD God commanded the man, saying, Of every tree of the garden thou mayest freely eat:

[17]But of the tree of the knowledge of good and evil, thou shalt not eat of it: for in the day that thou eatest thereof thou shalt surely die.

¹⁸And the LORD God said, It is not good that the man should be alone; I will make him an help meet for him.

¹⁹And out of the ground the LORD God formed every beast of the field, and every fowl of the air; and brought them unto Adam to see what he would call them: and whatsoever Adam called every living creature, that was the name thereof.

²⁰And Adam gave names to all cattle, and to the fowl of the air, and to every beast of the field; but for Adam there was not found an help meet for him.

²¹And the LORD God caused a deep sleep to fall upon Adam, and he slept: and he took one of his ribs, and closed up the flesh instead thereof;

²²And the rib, which the LORD God had taken from man, made he a woman, and brought her unto the man.

²³And Adam said, This is now bone of my bones, and flesh of my flesh: she shall be called Woman, because she was taken out of Man.

²⁴Therefore shall a man leave his father and his mother, and shall cleave unto his wife: and they shall be one flesh.

²⁵And they were both naked, the man and his wife, and were not ashamed.

CHAPTER 3

¹Now the serpent was more subtil than any beast of the field which the LORD God had made. And he said unto the woman, Yea, hath God said, Ye shall not eat of every tree of the garden?

²And the woman said unto the serpent, We may eat of the fruit of the trees of the garden:

³But of the fruit of the tree which is in the midst of the garden, God hath said, Ye shall not eat of it, neither shall ye touch it, lest ye die.

⁴And the serpent said unto the woman, Ye shall not surely die:

⁵For God doth know that in the day ye eat thereof, then your eyes shall be opened, and ye shall be as gods, knowing good and evil.

⁶And when the woman saw that the tree was good for food, and that it was pleasant to the eyes, and a tree to be desired to make one wise, she took of the fruit thereof, and did eat, and gave also unto her husband with her; and he did eat.

⁷And the eyes of them both were opened, and they knew that they were naked; and they sewed fig leaves together, and made themselves aprons.

⁸And they heard the voice of the LORD God walking in the garden

in the cool of the day: and Adam and his wife hid themselves from the presence of the LORD God amongst the trees of the garden.

⁹And the LORD God called unto Adam, and said unto him, Where art thou?

¹⁰And he said, I heard thy voice in the garden, and I was afraid, because I was naked; and I hid myself.

¹¹And he said, Who told thee that thou wast naked? Hast thou eaten of the tree, whereof I commanded thee that thou shouldest not eat?

¹²And the man said, The woman whom thou gavest to be with me, she gave me of the tree, and I did eat.

¹³And the LORD God said unto the woman, What is this that thou hast done? And the woman said, The serpent beguiled me, and I did eat.

¹⁴And the LORD God said unto the serpent, Because thou hast done this, thou art cursed above all cattle, and above every beast of the field; upon thy belly shalt thou go, and dust shalt thou eat all the days of thy life:

¹⁵And I will put enmity between thee and the woman, and between thy seed and her seed; it shall bruise thy head, and thou shalt bruise his heel.

¹⁶Unto the woman he said, I will greatly multiply thy sorrow and thy conception; in sorrow thou shalt bring forth children; and thy desire shall be to thy husband, and he shall rule over thee.

¹⁷And unto Adam he said, Because thou hast hearkened unto the voice of thy wife, and hast eaten of the tree, of which I commanded thee, saying, Thou shalt not eat of it: cursed is the ground for thy sake; in sorrow shalt thou eat of it all the days of thy life;

¹⁸Thorns also and thistles shall it bring forth to thee; and thou shalt eat the herb of the field;

¹⁹In the sweat of thy face shalt thou eat bread, till thou return unto the ground; for out of it wast thou taken: for dust thou art, and unto dust shalt thou return.

²⁰And Adam called his wife's name Eve; because she was the mother of all living.

²¹Unto Adam also and to his wife did the LORD God make coats of skins, and clothed them.

²²And the LORD God said, Behold, the man is become as one of us, to know good and evil: and now, lest he put forth his hand, and take also of the tree of life, and eat, and live for ever:

²³Therefore the LORD God sent him forth from the garden of Eden, to till the ground from whence he was taken.

^{24}So he drove out the man; and he placed at the east of the garden of Eden Cherubims, and a flaming sword which turned every way, to keep the way of the tree of life.

CHAPTER 4

^{1}And Adam knew Eve his wife; and she conceived, and bare Cain, and said, I have gotten a man from the LORD.

^{2}And she again bare his brother Abel. And Abel was a keeper of sheep, but Cain was a tiller of the ground.

^{3}And in process of time it came to pass, that Cain brought of the fruit of the ground an offering unto the LORD.

^{4}And Abel, he also brought of the firstlings of his flock and of the fat thereof. And the LORD had respect unto Abel and to his offering:

^{5}But unto Cain and to his offering he had not respect. And Cain was very wroth, and his countenance fell.

^{6}And the LORD said unto Cain, Why art thou wroth? and why is thy countenance fallen?

^{7}If thou doest well, shalt thou not be accepted? and if thou doest not well, sin lieth at the door. And unto thee shall be his desire, and thou shalt rule over him.

^{8}And Cain talked with Abel his brother: and it came to pass, when they were in the field, that Cain rose up against Abel his brother, and slew him.

^{9}And the LORD said unto Cain, Where is Abel thy brother? And he said, I know not: Am I my brother's keeper?

^{10}And he said, What hast thou done? the voice of thy brother's blood crieth unto me from the ground.

^{11}And now art thou cursed from the earth, which hath opened her mouth to receive thy brother's blood from thy hand;

^{12}When thou tillest the ground, it shall not henceforth yield unto thee her strength; a fugitive and a vagabond shalt thou be in the earth.

^{13}And Cain said unto the LORD, My punishment is greater than I can bear.

^{14}Behold, thou hast driven me out this day from the face of the earth; and from thy face shall I be hid; and I shall be a fugitive and a vagabond in the earth; and it shall come to pass, that every one that findeth me shall slay me.

^{15}And the LORD said unto him, Therefore whosoever slayeth Cain, vengeance shall be taken on him sevenfold. And the LORD set a mark upon Cain, lest any finding him should kill him.

¹⁶And Cain went out from the presence of the LORD, and dwelt in the land of Nod, on the east of Eden.

¹⁷And Cain knew his wife; and she conceived, and bare Enoch: and he builded a city, and called the name of the city, after the name of his son, Enoch.

¹⁸And unto Enoch was born Irad: and Irad begat Mehujael: and Mehujael begat Methusael: and Methusael begat Lamech.

¹⁹And Lamech took unto him two wives: the name of the one was Adah, and the name of the other Zillah.

²⁰And Adah bare Jabal: he was the father of such as dwell in tents, and of such as have cattle.

²¹And his brother's name was Jubal: he was the father of all such as handle the harp and organ.

²²And Zillah, she also bare Tubalcain, an instructer of every artificer in brass and iron: and the sister of Tubalcain was Naamah.

²³And Lamech said unto his wives, Adah and Zillah, Hear my voice; ye wives of Lamech, hearken unto my speech: for I have slain a man to my wounding, and a young man to my hurt.

²⁴If Cain shall be avenged sevenfold, truly Lamech seventy and sevenfold.

²⁵And Adam knew his wife again; and she bare a son, and called his name Seth: For God, said she, hath appointed me another seed instead of Abel, whom Cain slew.

²⁶And to Seth, to him also there was born a son; and he called his name Enos: then began men to call upon the name of the LORD.

CHAPTER 5

¹This is the book of the generations of Adam. In the day that God created man, in the likeness of God made he him;

²Male and female created he them; and blessed them, and called their name Adam, in the day when they were created.

³And Adam lived an hundred and thirty years, and begat a son in his own likeness, and after his image; and called his name Seth:

⁴And the days of Adam after he had begotten Seth were eight hundred years: and he begat sons and daughters:

⁵And all the days that Adam lived were nine hundred and thirty years: and he died.

⁶And Seth lived an hundred and five years, and begat Enos:

⁷And Seth lived after he begat Enos eight hundred and seven years, and begat sons and daughters:

⁸And all the days of Seth were nine hundred and twelve years: and he died.

⁹And Enos lived ninety years, and begat Cainan:

¹⁰And Enos lived after he begat Cainan eight hundred and fifteen years, and begat sons and daughters:

¹¹And all the days of Enos were nine hundred and five years: and he died.

¹²And Cainan lived seventy years and begat Mahalaleel:

¹³And Cainan lived after he begat Mahalaleel eight hundred and forty years, and begat sons and daughters:

¹⁴And all the days of Cainan were nine hundred and ten years: and he died.

¹⁵And Mahalaleel lived sixty and five years, and begat Jared:

¹⁶And Mahalaleel lived after he begat Jared eight hundred and thirty years, and begat sons and daughters:

¹⁷And all the days of Mahalaleel were eight hundred ninety and five years: and he died.

¹⁸And Jared lived an hundred sixty and two years, and he begat Enoch:

¹⁹And Jared lived after he begat Enoch eight hundred years, and begat sons and daughters:

²⁰And all the days of Jared were nine hundred sixty and two years: and he died.

²¹And Enoch lived sixty and five years, and begat Methuselah:

²²And Enoch walked with God after he begat Methuselah three hundred years, and begat sons and daughters:

²³And all the days of Enoch were three hundred sixty and five years:

²⁴And Enoch walked with God: and he was not; for God took him.

²⁵And Methuselah lived an hundred eighty and seven years, and begat Lamech.

²⁶And Methuselah lived after he begat Lamech seven hundred eighty and two years, and begat sons and daughters:

²⁷And all the days of Methuselah were nine hundred sixty and nine years: and he died.

²⁸And Lamech lived an hundred eighty and two years, and begat a son:

²⁹And he called his name Noah, saying, This same shall comfort us concerning our work and toil of our hands, because of the ground which the LORD hath cursed.

³⁰And Lamech lived after he begat Noah five hundred ninety and five years, and begat sons and daughters:

³¹And all the days of Lamech were seven hundred seventy and seven years: and he died.

³²And Noah was five hundred years old: and Noah begat Shem, Ham, and Japheth.

CHAPTER 6

¹And it came to pass, when men began to multiply on the face of the earth, and daughters were born unto them,

²That the sons of God saw the daughters of men that they were fair; and they took them wives of all which they chose.

³And the LORD said, My spirit shall not always strive with man, for that he also is flesh: yet his days shall be an hundred and twenty years.

⁴There were giants in the earth in those days; and also after that, when the sons of God came in unto the daughters of men, and they bare children to them, the same became mighty men which were of old, men of renown.

⁵And God saw that the wickedness of man was great in the earth, and that every imagination of the thoughts of his heart was only evil continually.

⁶And it repented the LORD that he had made man on the earth, and it grieved him at his heart.

⁷And the LORD said, I will destroy man whom I have created from the face of the earth; both man, and beast, and the creeping thing, and the fowls of the air; for it repenteth me that I have made them.

⁸But Noah found grace in the eyes of the LORD.

⁹These are the generations of Noah: Noah was a just man and perfect in his generations, and Noah walked with God.

¹⁰And Noah begat three sons, Shem, Ham, and Japheth.

¹¹The earth also was corrupt before God, and the earth was filled with violence.

¹²And God looked upon the earth, and, behold, it was corrupt; for all flesh had corrupted his way upon the earth.

¹³And God said unto Noah, The end of all flesh is come before me; for the earth is filled with violence through them; and, behold, I will destroy them with the earth.

¹⁴Make thee an ark of gopher wood; rooms shalt thou make in the ark, and shalt pitch it within and without with pitch.

¹⁵And this is the fashion which thou shalt make it of: The length of the ark shall be three hundred cubits, the breadth of it fifty cubits, and the height of it thirty cubits.

¹⁶A window shalt thou make to the ark, and in a cubit shalt thou finish it above; and the door of the ark shalt thou set in the side thereof; with lower, second, and third stories shalt thou make it.

¹⁷And, behold, I, even I, do bring a flood of waters upon the earth, to destroy all flesh, wherein is the breath of life, from under heaven; and every thing that is in the earth shall die.

¹⁸But with thee will I establish my covenant; and thou shalt come into the ark, thou, and thy sons, and thy wife, and thy sons' wives with thee.

¹⁹And of every living thing of all flesh, two of every sort shalt thou bring into the ark, to keep them alive with thee; they shall be male and female.

²⁰Of fowls after their kind, and of cattle after their kind, of every creeping thing of the earth after his kind, two of every sort shall come unto thee, to keep them alive.

²¹And take thou unto thee of all food that is eaten, and thou shalt gather it to thee; and it shall be for food for thee, and for them.

²²Thus did Noah; according to all that God commanded him, so did he.

CHAPTER 7

¹And the LORD said unto Noah, Come thou and all thy house into the ark; for thee have I seen righteous before me in this generation.

²Of every clean beast thou shalt take to thee by sevens, the male and his female: and of beasts that are not clean by two, the male and his female.

³Of fowls also of the air by sevens, the male and the female; to keep seed alive upon the face of all the earth.

⁴For yet seven days, and I will cause it to rain upon the earth forty days and forty nights; and every living substance that I have made will I destroy from off the face of the earth.

⁵And Noah did according unto all that the LORD commanded him.

⁶And Noah was six hundred years old when the flood of waters was upon the earth.

⁷And Noah went in, and his sons, and his wife, and his sons' wives with him, into the ark, because of the waters of the flood.

⁸Of clean beasts, and of beasts that are not clean, and of fowls, and of every thing that creepeth upon the earth,

⁹There went in two and two unto Noah into the ark, the male and the female, as God had commanded Noah.

¹⁰And it came to pass after seven days, that the waters of the flood were upon the earth.

¹¹In the six hundredth year of Noah's life, in the second month, the seventeenth day of the month, the same day were all the fountains of the great deep broken up, and the windows of heaven were opened.

¹²And the rain was upon the earth forty days and forty nights.

¹³In the selfsame day entered Noah, and Shem, and Ham, and Japheth, the sons of Noah, and Noah's wife, and the three wives of his sons with them, into the ark;

¹⁴They, and every beast after his kind, and all the cattle after their kind, and every creeping thing that creepeth upon the earth after his kind, and every fowl after his kind, every bird of every sort.

¹⁵And they went in unto Noah into the ark, two and two of all flesh, wherein is the breath of life.

¹⁶And they that went in, went in male and female of all flesh, as God had commanded him: and the LORD shut him in.

¹⁷And the flood was forty days upon the earth; and the waters increased, and bare up the ark, and it was lift up above the earth.

¹⁸And the waters prevailed, and were increased greatly upon the earth; and the ark went upon the face of the waters.

¹⁹And the waters prevailed exceedingly upon the earth; and all the high hills, that were under the whole heaven, were covered.

²⁰Fifteen cubits upward did the waters prevail; and the mountains were covered.

²¹And all flesh died that moved upon the earth, both of fowl, and of cattle, and of beast, and of every creeping thing that creepeth upon the earth, and every man:

²²All in whose nostrils was the breath of life, of all that was in the dry land, died.

²³And every living substance was destroyed which was upon the face of the ground, both man, and cattle, and the creeping things, and the fowl of the heaven; and they were destroyed from the earth: and Noah only remained alive, and they that were with him in the ark.

²⁴And the waters prevailed upon the earth an hundred and fifty days.

CHAPTER 8

¹And God remembered Noah, and every living thing, and all the cattle that was with him in the ark:

and God made a wind to pass over the earth, and the waters asswaged;

²The fountains also of the deep and the windows of heaven were stopped, and the rain from heaven was restrained;

³And the waters returned from off the earth continually: and after the end of the hundred and fifty days the waters were abated.

⁴And the ark rested in the seventh month, on the seventeenth day of the month, upon the mountains of Ararat.

⁵And the waters decreased continually until the tenth month: in the tenth month, on the first day of the month, were the tops of the mountains seen.

⁶And it came to pass at the end of forty days, that Noah opened the window of the ark which he had made:

⁷And he sent forth a raven, which went forth to and fro, until the waters were dried up from off the earth.

⁸Also he sent forth a dove from him, to see if the waters were abated from off the face of the ground;

⁹But the dove found no rest for the sole of her foot, and she returned unto him into the ark, for the waters were on the face of the whole earth: then he put forth his hand, and took her, and pulled her in unto him into the ark.

¹⁰And he stayed yet other seven days; and again he sent forth the dove out of the ark;

¹¹And the dove came in to him in the evening; and, lo, in her mouth was an olive leaf pluckt off: so Noah knew that the waters were abated from off the earth.

¹²And he stayed yet other seven days; and sent forth the dove; which returned not again unto him any more.

¹³And it came to pass in the six hundredth and first year, in the first month, the first day of the month, the waters were dried up from off the earth: and Noah removed the covering of the ark, and looked, and, behold, the face of the ground was dry.

¹⁴And in the second month, on the seven and twentieth day of the month, was the earth dried.

¹⁵And God spake unto Noah, saying,

¹⁶Go forth of the ark, thou, and thy wife, and thy sons, and thy sons' wives with thee.

¹⁷Bring forth with thee every living thing that is with thee, of all flesh, both of fowl, and of cattle, and of every creeping thing that creepeth upon the earth; that they may breed abundantly in the earth, and be fruitful, and multiply upon the earth.

¹⁸And Noah went forth, and his sons, and his wife, and his sons' wives with him:

¹⁹Every beast, every creeping thing, and every fowl, and whatsoever creepeth upon the earth, after their kinds, went forth out of the ark.

²⁰And Noah builded an altar unto the LORD; and took of every clean beast, and of every clean fowl, and offered burnt offerings on the altar.

²¹And the LORD smelled a sweet savour; and the LORD said in his heart, I will not again curse the ground any more for man's sake; for the imagination of man's heart is evil from his youth; neither will I again smite any more every thing living, as I have done.

²²While the earth remaineth, seedtime and harvest, and cold and heat, and summer and winter, and day and night shall not cease.

CHAPTER 9

¹And God blessed Noah and his sons, and said unto them, Be fruitful, and multiply, and replenish the earth.

²And the fear of you and the dread of you shall be upon every beast of the earth, and upon every fowl of the air, upon all that moveth upon the earth, and upon all the fishes of the sea; into your hand are they delivered.

³Every moving thing that liveth shall be meat for you; even as the green herb have I given you all things.

⁴But flesh with the life thereof, which is the blood thereof, shall ye not eat.

⁵And surely your blood of your lives will I require; at the hand of every beast will I require it, and at the hand of man; at the hand of every man's brother will I require the life of man.

⁶Whoso sheddeth man's blood, by man shall his blood be shed: for in the image of God made he man.

⁷And you, be ye fruitful, and multiply; bring forth abundantly in the earth, and multiply therein.

⁸And God spake unto Noah, and to his sons with him, saying,

⁹And I, behold, I establish my covenant with you, and with your seed after you;

¹⁰And with every living creature that is with you, of the fowl, of the cattle, and of every beast of the earth with you; from all that go out of the ark, to every beast of the earth.

¹¹And I will establish my covenant with you, neither shall all flesh be

cut off any more by the waters of a flood; neither shall there any more be a flood to destroy the earth.

¹²And God said, This is the token of the covenant which I make between me and you and every living creature that is with you, for perpetual generations:

¹³I do set my bow in the cloud, and it shall be for a token of a covenant between me and the earth.

¹⁴And it shall come to pass, when I bring a cloud over the earth, that the bow shall be seen in the cloud:

¹⁵And I will remember my covenant, which is between me and you and every living creature of all flesh; and the waters shall no more become a flood to destroy all flesh.

¹⁶And the bow shall be in the cloud; and I will look upon it, that I may remember the everlasting covenant between God and every living creature of all flesh that is upon the earth.

¹⁷And God said unto Noah, This is the token of the covenant, which I have established between me and all flesh that is upon the earth.

¹⁸And the sons of Noah, that went forth of the ark, were Shem, and Ham, and Japheth: and Ham is the father of Canaan.

¹⁹These are the three sons of Noah: and of them was the whole earth overspread.

²⁰And Noah began to be an husbandman, and he planted a vineyard:

²¹And he drank of the wine, and was drunken; and he was uncovered within his tent.

²²And Ham, the father of Canaan, saw the nakedness of his father, and told his two brethren without.

²³And Shem and Japheth took a garment, and laid it upon both their shoulders, and went backward, and covered the nakedness of their father; and their faces were backward, and they saw not their father's nakedness.

²⁴And Noah awoke from his wine, and knew what his younger son had done unto him.

²⁵And he said, Cursed be Canaan; a servant of servants shall he be unto his brethren.

²⁶And he said, Blessed be the LORD God of Shem; and Canaan shall be his servant.

²⁷God shall enlarge Japheth, and he shall dwell in the tents of Shem; and Canaan shall be his servant.

²⁸And Noah lived after the flood three hundred and fifty years.

²⁹And all the days of Noah were nine hundred and fifty years: and he died.

CHAPTER 10

¹Now these are the generations of the sons of Noah, Shem, Ham, and Japheth: and unto them were sons born after the flood.

²The sons of Japheth; Gomer, and Magog, and Madai, and Javan, and Tubal, and Meshech, and Tiras.

³And the sons of Gomer; Ashkenaz, and Riphath, and Togarmah.

⁴And the sons of Javan; Elishah, and Tarshish, Kittim, and Dodanim.

⁵By these were the isles of the Gentiles divided in their lands; every one after his tongue, after their families, in their nations.

⁶And the sons of Ham; Cush, and Mizraim, and Phut, and Canaan.

⁷And the sons of Cush; Seba, and Havilah, and Sabtah, and Raamah, and Sabtechah: and the sons of Raamah; Sheba, and Dedan.

⁸And Cush begat Nimrod: he began to be a mighty one in the earth.

⁹He was a mighty hunter before the LORD: wherefore it is said, Even as Nimrod the mighty hunter before the LORD.

¹⁰And the beginning of his kingdom was Babel, and Erech, and Accad, and Calneh, in the land of Shinar.

¹¹Out of that land went forth Asshur, and builded Nineveh, and the city Rehoboth, and Calah,

¹²And Resen between Nineveh and Calah: the same is a great city.

¹³And Mizraim begat Ludim, and Anamim, and Lehabim, and Naphtuhim,

¹⁴And Pathrusim, and Casluhim, (out of whom came Philistim,) and Caphtorim.

¹⁵And Canaan begat Sidon his first born, and Heth, ¹⁶And the Jebusite, and the Amorite, and the Girgasite,

¹⁷And the Hivite, and the Arkite, and the Sinite,

¹⁸And the Arvadite, and the Zemarite, and the Hamathite: and afterward were the families of the Canaanites spread abroad.

¹⁹And the border of the Canaanites was from Sidon, as thou comest to Gerar, unto Gaza; as thou goest, unto Sodom, and Gomorrah, and Admah, and Zeboim, even unto Lasha.

²⁰These are the sons of Ham, after their families, after their tongues, in their countries, and in their nations.

²¹Unto Shem also, the father of all the children of Eber, the brother of Japheth the elder, even to him were children born.

²²The children of Shem; Elam, and Asshur, and Arphaxad, and Lud, and Aram.

²³And the children of Aram; Uz, and Hul, and Gether, and Mash.

²⁴And Arphaxad begat Salah; and Salah begat Eber.

²⁵And unto Eber were born two sons: the name of one was Peleg; for in his days was the earth divided; and his brother's name was Joktan.

²⁶And Joktan begat Almodad, and Sheleph, and Hazarmaveth, and Jerah,

²⁷And Hadoram, and Uzal, and Diklah,

²⁸And Obal, and Abimael, and Sheba,

²⁹And Ophir, and Havilah, and Jobab: all these were the sons of Joktan.

³⁰And their dwelling was from Mesha, as thou goest unto Sephar a mount of the east.

³¹These are the sons of Shem, after their families, after their tongues, in their lands, after their nations.

³²These are the families of the sons of Noah, after their generations, in their nations: and by these were the nations divided in the earth after the flood.

CHAPTER 11

¹And the whole earth was of one language, and of one speech.

²And it came to pass, as they journeyed from the east, that they found a plain in the land of Shinar; and they dwelt there.

³And they said one to another, Go to, let us make brick, and burn them thoroughly. And they had brick for stone, and slime had they for morter.

⁴And they said, Go to, let us build us a city and a tower, whose top may reach unto heaven; and let us make us a name, lest we be scattered abroad upon the face of the whole earth.

⁵And the LORD came down to see the city and the tower, which the children of men builded.

⁶And the LORD said, Behold, the people is one, and they have all one language; and this they begin to do: and now nothing will be restrained from them, which they have imagined to do.

⁷Go to, let us go down, and there confound their language, that they may not understand one another's speech.

⁸So the LORD scattered them abroad from thence upon the face of all the earth: and they left off to build the city.

⁹Therefore is the name of it called Babel; because the LORD did there confound the language of all the earth: and from thence did the LORD scatter them abroad upon the face of all the earth.

¹⁰These are the generations of Shem: Shem was an hundred years old, and begat Arphaxad two years after the flood:

¹¹And Shem lived after he begat Arphaxad five hundred years, and begat sons and daughters.

¹²And Arphaxad lived five and thirty years, and begat Salah:

¹³And Arphaxad lived after he begat Salah four hundred and three years, and begat sons and daughters.

¹⁴And Salah lived thirty years, and begat Eber:

¹⁵And Salah lived after he begat Eber four hundred and three years, and begat sons and daughters.

¹⁶And Eber lived four and thirty years, and begat Peleg:

¹⁷And Eber lived after he begat Peleg four hundred and thirty years, and begat sons and daughters.

¹⁸And Peleg lived thirty years, and begat Reu:

¹⁹And Peleg lived after he begat Reu two hundred and nine years, and begat sons and daughters.

²⁰And Reu lived two and thirty years, and begat Serug:

²¹And Reu lived after he begat Serug two hundred and seven years, and begat sons and daughters.

²²And Serug lived thirty years, and begat Nahor:

²³And Serug lived after he begat Nahor two hundred years, and begat sons and daughters.

²⁴And Nahor lived nine and twenty years, and begat Terah:

²⁵And Nahor lived after he begat Terah an hundred and nineteen years, and begat sons and daughters.

²⁶And Terah lived seventy years, and begat Abram, Nahor, and Haran.

²⁷Now these are the generations of Terah: Terah begat Abram, Nahor, and Haran; and Haran begat Lot.

²⁸And Haran died before his father Terah in the land of his nativity, in Ur of the Chaldees.

²⁹And Abram and Nahor took them wives: the name of Abram's wife was Sarai; and the name of Nahor's wife, Milcah, the daughter of Haran, the father of Milcah, and the father of Iscah.

³⁰But Sarai was barren; she had no child.

³¹And Terah took Abram his son, and Lot the son of Haran his son's son, and Sarai his daughter in law, his son Abram's wife; and they

went forth with them from Ur of the Chaldees, to go into the land of Canaan; and they came unto Haran, and dwelt there.

³²And the days of Terah were two hundred and five years: and Terah died in Haran.

CHAPTER 12

¹Now the LORD had said unto Abram, Get thee out of thy country, and from thy kindred, and from thy father's house, unto a land that I will shew thee:

²And I will make of thee a great nation, and I will bless thee, and make thy name great; and thou shalt be a blessing:

³And I will bless them that bless thee, and curse him that curseth thee: and in thee shall all families of the earth be blessed.

⁴So Abram departed, as the LORD had spoken unto him; and Lot went with him: and Abram was seventy and five years old when he departed out of Haran.

⁵And Abram took Sarai his wife, and Lot his brother's son, and all their substance that they had gathered, and the souls that they had gotten in Haran; and they went forth to go into the land of Canaan;

and into the land of Canaan they came.

⁶And Abram passed through the land unto the place of Sichem, unto the plain of Moreh. And the Canaanite was then in the land.

⁷And the LORD appeared unto Abram, and said, Unto thy seed will I give this land: and there builded he an altar unto the LORD, who appeared unto him.

⁸And he removed from thence unto a mountain on the east of Bethel, and pitched his tent, having Bethel on the west, and Hai on the east: and there he builded an altar unto the LORD, and called upon the name of the LORD.

⁹And Abram journeyed, going on still toward the south.

¹⁰And there was a famine in the land: and Abram went down into Egypt to sojourn there; for the famine was grievous in the land.

¹¹And it came to pass, when he was come near to enter into Egypt, that he said unto Sarai his wife, Behold now, I know that thou art a fair woman to look upon:

¹²Therefore it shall come to pass, when the Egyptians shall see thee, that they shall say, This is his wife: and they will kill me, but they will save thee alive.

¹³Say, I pray thee, thou art my sister: that it may be well with me

for thy sake; and my soul shall live because of thee.

¹⁴And it came to pass, that, when Abram was come into Egypt, the Egyptians beheld the woman that she was very fair.

¹⁵The princes also of Pharaoh saw her, and commended her before Pharaoh: and the woman was taken into Pharaoh's house.

¹⁶And he entreated Abram well for her sake: and he had sheep, and oxen, and he asses, and menservants, and maidservants, and she asses, and camels.

¹⁷And the LORD plagued Pharaoh and his house with great plagues because of Sarai Abram's wife.

¹⁸And Pharaoh called Abram and said, What is this that thou hast done unto me? why didst thou not tell me that she was thy wife?

¹⁹Why saidst thou, She is my sister? so I might have taken her to me to wife: now therefore behold thy wife, take her, and go thy way.

²⁰And Pharaoh commanded his men concerning him: and they sent him away, and his wife, and all that he had.

CHAPTER 13

¹And Abram went up out of Egypt, he, and his wife, and all that he had, and Lot with him, into the south.

²And Abram was very rich in cattle, in silver, and in gold.

³And he went on his journeys from the south even to Bethel, unto the place where his tent had been at the beginning, between Bethel and Hai;

⁴Unto the place of the altar, which he had make there at the first: and there Abram called on the name of the LORD.

⁵And Lot also which went with Abram, had flocks, and herds, and tents.

⁶And the land was not able to bear them, that they might dwell together: for their substance was great, so that they could not dwell together.

⁷And there was a strife between the herdmen of Abram's cattle and the herdmen of Lot's cattle: and the Canaanite and the Perizzite dwelled then in the land.

⁸And Abram said unto Lot, Let there be no strife, I pray thee, between me and thee, and between my herdmen and thy herdmen; for we be brethren.

⁹Is not the whole land before thee? separate thyself, I pray thee, from me: if thou wilt take the left hand, then I will go to the right; or if thou depart to the right hand, then I will go to the left.

¹⁰And Lot lifted up his eyes, and beheld all the plain of Jordan, that it was well watered every where, before the LORD destroyed Sodom and Gomorrah, even as the garden of the LORD, like the land of Egypt, as thou comest unto Zoar.

¹¹Then Lot chose him all the plain of Jordan; and Lot journeyed east: and they separated themselves the one from the other.

¹²Abram dwelled in the land of Canaan, and Lot dwelled in the cities of the plain, and pitched his tent toward Sodom.

¹³But the men of Sodom were wicked and sinners before the LORD exceedingly.

¹⁴And the LORD said unto Abram, after that Lot was separated from him, Lift up now thine eyes, and look from the place where thou art northward, and southward, and eastward, and westward:

¹⁵For all the land which thou seest, to thee will I give it, and to thy seed for ever.

¹⁶And I will make thy seed as the dust of the earth: so that if a man can number the dust of the earth, then shall thy seed also be numbered.

¹⁷Arise, walk through the land in the length of it and in the breadth of it; for I will give it unto thee.

¹⁸Then Abram removed his tent, and came and dwelt in the plain of Mamre, which is in Hebron, and built there an altar unto the LORD.

CHAPTER 14

¹And it came to pass in the days of Amraphel king of Shinar, Arioch king of Ellasar, Chedorlaomer king of Elam, and Tidal king of nations;

²That these made war with Bera king of Sodom, and with Birsha king of Gomorrah, Shinab king of Admah, and Shemeber king of Zeboiim, and the king of Bela, which is Zoar.

³All these were joined together in the vale of Siddim, which is the salt sea.

⁴Twelve years they served Chedorlaomer, and in the thirteenth year they rebelled.

⁵And in the fourteenth year came Chedorlaomer, and the kings that were with him, and smote the Rephaims in Ashteroth Karnaim, and the Zuzims in Ham, and the Emins in Shaveh Kiriathaim,

⁶And the Horites in their mount Seir, unto Elparan, which is by the wilderness.

⁷And they returned, and came to Enmishpat, which is Kadesh, and smote all the country of the Amalekites, and also the Amorites, that dwelt in Hazezontamar.

⁸And there went out the king of Sodom, and the king of Gomorrah, and the king of Admah, and the king of Zeboiim, and the king of Bela (the same is Zoar;) and they joined battle with them in the vale of Siddim;

⁹With Chedorlaomer the king of Elam, and with Tidal king of nations, and Amraphel king of Shinar, and Arioch king of Ellasar; four kings with five.

¹⁰And the vale of Siddim was full of slimepits; and the kings of Sodom and Gomorrah fled, and fell there; and they that remained fled to the mountain.

¹¹And they took all the goods of Sodom and Gomorrah, and all their victuals, and went their way.

¹²And they took Lot, Abram's brother's son, who dwelt in Sodom, and his goods, and departed.

¹³And there came one that had escaped, and told Abram the Hebrew; for he dwelt in the plain of Mamre the Amorite, brother of Eshcol, and brother of Aner: and these were confederate with Abram.

¹⁴And when Abram heard that his brother was taken captive, he armed his trained servants, born in his own house, three hundred and eighteen, and pursued them unto Dan.

¹⁵And he divided himself against them, he and his servants, by night, and smote them, and pursued them unto Hobah, which is on the left hand of Damascus.

¹⁶And he brought back all the goods, and also brought again his brother Lot, and his goods, and the women also, and the people.

¹⁷And the king of Sodom went out to meet him after his return from the slaughter of Chedorlaomer, and of the kings that were with him, at the valley of Shaveh, which is the king's dale.

¹⁸And Melchizedek king of Salem brought forth bread and wine: and he was the priest of the most high God.

¹⁹And he blessed him, and said, Blessed be Abram of the most high God, possessor of heaven and earth:

²⁰And blessed be the most high God, which hath delivered thine enemies into thy hand. And he gave him tithes of all.

²¹And the king of Sodom said unto Abram, Give me the persons, and take the goods to thyself.

²²And Abram said to the king of Sodom, I have lift up mine hand unto the LORD, the most high God, the possessor of heaven and earth,

²³That I will not take from a thread even to a shoelatchet, and that I will not take any thing that is thine, lest thou shouldest say, I have made Abram rich:

²⁴Save only that which the young men have eaten, and the portion of the men which went with me, Aner, Eshcol, and Mamre; let them take their portion.

CHAPTER 15

¹After these things the word of the LORD came unto Abram in a vision, saying, Fear not, Abram: I am thy shield, and thy exceeding great reward.

²And Abram said, LORD God, what wilt thou give me, seeing I go childless, and the steward of my house is this Eliezer of Damascus?

³And Abram said, Behold, to me thou hast given no seed: and, lo, one born in my house is mine heir.

⁴And, behold, the word of the LORD came unto him, saying, This shall not be thine heir; but he that shall come forth out of thine own bowels shall be thine heir.

⁵And he brought him forth abroad, and said, Look now toward heaven, and tell the stars, if thou be able to number them: and he said unto him, So shall thy seed be.

⁶And he believed in the LORD; and he counted it to him for righteousness.

⁷And he said unto him, I am the LORD that brought thee out of Ur of the Chaldees, to give thee this land to inherit it.

⁸And he said, LORD God, whereby shall I know that I shall inherit it?

⁹And he said unto him, Take me an heifer of three years old, and a she goat of three years old, and a ram of three years old, and a turtledove, and a young pigeon.

¹⁰And he took unto him all these, and divided them in the midst, and laid each piece one against another: but the birds divided he not.

¹¹And when the fowls came down upon the carcases, Abram drove them away.

¹²And when the sun was going down, a deep sleep fell upon Abram; and, lo, an horror of great darkness fell upon him.

¹³And he said unto Abram, Know of a surety that thy seed shall be a stranger in a land that is not theirs, and shall serve them; and they shall afflict them four hundred years;

¹⁴And also that nation, whom they shall serve, will I judge: and afterward shall they come out with great substance.

¹⁵And thou shalt go to thy fathers in peace; thou shalt be buried in a good old age.

¹⁶But in the fourth generation they shall come hither again: for the iniquity of the Amorites is not yet full.

¹⁷And it came to pass, that, when the sun went down, and it was dark, behold a smoking furnace, and a burning lamp that passed between those pieces.

¹⁸In the same day the LORD made a covenant with Abram, saying, Unto thy seed have I given this land, from the river of Egypt unto the great river, the river Euphrates:

¹⁹The Kenites, and the Kenizzites, and the Kadmonites,

²⁰And the Hittites, and the Perizzites, and the Rephaims,

²¹And the Amorites, and the Canaanites, and the Girgashites, and the Jebusites.

CHAPTER 16

¹Now Sarai Abram's wife bare him no children: and she had an handmaid, an Egyptian, whose name was Hagar.

²And Sarai said unto Abram, Behold now, the LORD hath restrained me from bearing: I pray thee, go in unto my maid; it may be that I may obtain children by her. And Abram hearkened to the voice of Sarai.

³And Sarai Abram's wife took Hagar her maid the Egyptian, after Abram had dwelt ten years in the land of Canaan, and gave her to her husband Abram to be his wife.

⁴And he went in unto Hagar, and she conceived: and when she saw that she had conceived, her mistress was despised in her eyes.

⁵And Sarai said unto Abram, My wrong be upon thee: I have given my maid into thy bosom; and when she saw that she had conceived, I was despised in her eyes: the LORD judge between me and thee.

⁶But Abram said unto Sarai, Behold, thy maid is in thine hand; do to her as it pleaseth thee. And when Sarai dealt hardly with her, she fled from her face.

⁷And the angel of the LORD found her by a fountain of water in the wilderness, by the fountain in the way to Shur.

⁸And he said, Hagar, Sarai's maid, whence camest thou? and whither wilt thou go? And she said, I flee from the face of my mistress Sarai.

⁹And the angel of the LORD said unto her, Return to thy mistress, and submit thyself under her hands.

¹⁰And the angel of the LORD said unto her, I will multiply thy seed exceedingly, that it shall not be numbered for multitude.

¹¹And the angel of the LORD said unto her, Behold, thou art with child and shalt bear a son, and shalt call his name Ishmael; because the LORD hath heard thy affliction.

¹²And he will be a wild man; his hand will be against every man, and every man's hand against him; and he shall dwell in the presence of all his brethren.

¹³And she called the name of the LORD that spake unto her, Thou God seest me: for she said, Have I also here looked after him that seeth me?

¹⁴Wherefore the well was called Beer-lahai-roi; behold, it is between Kadesh and Bered.

¹⁵And Hagar bare Abram a son: and Abram called his son's name, which Hagar bare, Ishmael.

¹⁶And Abram was fourscore and six years old, when Hagar bare Ishmael to Abram.

CHAPTER 17

¹And when Abram was ninety years old and nine, the LORD appeared to Abram, and said unto him, I am the Almighty God; walk before me, and be thou perfect.

²And I will make my covenant between me and thee, and will multiply thee exceedingly.

³And Abram fell on his face: and God talked with him, saying,

⁴As for me, behold, my covenant is with thee, and thou shalt be a father of many nations.

⁵Neither shall thy name any more be called Abram, but thy name shall be Abraham; for a father of many nations have I made thee.

⁶And I will make thee exceeding fruitful, and I will make nations of thee, and kings shall come out of thee.

⁷And I will establish my covenant between me and thee and thy seed after thee in their generations for an everlasting covenant, to be a God unto thee, and to thy seed after thee.

⁸And I will give unto thee, and to thy seed after thee, the land wherein thou art a stranger, all the land of Canaan, for an everlasting possession; and I will be their God.

⁹And God said unto Abraham, Thou shalt keep my covenant

therefore, thou, and thy seed after thee in their generations.

¹⁰This is my covenant, which ye shall keep, between me and you and thy seed after thee; Every man child among you shall be circumcised.

¹¹And ye shall circumcise the flesh of your foreskin; and it shall be a token of the covenant betwixt me and you.

¹²And he that is eight days old shall be circumcised among you, every man child in your generations, he that is born in the house, or bought with money of any stranger, which is not of thy seed.

¹³He that is born in thy house, and he that is bought with thy money, must needs be circumcised: and my covenant shall be in your flesh for an everlasting covenant.

¹⁴And the uncircumcised man child whose flesh of his foreskin is not circumcised, that soul shall be cut off from his people; he hath broken my covenant.

¹⁵And God said unto Abraham, As for Sarai thy wife, thou shalt not call her name Sarai, but Sarah shall her name be.

¹⁶And I will bless her, and give thee a son also of her: yea, I will bless her, and she shall be a mother of nations; kings of people shall be of her.

¹⁷Then Abraham fell upon his face, and laughed, and said in his heart, Shall a child be born unto him that is an hundred years old? and shall Sarah, that is ninety years old, bear?

¹⁸And Abraham said unto God, O that Ishmael might live before thee!

¹⁹And God said, Sarah thy wife shall bear thee a son indeed; and thou shalt call his name Isaac: and I will establish my covenant with him for an everlasting covenant, and with his seed after him.

²⁰And as for Ishmael, I have heard thee: Behold, I have blessed him, and will make him fruitful, and will multiply him exceedingly; twelve princes shall he beget, and I will make him a great nation.

²¹But my covenant will I establish with Isaac, which Sarah shall bear unto thee at this set time in the next year.

²²And he left off talking with him, and God went up from Abraham.

²³And Abraham took Ishmael his son, and all that were born in his house, and all that were bought with his money, every male among the men of Abraham's house; and circumcised the flesh of their foreskin in the selfsame day, as God had said unto him.

²⁴And Abraham was ninety years old and nine, when he was circumcised in the flesh of his foreskin.

²⁵ And Ishmael his son was thirteen years old, when he was circumcised in the flesh of his foreskin.

²⁶ In the selfsame day was Abraham circumcised, and Ishmael his son.

²⁷ And all the men of his house, born in the house, and bought with money of the stranger, were circumcised with him.

CHAPTER 18

¹ And the LORD appeared unto him in the plains of Mamre: and he sat in the tent door in the heat of the day;

² And he lift up his eyes and looked, and, lo, three men stood by him: and when he saw them, he ran to meet them from the tent door, and bowed himself toward the ground,

³ And said, My LORD, if now I have found favour in thy sight, pass not away, I pray thee, from thy servant:

⁴ Let a little water, I pray you, be fetched, and wash your feet, and rest yourselves under the tree:

⁵ And I will fetch a morsel of bread, and comfort ye your hearts; after that ye shall pass on: for therefore are ye come to your servant. And they said, So do, as thou hast said.

⁶ And Abraham hastened into the tent unto Sarah, and said, Make ready quickly three measures of fine meal, knead it, and make cakes upon the hearth.

⁷ And Abraham ran unto the herd, and fetcht a calf tender and good, and gave it unto a young man; and he hasted to dress it.

⁸ And he took butter, and milk, and the calf which he had dressed, and set it before them; and he stood by them under the tree, and they did eat.

⁹ And they said unto him, Where is Sarah thy wife? And he said, Behold, in the tent.

¹⁰ And he said, I will certainly return unto thee according to the time of life; and, lo, Sarah thy wife shall have a son. And Sarah heard it in the tent door, which was behind him.

¹¹ Now Abraham and Sarah were old and well stricken in age; and it ceased to be with Sarah after the manner of women.

¹² Therefore Sarah laughed within herself, saying, After I am waxed old shall I have pleasure, my lord being old also?

¹³ And the LORD said unto Abraham, Wherefore did Sarah laugh, saying, Shall I of a surety bear a child, which am old?

¹⁴ Is any thing too hard for the LORD? At the time appointed I will

return unto thee, according to the time of life, and Sarah shall have a son.

¹⁵Then Sarah denied, saying, I laughed not; for she was afraid. And he said, Nay; but thou didst laugh.

¹⁶And the men rose up from thence, and looked toward Sodom: and Abraham went with them to bring them on the way.

¹⁷And the LORD said, Shall I hide from Abraham that thing which I do;

¹⁸Seeing that Abraham shall surely become a great and mighty nation, and all the nations of the earth shall be blessed in him?

¹⁹For I know him, that he will command his children and his household after him, and they shall keep the way of the LORD, to do justice and judgment; that the LORD may bring upon Abraham that which he hath spoken of him.

²⁰And the LORD said, Because the cry of Sodom and Gomorrah is great, and because their sin is very grievous;

²¹I will go down now, and see whether they have done altogether according to the cry of it, which is come unto me; and if not, I will know.

²²And the men turned their faces from thence, and went toward Sodom: but Abraham stood yet before the LORD.

²³And Abraham drew near, and said, Wilt thou also destroy the righteous with the wicked?

²⁴Peradventure there be fifty righteous within the city: wilt thou also destroy and not spare the place for the fifty righteous that are therein?

²⁵That be far from thee to do after this manner, to slay the righteous with the wicked: and that the righteous should be as the wicked, that be far from thee: Shall not the Judge of all the earth do right?

²⁶And the LORD said, If I find in Sodom fifty righteous within the city, then I will spare all the place for their sakes.

²⁷And Abraham answered and said, Behold now, I have taken upon me to speak unto the LORD, which am but dust and ashes:

²⁸Peradventure there shall lack five of the fifty righteous: wilt thou destroy all the city for lack of five? And he said, If I find there forty and five, I will not destroy it.

²⁹And he spake unto him yet again, and said, Peradventure there shall be forty found there. And he said, I will not do it for forty's sake.

³⁰And he said unto him, Oh let not the LORD be angry, and I will speak: Peradventure there shall thirty be found there. And he said, I will not do it, if I find thirty there.

³¹And he said, Behold now, I have taken upon me to speak unto the LORD: Peradventure there shall be twenty found there. And he said, I will not destroy it for twenty's sake.

³²And he said, Oh let not the LORD be angry, and I will speak yet but this once: Peradventure ten shall be found there. And he said, I will not destroy it for ten's sake.

³³And the LORD went his way, as soon as he had left communing with Abraham: and Abraham returned unto his place.

CHAPTER 19

¹And there came two angels to Sodom at even; and Lot sat in the gate of Sodom: and Lot seeing them rose up to meet them; and he bowed himself with his face toward the ground;

²And he said, Behold now, my lords, turn in, I pray you, into your servant's house, and tarry all night, and wash your feet, and ye shall rise up early, and go on your ways. And they said, Nay; but we will abide in the street all night.

³And he pressed upon them greatly; and they turned in unto him, and entered into his house;

and he made them a feast, and did bake unleavened bread, and they did eat.

⁴But before they lay down, the men of the city, even the men of Sodom, compassed the house round, both old and young, all the people from every quarter:

⁵And they called unto Lot, and said unto him, Where are the men which came in to thee this night? bring them out unto us, that we may know them.

⁶And Lot went out at the door unto them, and shut the door after him,

⁷And said, I pray you, brethren, do not so wickedly.

⁸Behold now, I have two daughters which have not known man; let me, I pray you, bring them out unto you, and do ye to them as is good in your eyes: only unto these men do nothing; for therefore came they under the shadow of my roof.

⁹And they said, Stand back. And they said again, This one fellow came in to sojourn, and he will needs be a judge: now will we deal worse with thee, than with them. And they pressed sore upon the man, even Lot, and came near to break the door.

¹⁰But the men put forth their hand, and pulled Lot into the house to them, and shut to the door.

11And they smote the men that were at the door of the house with blindness, both small and great: so that they wearied themselves to find the door.

12And the men said unto Lot, Hast thou here any besides? son in law, and thy sons, and thy daughters, and whatsoever thou hast in the city, bring them out of this place:

13For we will destroy this place, because the cry of them is waxen great before the face of the LORD; and the LORD hath sent us to destroy it.

14And Lot went out, and spake unto his sons in law, which married his daughters, and said, Up, get you out of this place; for the LORD will destroy this city. But he seemed as one that mocked unto his sons in law.

15And when the morning arose, then the angels hastened Lot, saying, Arise, take thy wife, and thy two daughters, which are here; lest thou be consumed in the iniquity of the city.

16And while he lingered, the men laid hold upon his hand, and upon the hand of his wife, and upon the hand of his two daughters; the LORD being merciful unto him: and they brought him forth, and set him without the city.

17And it came to pass, when they had brought them forth abroad, that he said, Escape for thy life; look not behind thee, neither stay thou in all the plain; escape to the mountain, lest thou be consumed.

18And Lot said unto them, Oh, not so, my LORD:

19Behold now, thy servant hath found grace in thy sight, and thou hast magnified thy mercy, which thou hast shewed unto me in saving my life; and I cannot escape to the mountain, lest some evil take me, and I die:

20Behold now, this city is near to flee unto, and it is a little one: Oh, let me escape thither, (is it not a little one?) and my soul shall live.

21And he said unto him, See, I have accepted thee concerning this thing also, that I will not overthrow this city, for the which thou hast spoken.

22Haste thee, escape thither; for I cannot do anything till thou be come thither. Therefore the name of the city was called Zoar.

23The sun was risen upon the earth when Lot entered into Zoar.

24Then the LORD rained upon Sodom and upon Gomorrah brimstone and fire from the LORD out of heaven;

25And he overthrew those cities, and all the plain, and all the inhabitants of the cities, and that which grew upon the ground.

26But his wife looked back from behind him, and she became a pillar of salt.

27And Abraham gat up early in the morning to the place where he stood before the LORD:

28And he looked toward Sodom and Gomorrah, and toward all the land of the plain, and beheld, and, lo, the smoke of the country went up as the smoke of a furnace.

29And it came to pass, when God destroyed the cities of the plain, that God remembered Abraham, and sent Lot out of the midst of the overthrow, when he overthrew the cities in the which Lot dwelt.

30And Lot went up out of Zoar, and dwelt in the mountain, and his two daughters with him; for he feared to dwell in Zoar: and he dwelt in a cave, he and his two daughters.

31And the firstborn said unto the younger, Our father is old, and there is not a man in the earth to come in unto us after the manner of all the earth:

32Come, let us make our father drink wine, and we will lie with him, that we may preserve seed of our father.

33And they made their father drink wine that night: and the firstborn went in, and lay with her father; and he perceived not when she lay down, nor when she arose.

34And it came to pass on the morrow, that the firstborn said unto the younger, Behold, I lay yesternight with my father: let us make him drink wine this night also; and go thou in, and lie with him, that we may preserve seed of our father.

35And they made their father drink wine that night also: and the younger arose, and lay with him; and he perceived not when she lay down, nor when she arose.

36Thus were both the daughters of Lot with child by their father.

37And the first born bare a son, and called his name Moab: the same is the father of the Moabites unto this day.

38And the younger, she also bare a son, and called his name Benammi: the same is the father of the children of Ammon unto this day.

CHAPTER 20

1And Abraham journeyed from thence toward the south country, and dwelled between Kadesh and Shur, and sojourned in Gerar.

2And Abraham said of Sarah his wife, She is my sister: and Abimelech king of Gerar sent, and took Sarah.

³But God came to Abimelech in a dream by night, and said to him, Behold, thou art but a dead man, for the woman which thou hast taken; for she is a man's wife.

⁴But Abimelech had not come near her: and he said, LORD, wilt thou slay also a righteous nation?

⁵Said he not unto me, She is my sister? and she, even she herself said, He is my brother: in the integrity of my heart and innocency of my hands have I done this.

⁶And God said unto him in a dream, Yea, I know that thou didst this in the integrity of thy heart; for I also withheld thee from sinning against me: therefore suffered I thee not to touch her.

⁷Now therefore restore the man his wife; for he is a prophet, and he shall pray for thee, and thou shalt live: and if thou restore her not, know thou that thou shalt surely die, thou, and all that are thine.

⁸Therefore Abimelech rose early in the morning, and called all his servants, and told all these things in their ears: and the men were sore afraid.

⁹Then Abimelech called Abraham, and said unto him, What hast thou done unto us? and what have I offended thee, that thou hast brought on me and on my kingdom a great sin? thou hast done deeds unto me that ought not to be done.

¹⁰And Abimelech said unto Abraham, What sawest thou, that thou hast done this thing?

¹¹And Abraham said, Because I thought, Surely the fear of God is not in this place; and they will slay me for my wife's sake.

¹²And yet indeed she is my sister; she is the daughter of my father, but not the daughter of my mother; and she became my wife.

¹³And it came to pass, when God caused me to wander from my father's house, that I said unto her, This is thy kindness which thou shalt shew unto me; at every place whither we shall come, say of me, He is my brother.

¹⁴And Abimelech took sheep, and oxen, and menservants, and womenservants, and gave them unto Abraham, and restored him Sarah his wife.

¹⁵And Abimelech said, Behold, my land is before thee: dwell where it pleaseth thee.

¹⁶And unto Sarah he said, Behold, I have given thy brother a thousand pieces of silver: behold, he is to thee a covering of the eyes, unto all that are with thee, and with all other: thus she was reproved.

¹⁷So Abraham prayed unto God: and God healed Abimelech, and his wife, and his maidservants; and they bare children.

¹⁸For the LORD had fast closed up all the wombs of the house of Abimelech, because of Sarah Abraham's wife.

CHAPTER 21

¹And the LORD visited Sarah as he had said, and the LORD did unto Sarah as he had spoken.

²For Sarah conceived, and bare Abraham a son in his old age, at the set time of which God had spoken to him.

³And Abraham called the name of his son that was born unto him, whom Sarah bare to him, Isaac.

⁴And Abraham circumcised his son Isaac being eight days old, as God had commanded him.

⁵And Abraham was an hundred years old, when his son Isaac was born unto him.

⁶And Sarah said, God hath made me to laugh, so that all that hear will laugh with me.

⁷And she said, Who would have said unto Abraham, that Sarah should have given children suck? for I have born him a son in his old age.

⁸And the child grew, and was weaned: and Abraham made a great feast the same day that Isaac was weaned.

⁹And Sarah saw the son of Hagar the Egyptian, which she had born unto Abraham, mocking.

¹⁰Wherefore she said unto Abraham, Cast out this bondwoman and her son: for the son of this bondwoman shall not be heir with my son, even with Isaac.

¹¹And the thing was very grievous in Abraham's sight because of his son.

¹²And God said unto Abraham, Let it not be grievous in thy sight because of the lad, and because of thy bondwoman; in all that Sarah hath said unto thee, hearken unto her voice; for in Isaac shall thy seed be called.

¹³And also of the son of the bondwoman will I make a nation, because he is thy seed.

¹⁴And Abraham rose up early in the morning, and took bread, and a bottle of water, and gave it unto Hagar, putting it on her shoulder, and the child, and sent her away: and she departed, and wandered in the wilderness of Beer-sheba.

¹⁵And the water was spent in the bottle, and she cast the child under one of the shrubs.

¹⁶And she went, and sat her down over against him a good way off, as it were a bow shot: for she said, Let me not see the death of the child. And she sat over against him, and lift up her voice, and wept.

¹⁷And God heard the voice of the lad; and the angel of God called to Hagar out of heaven, and said unto her, What aileth thee, Hagar? fear not; for God hath heard the voice of the lad where he is.

¹⁸Arise, lift up the lad, and hold him in thine hand; for I will make him a great nation.

¹⁹And God opened her eyes, and she saw a well of water; and she went, and filled the bottle with water, and gave the lad drink.

²⁰And God was with the lad; and he grew, and dwelt in the wilderness, and became an archer.

²¹And he dwelt in the wilderness of Paran: and his mother took him a wife out of the land of Egypt.

²²And it came to pass at that time, that Abimelech and Phichol the chief captain of his host spake unto Abraham, saying, God is with thee in all that thou doest:

²³Now therefore swear unto me here by God that thou wilt not deal falsely with me, nor with my son, nor with my son's son: but according to the kindness that I have done unto thee, thou shalt do unto me, and to the land wherein thou hast sojourned.

²⁴And Abraham said, I will swear.

²⁵And Abraham reproved Abimelech because of a well of water, which Abimelech's servants had violently taken away.

²⁶And Abimelech said, I wot not who hath done this thing; neither didst thou tell me, neither yet heard I of it, but to day.

²⁷And Abraham took sheep and oxen, and gave them unto Abimelech; and both of them made a covenant.

²⁸And Abraham set seven ewe lambs of the flock by themselves.

²⁹And Abimelech said unto Abraham, What mean these seven ewe lambs which thou hast set by themselves?

³⁰And he said, For these seven ewe lambs shalt thou take of my hand, that they may be a witness unto me, that I have digged this well.

³¹Wherefore he called that place Beer-sheba; because there they sware both of them.

³²Thus they made a covenant at Beer-sheba: then Abimelech rose up, and Phichol the chief captain of his host, and they returned into the land of the Philistines.

³³And Abraham planted a grove in Beer-sheba, and called there on the name of the LORD, the everlasting God.

³⁴And Abraham sojourned in the Philistines' land many days.

CHAPTER 22

¹And it came to pass after these things, that God did tempt Abraham, and said unto him, Abraham: and he said, Behold, here I am.

²And he said, Take now thy son, thine only son Isaac, whom thou lovest, and get thee into the land of Moriah; and offer him there for a burnt offering upon one of the mountains which I will tell thee of.

³And Abraham rose up early in the morning, and saddled his ass, and took two of his young men with him, and Isaac his son, and clave the wood for the burnt offering, and rose up, and went unto the place of which God had told him.

⁴Then on the third day Abraham lifted up his eyes, and saw the place afar off.

⁵And Abraham said unto his young men, Abide ye here with the ass; and I and the lad will go yonder and worship, and come again to you.

⁶And Abraham took the wood of the burnt offering, and laid it upon Isaac his son; and he took the fire in his hand, and a knife; and they went both of them together.

⁷And Isaac spake unto Abraham his father, and said, My father: and he said, Here am I, my son. And he said, Behold the fire and the wood: but where is the lamb for a burnt offering?

⁸And Abraham said, My son, God will provide himself a lamb for a burnt offering: so they went both of them together.

⁹And they came to the place which God had told him of; and Abraham built an altar there, and laid the wood in order, and bound Isaac his son, and laid him on the altar upon the wood.

¹⁰And Abraham stretched forth his hand, and took the knife to slay his son.

¹¹And the angel of the LORD called unto him out of heaven, and said, Abraham, Abraham: and he said, Here am I.

¹²And he said, Lay not thine hand upon the lad, neither do thou any thing unto him: for now I know that thou fearest God, seeing thou hast not withheld thy son, thine only son from me.

¹³And Abraham lifted up his eyes, and looked, and behold behind him a ram caught in a thicket by his horns: and Abraham went and took the ram, and offered him up for a burnt offering in the stead of his son.

¹⁴And Abraham called the name of that place Jehovah-jireh: as it is said to this day, In the mount of the LORD it shall be seen.

¹⁵And the angel of the LORD called unto Abraham out of heaven the second time,

¹⁶And said, By myself have I sworn, saith the LORD, for because thou hast done this thing, and hast not withheld thy son, thine only son:

¹⁷That in blessing I will bless thee, and in multiplying I will multiply thy seed as the stars of the heaven, and as the sand which is upon the sea shore; and thy seed shall possess the gate of his enemies;

¹⁸And in thy seed shall all the nations of the earth be blessed; because thou hast obeyed my voice.

¹⁹So Abraham returned unto his young men, and they rose up and went together to Beer-sheba, and Abraham dwelt at Beer-sheba.

²⁰And it came to pass after these things, that it was told Abraham, saying, Behold, Milcah, she hath also born children unto thy brother Nahor;

²¹Huz his firstborn, and Buz his brother, and Kemuel the father of Aram,

²²And Chesed, and Hazo, and Pildash, and Jidlaph, and Bethuel.

²³And Bethuel begat Rebekah: these eight Milcah did bear to Nahor, Abraham's brother.

²⁴And his concubine, whose name was Reumah, she bare also Tebah, and Gaham, and Thahash, and Maachah.

CHAPTER 23

¹And Sarah was an hundred and seven and twenty years old: these were the years of the life of Sarah.

²And Sarah died in Kirjath-arba; the same is Hebron in the land of Canaan: and Abraham came to mourn for Sarah, and to weep for her.

³And Abraham stood up from before his dead, and spake unto the sons of Heth, saying,

⁴I am a stranger and a sojourner with you: give me a possession of a buryingplace with you, that I may bury my dead out of my sight.

⁵And the children of Heth answered Abraham, saying unto him,

⁶Hear us, my lord: thou art a mighty prince among us: in the choice of our sepulchres bury thy dead; none of us shall withhold from thee his sepulchre, but that thou mayest bury thy dead.

⁷And Abraham stood up, and bowed himself to the people of the land, even to the children of Heth.

⁸And he communed with them, saying, If it be your mind that I should bury my dead out of my sight; hear me, and intreat for me to Ephron the son of Zohar,

⁹That he may give me the cave of Machpelah, which he hath, which

is in the end of his field; for as much money as it is worth he shall give it me for a possession of a buryingplace amongst you.

¹⁰And Ephron dwelt among the children of Heth: and Ephron the Hittite answered Abraham in the audience of the children of Heth, even of all that went in at the gate of his city, saying,

¹¹Nay, my lord, hear me: the field give I thee, and the cave that is therein, I give it thee; in the presence of the sons of my people give I it thee: bury thy dead.

¹²And Abraham bowed down himself before the people of the land.

¹³And he spake unto Ephron in the audience of the people of the land, saying, But if thou wilt give it, I pray thee, hear me: I will give thee money for the field; take it of me, and I will bury my dead there.

¹⁴And Ephron answered Abraham, saying unto him,

¹⁵My lord, hearken unto me: the land is worth four hundred shekels of silver; what is that betwixt me and thee? bury therefore thy dead.

¹⁶And Abraham hearkened unto Ephron; and Abraham weighed to Ephron the silver, which he had named in the audience of the sons of Heth, four hundred shekels of silver, current money with the merchant.

¹⁷And the field of Ephron which was in Machpelah, which was before Mamre, the field, and the cave which was therein, and all the trees that were in the field, that were in all the borders round about, were made sure

¹⁸Unto Abraham for a possession in the presence of the children of Heth, before all that went in at the gate of his city.

¹⁹And after this, Abraham buried Sarah his wife in the cave of the field of Machpelah before Mamre: the same is Hebron in the land of Canaan.

²⁰And the field, and the cave that is therein, were made sure unto Abraham for a possession of a buryingplace by the sons of Heth.

CHAPTER 24

¹And Abraham was old, and well stricken in age: and the LORD had blessed Abraham in all things.

²And Abraham said unto his eldest servant of his house, that ruled over all that he had, Put, I pray thee, thy hand under my thigh:

³And I will make thee swear by the LORD, the God of heaven, and the God of the earth, that thou shalt not take a wife unto my son of the

daughters of the Canaanites, among whom I dwell:

⁴But thou shalt go unto my country, and to my kindred, and take a wife unto my son Isaac.

⁵And the servant said unto him, Peradventure the woman will not be willing to follow me unto this land: must I needs bring thy son again unto the land from whence thou camest?

⁶And Abraham said unto him, Beware thou that thou bring not my son thither again.

⁷The LORD God of heaven, which took me from my father's house, and from the land of my kindred, and which spake unto me, and that sware unto me, saying, Unto thy seed will I give this land; he shall send his angel before thee, and thou shalt take a wife unto my son from thence.

⁸And if the woman will not be willing to follow thee, then thou shalt be clear from this my oath: only bring not my son thither again.

⁹And the servant put his hand under the thigh of Abraham his master, and sware to him concerning that matter.

¹⁰And the servant took ten camels of the camels of his master, and departed; for all the goods of his master were in his hand: and he arose, and went to Mesopotamia, unto the city of Nahor.

¹¹And he made his camels to kneel down without the city by a well of water at the time of the evening, even the time that women go out to draw water.

¹²And he said O LORD God of my master Abraham, I pray thee, send me good speed this day, and shew kindness unto my master Abraham.

¹³Behold, I stand here by the well of water; and the daughters of the men of the city come out to draw water:

¹⁴And let it come to pass, that the damsel to whom I shall say, Let down thy pitcher, I pray thee, that I may drink; and she shall say, Drink, and I will give thy camels drink also: let the same be she that thou hast appointed for thy servant Isaac; and thereby shall I know that thou hast shewed kindness unto my master.

¹⁵And it came to pass, before he had done speaking, that, behold, Rebekah came out, who was born to Bethuel, son of Milcah, the wife of Nahor, Abraham's brother, with her pitcher upon her shoulder.

¹⁶And the damsel was very fair to look upon, a virgin, neither had any man known her: and she went down to the well, and filled her pitcher, and came up.

¹⁷And the servant ran to meet her, and said, Let me, I pray thee, drink a little water of thy pitcher.

¹⁸And she said, Drink, my lord: and she hasted, and let down her pitcher upon her hand, and gave him drink.

¹⁹And when she had done giving him drink, she said, I will draw water for thy camels also, until they have done drinking.

²⁰And she hasted, and emptied her pitcher into the trough, and ran again unto the well to draw water, and drew for all his camels.

²¹And the man wondering at her held his peace, to wit whether the LORD had made his journey prosperous or not.

²²And it came to pass, as the camels had done drinking, that the man took a golden earring of half a shekel weight, and two bracelets for her hands of ten shekels weight of gold;

²³And said, Whose daughter art thou? tell me, I pray thee: is there room in thy father's house for us to lodge in?

²⁴And she said unto him, I am the daughter of Bethuel the son of Milcah, which she bare unto Nahor.

²⁵She said moreover unto him, We have both straw and provender enough, and room to lodge in.

²⁶And the man bowed down his head, and worshipped the LORD.

²⁷And he said, Blessed be the LORD God of my master Abraham, who hath not left destitute my master of his mercy and his truth: I being in the way, the LORD led me to the house of my master's brethren.

²⁸And the damsel ran, and told them of her mother's house these things.

²⁹And Rebekah had a brother, and his name was Laban: and Laban ran out unto the man, unto the well.

³⁰And it came to pass, when he saw the earring and bracelets upon his sister's hands, and when he heard the words of Rebekah his sister, saying, Thus spake the man unto me; that he came unto the man; and, behold, he stood by the camels at the well.

³¹And he said, Come in, thou blessed of the LORD; wherefore standest thou without? for I have prepared the house, and room for the camels.

³²And the man came into the house: and he ungirded his camels, and gave straw and provender for the camels, and water to wash his feet, and the men's feet that were with him.

³³And there was set meat before him to eat: but he said, I will not eat, until I have told mine errand. And he said, Speak on.

³⁴And he said, I am Abraham's servant.

35And the LORD hath blessed my master greatly; and he is become great: and he hath given him flocks, and herds, and silver, and gold, and menservants, and maidservants, and camels, and asses.

36And Sarah my master's wife bare a son to my master when she was old: and unto him hath he given all that he hath.

37And my master made me swear, saying, Thou shalt not take a wife to my son of the daughters of the Canaanites, in whose land I dwell:

38But thou shalt go unto my father's house, and to my kindred, and take a wife unto my son.

39And I said unto my master, Peradventure the woman will not follow me.

40And he said unto me, The LORD, before whom I walk, will send his angel with thee, and prosper thy way; and thou shalt take a wife for my son of my kindred, and of my father's house:

41Then shalt thou be clear from this my oath, when thou comest to my kindred; and if they give not thee one, thou shalt be clear from my oath.

42And I came this day unto the well, and said, O LORD God of my master Abraham, if now thou do prosper my way which I go:

43Behold, I stand by the well of water; and it shall come to pass, that when the virgin cometh forth to draw water, and I say to her, Give me, I pray thee, a little water of thy pitcher to drink;

44And she say to me, Both drink thou, and I will also draw for thy camels: let the same be the woman whom the LORD hath appointed out for my master's son.

45And before I had done speaking in mine heart, behold, Rebekah came forth with her pitcher on her shoulder; and she went down unto the well, and drew water: and I said unto her, Let me drink, I pray thee.

46And she made haste, and let down her pitcher from her shoulder, and said, Drink, and I will give thy camels drink also: so I drank, and she made the camels drink also.

47And I asked her, and said, Whose daughter art thou? And she said, the daughter of Bethuel, Nahor's son, whom Milcah bare unto him: and I put the earring upon her face, and the bracelets upon her hands.

48And I bowed down my head, and worshipped the LORD, and blessed the LORD God of my master Abraham, which had led me in the right way to take my master's brother's daughter unto his son.

49And now if ye will deal kindly and truly with my master, tell me: and if not, tell me; that I may turn to the right hand, or to the left.

⁵⁰Then Laban and Bethuel answered and said, The thing proceedeth from the LORD: we cannot speak unto thee bad or good.

⁵¹Behold, Rebekah is before thee, take her, and go, and let her be thy master's son's wife, as the LORD hath spoken.

⁵²And it came to pass, that, when Abraham's servant heard their words, he worshipped the LORD, bowing himself to the earth.

⁵³And the servant brought forth jewels of silver, and jewels of gold, and raiment, and gave them to Rebekah: he gave also to her brother and to her mother precious things.

⁵⁴And they did eat and drink, he and the men that were with him, and tarried all night; and they rose up in the morning, and he said, Send me away unto my master.

⁵⁵And her brother and her mother said, Let the damsel abide with us a few days, at the least ten; after that she shall go.

⁵⁶And he said unto them, Hinder me not, seeing the LORD hath prospered my way; send me away that I may go to my master.

⁵⁷And they said, We will call the damsel, and enquire at her mouth.

⁵⁸And they called Rebekah, and said unto her, Wilt thou go with this man? And she said, I will go.

⁵⁹And they sent away Rebekah their sister, and her nurse, and Abraham's servant, and his men.

⁶⁰And they blessed Rebekah, and said unto her, Thou art our sister, be thou the mother of thousands of millions, and let thy seed possess the gate of those which hate them.

⁶¹And Rebekah arose, and her damsels, and they rode upon the camels, and followed the man: and the servant took Rebekah, and went his way.

⁶²And Isaac came from the way of the well Lahai-roi; for he dwelt in the south country.

⁶³And Isaac went out to meditate in the field at the eventide: and he lifted up his eyes, and saw, and, behold, the camels were coming.

⁶⁴And Rebekah lifted up her eyes, and when she saw Isaac, she lighted off the camel.

⁶⁵For she had said unto the servant, What man is this that walketh in the field to meet us? And the servant had said, It is my master: therefore she took a vail, and covered herself.

⁶⁶And the servant told Isaac all things that he had done.

⁶⁷And Isaac brought her into his mother Sarah's tent, and took Rebekah, and she became his wife; and he loved her: and Isaac was comforted after his mother's death.

CHAPTER 25

¹Then again Abraham took a wife, and her name was Keturah.

²And she bare him Zimran, and Jokshan, and Medan, and Midian, and Ishbak, and Shuah.

³And Jokshan begat Sheba, and Dedan. And the sons of Dedan were Asshurim, and Letushim, and Leummim.

⁴And the sons of Midian; Ephah, and Epher, and Hanoch, and Abidah, and Eldaah. All these were the children of Keturah.

⁵And Abraham gave all that he had unto Isaac.

⁶But unto the sons of the concubines, which Abraham had, Abraham gave gifts, and sent them away from Isaac his son, while he yet lived, eastward, unto the east country.

⁷And these are the days of the years of Abraham's life which he lived, an hundred threescore and fifteen years.

⁸Then Abraham gave up the ghost, and died in a good old age, an old man, and full of years; and was gathered to his people.

⁹And his sons Isaac and Ishmael buried him in the cave of Machpelah, in the field of Ephron the son of Zohar the Hittite, which is before Mamre;

¹⁰The field which Abraham purchased of the sons of Heth: there was Abraham buried, and Sarah his wife.

¹¹And it came to pass after the death of Abraham, that God blessed his son Isaac; and Isaac dwelt by the well Lahai-roi.

¹²Now these are the generations of Ishmael, Abraham's son, whom Hagar the Egyptian, Sarah's handmaid, bare unto Abraham:

¹³And these are the names of the sons of Ishmael, by their names, according to their generations: the firstborn of Ishmael, Nebajoth; and Kedar, and Adbeel, and Mibsam,

¹⁴And Mishma, and Dumah, and Massa,

¹⁵Hadar, and Tema, Jetur, Naphish, and Kedemah:

¹⁶These are the sons of Ishmael, and these are their names, by their towns, and by their castles; twelve princes according to their nations.

¹⁷And these are the years of the life of Ishmael, an hundred and thirty and seven years: and he gave up the ghost and died; and was gathered unto his people.

¹⁸And they dwelt from Havilah unto Shur, that is before Egypt, as thou goest toward Assyria: and he died in the presence of all his brethren.

¹⁹And these are the generations

of Isaac, Abraham's son: Abraham begat Isaac:

²⁰And Isaac was forty years old when he took Rebekah to wife, the daughter of Bethuel the Syrian of Padan-aram, the sister to Laban the Syrian.

²¹And Isaac intreated the LORD for his wife, because she was barren: and the LORD was intreated of him, and Rebekah his wife conceived.

²²And the children struggled together within her; and she said, If it be so, why am I thus? And she went to enquire of the LORD.

²³And the LORD said unto her, Two nations are in thy womb, and two manner of people shall be separated from thy bowels; and the one people shall be stronger than the other people; and the elder shall serve the younger.

²⁴And when her days to be delivered were fulfilled, behold, there were twins in her womb.

²⁵And the first came out red, all over like an hairy garment; and they called his name Esau.

²⁶And after that came his brother out, and his hand took hold on Esau's heel; and his name was called Jacob: and Isaac was threescore years old when she bare them.

²⁷And the boys grew: and Esau was a cunning hunter, a man of the field; and Jacob was a plain man, dwelling in tents.

²⁸And Isaac loved Esau, because he did eat of his venison: but Rebekah loved Jacob.

²⁹And Jacob sod pottage: and Esau came from the field, and he was faint:

³⁰And Esau said to Jacob, Feed me, I pray thee, with that same red pottage; for I am faint: therefore was his name called Edom.

³¹And Jacob said, Sell me this day thy birthright.

³²And Esau said, Behold, I am at the point to die: and what profit shall this birthright do to me?

³³And Jacob said, Swear to me this day; and he sware unto him: and he sold his birthright unto Jacob.

³⁴Then Jacob gave Esau bread and pottage of lentiles; and he did eat and drink, and rose up, and went his way: thus Esau despised his birthright.

CHAPTER 26

¹And there was a famine in the land, beside the first famine that was in the days of Abraham. And Isaac went unto Abimelech king of the Philistines unto Gerar.

²And the LORD appeared unto him, and said, Go not down into

Egypt; dwell in the land which I shall tell thee of:

³Sojourn in this land, and I will be with thee, and will bless thee; for unto thee, and unto thy seed, I will give all these countries, and I will perform the oath which I sware unto Abraham thy father;

⁴And I will make thy seed to multiply as the stars of heaven, and will give unto thy seed all these countries; and in thy seed shall all the nations of the earth be blessed;

⁵Because that Abraham obeyed my voice, and kept my charge, my commandments, my statutes, and my laws.

⁶And Isaac dwelt in Gerar:

⁷And the men of the place asked him of his wife; and he said, She is my sister: for he feared to say, She is my wife; lest, said he, the men of the place should kill me for Rebekah; because she was fair to look upon.

⁸And it came to pass, when he had been there a long time, that Abimelech king of the Philistines looked out at a window, and saw, and, behold, Isaac was sporting with Rebekah his wife.

⁹And Abimelech called Isaac, and said, Behold, of a surety she is thy wife; and how saidst thou, She is my sister? And Isaac said unto him, Because I said, Lest I die for her.

¹⁰And Abimelech said, What is this thou hast done unto us? one of the people might lightly have lien with thy wife, and thou shouldest have brought guiltiness upon us.

¹¹And Abimelech charged all his people, saying, He that toucheth this man or his wife shall surely be put to death.

¹²Then Isaac sowed in that land, and received in the same year an hundredfold: and the LORD blessed him.

¹³And the man waxed great, and went forward, and grew until he became very great:

¹⁴For he had possession of flocks, and possession of herds, and great store of servants: and the Philistines envied him.

¹⁵For all the wells which his father's servants had digged in the days of Abraham his father, the Philistines had stopped them, and filled them with earth.

¹⁶And Abimelech said unto Isaac, Go from us; for thou art much mightier than we.

¹⁷And Isaac departed thence, and pitched his tent in the valley of Gerar, and dwelt there.

¹⁸And Isaac digged again the wells of water, which they had digged in the days of Abraham his father; for the Philistines had stopped them after the death of Abraham: and he

called their names after the names by which his father had called them.

¹⁹And Isaac's servants digged in the valley, and found there a well of springing water.

²⁰And the herdmen of Gerar did strive with Isaac's herdmen, saying, The water is ours: and he called the name of the well Esek; because they strove with him.

²¹And they digged another well, and strove for that also: and he called the name of it Sitnah.

²²And he removed from thence, and digged another well; and for that they strove not: and he called the name of it Rehoboth; and he said, For now the LORD hath made room for us, and we shall be fruitful in the land.

²³And he went up from thence to Beer-sheba.

²⁴And the LORD appeared unto him the same night, and said, I am the God of Abraham thy father: fear not, for I am with thee, and will bless thee, and multiply thy seed for my servant Abraham's sake.

²⁵And he builded an altar there, and called upon the name of the LORD, and pitched his tent there: and there Isaac's servants digged a well.

²⁶Then Abimelech went to him from Gerar, and Ahuzzath one of his friends, and Phichol the chief captain of his army.

²⁷And Isaac said unto them, Wherefore come ye to me, seeing ye hate me, and have sent me away from you?

²⁸And they said, We saw certainly that the LORD was with thee: and we said, Let there be now an oath betwixt us, even betwixt us and thee, and let us make a covenant with thee;

²⁹That thou wilt do us no hurt, as we have not touched thee, and as we have done unto thee nothing but good, and have sent thee away in peace: thou art now the blessed of the LORD.

³⁰And he made them a feast, and they did eat and drink.

³¹And they rose up betimes in the morning, and sware one to another: and Isaac sent them away, and they departed from him in peace.

³²And it came to pass the same day, that Isaac's servants came, and told him concerning the well which they had digged, and said unto him, We have found water.

³³And he called it Shebah: therefore the name of the city is Beer-sheba unto this day.

³⁴And Esau was forty years old when he took to wife Judith the daughter of Beeri the Hittite, and Bashemath the daughter of Elon the Hittite:

³⁵Which were a grief of mind unto Isaac and to Rebekah.

CHAPTER 27

¹And it came to pass, that when Isaac was old, and his eyes were dim, so that he could not see, he called Esau his eldest son, and said unto him, My son: and he said unto him, Behold, here am I.

²And he said, Behold now, I am old, I know not the day of my death:

³Now therefore take, I pray thee, thy weapons, thy quiver and thy bow, and go out to the field, and take me some venison;

⁴And make me savoury meat, such as I love, and bring it to me, that I may eat; that my soul may bless thee before I die.

⁵And Rebekah heard when Isaac spake to Esau his son. And Esau went to the field to hunt for venison, and to bring it.

⁶And Rebekah spake unto Jacob her son, saying, Behold, I heard thy father speak unto Esau thy brother, saying,

⁷Bring me venison, and make me savoury meat, that I may eat, and bless thee before the LORD before my death.

⁸Now therefore, my son, obey my voice according to that which I command thee.

⁹Go now to the flock, and fetch me from thence two good kids of the goats; and I will make them savoury meat for thy father, such as he loveth:

¹⁰And thou shalt bring it to thy father, that he may eat, and that he may bless thee before his death.

¹¹And Jacob said to Rebekah his mother, Behold, Esau my brother is a hairy man, and I am a smooth man:

¹²My father peradventure will feel me, and I shall seem to him as a deceiver; and I shall bring a curse upon me, and not a blessing.

¹³And his mother said unto him, Upon me be thy curse, my son: only obey my voice, and go fetch me them.

¹⁴And he went, and fetched, and brought them to his mother: and his mother made savoury meat, such as his father loved.

¹⁵And Rebekah took goodly raiment of her eldest son Esau, which were with her in the house, and put them upon Jacob her younger son:

¹⁶And she put the skins of the kids of the goats upon his hands, and upon the smooth of his neck:

¹⁷And she gave the savoury meat and the bread, which she had prepared, into the hand of her son Jacob.

¹⁸And he came unto his father, and said, My father: and he said, Here am I; who art thou, my son?

^{19}And Jacob said unto his father, I am Esau thy first born; I have done according as thou badest me: arise, I pray thee, sit and eat of my venison, that thy soul may bless me.

^{20}And Isaac said unto his son, How is it that thou hast found it so quickly, my son? And he said, Because the LORD thy God brought it to me.

^{21}And Isaac said unto Jacob, Come near, I pray thee, that I may feel thee, my son, whether thou be my very son Esau or not.

^{22}And Jacob went near unto Isaac his father; and he felt him, and said, The voice is Jacob's voice, but the hands are the hands of Esau.

^{23}And he discerned him not, because his hands were hairy, as his brother Esau's hands: so he blessed him.

^{24}And he said, Art thou my very son Esau? And he said, I am.

^{25}And he said, Bring it near to me, and I will eat of my son's venison, that my soul may bless thee. And he brought it near to him, and he did eat: and he brought him wine and he drank.

^{26}And his father Isaac said unto him, Come near now, and kiss me, my son.

^{27}And he came near, and kissed him: and he smelled the smell of his raiment, and blessed him, and said, See, the smell of my son is as the smell of a field which the LORD hath blessed:

^{28}Therefore God give thee of the dew of heaven, and the fatness of the earth, and plenty of corn and wine:

^{29}Let people serve thee, and nations bow down to thee: be lord over thy brethren, and let thy mother's sons bow down to thee: cursed be every one that curseth thee, and blessed be he that blesseth thee.

^{30}And it came to pass, as soon as Isaac had made an end of blessing Jacob, and Jacob was yet scarce gone out from the presence of Isaac his father, that Esau his brother came in from his hunting.

^{31}And he also had made savoury meat, and brought it unto his father, and said unto his father, Let my father arise, and eat of his son's venison, that thy soul may bless me.

^{32}And Isaac his father said unto him, Who art thou? And he said, I am thy son, thy firstborn Esau.

^{33}And Isaac trembled very exceedingly, and said, Who? where is he that hath taken venison, and brought it me, and I have eaten of all before thou camest, and have blessed him? yea, and he shall be blessed.

³⁴And when Esau heard the words of his father, he cried with a great and exceeding bitter cry, and said unto his father, Bless me, even me also, O my father.

³⁵And he said, Thy brother came with subtilty, and hath taken away thy blessing.

³⁶And he said, Is not he rightly named Jacob? for he hath supplanted me these two times: he took away my birthright; and, behold, now he hath taken away my blessing. And he said, Hast thou not reserved a blessing for me?

³⁷And Isaac answered and said unto Esau, Behold, I have made him thy lord, and all his brethren have I given to him for servants; and with corn and wine have I sustained him: and what shall I do now unto thee, my son?

³⁸And Esau said unto his father, Hast thou but one blessing, my father? bless me, even me also, O my father. And Esau lifted up his voice, and wept.

³⁹And Isaac his father answered and said unto him, Behold, thy dwelling shall be the fatness of the earth, and of the dew of heaven from above;

⁴⁰And by thy sword shalt thou live, and shalt serve thy brother; and it shall come to pass when thou shalt have the dominion, that thou shalt break his yoke from off thy neck.

⁴¹And Esau hated Jacob because of the blessing wherewith his father blessed him: and Esau said in his heart, The days of mourning for my father are at hand; then will I slay my brother Jacob.

⁴²And these words of Esau her elder son were told to Rebekah: and she sent and called Jacob her younger son, and said unto him, Behold, thy brother Esau, as touching thee, doth comfort himself, purposing to kill thee.

⁴³Now therefore, my son, obey my voice; arise, flee thou to Laban my brother to Haran;

⁴⁴And tarry with him a few days, until thy brother's fury turn away;

⁴⁵Until thy brother's anger turn away from thee, and he forget that which thou hast done to him: then I will send, and fetch thee from thence: why should I be deprived also of you both in one day?

⁴⁶And Rebekah said to Isaac, I am weary of my life because of the daughters of Heth: if Jacob take a wife of the daughters of Heth, such as these which are of the daughters of the land, what good shall my life do me?

CHAPTER 28

¹And Isaac called Jacob, and blessed him, and charged him, and said unto him, Thou shalt not take a wife of the daughters of Canaan.

²Arise, go to Padan-aram, to the house of Bethuel thy mother's father; and take thee a wife from thence of the daughers of Laban thy mother's brother.

³And God Almighty bless thee, and make thee fruitful, and multiply thee, that thou mayest be a multitude of people;

⁴And give thee the blessing of Abraham, to thee, and to thy seed with thee; that thou mayest inherit the land wherein thou art a stranger, which God gave unto Abraham.

⁵And Isaac sent away Jacob: and he went to Padan-aram unto Laban, son of Bethuel the Syrian, the brother of Rebekah, Jacob's and Esau's mother.

⁶When Esau saw that Isaac had blessed Jacob, and sent him away to Padan-aram, to take him a wife from thence; and that as he blessed him he gave him a charge, saying, Thou shalt not take a wife of the daughers of Canaan;

⁷And that Jacob obeyed his father and his mother, and was gone to Padan-aram;

⁸And Esau seeing that the daughters of Canaan pleased not Isaac his father;

⁹Then went Esau unto Ishmael, and took unto the wives which he had Mahalath the daughter of Ishmael Abraham's son, the sister of Nebajoth, to be his wife.

¹⁰And Jacob went out from Beer-sheba, and went toward Haran.

¹¹And he lighted upon a certain place, and tarried there all night, because the sun was set; and he took of the stones of that place, and put them for his pillows, and lay down in that place to sleep.

¹²And he dreamed, and behold a ladder set up on the earth, and the top of it reached to heaven: and behold the angels of God ascending and descending on it.

¹³And, behold, the LORD stood above it, and said, I am the LORD God of Abraham thy father, and the God of Isaac: the land whereon thou liest, to thee will I give it, and to thy seed;

¹⁴And thy seed shall be as the dust of the earth, and thou shalt spread abroad to the west, and to the east, and to the north, and to the south: and in thee and in thy seed shall all the families of the earth be blessed.

¹⁵And, behold, I am with thee, and will keep thee in all places whither thou goest, and will bring thee again

into this land; for I will not leave thee, until I have done that which I have spoken to thee of.

¹⁶And Jacob awaked out of his sleep, and he said, Surely the LORD is in this place; and I knew it not.

¹⁷And he was afraid, and said, How dreadful is this place! this is none other but the house of God, and this is the gate of heaven.

¹⁸And Jacob rose up early in the morning, and took the stone that he had put for his pillows, and set it up for a pillar, and poured oil upon the top of it.

¹⁹And he called the name of that place Bethel: but the name of that city was called Luz at the first.

²⁰And Jacob vowed a vow, saying, If God will be with me, and will keep me in this way that I go, and will give me bread to eat, and raiment to put on,

²¹So that I come again to my father's house in peace; then shall the LORD be my God:

²²And this stone, which I have set for a pillar, shall be God's house: and of all that thou shalt give me I will surely give the tenth unto thee.

CHAPTER 29

¹Then Jacob went on his journey, and came into the land of the people of the east.

²And he looked, and behold a well in the field, and, lo, there were three flocks of sheep lying by it; for out of that well they watered the flocks: and a great stone was upon the well's mouth.

³And thither were all the flocks gathered: and they rolled the stone from the well's mouth, and watered the sheep, and put the stone again upon the well's mouth in his place.

⁴And Jacob said unto them, My brethren, whence be ye? And they said, Of Haran are we.

⁵And he said unto them, Know ye Laban the son of Nahor? And they said, We know him.

⁶And he said unto them, Is he well? And they said, He is well: and, behold, Rachel his daughter cometh with the sheep.

⁷And he said, Lo, it is yet high day, neither is it time that the cattle should be gathered together: water ye the sheep, and go and feed them.

⁸And they said, We cannot, until all the flocks be gathered together, and till they roll the stone from the well's mouth; then we water the sheep.

⁹And while he yet spake with them, Rachel came with her father's sheep; for she kept them.

¹⁰And it came to pass, when Jacob saw Rachel the daughter of Laban his mother's brother, and the sheep of Laban his mother's brother, that Jacob went near, and rolled the stone from the well's mouth, and watered the flock of Laban his mother's brother.

¹¹And Jacob kissed Rachel, and lifted up his voice, and wept.

¹²And Jacob told Rachel that he was her father's brother, and that he was Rebekah's son: and she ran and told her father.

¹³And it came to pass, when Laban heard the tidings of Jacob his sister's son, that he ran to meet him, and embraced him, and kissed him, and brought him to his house. And he told Laban all these things.

¹⁴And Laban said to him, Surely thou art my bone and my flesh. And he abode with him the space of a month.

¹⁵And Laban said unto Jacob, Because thou art my brother, shouldest thou therefore serve me for nought? tell me, what shall thy wages be?

¹⁶And Laban had two daughters: the name of the elder was Leah, and the name of the younger was Rachel.

¹⁷Leah was tender eyed; but Rachel was beautiful and well favoured.

¹⁸And Jacob loved Rachel; and said, I will serve thee seven years for Rachel thy younger daughter.

¹⁹And Laban said, It is better that I give her to thee, than that I should give her to another man: abide with me.

²⁰And Jacob served seven years for Rachel; and they seemed unto him but a few days, for the love he had to her.

²¹And Jacob said unto Laban, Give me my wife, for my days are fulfilled, that I may go in unto her.

²²And Laban gathered together all the men of the place, and made a feast.

²³And it came to pass in the evening, that he took Leah his daughter, and brought her to him; and he went in unto her.

²⁴And Laban gave unto his daughter Leah Zilpah his maid for an handmaid.

²⁵And it came to pass, that in the morning, behold, it was Leah: and he said to Laban, What is this thou hast done unto me? did not I serve with thee for Rachel? wherefore then hast thou beguiled me?

²⁶And Laban said, It must not be so done in our country, to give the younger before the firstborn.

^{27}Fulfil her week, and we will give thee this also for the service which thou shalt serve with me yet seven other years.

^{28}And Jacob did so, and fulfilled her week: and he gave him Rachel his daughter to wife also.

^{29}And Laban gave to Rachel his daughter Bilhah his handmaid to be her maid.

^{30}And he went in also unto Rachel, and he loved also Rachel more than Leah, and served with him yet seven other years.

^{31}And when the LORD saw that Leah was hated, he opened her womb: but Rachel was barren.

^{32}And Leah conceived, and bare a son, and she called his name Reuben: for she said, Surely the LORD hath looked upon my affliction; now therefore my husband will love me.

^{33}And she conceived again, and bare a son; and said, Because the LORD hath heard I was hated, he hath therefore given me this son also: and she called his name Simeon.

^{34}And she conceived again, and bare a son; and said, Now this time will my husband be joined unto me, because I have born him three sons: therefore was his name called Levi.

^{35}And she conceived again, and bare a son: and she said, Now will I praise the LORD: therefore she called his name Judah; and left bearing.

CHAPTER 30

^{1}And when Rachel saw that she bare Jacob no children, Rachel envied her sister; and said unto Jacob, Give me children, or else I die.

^{2}And Jacob's anger was kindled against Rachel: and he said, Am I in God's stead, who hath withheld from thee the fruit of the womb?

^{3}And she said, Behold my maid Bilhah, go in unto her; and she shall bear upon my knees, that I may also have children by her.

^{4}And she gave him Bilhah her handmaid to wife: and Jacob went in unto her.

^{5}And Bilhah conceived, and bare Jacob a son.

^{6}And Rachel said, God hath judged me, and hath also heard my voice, and hath given me a son: therefore called she his name Dan.

^{7}And Bilhah Rachel's maid conceived again, and bare Jacob a second son.

^{8}And Rachel said, With great wrestlings have I wrestled with my sister, and I have prevailed: and she called his name Naphtali.

⁹When Leah saw that she had left bearing, she took Zilpah her maid, and gave her Jacob to wife.

¹⁰And Zilpah Leah's maid bare Jacob a son.

¹¹And Leah said, A troop cometh: and she called his name Gad.

¹²And Zilpah Leah's maid bare Jacob a second son.

¹³And Leah said, Happy am I, for the daughters will call me blessed: and she called his name Asher.

¹⁴And Reuben went in the days of wheat harvest, and found mandrakes in the field, and brought them unto his mother Leah. Then Rachel said to Leah, Give me, I pray thee, of thy son's mandrakes.

¹⁵And she said unto her, Is it a small matter that thou hast taken my husband? and wouldest thou take away my son's mandrakes also? And Rachel said, Therefore he shall lie with thee to night for thy son's mandrakes.

¹⁶And Jacob came out of the field in the evening, and Leah went out to meet him, and said, Thou must come in unto me; for surely I have hired thee with my son's mandrakes. And he lay with her that night.

¹⁷And God hearkened unto Leah, and she conceived, and bare Jacob the fifth son.

¹⁸And Leah said, God hath given me my hire, because I have given my maiden to my husband: and she called his name Issachar.

¹⁹And Leah conceived again, and bare Jacob the sixth son.

²⁰And Leah said, God hath endued me with a good dowry; now will my husband dwell with me, because I have born him six sons: and she called his name Zebulun.

²¹And afterwards she bare a daughter, and called her name Dinah.

²²And God remembered Rachel, and God hearkened to her, and opened her womb.

²³And she conceived, and bare a son; and said, God hath taken away my reproach:

²⁴And she called his name Joseph; and said, The LORD shall add to me another son.

²⁵And it came to pass, when Rachel had born Joseph, that Jacob said unto Laban, Send me away, that I may go unto mine own place, and to my country.

²⁶Give me my wives and my children, for whom I have served thee, and let me go: for thou knowest my service which I have done thee.

²⁷And Laban said unto him, I pray thee, if I have found favour in thine eyes, tarry: for I have learned by experience that the LORD hath blessed me for thy sake.

²⁸And he said, Appoint me thy wages, and I will give it.

²⁹And he said unto him, Thou knowest how I have served thee, and how thy cattle was with me.

³⁰For it was little which thou hadst before I came, and it is now increased unto a multitude; and the LORD hath blessed thee since my coming: and now when shall I provide for mine own house also?

³¹And he said, What shall I give thee? And Jacob said, Thou shalt not give me any thing: if thou wilt do this thing for me, I will again feed and keep thy flock.

³²I will pass through all thy flock to day, removing from thence all the speckled and spotted cattle, and all the brown cattle among the sheep, and the spotted and speckled among the goats: and of such shall be my hire.

³³So shall my righteousness answer for me in time to come, when it shall come for my hire before thy face: every one that is not speckled and spotted among the goats, and brown among the sheep, that shall be counted stolen with me.

³⁴And Laban said, Behold, I would it might be according to thy word.

³⁵And he removed that day the he goats that were ringstraked and spotted, and all the she goats that were speckled and spotted, and every one that had some white in it, and all the brown among the sheep, and gave them into the hand of his sons.

³⁶And he set three days' journey betwixt himself and Jacob: and Jacob fed the rest of Laban's flocks.

³⁷And Jacob took him rods of green poplar, and of the hazel and chesnut tree; and pilled white strakes in them, and made the white appear which was in the rods.

³⁸And he set the rods which he had pilled before the flocks in the gutters in the watering troughs when the flocks came to drink, that they should conceive when they came to drink.

³⁹And the flocks conceived before the rods, and brought forth cattle ringstraked, speckled, and spotted.

⁴⁰And Jacob did separate the lambs, and set the faces of the flocks toward the ringstraked, and all the brown in the flock of Laban; and he put his own flocks by themselves, and put them not unto Laban's cattle.

⁴¹And it came to pass, whensoever the stronger cattle did conceive, that Jacob laid the rods before the eyes of the cattle in the gutters, that they might conceive among the rods.

⁴²But when the cattle were feeble, he put them not in: so the feebler

were Laban's, and the stronger Jacob's.

⁴³And the man increased exceedingly, and had much cattle, and maidservants, and menservants, and camels, and asses.

CHAPTER 31

¹And he heard the words of Laban's sons, saying, Jacob hath taken away all that was our father's; and of that which was our father's hath he gotten all this glory.

²And Jacob beheld the countenance of Laban, and, behold, it was not toward him as before.

³And the LORD said unto Jacob, Return unto the land of thy fathers, and to thy kindred; and I will be with thee.

⁴And Jacob sent and called Rachel and Leah to the field unto his flock,

⁵And said unto them, I see your father's countenance, that it is not toward me as before; but the God of my father hath been with me.

⁶And ye know that with all my power I have served your father.

⁷And your father hath deceived me, and changed my wages ten times; but God suffered him not to hurt me.

⁸If he said thus, The speckled shall be thy wages; then all the cattle bare speckled: and if he said thus, The ringstraked shall be thy hire; then bare all the cattle ringstraked.

⁹Thus God hath taken away the cattle of your father, and given them to me.

¹⁰And it came to pass at the time that the cattle conceived, that I lifted up mine eyes, and saw in a dream, and, behold, the rams which leaped upon the cattle were ringstraked, speckled, and grisled.

¹¹And the angel of God spake unto me in a dream, saying, Jacob: And I said, Here am I.

¹²And he said, Lift up now thine eyes, and see, all the rams which leap upon the cattle are ringstraked, speckled, and grisled: for I have seen all that Laban doeth unto thee.

¹³I am the God of Bethel, where thou anointedst the pillar, and where thou vowedst a vow unto me: now arise, get thee out from this land, and return unto the land of thy kindred.

¹⁴And Rachel and Leah answered and said unto him, Is there yet any portion or inheritance for us in our father's house?

¹⁵Are we not counted of him strangers? for he hath sold us, and hath quite devoured also our money.

¹⁶For all the riches which God hath taken from our father, that is ours, and our children's: now then, whatsoever God hath said unto thee, do.

¹⁷Then Jacob rose up, and set his sons and his wives upon camels;

¹⁸And he carried away all his cattle, and all his goods which he had gotten, the cattle of his getting, which he had gotten in Padan-aram, for to go to Isaac his father in the land of Canaan.

¹⁹And Laban went to shear his sheep: and Rachel had stolen the images that were her father's.

²⁰And Jacob stole away unawares to Laban the Syrian, in that he told him not that he fled.

²¹So he fled with all that he had; and he rose up, and passed over the river, and set his face toward the mount Gilead.

²²And it was told Laban on the third day that Jacob was fled.

²³And he took his brethren with him, and pursued after him seven days' journey; and they overtook him in the mount Gilead.

²⁴And God came to Laban the Syrian in a dream by night, and said unto him, Take heed that thou speak not to Jacob either good or bad.

²⁵Then Laban overtook Jacob. Now Jacob had pitched his tent in the mount: and Laban with his brethren pitched in the mount of Gilead.

²⁶And Laban said to Jacob, What hast thou done, that thou hast stolen away unawares to me, and carried away my daughters, as captives taken with the sword?

²⁷Wherefore didst thou flee away secretly, and steal away from me; and didst not tell me, that I might have sent thee away with mirth, and with songs, with tabret, and with harp?

²⁸And hast not suffered me to kiss my sons and my daughters? thou hast now done foolishly in so doing.

²⁹It is in the power of my hand to do you hurt: but the God of your father spake unto me yesternight, saying, Take thou heed that thou speak not to Jacob either good or bad.

³⁰And now, though thou wouldest needs be gone, because thou sore longedst after thy father's house, yet wherefore hast thou stolen my gods?

³¹And Jacob answered and said to Laban, Because I was afraid: for I said, Peradventure thou wouldest take by force thy daughters from me.

³²With whomsoever thou findest thy gods, let him not live: before our brethren discern thou what is thine with me, and take it to thee.

For Jacob knew not that Rachel had stolen them.

³³And Laban went into Jacob's tent, and into Leah's tent, and into the two maidservants' tents; but he found them not. Then went he out of Leah's tent, and entered into Rachel's tent.

³⁴Now Rachel had taken the images, and put them in the camel's furniture, and sat upon them. And Laban searched all the tent, but found them not.

³⁵And she said to her father, Let it not displease my lord that I cannot rise up before thee; for the custom of women is upon me. And he searched but found not the images.

³⁶And Jacob was wroth, and chode with Laban: and Jacob answered and said to Laban, What is my trespass? what is my sin, that thou hast so hotly pursued after me?

³⁷Whereas thou hast searched all my stuff, what hast thou found of all thy household stuff? set it here before my brethren and thy brethren, that they may judge betwixt us both.

³⁸This twenty years have I been with thee; thy ewes and thy she goats have not cast their young, and the rams of thy flock have I not eaten.

³⁹That which was torn of beasts I brought not unto thee; I bare the loss of it; of my hand didst thou require it, whether stolen by day, or stolen by night.

⁴⁰Thus I was; in the day the drought consumed me, and the frost by night; and my sleep departed from mine eyes.

⁴¹Thus have I been twenty years in thy house; I served thee fourteen years for thy two daughters, and six years for thy cattle: and thou hast changed my wages ten times.

⁴²Except the God of my father, the God of Abraham, and the fear of Isaac, had been with me, surely thou hadst sent me away now empty. God hath seen mine affliction and the labour of my hands, and rebuked thee yesternight.

⁴³And Laban answered and said unto Jacob, These daughters are my daughters, and these children are my children, and these cattle are my cattle, and all that thou seest is mine: and what can I do this day unto these my daughters, or unto their children which they have born?

⁴⁴Now therefore come thou, let us make a covenant, I and thou; and let it be for a witness between me and thee.

⁴⁵And Jacob took a stone, and set it up for a pillar.

⁴⁶And Jacob said unto his brethren, Gather stones; and they took stones, and made an heap: and they did eat there upon the heap.

⁴⁷And Laban called it Jegarsahadutha: but Jacob called it Galeed.

⁴⁸And Laban said, This heap is a witness between me and thee this day. Therefore was the name of it called Galeed;

⁴⁹And Mizpah; for he said, The LORD watch between me and thee, when we are absent one from another.

⁵⁰If thou shalt afflict my daughters, or if thou shalt take other wives beside my daughters, no man is with us; see, God is witness betwixt me and thee.

⁵¹And Laban said to Jacob, Behold this heap, and behold this pillar, which I have cast betwixt me and thee:

⁵²This heap be witness, and this pillar be witness, that I will not pass over this heap to thee, and that thou shalt not pass over this heap and this pillar unto me, for harm.

⁵³The God of Abraham, and the God of Nahor, the God of their father, judge betwixt us. And Jacob sware by the fear of his father Isaac.

⁵⁴Then Jacob offered sacrifice upon the mount, and called his brethren to eat bread: and they did eat bread, and tarried all night in the mount.

⁵⁵And early in the morning Laban rose up, and kissed his sons and his daughters, and blessed them: and Laban departed, and returned unto his place.

CHAPTER 32

¹And Jacob went on his way, and the angels of God met him.

²And when Jacob saw them, he said, This is God's host: and he called the name of that place Mahanaim.

³And Jacob sent messengers before him to Esau his brother unto the land of Seir, the country of Edom.

⁴And he commanded them, saying, Thus shall ye speak unto my lord Esau; Thy servant Jacob saith thus, I have sojourned with Laban, and stayed there until now:

⁵And I have oxen, and asses, flocks, and menservants, and womenservants: and I have sent to tell my lord, that I may find grace in thy sight.

⁶And the messengers returned to Jacob, saying, We came to thy brother Esau, and also he cometh to meet thee, and four hundred men with him.

⁷Then Jacob was greatly afraid and distressed: and he divided the people that was with him, and the flocks, and herds, and the camels, into two bands;

⁸And said, If Esau come to the one company, and smite it, then the other company which is left shall escape.

⁹And Jacob said, O God of my father Abraham, and God of my father Isaac, the LORD which saidst unto me, Return unto thy country, and to thy kindred, and I will deal well with thee:

¹⁰I am not worthy of the least of all the mercies, and of all the truth, which thou hast shewed unto thy servant; for with my staff I passed over this Jordan; and now I am become two bands.

¹¹Deliver me, I pray thee, from the hand of my brother, from the hand of Esau: for I fear him, lest he will come and smite me, and the mother with the children.

¹²And thou saidst, I will surely do thee good, and make thy seed as the sand of the sea, which cannot be numbered for multitude.

¹³And he lodged there that same night; and took of that which came to his hand a present for Esau his brother;

¹⁴Two hundred she goats, and twenty he goats, two hundred ewes, and twenty rams,

¹⁵Thirty milch camels with their colts, forty kine, and ten bulls, twenty she asses, and ten foals.

¹⁶And he delivered them into the hand of his servants, every drove by themselves; and said unto his servants, Pass over before me, and put a space betwixt drove and drove.

¹⁷And he commanded the foremost, saying, When Esau my brother meeteth thee, and asketh thee, saying, Whose art thou? and whither goest thou? and whose are these before thee?

¹⁸Then thou shalt say, They be thy servant Jacob's; it is a present sent unto my lord Esau: and, behold, also he is behind us.

¹⁹And so commanded he the second, and the third, and all that followed the droves, saying, On this manner shall ye speak unto Esau, when ye find him.

²⁰And say ye moreover, Behold, thy servant Jacob is behind us. For he said, I will appease him with the present that goeth before me, and afterward I will see his face; peradventure he will accept of me.

²¹So went the present over before him: and himself lodged that night in the company.

²²And he rose up that night, and took his two wives, and his two womenservants, and his eleven sons, and passed over the ford Jabbok.

²³And he took them, and sent them over the brook, and sent over that he had.

²⁴And Jacob was left alone; and

Genesis

there wrestled a man with him until the breaking of the day.

²⁵And when he saw that he prevailed not against him, he touched the hollow of his thigh; and the hollow of Jacob's thigh was out of joint, as he wrestled with him.

²⁶And he said, Let me go, for the day breaketh. And he said, I will not let thee go, except thou bless me.

²⁷And he said unto him, What is thy name? And he said, Jacob.

²⁸And he said, Thy name shall be called no more Jacob, but Israel: for as a prince hast thou power with God and with men, and hast prevailed.

²⁹And Jacob asked him, and said, Tell me, I pray thee, thy name. And he said, Wherefore is it that thou dost ask after my name? And he blessed him there.

³⁰And Jacob called the name of the place Peniel: for I have seen God face to face, and my life is preserved.

³¹And as he passed over Penuel the sun rose upon him, and he halted upon his thigh.

³²Therefore the children of Israel eat not of the sinew which shrank, which is upon the hollow of the thigh, unto this day: because he touched the hollow of Jacob's thigh in the sinew that shrank.

CHAPTER 33

¹And Jacob lifted up his eyes, and looked, and, behold, Esau came, and with him four hundred men. And he divided the children unto Leah, and unto Rachel, and unto the two handmaids.

²And he put the handmaids and their children foremost, and Leah and her children after, and Rachel and Joseph hindermost.

³And he passed over before them, and bowed himself to the ground seven times, until he came near to his brother.

⁴And Esau ran to meet him, and embraced him, and fell on his neck, and kissed him: and they wept.

⁵And he lifted up his eyes, and saw the women and the children; and said, Who are those with thee? And he said, The children which God hath graciously given thy servant.

⁶Then the handmaidens came near, they and their children, and they bowed themselves.

⁷And Leah also with her children came near, and bowed themselves: and after came Joseph near and Rachel, and they bowed themselves.

⁸And he said, What meanest thou by all this drove which I met? And he said, These are to find grace in the sight of my lord.

⁹And Esau said, I have enough, my brother; keep that thou hast unto thyself.

¹⁰And Jacob said, Nay, I pray thee, if now I have found grace in thy sight, then receive my present at my hand: for therefore I have seen thy face, as though I had seen the face of God, and thou wast pleased with me.

¹¹Take, I pray thee, my blessing that is brought to thee; because God hath dealt graciously with me, and because I have enough. And he urged him, and he took it.

¹²And he said, Let us take our journey, and let us go, and I will go before thee.

¹³And he said unto him, My lord knoweth that the children are tender, and the flocks and herds with young are with me: and if men should overdrive them one day, all the flock will die.

¹⁴Let my lord, I pray thee, pass over before his servant: and I will lead on softly, according as the cattle that goeth before me and the children be able to endure, until I come unto my lord unto Seir.

¹⁵And Esau said, Let me now leave with thee some of the folk that are with me. And he said, What needeth it? let me find grace in the sight of my lord.

¹⁶So Esau returned that day on his way unto Seir.

¹⁷And Jacob journeyed to Succoth, and built him an house, and made booths for his cattle: therefore the name of the place is called Succoth.

¹⁸And Jacob came to Shalem, a city of Shechem, which is in the land of Canaan, when he came from Padan-aram; and pitched his tent before the city.

¹⁹And he bought a parcel of a field, where he had spread his tent, at the hand of the children of Hamor, Shechem's father, for an hundred pieces of money.

²⁰And he erected there an altar, and called it Elel0heIsrael.

CHAPTER 34

¹And Dinah the daughter of Leah, which she bare unto Jacob, went out to see the daughters of the land.

²And when Shechem the son of Hamor the Hivite, prince of the country, saw her, he took her, and lay with her, and defiled her.

³And his soul clave unto Dinah the daughter of Jacob, and he loved the damsel, and spake kindly unto the damsel.

⁴And Shechem spake unto his father Hamor, saying, Get me this damsel to wife.

⁵And Jacob heard that he had defiled Dinah his daughter: now his sons were with his cattle in the field: and Jacob held his peace until they were come.

⁶And Hamor the father of Shechem went out unto Jacob to commune with him.

⁷And the sons of Jacob came out of the field when they heard it: and the men were grieved, and they were very wroth, because he had wrought folly in Israel in lying with Jacob's daughter: which thing ought not to be done.

⁸And Hamor communed with them, saying, The soul of my son Shechem longeth for your daughter: I pray you give her him to wife.

⁹And make ye marriages with us, and give your daughters unto us, and take our daughters unto you.

¹⁰And ye shall dwell with us: and the land shall be before you; dwell and trade ye therein, and get you possessions therein.

¹¹And Shechem said unto her father and unto her brethren, Let me find grace in your eyes, and what ye shall say unto me I will give.

¹²Ask me never so much dowry and gift, and I will give according as ye shall say unto me: but give me the damsel to wife.

¹³And the sons of Jacob answered Shechem and Hamor his father deceitfully, and said, because he had defiled Dinah their sister:

¹⁴And they said unto them, We cannot do this thing, to give our sister to one that is uncircumcised; for that were a reproach unto us:

¹⁵But in this will we consent unto you: If ye will be as we be, that every male of you be circumcised;

¹⁶Then will we give our daughters unto you, and we will take your daughters to us, and we will dwell with you, and we will become one people.

¹⁷But if ye will not hearken unto us, to be circumcised; then will we take our daughter, and we will be gone.

¹⁸And their words pleased Hamor, and Shechem Hamor's son.

¹⁹And the young man deferred not to do the thing, because he had delight in Jacob's daughter: and he was more honourable than all the house of his father.

²⁰And Hamor and Shechem his son came unto the gate of their city, and communed with the men of their city, saying,

²¹These men are peaceable with us; therefore let them dwell in the land, and trade therein; for the land, behold, it is large enough for them; let us take their daughters to us for wives, and let us give them our daughters.

²²Only herein will the men consent unto us for to dwell with us, to be one people, if every male among us be circumcised, as they are circumcised.

²³Shall not their cattle and their substance and every beast of theirs be our's? only let us consent unto them, and they will dwell with us.

²⁴And unto Hamor and unto Shechem his son hearkened all that went out of the gate of his city; and every male was circumcised, all that went out of the gate of his city.

²⁵And it came to pass on the third day, when they were sore, that two of the sons of Jacob, Simeon and Levi, Dinah's brethren, took each man his sword, and came upon the city boldly, and slew all the males.

²⁶And they slew Hamor and Shechem his son with the edge of the sword, and took Dinah out of Shechem's house, and went out.

²⁷The sons of Jacob came upon the slain, and spoiled the city, because they had defiled their sister.

²⁸They took their sheep, and their oxen, and their asses, and that which was in the city, and that which was in the field,

²⁹And all their wealth, and all their little ones, and their wives took they captive, and spoiled even all that was in the house.

³⁰And Jacob said to Simeon and Levi, Ye have troubled me to make me to stink among the inhabitants of the land, among the Canaanites and the Perizzites: and I being few in number, they shall gather themselves together against me, and slay me; and I shall be destroyed, I and my house.

³¹And they said, Should he deal with our sister as with an harlot?

CHAPTER 35

¹And God said unto Jacob, Arise, go up to Bethel, and dwell there: and make there an altar unto God, that appeared unto thee when thou fleddest from the face of Esau thy brother.

²Then Jacob said unto his household, and to all that were with him, Put away the strange gods that are among you, and be clean, and change your garments:

³And let us arise, and go up to Bethel; and I will make there an altar unto God, who answered me in the day of my distress, and was with me in the way which I went.

⁴And they gave unto Jacob all the strange gods which were in their hand, and all their earrings which were in their ears; and Jacob hid

them under the oak which was by Shechem.

⁵And they journeyed: and the terror of God was upon the cities that were round about them, and they did not pursue after the sons of Jacob.

⁶So Jacob came to Luz, which is in the land of Canaan, that is, Bethel, he and all the people that were with him.

⁷And he built there an altar, and called the place El-beth-el: because there God appeared unto him, when he fled from the face of his brother.

⁸But Deborah Rebekah's nurse died, and she was buried beneath Bethel under an oak: and the name of it was called Allon-bachuth.

⁹And God appeared unto Jacob again, when he came out of Padan-aram, and blessed him.

¹⁰And God said unto him, Thy name is Jacob: thy name shall not be called any more Jacob, but Israel shall be thy name: and he called his name Israel.

¹¹And God said unto him, I am God Almighty: be fruitful and multiply; a nation and a company of nations shall be of thee, and kings shall come out of thy loins;

¹²And the land which I gave Abraham and Isaac, to thee I will give it, and to thy seed after thee will I give the land.

¹³And God went up from him in the place where he talked with him.

¹⁴And Jacob set up a pillar in the place where he talked with him, even a pillar of stone: and he poured a drink offering thereon, and he poured oil thereon.

¹⁵And Jacob called the name of the place where God spake with him, Bethel.

¹⁶And they journeyed from Bethel; and there was but a little way to come to Ephrath: and Rachel travailed, and she had hard labour.

¹⁷And it came to pass, when she was in hard labour, that the midwife said unto her, Fear not; thou shalt have this son also.

¹⁸And it came to pass, as her soul was in departing, (for she died) that she called his name Benoni: but his father called him Ben-jamin.

¹⁹And Rachel died, and was buried in the way to Ephrath, which is Bethlehem.

²⁰And Jacob set a pillar upon her grave: that is the pillar of Rachel's grave unto this day.

²¹And Israel journeyed, and spread his tent beyond the tower of Edar.

²²And it came to pass, when Israel dwelt in that land, that Reuben went and lay with Bilhah his father's concubine: and Israel heard it. Now the sons of Jacob were twelve:

²³The sons of Leah; Reuben, Jacob's firstborn, and Simeon, and Levi, and Judah, and Issachar, and Zebulun:

²⁴The sons of Rachel; Joseph, and Ben-jamin:

²⁵And the sons of Bilhah, Rachel's handmaid; Dan, and Naphtali:

²⁶And the sons of Zilpah, Leah's handmaid: Gad, and Asher: these are the sons of Jacob, which were born to him in Padan-aram.

²⁷And Jacob came unto Isaac his father unto Mamre, unto the city of Arbah, which is Hebron, where Abraham and Isaac sojourned.

²⁸And the days of Isaac were an hundred and fourscore years.

²⁹And Isaac gave up the ghost, and died, and was gathered unto his people, being old and full of days: and his sons Esau and Jacob buried him.

CHAPTER 36

¹Now these are the generations of Esau, who is Edom.

²Esau took his wives of the daughters of Canaan; Adah the daughter of Elon the Hittite, and Aholibamah the daughter of Anah the daughter of Zibeon the Hivite;

³And Bashemath Ishmael's daughter, sister of Nebajoth.

⁴And Adah bare to Esau Eliphaz; and Bashemath bare Reuel;

⁵And Aholibamah bare Jeush, and Jaalam, and Korah: these are the sons of Esau, which were born unto him in the land of Canaan.

⁶And Esau took his wives, and his sons, and his daughters, and all the persons of his house, and his cattle, and all his beasts, and all his substance, which he had got in the land of Canaan; and went into the country from the face of his brother Jacob.

⁷For their riches were more than that they might dwell together; and the land wherein they were strangers could not bear them because of their cattle.

⁸Thus dwelt Esau in mount Seir: Esau is Edom.

⁹And these are the generations of Esau the father of the Edomites in mount Seir:

¹⁰These are the names of Esau's sons; Eliphaz the son of Adah the wife of Esau, Reuel the son of Bashemath the wife of Esau.

¹¹And the sons of Eliphaz were Teman, Omar, Zepho, and Gatam, and Kenaz.

¹²And Timna was concubine to Eliphaz Esau's son; and she bare to Eliphaz Amalek: these were the sons of Adah Esau's wife.

¹³And these are the sons of Reuel; Nahath, and Zerah, Shammah, and

Mizzah: these were the sons of Bashemath Esau's wife.

¹⁴And these were the sons of Aholibamah, the daughter of Anah the daughter of Zibeon, Esau's wife: and she bare to Esau Jeush, and Jaalam, and Korah.

¹⁵These were dukes of the sons of Esau: the sons of Eliphaz the firstborn son of Esau; duke Teman, duke Omar, duke Zepho, duke Kenaz,

¹⁶Duke Korah, duke Gatam, and duke Amalek: these are the dukes that came of Eliphaz in the land of Edom; these were the sons of Adah.

¹⁷And these are the sons of Reuel Esau's son; duke Nahath, duke Zerah, duke Shammah, duke Mizzah: these are the dukes that came of Reuel in the land of Edom; these are the sons of Bashemath Esau's wife.

¹⁸And these are the sons of Aholibamah Esau's wife; duke Jeush, duke Jaalam, duke Korah: these were the dukes that came of Aholibamah the daughter of Anah, Esau's wife.

¹⁹These are the sons of Esau, who is Edom, and these are their dukes.

²⁰These are the sons of Seir the Horite, who inhabited the land; Lotan, and Shobal, and Zibeon, and Anah,

²¹And Dishon, and Ezer, and Dishan: these are the dukes of the Horites, the children of Seir in the land of Edom.

²²And the children of Lotan were Hori and Hemam; and Lotan's sister was Timna.

²³And the children of Shobal were these; Alvan, and Manahath, and Ebal, Shepho, and Onam.

²⁴And these are the children of Zibeon; both Ajah, and Anah: this was that Anah that found the mules in the wilderness, as he fed the asses of Zibeon his father.

²⁵And the children of Anah were these; Dishon, and Aholibamah the daughter of Anah.

²⁶And these are the children of Dishon; Hemdan, and Eshban, and Ithran, and Cheran.

²⁷The children of Ezer are these; Bilhan, and Zaavan, and Akan.

²⁸The children of Dishan are these; Uz, and Aran.

²⁹These are the dukes that came of the Horites; duke Lotan, duke Shobal, duke Zibeon, duke Anah,

³⁰Duke Dishon, duke Ezer, duke Dishan: these are the dukes that came of Hori, among their dukes in the land of Seir.

³¹And these are the kings that reigned in the land of Edom, before there reigned any king over the children of Israel.

³²And Bela the son of Beor reigned in Edom: and the name of his city was Dinhabah.

³³And Bela died, and Jobab the son of Zerah of Bozrah reigned in his stead.

³⁴And Jobab died, and Husham of the land of Temani reigned in his stead.

³⁵And Husham died, and Hadad the son of Bedad, who smote Midian in the field of Moab, reigned in his stead: and the name of his city was Avith.

³⁶And Hadad died, and Samlah of Masrekah reigned in his stead.

³⁷And Samlah died, and Saul of Rehoboth by the river reigned in his stead.

³⁸And Saul died, and Baal-hanan the son of Achbor reigned in his stead.

³⁹And Baal-hanan the son of Achbor died, and Hadar reigned in his stead: and the name of his city was Pau; and his wife's name was Mehetabel, the daughter of Matred, the daughter of Mezahab.

⁴⁰And these are the names of the dukes that came of Esau, according to their families, after their places, by their names; duke Timnah, duke Alvah, duke Jetheth,

⁴¹Duke Aholibamah, duke Elah, duke Pinon,

⁴²Duke Kenaz, duke Teman, duke Mibzar,

⁴³Duke Magdiel, duke Iram: these be the dukes of Edom, according to their habitations in the land of their possession: he is Esau the father of the Edomites.

Chapter 37

¹And Jacob dwelt in the land wherein his father was a stranger, in the land of Canaan.

²These are the generations of Jacob. Joseph, being seventeen years old, was feeding the flock with his brethren; and the lad was with the sons of Bilhah, and with the sons of Zilpah, his father's wives: and Joseph brought unto his father their evil report.

³Now Israel loved Joseph more than all his children, because he was the son of his old age: and he made him a coat of many colours.

⁴And when his brethren saw that their father loved him more than all his brethren, they hated him, and could not speak peaceably unto him.

⁵And Joseph dreamed a dream, and he told it his brethren: and they hated him yet the more.

⁶And he said unto them, Hear, I pray you, this dream which I have dreamed:

⁷For, behold, we were binding sheaves in the field, and, lo, my sheaf arose, and also stood upright; and, behold, your sheaves stood round about, and made obeisance to my sheaf.

⁸And his brethren said to him, Shalt thou indeed reign over us? or shalt thou indeed have dominion over us? And they hated him yet the more for his dreams, and for his words.

⁹And he dreamed yet another dream, and told it his brethren, and said, Behold, I have dreamed a dream more; and, behold, the sun and the moon and the eleven stars made obeisance to me.

¹⁰And he told it to his father, and to his brethren: and his father rebuked him, and said unto him, What is this dream that thou hast dreamed? Shall I and thy mother and thy brethren indeed come to bow down ourselves to thee to the earth?

¹¹And his brethren envied him; but his father observed the saying.

¹²And his brethren went to feed their father's flock in Shechem.

¹³And Israel said unto Joseph, Do not thy brethren feed the flock in Shechem? come, and I will send thee unto them. And he said to him, Here am I.

¹⁴And he said to him, Go, I pray thee, see whether it be well with thy brethren, and well with the flocks; and bring me word again. So he sent him out of the vale of Hebron, and he came to Shechem.

¹⁵And a certain man found him, and, behold, he was wandering in the field: and the man asked him, saying, What seekest thou?

¹⁶And he said, I seek my brethren: tell me, I pray thee, where they feed their flocks.

¹⁷And the man said, They are departed hence; for I heard them say, Let us go to Dothan. And Joseph went after his brethren, and found them in Dothan.

¹⁸And when they saw him afar off, even before he came near unto them, they conspired against him to slay him.

¹⁹And they said one to another, Behold, this dreamer cometh.

²⁰Come now therefore, and let us slay him, and cast him into some pit, and we will say, Some evil beast hath devoured him: and we shall see what will become of his dreams.

²¹And Reuben heard it, and he delivered him out of their hands; and said, Let us not kill him.

²²And Reuben said unto them, Shed no blood, but cast him into

this pit that is in the wilderness, and lay no hand upon him; that he might rid him out of their hands, to deliver him to his father again.

²³And it came to pass, when Joseph was come unto his brethren, that they stript Joseph out of his coat, his coat of many colours that was on him;

²⁴And they took him, and cast him into a pit: and the pit was empty, there was no water in it.

²⁵And they sat down to eat bread: and they lifted up their eyes and looked, and, behold, a company of Ishmeelites came from Gilead with their camels bearing spicery and balm and myrrh, going to carry it down to Egypt.

²⁶And Judah said unto his brethren, What profit is it if we slay our brother, and conceal his blood?

²⁷Come, and let us sell him to the Ishmeelites, and let not our hand be upon him; for he is our brother and our flesh. And his brethren were content.

²⁸Then there passed by Midianites merchantmen; and they drew and lifted up Joseph out of the pit, and sold Joseph to the Ishmeelites for twenty pieces of silver: and they brought Joseph into Egypt.

²⁹And Reuben returned unto the pit; and, behold, Joseph was not in the pit; and he rent his clothes.

³⁰And he returned unto his brethren, and said, The child is not; and I, whither shall I go?

³¹And they took Joseph's coat, and killed a kid of the goats, and dipped the coat in the blood;

³²And they sent the coat of many colours, and they brought it to their father; and said, This have we found: know now whether it be thy son's coat or no.

³³And he knew it, and said, It is my son's coat; an evil beast hath devoured him; Joseph is without doubt rent in pieces.

³⁴And Jacob rent his clothes, and put sackcloth upon his loins, and mourned for his son many days.

³⁵And all his sons and all his daughters rose up to comfort him; but he refused to be comforted; and he said, For I will go down into the grave unto my son mourning. Thus his father wept for him.

³⁶And the Midianites sold him into Egypt unto Potiphar, an officer of Pharaoh's, and captain of the guard.

CHAPTER 38

¹And it came to pass at that time, that Judah went down from his brethren, and turned in to a certain Adullamite, whose name was Hirah.

²And Judah saw there a daughter of a certain Canaanite, whose name was Shuah; and he took her, and went in unto her.

³And she conceived, and bare a son; and he called his name Er.

⁴And she conceived again, and bare a son; and she called his name Onan.

⁵And she yet again conceived, and bare a son; and called his name Shelah: and he was at Chezib, when she bare him.

⁶And Judah took a wife for Er his firstborn, whose name was Tamar.

⁷And Er, Judah's firstborn, was wicked in the sight of the LORD; and the LORD slew him.

⁸And Judah said unto Onan, Go in unto thy brother's wife, and marry her, and raise up seed to thy brother.

⁹And Onan knew that the seed should not be his; and it came to pass, when he went in unto his brother's wife, that he spilled it on the ground, lest that he should give seed to his brother.

¹⁰And the thing which he did displeased the LORD: wherefore he slew him also.

¹¹Then said Judah to Tamar his daughter in law, Remain a widow at thy father's house, till Shelah my son be grown: for he said, Lest peradventure he die also, as his brethren did. And Tamar went and dwelt in her father's house.

¹²And in process of time the daughter of Shuah Judah's wife died; and Judah was comforted, and went up unto his sheepshearers to Timnath, he and his friend Hirah the Adullamite.

¹³And it was told Tamar, saying, Behold thy father in law goeth up to Timnath to shear his sheep.

¹⁴And she put her widow's garments off from her, and covered her with a vail, and wrapped herself, and sat in an open place, which is by the way to Timnath; for she saw that Shelah was grown, and she was not given unto him to wife.

¹⁵When Judah saw her he thought her to be an harlot; because she had covered her face.

¹⁶And he turned unto her by the way, and said, Go to, I pray thee, let me come in unto thee; (for he knew not that she was his daughter in law.) And she said, What wilt thou give me, that thou mayest come in unto me?

¹⁷And he said, I will send thee a kid from the flock. And she said, Wilt thou give me a pledge, till thou send it?

¹⁸And he said, What pledge shall I give thee? And she said, Thy signet, and thy bracelets, and thy staff that is in thine hand. And he gave it

her, and came in unto her, and she conceived by him.

¹⁹And she arose, and went away, and laid by her vail from her, and put on the garments of her widowhood.

²⁰And Judah sent the kid by the hand of his friend the Adullamite, to receive his pledge from the woman's hand: but he found her not.

²¹Then he asked the men of that place, saying, Where is the harlot, that was openly by the way side? And they said, There was no harlot in this place.

²²And he returned to Judah, and said, I cannot find her; and also the men of the place said, that there was no harlot in this place.

²³And Judah said, Let her take it to her, lest we be shamed: behold, I sent this kid, and thou hast not found her.

²⁴And it came to pass about three months after, that it was told Judah, saying, Tamar thy daughter in law hath played the harlot; and also, behold, she is with child by whoredom. And Judah said, Bring her forth, and let her be burnt.

²⁵When she was brought forth, she sent to her father in law, saying, By the man, whose these are, am I with child: and she said, Discern, I pray thee, whose are these, the signet, and bracelets, and staff.

²⁶And Judah acknowledged them, and said, She hath been more righteous than I; because that I gave her not to Shelah my son. And he knew her again no more.

²⁷And it came to pass in the time of her travail, that, behold, twins were in her womb.

²⁸And it came to pass, when she travailed, that the one put out his hand: and the midwife took and bound upon his hand a scarlet thread, saying, This came out first.

²⁹And it came to pass, as he drew back his hand, that, behold, his brother came out: and she said, How hast thou broken forth? this breach be upon thee: therefore his name was called Pharez.

³⁰And afterward came out his brother, that had the scarlet thread upon his hand: and his name was called Zarah.

CHAPTER 39

¹And Joseph was brought down to Egypt; and Potiphar, an officer of Pharaoh, captain of the guard, an Egyptian, bought him of the hands of the Ishmeelites, which had brought him down thither.

²And the LORD was with Joseph, and he was a prosperous man; and

he was in the house of his master the Egyptian.

³And his master saw that the LORD was with him, and that the LORD made all that he did to prosper in his hand.

⁴And Joseph found grace in his sight, and he served him: and he made him overseer over his house, and all that he had he put into his hand.

⁵And it came to pass from the time that he had made him overseer in his house, and over all that he had, that the LORD blessed the Egyptian's house for Joseph's sake; and the blessing of the LORD was upon all that he had in the house, and in the field.

⁶And he left all that he had in Joseph's hand; and he knew not ought he had, save the bread which he did eat. And Joseph was a goodly person, and well favoured.

⁷And it came to pass after these things, that his master's wife cast her eyes upon Joseph; and she said, Lie with me.

⁸But he refused, and said unto his master's wife, Behold, my master wotteth not what is with me in the house, and he hath committed all that he hath to my hand;

⁹There is none greater in this house than I; neither hath he kept back any thing from me but thee, because thou art his wife: how then can I do this great wickedness, and sin against God?

¹⁰And it came to pass, as she spake to Joseph day by day, that he hearkened not unto her, to lie by her, or to be with her.

¹¹And it came to pass about this time, that Joseph went into the house to do his business; and there was none of the men of the house there within.

¹²And she caught him by his garment, saying, Lie with me: and he left his garment in her hand, and fled, and got him out.

¹³And it came to pass, when she saw that he had left his garment in her hand, and was fled forth,

¹⁴That she called unto the men of her house, and spake unto them, saying, See, he hath brought in an Hebrew unto us to mock us; he came in unto me to lie with me, and I cried with a loud voice:

¹⁵And it came to pass, when he heard that I lifted up my voice and cried, that he left his garment with me, and fled, and got him out.

¹⁶And she laid up his garment by her, until his lord came home.

¹⁷And she spake unto him according to these words, saying, The Hebrew servant, which thou hast brought unto us, came in unto me to mock me:

¹⁸And it came to pass, as I lifted up my voice and cried, that he left his garment with me, and fled out.

¹⁹And it came to pass, when his master heard the words of his wife, which she spake unto him, saying, After this manner did thy servant to me; that his wrath was kindled.

²⁰And Joseph's master took him, and put him into the prison, a place where the king's prisoners were bound: and he was there in the prison.

²¹But the LORD was with Joseph, and shewed him mercy, and gave him favour in the sight of the keeper of the prison.

²²And the keeper of the prison committed to Joseph's hand all the prisoners that were in the prison; and whatsoever they did there, he was the doer of it.

²³The keeper of the prison looked not to any thing that was under his hand; because the LORD was with him, and that which he did, the LORD made it to prosper.

CHAPTER 40

¹And it came to pass after these things, that the butler of the king of Egypt and his baker had offended their lord the king of Egypt.

²And Pharaoh was wroth against two of his officers, against the chief of the butlers, and against the chief of the bakers.

³And he put them in ward in the house of the captain of the guard, into the prison, the place where Joseph was bound.

⁴And the captain of the guard charged Joseph with them, and he served them: and they continued a season in ward.

⁵And they dreamed a dream both of them, each man his dream in one night, each man according to the interpretation of his dream, the butler and the baker of the king of Egypt, which were bound in the prison.

⁶And Joseph came in unto them in the morning, and looked upon them, and, behold, they were sad.

⁷And he asked Pharaoh's officers that were with him in the ward of his lord's house, saying, Wherefore look ye so sadly to day?

⁸And they said unto him, We have dreamed a dream, and there is no interpreter of it. And Joseph said unto them, Do not interpretations belong to God? tell me them, I pray you.

⁹And the chief butler told his dream to Joseph, and said to him, In my dream, behold, a vine was before me;

¹⁰And in the vine were three branches: and it was as though it budded, and her blossoms shot forth; and the clusters thereof brought forth ripe grapes:

¹¹And Pharaoh's cup was in my hand: and I took the grapes, and pressed them into Pharaoh's cup, and I gave the cup into Pharaoh's hand.

¹²And Joseph said unto him, This is the interpretation of it: The three branches are three days:

¹³Yet within three days shall Pharaoh lift up thine head, and restore thee unto thy place: and thou shalt deliver Pharaoh's cup into his hand, after the former manner when thou wast his butler.

¹⁴But think on me when it shall be well with thee, and shew kindness, I pray thee, unto me, and make mention of me unto Pharaoh, and bring me out of this house:

¹⁵For indeed I was stolen away out of the land of the Hebrews: and here also have I done nothing that they should put me into the dungeon.

¹⁶When the chief baker saw that the interpretation was good, he said unto Joseph, I also was in my dream, and, behold, I had three white baskets on my head:

¹⁷And in the uppermost basket there was of all manner of bakemeats for Pharaoh; and the birds did eat them out of the basket upon my head.

¹⁸And Joseph answered and said, This is the interpretation thereof: The three baskets are three days:

¹⁹Yet within three days shall Pharaoh lift up thy head from off thee, and shall hang thee on a tree; and the birds shall eat thy flesh from off thee.

²⁰And it came to pass the third day, which was Pharaoh's birthday, that he made a feast unto all his servants: and he lifted up the head of the chief butler and of the chief baker among his servants.

²¹And he restored the chief butler unto his butlership again; and he gave the cup into Pharaoh's hand:

²²But he hanged the chief baker: as Joseph had interpreted to them.

²³Yet did not the chief butler remember Joseph, but forgat him.

CHAPTER 41

¹And it came to pass at the end of two full years, that Pharaoh dreamed: and, behold, he stood by the river.

²And, behold, there came up out of the river seven well favoured kine and fatfleshed; and they fed in a meadow.

³And, behold, seven other kine came up after them out of the river, ill favoured and leanfleshed; and stood by the other kine upon the brink of the river.

⁴And the ill favoured and leanfleshed kine did eat up the seven well favoured and fat kine. So Pharaoh awoke.

⁵And he slept and dreamed the second time: and, behold, seven ears of corn came up upon one stalk, rank and good.

⁶And, behold, seven thin ears and blasted with the east wind sprung up after them.

⁷And the seven thin ears devoured the seven rank and full ears. And Pharaoh awoke, and, behold, it was a dream.

⁸And it came to pass in the morning that his spirit was troubled; and he sent and called for all the magicians of Egypt, and all the wise men thereof: and Pharaoh told them his dream; but there was none that could interpret them unto Pharaoh.

⁹Then spake the chief butler unto Pharaoh, saying, I do remember my faults this day:

¹⁰Pharaoh was wroth with his servants, and put me in ward in the captain of the guard's house, both me and the chief baker:

¹¹And we dreamed a dream in one night, I and he; we dreamed each man according to the interpretation of his dream.

¹²And there was there with us a young man, an Hebrew, servant to the captain of the guard; and we told him, and he interpreted to us our dreams; to each man according to his dream he did interpret.

¹³And it came to pass, as he interpreted to us, so it was; me he restored unto mine office, and him he hanged.

¹⁴Then Pharaoh sent and called Joseph, and they brought him hastily out of the dungeon: and he shaved himself, and changed his raiment, and came in unto Pharaoh.

¹⁵And Pharaoh said unto Joseph, I have dreamed a dream, and there is none that can interpret it: and I have heard say of thee, that thou canst understand a dream to interpret it.

¹⁶And Joseph answered Pharaoh, saying, It is not in me: God shall give Pharaoh an answer of peace.

¹⁷And Pharaoh said unto Joseph, In my dream, behold, I stood upon the bank of the river:

¹⁸And, behold, there came up out of the river seven kine, fatfleshed and well favoured; and they fed in a meadow:

¹⁹And, behold, seven other kine came up after them, poor and very ill favoured and leanfleshed, such as

I never saw in all the land of Egypt for badness:

²⁰And the lean and the ill favoured kine did eat up the first seven fat kine:

²¹And when they had eaten them up, it could not be known that they had eaten them; but they were still ill favoured, as at the beginning. So I awoke.

²²And I saw in my dream, and, behold, seven ears came up in one stalk, full and good:

²³And, behold, seven ears, withered, thin, and blasted with the east wind, sprung up after them:

²⁴And the thin ears devoured the seven good ears: and I told this unto the magicians; but there was none that could declare it to me.

²⁵And Joseph said unto Pharaoh, The dream of Pharaoh is one: God hath shewed Pharaoh what he is about to do.

²⁶The seven good kine are seven years; and the seven good ears are seven years: the dream is one.

²⁷And the seven thin and ill favoured kine that came up after them are seven years; and the seven empty ears blasted with the east wind shall be seven years of famine.

²⁸This is the thing which I have spoken unto Pharaoh: What God is about to do he sheweth unto Pharaoh.

²⁹Behold, there come seven years of great plenty throughout all the land of Egypt:

³⁰And there shall arise after them seven years of famine; and all the plenty shall be forgotten in the land of Egypt; and the famine shall consume the land;

³¹And the plenty shall not be known in the land by reason of that famine following; for it shall be very grievous.

³²And for that the dream was doubled unto Pharaoh twice; it is because the thing is established by God, and God will shortly bring it to pass.

³³Now therefore let Pharaoh look out a man discreet and wise, and set him over the land of Egypt.

³⁴Let Pharaoh do this, and let him appoint officers over the land, and take up the fifth part of the land of Egypt in the seven plenteous years.

³⁵And let them gather all the food of those good years that come, and lay up corn under the hand of Pharaoh, and let them keep food in the cities.

³⁶And that food shall be for store to the land against the seven years of famine, which shall be in the land of Egypt; that the land perish not through the famine.

³⁷And the thing was good in the eyes of Pharaoh, and in the eyes of all his servants.

38And Pharaoh said unto his servants, Can we find such a one as this is, a man in whom the Spirit of God is?

39And Pharaoh said unto Joseph, Forasmuch as God hath shewed thee all this, there is none so discreet and wise as thou art:

40Thou shalt be over my house, and according unto thy word shall all my people be ruled: only in the throne will I be greater than thou.

41And Pharaoh said unto Joseph, See, I have set thee over all the land of Egypt.

42And Pharaoh took off his ring from his hand, and put it upon Joseph's hand, and arrayed him in vestures of fine linen, and put a gold chain about his neck;

43And he made him to ride in the second chariot which he had; and they cried before him, Bow the knee: and he made him ruler over all the land of Egypt.

44And Pharaoh said unto Joseph, I am Pharaoh, and without thee shall no man lift up his hand or foot in all the land of Egypt.

45And Pharaoh called Joseph's name Zaphnath-paaneah; and he gave him to wife Asenath the daughter of Poti-pherah priest of On. And Joseph went out over all the land of Egypt.

46And Joseph was thirty years old when he stood before Pharaoh king of Egypt. And Joseph went out from the presence of Pharaoh, and went throughout all the land of Egypt.

47And in the seven plenteous years the earth brought forth by handfuls.

48And he gathered up all the food of the seven years, which were in the land of Egypt, and laid up the food in the cities: the food of the field, which was round about every city, laid he up in the same.

49And Joseph gathered corn as the sand of the sea, very much, until he left numbering; for it was without number.

50And unto Joseph were born two sons before the years of famine came, which Asenath the daughter of Poti-pherah priest of On bare unto him.

51And Joseph called the name of the firstborn Manasseh: For God, said he, hath made me forget all my toil, and all my father's house.

52And the name of the second called he Ephraim: For God hath caused me to be fruitful in the land of my affliction.

53And the seven years of plenteousness, that was in the land of Egypt, were ended.

54And the seven years of dearth began to come, according as Joseph had said: and the dearth was in all lands; but in all the land of Egypt there was bread.

⁵⁵And when all the land of Egypt was famished, the people cried to Pharaoh for bread: and Pharaoh said unto all the Egyptians, Go unto Joseph; what he saith to you, do.

⁵⁶And the famine was over all the face of the earth: and Joseph opened all the storehouses, and sold unto the Egyptians; and the famine waxed sore in the land of Egypt.

⁵⁷And all countries came into Egypt to Joseph for to buy corn; because that the famine was so sore in all lands.

CHAPTER 42

¹Now when Jacob saw that there was corn in Egypt, Jacob said unto his sons, Why do ye look one upon another?

²And he said, Behold, I have heard that there is corn in Egypt: get you down thither, and buy for us from thence; that we may live, and not die.

³And Joseph's ten brethren went down to buy corn in Egypt.

⁴But Ben-jamin, Joseph's brother, Jacob sent not with his brethren; for he said, Lest peradventure mischief befall him.

⁵And the sons of Israel came to buy corn among those that came: for the famine was in the land of Canaan.

⁶And Joseph was the governor over the land, and he it was that sold to all the people of the land: and Joseph's brethren came, and bowed down themselves before him with their faces to the earth.

⁷And Joseph saw his brethren, and he knew them, but made himself strange unto them, and spake roughly unto them; and he said unto them, Whence come ye? And they said, From the land of Canaan to buy food.

⁸And Joseph knew his brethren, but they knew not him.

⁹And Joseph remembered the dreams which he dreamed of them, and said unto them, Ye are spies; to see the nakedness of the land ye are come.

¹⁰And they said unto him, Nay, my lord, but to buy food are thy servants come.

¹¹We are all one man's sons; we are true men, thy servants are no spies.

¹²And he said unto them, Nay, but to see the nakedness of the land ye are come.

¹³And they said, Thy servants are twelve brethren, the sons of one

man in the land of Canaan; and, behold, the youngest is this day with our father, and one is not.

¹⁴And Joseph said unto them, That is it that I spake unto you, saying, Ye are spies:

¹⁵Hereby ye shall be proved: By the life of Pharaoh ye shall not go forth hence, except your youngest brother come hither.

¹⁶Send one of you, and let him fetch your brother, and ye shall be kept in prison, that your words may be proved, whether there be any truth in you: or else by the life of Pharaoh surely ye are spies.

¹⁷And he put them all together into ward three days.

¹⁸And Joseph said unto them the third day, This do, and live; for I fear God:

¹⁹If ye be true men, let one of your brethren be bound in the house of your prison: go ye, carry corn for the famine of your houses:

²⁰But bring your youngest brother unto me; so shall your words be verified, and ye shall not die. And they did so.

²¹And they said one to another, We are verily guilty concerning our brother, in that we saw the anguish of his soul, when he besought us, and we would not hear; therefore is this distress come upon us.

²²And Reuben answered them, saying, Spake I not unto you, saying, Do not sin against the child; and ye would not hear? therefore, behold, also his blood is required.

²³And they knew not that Joseph understood them; for he spake unto them by an interpreter.

²⁴And he turned himself about from them, and wept; and returned to them again, and communed with them, and took from them Simeon, and bound him before their eyes.

²⁵Then Joseph commanded to fill their sacks with corn, and to restore every man's money into his sack, and to give them provision for the way: and thus did he unto them.

²⁶And they laded their asses with the corn, and departed thence.

²⁷And as one of them opened his sack to give his ass provender in the inn, he espied his money; for, behold, it was in his sack's mouth.

²⁸And he said unto his brethren, My money is restored; and, lo, it is even in my sack: and their heart failed them, and they were afraid, saying one to another, What is this that God hath done unto us?

²⁹And they came unto Jacob their father unto the land of Canaan, and told him all that befell unto them; saying,

³⁰The man, who is the lord of the

land, spake roughly to us, and took us for spies of the country.

³¹And we said unto him, We are true men; we are no spies:

³²We be twelve brethren, sons of our father; one is not, and the youngest is this day with our father in the land of Canaan.

³³And the man, the lord of the country, said unto us, Hereby shall I know that ye are true men; leave one of your brethren here with me, and take food for the famine of your households, and be gone:

³⁴And bring your youngest brother unto me: then shall I know that ye are no spies, but that ye are true men: so will I deliver you your brother, and ye shall traffick in the land.

³⁵And it came to pass as they emptied their sacks, that, behold, every man's bundle of money was in his sack: and when both they and their father saw the bundles of money, they were afraid.

³⁶And Jacob their father said unto them, Me have ye bereaved of my children: Joseph is not, and Simeon is not, and ye will take Ben-jamin away: all these things are against me.

³⁷And Reuben spake unto his father, saying, Slay my two sons, if I bring him not to thee: deliver him into my hand, and I will bring him to thee again.

³⁸And he said, My son shall not go down with you; for his brother is dead, and he is left alone: if mischief befall him by the way in the which ye go, then shall ye bring down my gray hairs with sorrow to the grave.

CHAPTER 43

¹And the famine was sore in the land.

²And it came to pass, when they had eaten up the corn which they had brought out of Egypt, their father said unto them, Go again, buy us a little food.

³And Judah spake unto him, saying, The man did solemnly protest unto us, saying, Ye shall not see my face, except your brother be with you.

⁴If thou wilt send our brother with us, we will go down and buy thee food:

⁵But if thou wilt not send him, we will not go down: for the man said unto us, Ye shall not see my face, except your brother be with you.

⁶And Israel said, Wherefore dealt ye so ill with me, as to tell the man whether ye had yet a brother?

⁷And they said, The man asked us straitly of our state, and of our

kindred, saying, Is your father yet alive? have ye another brother? and we told him according to the tenor of these words: could we certainly know that he would say, Bring your brother down?

⁸And Judah said unto Israel his father, Send the lad with me, and we will arise and go; that we may live, and not die, both we, and thou, and also our little ones.

⁹I will be surety for him; of my hand shalt thou require him: if I bring him not unto thee, and set him before thee, then let me bear the blame for ever:

¹⁰For except we had lingered, surely now we had returned this second time.

¹¹And their father Israel said unto them, If it must be so now, do this; take of the best fruits in the land in your vessels, and carry down the man a present, a little balm, and a little honey, spices, and myrrh, nuts, and almonds:

¹²And take double money in your hand; and the money that was brought again in the mouth of your sacks, carry it again in your hand; peradventure it was an oversight:

¹³Take also your brother, and arise, go again unto the man:

¹⁴And God Almighty give you mercy before the man, that he may send away your other brother, and Ben-jamin. If I be bereaved of my children, I am bereaved.

¹⁵And the men took that present, and they took double money in their hand and Ben-jamin; and rose up, and went down to Egypt, and stood before Joseph.

¹⁶And when Joseph saw Ben-jamin with them, he said to the ruler of his house, Bring these men home, and slay, and make ready; for these men shall dine with me at noon.

¹⁷And the man did as Joseph bade; and the man brought the men into Joseph's house.

¹⁸And the men were afraid, because they were brought into Joseph's house; and they said, Because of the money that was returned in our sacks at the first time are we brought in; that he may seek occasion against us, and fall upon us, and take us for bondmen, and our asses.

¹⁹And they came near to the steward of Joseph's house, and they communed with him at the door of the house,

²⁰And said, O sir, we came indeed down at the first time to buy food:

²¹And it came to pass, when we came to the inn, that we opened our sacks, and, behold, every man's money was in the mouth of his sack, our money in full weight: and we have brought it again in our hand.

²²And other money have we brought down in our hands to buy food: we cannot tell who put our money in our sacks.

²³And he said, Peace be to you, fear not: your God, and the God of your father, hath given you treasure in your sacks: I had your money. And he brought Simeon out unto them.

²⁴And the man brought the men into Joseph's house, and gave them water, and they washed their feet; and he gave their asses provender.

²⁵And they made ready the present against Joseph came at noon: for they heard that they should eat bread there.

²⁶And when Joseph came home, they brought him the present which was in their hand into the house, and bowed themselves to him to the earth.

²⁷And he asked them of their welfare, and said, Is your father well, the old man of whom ye spake? Is he yet alive?

²⁸And they answered, Thy servant our father is in good health, he is yet alive. And they bowed down their heads, and made obeisance.

²⁹And he lifted up his eyes, and saw his brother Ben-jamin, his mother's son, and said, Is this your younger brother, of whom ye spake unto me? And he said, God be gracious unto thee, my son.

³⁰And Joseph made haste; for his bowels did yearn upon his brother: and he sought where to weep; and he entered into his chamber, and wept there.

³¹And he washed his face, and went out, and refrained himself, and said, Set on bread.

³²And they set on for him by himself, and for them by themselves, and for the Egyptians, which did eat with him, by themselves: because the Egyptians might not eat bread with the Hebrews; for that is an abomination unto the Egyptians.

³³And they sat before him, the firstborn according to his birthright, and the youngest according to his youth: and the men marvelled one at another.

³⁴And he took and sent messes unto them from before him: but Ben-jamin's mess was five times so much as any of theirs. And they drank, and were merry with him.

CHAPTER 44

¹And he commanded the steward of his house, saying, Fill the men's sacks with food, as much as they can carry, and put every man's money in his sack's mouth.

²And put my cup, the silver cup, in the sack's mouth of the youngest, and his corn money. And he did according to the word that Joseph had spoken.

³As soon as the morning was light, the men were sent away, they and their asses.

⁴And when they were gone out of the city, and not yet far off, Joseph said unto his steward, Up, follow after the men; and when thou dost overtake them, say unto them, Wherefore have ye rewarded evil for good?

⁵Is not this it in which my lord drinketh, and whereby indeed he divineth? ye have done evil in so doing.

⁶And he overtook them, and he spake unto them these same words.

⁷And they said unto him, Wherefore saith my lord these words? God forbid that thy servants should do according to this thing:

⁸Behold, the money, which we found in our sacks' mouths, we brought again unto thee out of the land of Canaan: how then should we steal out of thy lord's house silver or gold?

⁹With whomsoever of thy servants it be found, both let him die, and we also will be my lord's bondmen.

¹⁰And he said, Now also let it be according unto your words: he with whom it is found shall be my servant; and ye shall be blameless.

¹¹Then they speedily took down every man his sack to the ground, and opened every man his sack.

¹²And he searched, and began at the eldest, and left at the youngest: and the cup was found in Benjamin's sack.

¹³Then they rent their clothes, and laded every man his ass, and returned to the city.

¹⁴And Judah and his brethren came to Joseph's house; for he was yet there: and they fell before him on the ground.

¹⁵And Joseph said unto them, What deed is this that ye have done? wot ye not that such a man as I can certainly divine?

¹⁶And Judah said, What shall we say unto my lord? what shall we speak? or how shall we clear ourselves? God hath found out the iniquity of thy servants: behold, we are my lord's servants, both we, and he also with whom the cup is found.

¹⁷And he said, God forbid that I should do so: but the man in whose hand the cup is found, he shall be my servant; and as for you, get you up in peace unto your father.

¹⁸Then Judah came near unto

him, and said, Oh my lord, let thy servant, I pray thee, speak a word in my lord's ears, and let not thine anger burn against thy servant: for thou art even as Pharaoh.

¹⁹My lord asked his servants, saying, Have ye a father, or a brother?

²⁰And we said unto my lord, We have a father, an old man, and a child of his old age, a little one; and his brother is dead, and he alone is left of his mother, and his father loveth him.

²¹And thou saidst unto thy servants, Bring him down unto me, that I may set mine eyes upon him.

²²And we said unto my lord, The lad cannot leave his father: for if he should leave his father, his father would die.

²³And thou saidst unto thy servants, Except your youngest brother come down with you, ye shall see my face no more.

²⁴And it came to pass when we came up unto thy servant my father, we told him the words of my lord.

²⁵And our father said, Go again, and buy us a little food.

²⁶And we said, We cannot go down: if our youngest brother be with us, then will we go down: for we may not see the man's face, except our youngest brother be with us.

²⁷And thy servant my father said unto us, Ye know that my wife bare me two sons:

²⁸And the one went out from me, and I said, Surely he is torn in pieces; and I saw him not since:

²⁹And if ye take this also from me, and mischief befall him, ye shall bring down my gray hairs with sorrow to the grave.

³⁰Now therefore when I come to thy servant my father, and the lad be not with us; seeing that his life is bound up in the lad's life;

³¹It shall come to pass, when he seeth that the lad is not with us, that he will die: and thy servants shall bring down the gray hairs of thy servant our father with sorrow to the grave.

³²For thy servant became surety for the lad unto my father, saying, If I bring him not unto thee, then I shall bear the blame to my father for ever.

³³Now therefore, I pray thee, let thy servant abide instead of the lad a bondman to my lord; and let the lad go up with his brethren.

³⁴For how shall I go up to my father, and the lad be not with me? lest peradventure I see the evil that shall come on my father.

CHAPTER 45

^{1}Then Joseph could not refrain himself before all them that stood by him; and he cried, Cause every man to go out from me. And there stood no man with him, while Joseph made himself known unto his brethren.

^{2}And he wept aloud: and the Egyptians and the house of Pharaoh heard.

^{3}And Joseph said unto his brethren, I am Joseph; doth my father yet live? And his brethren could not answer him; for they were troubled at his presence.

^{4}And Joseph said unto his brethren, Come near to me, I pray you. And they came near. And he said, I am Joseph your brother, whom ye sold into Egypt.

^{5}Now therefore be not grieved, nor angry with yourselves, that ye sold me hither: for God did send me before you to preserve life.

^{6}For these two years hath the famine been in the land: and yet there are five years, in the which there shall neither be earing nor harvest.

^{7}And God sent me before you to preserve you a posterity in the earth, and to save your lives by a great deliverance.

^{8}So now it was not you that sent me hither, but God: and he hath made me a father to Pharaoh, and lord of all his house, and a ruler throughout all the land of Egypt.

^{9}Haste ye, and go up to my father, and say unto him, Thus saith thy son Joseph, God hath made me lord of all Egypt: come down unto me, tarry not:

^{10}And thou shalt dwell in the land of Goshen, and thou shalt be near unto me, thou, and thy children, and thy children's children, and thy flocks, and thy herds, and all that thou hast:

^{11}And there will I nourish thee; for yet there are five years of famine; lest thou, and thy household, and all that thou hast, come to poverty.

^{12}And, behold, your eyes see, and the eyes of my brother Ben-jamin, that it is my mouth that speaketh unto you.

^{13}And ye shall tell my father of all my glory in Egypt, and of all that ye have seen; and ye shall haste and bring down my father hither.

^{14}And he fell upon his brother Ben-jamin's neck, and wept; and Ben-jamin wept upon his neck.

^{15}Moreover he kissed all his brethren, and wept upon them: and after that his brethren talked with him.

¹⁶And the fame thereof was heard in Pharaoh's house, saying, Joseph's brethren are come: and it pleased Pharaoh well, and his servants.

¹⁷And Pharaoh said unto Joseph, Say unto thy brethren, This do ye; lade your beasts, and go, get you unto the land of Canaan;

¹⁸And take your father and your households, and come unto me: and I will give you the good of the land of Egypt, and ye shall eat the fat of the land.

¹⁹Now thou art commanded, this do ye; take you wagons out of the land of Egypt for your little ones, and for your wives, and bring your father, and come.

²⁰Also regard not your stuff; for the good of all the land of Egypt is yours.

²¹And the children of Israel did so: and Joseph gave them wagons, according to the commandment of Pharaoh, and gave them provision for the way.

²²To all of them he gave each man changes of raiment; but to Ben-jamin he gave three hundred pieces of silver, and five changes of raiment.

²³And to his father he sent after this manner; ten asses laden with the good things of Egypt, and ten she asses laden with corn and bread and meat for his father by the way.

²⁴So he sent his brethren away, and they departed: and he said unto them, See that ye fall not out by the way.

²⁵And they went up out of Egypt, and came into the land of Canaan unto Jacob their father,

²⁶And told him, saying, Joseph is yet alive, and he is governor over all the land of Egypt. And Jacob's heart fainted, for he believed them not.

²⁷And they told him all the words of Joseph, which he had said unto them: and when he saw the wagons which Joseph had sent to carry him, the spirit of Jacob their father revived:

²⁸And Israel said, It is enough; Joseph my son is yet alive: I will go and see him before I die.

CHAPTER 46

¹And Israel took his journey with all that he had, and came to Beer-sheba, and offered sacrifices unto the God of his father Isaac.

²And God spake unto Israel in the visions of the night, and said, Jacob, Jacob. And he said, Here am I.

³And he said, I am God, the God of thy father: fear not to go down

into Egypt; for I will there make of thee a great nation:

⁴I will go down with thee into Egypt; and I will also surely bring thee up again: and Joseph shall put his hand upon thine eyes.

⁵And Jacob rose up from Beersheba: and the sons of Israel carried Jacob their father, and their little ones, and their wives, in the wagons which Pharaoh had sent to carry him.

⁶And they took their cattle, and their goods, which they had gotten in the land of Canaan, and came into Egypt, Jacob, and all his seed with him:

⁷His sons, and his sons' sons with him, his daughters, and his sons' daughters, and all his seed brought he with him into Egypt.

⁸And these are the names of the children of Israel, which came into Egypt, Jacob and his sons: Reuben, Jacob's firstborn.

⁹And the sons of Reuben; Hanoch, and Phallu, and Hezron, and Carmi.

¹⁰And the sons of Simeon; Jemuel, and Jamin, and Ohad, and Jachin, and Zohar, and Shaul the son of a Canaanitish woman.

¹¹And the sons of Levi; Gershon, Kohath, and Merari.

¹²And the sons of Judah; Er, and Onan, and Shelah, and Pharez, and Zarah: but Er and Onan died in the land of Canaan. And the sons of Pharez were Hezron and Hamul.

¹³And the sons of Issachar; Tola, and Phuvah, and Job, and Shimron.

¹⁴And the sons of Zebulun; Sered, and Elon, and Jahleel.

¹⁵These be the sons of Leah, which she bare unto Jacob in Padanaram, with his daughter Dinah: all the souls of his sons and his daughters were thirty and three.

¹⁶And the sons of Gad; Ziphion, and Haggi, Shuni, and Ezbon, Eri, and Arodi, and Areli.

¹⁷And the sons of Asher; Jimnah, and Ishuah, and Isui, and Beriah, and Serah their sister: and the sons of Beriah; Heber, and Malchiel.

¹⁸These are the sons of Zilpah, whom Laban gave to Leah his daughter, and these she bare unto Jacob, even sixteen souls.

¹⁹The sons of Rachel Jacob's wife; Joseph, and Ben-jamin.

²⁰And unto Joseph in the land of Egypt were born Manasseh and Ephraim, which Asenath the daughter of Poti-pherah priest of On bare unto him.

²¹And the sons of Ben-jamin were Belah, and Becher, and Ashbel, Gera, and Naaman, Ehi, and Rosh, Muppim, and Huppim, and Ard.

²²These are the sons of Rachel, which were born to Jacob: all the souls were fourteen.

²³And the sons of Dan; Hushim.

²⁴And the sons of Naphtali; Jahzeel, and Guni, and Jezer, and Shillem.

²⁵These are the sons of Bilhah, which Laban gave unto Rachel his daughter, and she bare these unto Jacob: all the souls were seven.

²⁶All the souls that came with Jacob into Egypt, which came out of his loins, besides Jacob's sons' wives, all the souls were threescore and six;

²⁷And the sons of Joseph, which were born him in Egypt, were two souls: all the souls of the house of Jacob, which came into Egypt, were threescore and ten.

²⁸And he sent Judah before him unto Joseph, to direct his face unto Goshen; and they came into the land of Goshen.

²⁹And Joseph made ready his chariot, and went up to meet Israel his father, to Goshen, and presented himself unto him; and he fell on his neck, and wept on his neck a good while.

³⁰And Israel said unto Joseph, Now let me die, since I have seen thy face, because thou art yet alive.

³¹And Joseph said unto his brethren, and unto his father's house, I will go up, and shew Pharaoh, and say unto him, My brethren, and my father's house, which were in the land of Canaan, are come unto me;

³²And the men are shepherds, for their trade hath been to feed cattle; and they have brought their flocks, and their herds, and all that they have.

³³And it shall come to pass, when Pharaoh shall call you, and shall say, What is your occupation?

³⁴That ye shall say, Thy servants' trade hath been about cattle from our youth even until now, both we, and also our fathers: that ye may dwell in the land of Goshen; for every shepherd is an abomination unto the Egyptians.

CHAPTER 47

¹Then Joseph came and told Pharaoh, and said, My father and my brethren, and their flocks, and their herds, and all that they have, are come out of the land of Canaan; and, behold, they are in the land of Goshen.

²And he took some of his brethren, even five men, and presented them unto Pharaoh.

³And Pharaoh said unto his brethren, What is your occupation? And they said unto Pharaoh, Thy servants are shepherds, both we, and also our fathers.

⁴They said morever unto

Pharaoh, For to sojourn in the land are we come; for thy servants have no pasture for their flocks; for the famine is sore in the land of Canaan: now therefore, we pray thee, let thy servants dwell in the land of Goshen.

5 And Pharaoh spake unto Joseph, saying, Thy father and thy brethren are come unto thee:

6 The land of Egypt is before thee; in the best of the land make thy father and brethren to dwell; in the land of Goshen let them dwell: and if thou knowest any men of activity among them, then make them rulers over my cattle.

7 And Joseph brought in Jacob his father, and set him before Pharaoh: and Jacob blessed Pharaoh.

8 And Pharaoh said unto Jacob, How old art thou?

9 And Jacob said unto Pharaoh, The days of the years of my pilgrimage are an hundred and thirty years: few and evil have the days of the years of my life been, and have not attained unto the days of the years of the life of my fathers in the days of their pilgrimage.

10 And Jacob blessed Pharaoh, and went out from before Pharaoh.

11 And Joseph placed his father and his brethren, and gave them a possession in the land of Egypt, in the best of the land, in the land of Rameses, as Pharaoh had commanded.

12 And Joseph nourished his father, and his brethren, and all his father's household, with bread, according to their families.

13 And there was no bread in all the land; for the famine was very sore, so that the land of Egypt and all the land of Canaan fainted by reason of the famine.

14 And Joseph gathered up all the money that was found in the land of Egypt, and in the land of Canaan, for the corn which they bought: and Joseph brought the money into Pharaoh's house.

15 And when money failed in the land of Egypt, and in the land of Canaan, all the Egyptians came unto Joseph, and said, Give us bread: for why should we die in thy presence? for the money faileth.

16 And Joseph said, Give your cattle; and I will give you for your cattle, if money fail.

17 And they brought their cattle unto Joseph: and Joseph gave them bread in exchange for horses, and for the flocks, and for the cattle of the herds, and for the asses: and he fed them with bread for all their cattle for that year.

18 When that year was ended, they came unto him the second year, and said unto him, We will not hide it

from my lord, how that our money is spent; my lord also hath our herds of cattle; there is not ought left in the sight of my lord, but our bodies, and our lands:

¹⁹Wherefore shall we die before thine eyes, both we and our land? buy us and our land for bread, and we and our land will be servants unto Pharaoh: and give us seed, that we may live, and not die, that the land be not desolate.

²⁰And Joseph bought all the land of Egypt for Pharaoh; for the Egyptians sold every man his field, because the famine prevailed over them: so the land became Pharaoh's.

²¹And as for the people, he removed them to cities from one end of the borders of Egypt even to the other end thereof.

²²Only the land of the priests bought he not; for the priests had a portion assigned them of Pharaoh, and did eat their portion which Pharaoh gave them: wherefore they sold not their lands.

²³Then Joseph said unto the people, Behold, I have bought you this day and your land for Pharaoh: lo, here is seed for you, and ye shall sow the land.

²⁴And it shall come to pass in the increase, that ye shall give the fifth part unto Pharaoh, and four parts shall be your own, for seed of the field, and for your food, and for them of your households, and for food for your little ones.

²⁵And they said, Thou hast saved our lives: let us find grace in the sight of my lord, and we will be Pharaoh's servants.

²⁶And Joseph made it a law over the land of Egypt unto this day, that Pharaoh should have the fifth part, except the land of the priests only, which became not Pharaoh's.

²⁷And Israel dwelt in the land of Egypt, in the country of Goshen; and they had possessions therein, and grew, and multiplied exceedingly.

²⁸And Jacob lived in the land of Egypt seventeen years: so the whole age of Jacob was an hundred forty and seven years.

²⁹And the time drew nigh that Israel must die: and he called his son Joseph, and said unto him, If now I have found grace in thy sight, put, I pray thee, thy hand under my thigh, and deal kindly and truly with me; bury me not, I pray thee, in Egypt:

³⁰But I will lie with my fathers, and thou shalt carry me out of Egypt, and bury me in their buryingplace. And he said, I will do as thou hast said.

³¹And he said, Swear unto me. And he sware unto him. And Israel bowed himself upon the bed's head.

CHAPTER 48

¹And it came to pass after these things, that one told Joseph, Behold, thy father is sick: and he took with him his two sons, Manasseh and Ephraim.

²And one told Jacob, and said, Behold, thy son Joseph cometh unto thee: and Israel strengthened himself, and sat upon the bed.

³And Jacob said unto Joseph, God Almighty appeared unto me at Luz in the land of Canaan, and blessed me,

⁴And said unto me, Behold, I will make thee fruitful, and multiply thee, and I will make of thee a multitude of people; and will give this land to thy seed after thee for an everlasting possession.

⁵And now thy two sons, Ephraim and Manasseh, which were born unto thee in the land of Egypt before I came unto thee into Egypt, are mine; as Reuben and Simeon, they shall be mine.

⁶And thy issue, which thou begettest after them, shall be thine, and shall be called after the name of their brethren in their inheritance.

⁷And as for me, when I came from Padan, Rachel died by me in the land of Canaan in the way, when yet there was but a little way to come unto Ephrath: and I buried her there in the way of Ephrath; the same is Bethlehem.

⁸And Israel beheld Joseph's sons, and said, Who are these?

⁹And Joseph said unto his father, They are my sons, whom God hath given me in this place. And he said, Bring them, I pray thee, unto me, and I will bless them.

¹⁰Now the eyes of Israel were dim for age, so that he could not see. And he brought them near unto him; and he kissed them, and embraced them.

¹¹And Israel said unto Joseph, I had not thought to see thy face: and, lo, God hath shewed me also thy seed.

¹²And Joseph brought them out from between his knees, and he bowed himself with his face to the earth.

¹³And Joseph took them both, Ephraim in his right hand toward Israel's left hand, and Manasseh in his left hand toward Israel's right hand, and brought them near unto him.

¹⁴And Israel stretched out his right hand, and laid it upon Ephraim's head, who was the younger, and his left hand upon Manasseh's head, guiding his hands wittingly; for Manasseh was the firstborn.

¹⁵And he blessed Joseph, and said, God, before whom my fathers

Abraham and Isaac did walk, the God which fed me all my life long unto this day,

¹⁶The Angel which redeemed me from all evil, bless the lads; and let my name be named on them, and the name of my fathers Abraham and Isaac; and let them grow into a multitude in the midst of the earth.

¹⁷And when Joseph saw that his father laid his right hand upon the head of Ephraim, it displeased him: and he held up his father's hand, to remove it from Ephraim's head unto Manasseh's head.

¹⁸And Joseph said unto his father, Not so, my father: for this is the firstborn; put thy right hand upon his head.

¹⁹And his father refused, and said, I know it, my son, I know it: he also shall become a people, and he also shall be great: but truly his younger brother shall be greater than he, and his seed shall become a multitude of nations.

²⁰And he blessed them that day, saying, In thee shall Israel bless, saying, God make thee as Ephraim and as Manasseh: and he set Ephraim before Manasseh.

²¹And Israel said unto Joseph, Behold, I die: but God shall be with you, and bring you again unto the land of your fathers.

²²Moreover I have given to thee one portion above thy brethren, which I took out of the hand of the Amorite with my sword and with my bow.

CHAPTER 49

¹And Jacob called unto his sons, and said, Gather yourselves together, that I may tell you that which shall befall you in the last days.

²Gather yourselves together, and hear, ye sons of Jacob; and hearken unto Israel your father.

³Reuben, thou art my firstborn, my might, and the beginning of my strength, the excellency of dignity, and the excellency of power:

⁴Unstable as water, thou shalt not excel; because thou wentest up to thy father's bed; then defiledst thou it: he went up to my couch.

⁵Simeon and Levi are brethren; instruments of cruelty are in their habitations.

⁶O my soul, come not thou into their secret; unto their assembly, mine honour, be not thou united: for in their anger they slew a man, and in their selfwill they digged down a wall.

⁷Cursed be their anger, for it was fierce; and their wrath, for it was cruel: I will divide them in Jacob, and scatter them in Israel.

⁸Judah, thou art he whom thy brethren shall praise: thy hand shall be in the neck of thine enemies; thy father's children shall bow down before thee.

⁹Judah is a lion's whelp: from the prey, my son, thou art gone up: he stooped down, he couched as a lion, and as an old lion; who shall rouse him up?

¹⁰The sceptre shall not depart from Judah, nor a lawgiver from between his feet, until Shiloh come; and unto him shall the gathering of the people be.

¹¹Binding his foal unto the vine, and his ass's colt unto the choice vine; he washed his garments in wine, and his clothes in the blood of grapes:

¹²His eyes shall be red with wine, and his teeth white with milk.

¹³Zebulun shall dwell at the haven of the sea; and he shall be for an haven of ships; and his border shall be unto Zidon.

¹⁴Issachar is a strong ass couching down between two burdens:

¹⁵And he saw that rest was good, and the land that it was pleasant; and bowed his shoulder to bear, and became a servant unto tribute.

¹⁶Dan shall judge his people, as one of the tribes of Israel.

¹⁷Dan shall be a serpent by the way, an adder in the path, that biteth the horse heels, so that his rider shall fall backward.

¹⁸I have waited for thy salvation, O LORD.

¹⁹Gad, a troop shall overcome him: but he shall overcome at the last.

²⁰Out of Asher his bread shall be fat, and he shall yield royal dainties.

²¹Naphtali is a hind let loose: he giveth goodly words.

²²Joseph is a fruitful bough, even a fruitful bough by a well; whose branches run over the wall:

²³The archers have sorely grieved him, and shot at him, and hated him:

²⁴But his bow abode in strength, and the arms of his hands were made strong by the hands of the mighty God of Jacob; (from thence is the shepherd, the stone of Israel:)

²⁵Even by the God of thy father, who shall help thee; and by the Almighty, who shall bless thee with blessings of heaven above, blessings of the deep that lieth under, blessings of the breasts, and of the womb:

²⁶The blessings of thy father have prevailed above the blessings of my progenitors unto the utmost bound of the everlasting hills: they shall be on the head of Joseph, and on the crown of the head of him that was separate from his brethren.

²⁷Ben-jamin shall ravin as a wolf: in the morning he shall devour the prey, and at night he shall divide the spoil.

²⁸All these are the twelve tribes of Israel: and this is it that their father spake unto them, and blessed them; every one according to his blessing he blessed them.

²⁹And he charged them, and said unto them, I am to be gathered unto my people: bury me with my fathers in the cave that is in the field of Ephron the Hittite,

³⁰In the cave that is in the field of Machpelah, which is before Mamre, in the land of Canaan, which Abraham bought with the field of Ephron the Hittite for a possession of a buryingplace.

³¹There they buried Abraham and Sarah his wife; there they buried Isaac and Rebekah his wife; and there I buried Leah.

³²The purchase of the field and of the cave that is therein was from the children of Heth.

³³And when Jacob had made an end of commanding his sons, he gathered up his feet into the bed, and yielded up the ghost, and was gathered unto his people.

CHAPTER 50

¹And Joseph fell upon his father's face, and wept upon him, and kissed him.

²And Joseph commanded his servants the physicians to embalm his father: and the physicians embalmed Israel.

³And forty days were fulfilled for him; for so are fulfilled the days of those which are embalmed: and the Egyptians mourned for him threescore and ten days.

⁴And when the days of his mourning were past, Joseph spake unto the house of Pharaoh, saying, If now I have found grace in your eyes, speak, I pray you, in the ears of Pharaoh, saying,

⁵My father made me swear, saying, Lo, I die: in my grave which I have digged for me in the land of Canaan, there shalt thou bury me. Now therefore let me go up, I pray thee, and bury my father, and I will come again.

⁶And Pharaoh said, Go up, and bury thy father, according as he made thee swear.

⁷And Joseph went up to bury his father: and with him went up all the servants of Pharaoh, the elders of his house, and all the elders of the land of Egypt,

8 And all the house of Joseph, and his brethren, and his father's house: only their little ones, and their flocks, and their herds, they left in the land of Goshen.

9 And there went up with him both chariots and horsemen: and it was a very great company.

10 And they came to the threshingfloor of Atad, which is beyond Jordan, and there they mourned with a great and very sore lamentation: and he made a mourning for his father seven days.

11 And when the inhabitants of the land, the Canaanites, saw the mourning in the floor of Atad, they said, This is a grievous mourning to the Egyptians: wherefore the name of it was called Abelmizraim, which is beyond Jordan.

12 And his sons did unto him according as he commanded them:

13 For his sons carried him into the land of Canaan, and buried him in the cave of the field of Machpelah, which Abraham bought with the field for a possession of a buryingplace of Ephron the Hittite, before Mamre.

14 And Joseph returned into Egypt, he, and his brethren, and all that went up with him to bury his father, after he had buried his father.

15 And when Joseph's brethren saw that their father was dead, they said, Joseph will peradventure hate us, and will certainly requite us all the evil which we did unto him.

16 And they sent a messenger unto Joseph, saying, Thy father did command before he died, saying,

17 So shall ye say unto Joseph, Forgive, I pray thee now, the trespass of thy brethren, and their sin; for they did unto thee evil: and now, we pray thee, forgive the trespass of the servants of the God of thy father. And Joseph wept when they spake unto him.

18 And his brethren also went and fell down before his face; and they said, Behold, we be thy servants.

19 And Joseph said unto them, Fear not: for am I in the place of God?

20 But as for you, ye thought evil against me; but God meant it unto good, to bring to pass, as it is this day, to save much people alive.

21 Now therefore fear ye not: I will nourish you, and your little ones. And he comforted them, and spake kindly unto them.

22 And Joseph dwelt in Egypt, he, and his father's house: and Joseph lived an hundred and ten years.

23 And Joseph saw Ephraim's children of the third generation: the children also of Machir the son of Manasseh were brought up upon Joseph's knees.

²⁴And Joseph said unto his brethren, I die: and God will surely visit you, and bring you out of this land unto the land which he sware to Abraham, to Isaac, and to Jacob.

²⁵And Joseph took an oath of the children of Israel, saying, God will surely visit you, and ye shall carry up my bones from hence.

²⁶So Joseph died, being an hundred and ten years old: and they embalmed him, and he was put in a coffin in Egypt.

EXODUS

שמות

CHAPTER 1

¹Now these are the names of the children of Israel, which came into Egypt; every man and his household came with Jacob.

²Reuben, Simeon, Levi, and Judah,

³Issachar, Zebulun, and Benjamin,

⁴Dan, and Naphtali, Gad, and Asher.

⁵And all the souls that came out of the loins of Jacob were seventy souls: for Joseph was in Egypt already.

⁶And Joseph died, and all his brethren, and all that generation.

⁷And the children of Israel were fruitful, and increased abundantly, and multiplied, and waxed exceeding mighty; and the land was filled with them.

⁸Now there arose up a new king over Egypt, which knew not Joseph.

⁹And he said unto his people, Behold, the people of the children of Israel are more and mightier than we:

¹⁰Come on, let us deal wisely with them; lest they multiply, and it come to pass, that, when there falleth out any war, they join also unto our enemies, and fight against us, and so get them up out of the land.

¹¹Therefore they did set over them taskmasters to afflict them with their burdens. And they built for Pharaoh treasure cities, Pithom and Raamses.

¹²But the more they afflicted them, the more they multiplied and grew. And they were grieved because of the children of Israel.

¹³And the Egyptians made the children of Israel to serve with rigour:

¹⁴And they made their lives bitter with hard bondage, in morter, and in brick, and in all manner of service in the field: all their service, wherein they made them serve, was with rigour.

¹⁵And the king of Egypt spake to the Hebrew midwives, of which the name of the one was Shiphrah, and the name of the other Puah:

¹⁶And he said, When ye do the office of a midwife to the Hebrew women, and see them upon the stools; if it be a son, then ye shall kill him: but if it be a daughter, then she shall live.

17But the midwives feared God, and did not as the king of Egypt commanded them, but saved the men children alive.

18And the king of Egypt called for the midwives, and said unto them, Why have ye done this thing, and have saved the men children alive?

19And the midwives said unto Pharaoh, Because the Hebrew women are not as the Egyptian women; for they are lively, and are delivered ere the midwives come in unto them.

20Therefore God dealt well with the midwives: and the people multiplied, and waxed very mighty.

21And it came to pass, because the midwives feared God, that he made them houses.

22And Pharaoh charged all his people, saying, Every son that is born ye shall cast into the river, and every daughter ye shall save alive.

CHAPTER 2

1And there went a man of the house of Levi, and took to wife a daughter of Levi.

2And the woman conceived, and bare a son: and when she saw him that he was a goodly child, she hid him three months.

3And when she could not longer hide him, she took for him an ark of bulrushes, and daubed it with slime and with pitch, and put the child therein; and she laid it in the flags by the river's brink.

4And his sister stood afar off, to wit what would be done to him.

5And the daughter of Pharaoh came down to wash herself at the river; and her maidens walked along by the river's side; and when she saw the ark among the flags, she sent her maid to fetch it.

6And when she had opened it, she saw the child: and, behold, the babe wept. And she had compassion on him, and said, This is one of the Hebrews' children.

7Then said his sister to Pharaoh's daughter, Shall I go and call to thee a nurse of the Hebrew women, that she may nurse the child for thee?

8And Pharaoh's daughter said to her, Go. And the maid went and called the child's mother.

9And Pharaoh's daughter said unto her, Take this child away, and nurse it for me, and I will give thee thy wages. And the women took the child, and nursed it.

10And the child grew, and she brought him unto Pharaoh's daughter, and he became her son. And she called his name Moses: and she said, Because I drew him out of the water.

¹¹And it came to pass in those days, when Moses was grown, that he went out unto his brethren, and looked on their burdens: and he spied an Egyptian smiting an Hebrew, one of his brethren.

¹²And he looked this way and that way, and when he saw that there was no man, he slew the Egyptian, and hid him in the sand.

¹³And when he went out the second day, behold, two men of the Hebrews strove together: and he said to him that did the wrong, Wherefore smitest thou thy fellow?

¹⁴And he said, Who made thee a prince and a judge over us? intendest thou to kill me, as thou killedst the Egyptian? And Moses feared, and said, Surely this thing is known.

¹⁵Now when Pharaoh heard this thing, he sought to slay Moses. But Moses fled from the face of Pharaoh, and dwelt in the land of Midian: and he sat down by a well.

¹⁶Now the priest of Midian had seven daughters: and they came and drew water, and filled the troughs to water their father's flock.

¹⁷And the shepherds came and drove them away: but Moses stood up and helped them, and watered their flock.

¹⁸And when they came to Reuel their father, he said, How is it that ye are come so soon to day?

¹⁹And they said, An Egyptian delivered us out of the hand of the shepherds, and also drew water enough for us, and watered the flock.

²⁰And he said unto his daughters, And where is he? why is it that ye have left the man? call him, that he may eat bread.

²¹And Moses was content to dwell with the man: and he gave Moses Zipporah his daughter.

²²And she bare him a son, and he called his name Gershom: for he said, I have been a stranger in a strange land.

²³And it came to pass in process of time, that the king of Egypt died: and the children of Israel sighed by reason of the bondage, and they cried, and their cry came up unto God by reason of the bondage.

²⁴And God heard their groaning, and God remembered his covenant with Abraham, with Isaac, and with Jacob.

²⁵And God looked upon the children of Israel, and God had respect unto them.

CHAPTER 3

¹Now Moses kept the flock of Jethro his father in law, the priest of Midian: and he led the flock to the backside of the desert, and came to the mountain of God, even to Horeb.

²And the angel of the LORD appeared unto him in a flame of fire out of the midst of a bush: and he looked, and, behold, the bush burned with fire, and the bush was not consumed.

³And Moses said, I will now turn aside, and see this great sight, why the bush is not burnt.

⁴And when the LORD saw that he turned aside to see, God called unto him out of the midst of the bush, and said, Moses, Moses. And he said, Here am I.

⁵And he said, Draw not nigh hither: put off thy shoes from off thy feet, for the place whereon thou standest is holy ground.

⁶Moreover he said, I am the God of thy father, the God of Abraham, the God of Isaac, and the God of Jacob. And Moses hid his face; for he was afraid to look upon God.

⁷And the LORD said, I have surely seen the affliction of my people which are in Egypt, and have heard their cry by reason of their taskmasters; for I know their sorrows;

⁸And I am come down to deliver them out of the hand of the Egyptians, and to bring them up out of that land unto a good land and a large, unto a land flowing with milk and honey; unto the place of the Canaanites, and the Hittites, and the Amorites, and the Perizzites, and the Hivites, and the Jebusites.

⁹Now therefore, behold, the cry of the children of Israel is come unto me: and I have also seen the oppression wherewith the Egyptians oppress them.

¹⁰Come now therefore, and I will send thee unto Pharaoh, that thou mayest bring forth my people the children of Israel out of Egypt.

¹¹And Moses said unto God, Who am I, that I should go unto Pharaoh, and that I should bring forth the children of Israel out of Egypt?

¹²And he said, Certainly I will be with thee; and this shall be a token unto thee, that I have sent thee: When thou hast brought forth the people out of Egypt, ye shall serve God upon this mountain.

¹³And Moses said unto God, Behold, when I come unto the children of Israel, and shall say unto them, The God of your fathers hath sent me unto you; and they shall say

to me, What is his name? what shall I say unto them?

¹⁴And God said unto Moses, I AM THAT I AM: and he said, Thus shalt thou say unto the children of Israel, I AM hath sent me unto you.

¹⁵And God said moreover unto Moses, Thus shalt thou say unto the children of Israel, the LORD God of your fathers, the God of Abraham, the God of Isaac, and the God of Jacob, hath sent me unto you: this is my name for ever, and this is my memorial unto all generations.

¹⁶Go, and gather the elders of Israel together, and say unto them, The LORD God of your fathers, the God of Abraham, of Isaac, and of Jacob, appeared unto me, saying, I have surely visited you, and seen that which is done to you in Egypt:

¹⁷And I have said, I will bring you up out of the affliction of Egypt unto the land of the Canaanites, and the Hittites, and the Amorites, and the Perizzites, and the Hivites, and the Jebusites, unto a land flowing with milk and honey.

¹⁸And they shall hearken to thy voice: and thou shalt come, thou and the elders of Israel, unto the king of Egypt, and ye shall say unto him, The LORD God of the Hebrews hath met with us: and now let us go, we beseech thee, three

days' journey into the wilderness, that we may sacrifice to the LORD our God.

¹⁹And I am sure that the king of Egypt will not let you go, no, not by a mighty hand.

²⁰And I will stretch out my hand, and smite Egypt with all my wonders which I will do in the midst thereof: and after that he will let you go.

²¹And I will give this people favour in the sight of the Egyptians: and it shall come to pass, that, when ye go, ye shall not go empty.

²²But every woman shall borrow of her neighbour, and of her that sojourneth in her house, jewels of silver, and jewels of gold, and raiment: and ye shall put them upon your sons, and upon your daughters; and ye shall spoil the Egyptians.

CHAPTER 4

¹And Moses answered and said, But, behold, they will not believe me, nor hearken unto my voice: for they will say, The LORD hath not appeared unto thee.

²And the LORD said unto him, What is that in thine hand? And he said, A rod.

³And he said, Cast it on the ground. And he cast it on the

ground, and it became a serpent; and Moses fled from before it.

⁴And the LORD said unto Moses, Put forth thine hand, and take it by the tail. And he put forth his hand, and caught it, and it became a rod in his hand:

⁵That they may believe that the LORD God of their fathers, the God of Abraham, the God of Isaac, and the God of Jacob, hath appeared unto thee.

⁶And the LORD said furthermore unto him, Put now thine hand into thy bosom. And he put his hand into his bosom: and when he took it out, behold, his hand was leprous as snow.

⁷And he said, Put thine hand into thy bosom again. And he put his hand into his bosom again; and plucked it out of his bosom, and, behold, it was turned again as his other flesh.

⁸And it shall come to pass, if they will not believe thee, neither hearken to the voice of the first sign, that they will believe the voice of the latter sign.

⁹And it shall come to pass, if they will not believe also these two signs, neither hearken unto thy voice, that thou shalt take of the water of the river, and pour it upon the dry land: and the water which thou takest out of the river shall become blood upon the dry land.

¹⁰And Moses said unto the LORD, O my LORD, I am not eloquent, neither heretofore, nor since thou hast spoken unto thy servant: but I am slow of speech, and of a slow tongue.

¹¹And the LORD said unto him, Who hath made man's mouth? or who maketh the dumb, or deaf, or the seeing, or the blind? have not I the LORD?

¹²Now therefore go, and I will be with thy mouth, and teach thee what thou shalt say.

¹³And he said, O my LORD, send, I pray thee, by the hand of him whom thou wilt send.

¹⁴And the anger of the LORD was kindled against Moses, and he said, Is not Aaron the Levite thy brother? I know that he can speak well. And also, behold, he cometh forth to meet thee: and when he seeth thee, he will be glad in his heart.

¹⁵And thou shalt speak unto him, and put words in his mouth: and I will be with thy mouth, and with his mouth, and will teach you what ye shall do.

¹⁶And he shall be thy spokesman unto the people: and he shall be, even he shall be to thee instead of a mouth, and thou shalt be to him instead of God.

¹⁷And thou shalt take this rod in thine hand, wherewith thou shalt do signs.

¹⁸And Moses went and returned to Jethro his father in law, and said unto him, Let me go, I pray thee, and return unto my brethren which are in Egypt, and see whether they be yet alive. And Jethro said to Moses, Go in peace.

¹⁹And the LORD said unto Moses in Midian, Go, return into Egypt: for all the men are dead which sought thy life.

²⁰And Moses took his wife and his sons, and set them upon an ass, and he returned to the land of Egypt: and Moses took the rod of God in his hand.

²¹And the LORD said unto Moses, When thou goest to return into Egypt, see that thou do all those wonders before Pharaoh, which I have put in thine hand: but I will harden his heart, that he shall not let the people go.

²²And thou shalt say unto Pharaoh, Thus saith the LORD, Israel is my son, even my firstborn:

²³And I say unto thee, Let my son go, that he may serve me: and if thou refuse to let him go, behold, I will slay thy son, even thy firstborn.

²⁴And it came to pass by the way in the inn, that the LORD met him, and sought to kill him.

²⁵Then Zipporah took a sharp stone, and cut off the foreskin of her son, and cast it at his feet, and said, Surely a bloody husband art thou to me.

²⁶So he let him go: then she said, A bloody husband thou art, because of the circumcision.

²⁷And the LORD said to Aaron, Go into the wilderness to meet Moses. And he went, and met him in the mount of God, and kissed him.

²⁸And Moses told Aaron all the words of the LORD who had sent him, and all the signs which he had commanded him.

²⁹And Moses and Aaron went and gathered together all the elders of the children of Israel:

³⁰And Aaron spake all the words which the LORD had spoken unto Moses, and did the signs in the sight of the people.

³¹And the people believed: and when they heard that the LORD had visited the children of Israel, and that he had looked upon their affliction, then they bowed their heads and worshipped.

CHAPTER 5

¹And afterward Moses and Aaron went in, and told Pharaoh, Thus saith the LORD God of Israel, Let my people go, that they may hold a feast unto me in the wilderness.

²And Pharaoh said, Who is the LORD, that I should obey his voice to let Israel go? I know not the LORD, neither will I let Israel go.

³And they said, The God of the Hebrews hath met with us: let us go, we pray thee, three days' journey into the desert, and sacrifice unto the LORD our God; lest he fall upon us with pestilence, or with the sword.

⁴And the king of Egypt said unto them, Wherefore do ye, Moses and Aaron, let the people from their works? get you unto your burdens.

⁵And Pharaoh said, Behold, the people of the land now are many, and ye make them rest from their burdens.

⁶And Pharaoh commanded the same day the taskmasters of the people, and their officers, saying,

⁷Ye shall no more give the people straw to make brick, as heretofore: let them go and gather straw for themselves.

⁸And the tale of the bricks, which they did make heretofore, ye shall lay upon them; ye shall not diminish ought thereof: for they be idle; therefore they cry, saying, Let us go and sacrifice to our God.

⁹Let there more work be laid upon the men, that they may labour therein; and let them not regard vain words.

¹⁰And the taskmasters of the people went out, and their officers, and they spake to the people, saying, Thus saith Pharaoh, I will not give you straw.

¹¹Go ye, get you straw where ye can find it: yet not ought of your work shall be diminished.

¹²So the people were scattered abroad throughout all the land of Egypt to gather stubble instead of straw.

¹³And the taskmasters hasted them, saying, Fulfil your works, your daily tasks, as when there was straw.

¹⁴And the officers of the children of Israel, which Pharaoh's taskmasters had set over them, were beaten, and demanded, Wherefore have ye not fulfilled your task in making brick both yesterday and to day, as heretofore?

¹⁵Then the officers of the children of Israel came and cried unto Pharaoh, saying, Wherefore dealest thou thus with thy servants?

¹⁶There is no straw given unto thy servants, and they say to us, Make brick: and, behold, thy servants are beaten; but the fault is in thine own people.

¹⁷But he said, Ye are idle, ye are idle: therefore ye say, Let us go and do sacrifice to the LORD.

¹⁸Go therefore now, and work; for

there shall no straw be given you, yet shall ye deliver the tale of bricks.

¹⁹And the officers of the children of Israel did see that they were in evil case, after it was said, Ye shall not minish ought from your bricks of your daily task.

²⁰And they met Moses and Aaron, who stood in the way, as they came forth from Pharaoh:

²¹And they said unto them, The LORD look upon you, and judge; because ye have made our savour to be abhorred in the eyes of Pharaoh, and in the eyes of his servants, to put a sword in their hand to slay us.

²²And Moses returned unto the LORD, and said, LORD, wherefore hast thou so evil entreated this people? why is it that thou hast sent me?

²³For since I came to Pharaoh to speak in thy name, he hath done evil to this people; neither hast thou delivered thy people at all.

CHAPTER 6

¹Then the LORD said unto Moses, Now shalt thou see what I will do to Pharaoh: for with a strong hand shall he let them go, and with a strong hand shall he drive them out of his land.

²And God spake unto Moses, and said unto him, I am the LORD:

³And I appeared unto Abraham, unto Isaac, and unto Jacob, by the name of God Almighty, but by my name JEHOVAH was I not known to them.

⁴And I have also established my covenant with them, to give them the land of Canaan, the land of their pilgrimage, wherein they were strangers.

⁵And I have also heard the groaning of the children of Israel, whom the Egyptians keep in bondage; and I have remembered my covenant.

⁶Wherefore say unto the children of Israel, I am the LORD, and I will bring you out from under the burdens of the Egyptians, and I will rid you out of their bondage, and I will redeem you with a stretched out arm, and with great judgments:

⁷And I will take you to me for a people, and I will be to you a God: and ye shall know that I am the LORD your God, which bringeth you out from under the burdens of the Egyptians.

⁸And I will bring you in unto the land, concerning the which I did swear to give it to Abraham, to Isaac, and to Jacob; and I will give it you for an heritage: I am the LORD.

⁹And Moses spake so unto the children of Israel: but they hearkened not unto Moses for anguish of spirit, and for cruel bondage.

¹⁰And the LORD spake unto Moses, saying,

¹¹Go in, speak unto Pharaoh king of Egypt, that he let the children of Israel go out of his land.

¹²And Moses spake before the LORD, saying, Behold, the children of Israel have not hearkened unto me; how then shall Pharaoh hear me, who am of uncircumcised lips?

¹³And the LORD spake unto Moses and unto Aaron, and gave them a charge unto the children of Israel, and unto Pharaoh king of Egypt, to bring the children of Israel out of the land of Egypt.

¹⁴These be the heads of their fathers' houses: The sons of Reuben the firstborn of Israel; Hanoch, and Pallu, Hezron, and Carmi: these be the families of Reuben.

¹⁵And the sons of Simeon; Jemuel, and Jamin, and Ohad, and Jachin, and Zohar, and Shaul the son of a Canaanitish woman: these are the families of Simeon.

¹⁶And these are the names of the sons of Levi according to their generations; Gershon, and Kohath, and Merari: and the years of the life of Levi were an hundred thirty and seven years.

¹⁷The sons of Gershon; Libni, and Shimi, according to their families.

¹⁸And the sons of Kohath; Amram, and Izhar, and Hebron, and Uzziel: and the years of the life of Kohath were an hundred thirty and three years.

¹⁹And the sons of Merari; Mahali and Mushi: these are the families of Levi according to their generations.

²⁰And Amram took him Jochebed his father's sister to wife; and she bare him Aaron and Moses: and the years of the life of Amram were an hundred and thirty and seven years.

²¹And the sons of Izhar; Korah, and Nepheg, and Zichri.

²²And the sons of Uzziel; Mishael, and Elzaphan, and Zithri.

²³And Aaron took him Elisheba, daughter of Amminadab, sister of Naashon, to wife; and she bare him Nadab, and Abihu, Eleazar, and Ithamar.

²⁴And the sons of Korah; Assir, and Elkanah, and Abiasaph: these are the families of the Korhites.

²⁵And Eleazar Aaron's son took him one of the daughters of Putiel to wife; and she bare him Phinehas: these are the heads of the fathers of the Levites according to their families.

²⁶These are that Aaron and Moses, to whom the LORD said, Bring out the children of Israel from the land of Egypt according to their armies.

²⁷These are they which spake to Pharaoh king of Egypt, to bring out the children of Israel from Egypt: these are that Moses and Aaron.

²⁸And it came to pass on the day when the LORD spake unto Moses in the land of Egypt,

²⁹That the LORD spake unto Moses, saying, I am the LORD: speak thou unto Pharaoh king of Egypt all that I say unto thee.

³⁰And Moses said before the LORD, Behold, I am of uncircumcised lips, and how shall Pharaoh hearken unto me?

CHAPTER 7

¹And the LORD said unto Moses, See, I have made thee a god to Pharaoh: and Aaron thy brother shall be thy prophet.

²Thou shalt speak all that I command thee: and Aaron thy brother shall speak unto Pharaoh, that he send the children of Israel out of his land.

³And I will harden Pharaoh's heart, and multiply my signs and my wonders in the land of Egypt.

⁴But Pharaoh shall not hearken unto you, that I may lay my hand upon Egypt, and bring forth mine armies, and my people the children of Israel, out of the land of Egypt by great judgments.

⁵And the Egyptians shall know that I am the LORD, when I stretch forth mine hand upon Egypt, and bring out the children of Israel from among them.

⁶And Moses and Aaron did as the LORD commanded them, so did they.

⁷And Moses was fourscore years old, and Aaron fourscore and three years old, when they spake unto Pharaoh.

⁸And the LORD spake unto Moses and unto Aaron, saying,

⁹When Pharaoh shall speak unto you, saying, Shew a miracle for you: then thou shalt say unto Aaron, Take thy rod, and cast it before Pharaoh, and it shall become a serpent.

¹⁰And Moses and Aaron went in unto Pharaoh, and they did so as the LORD had commanded: and Aaron cast down his rod before Pharaoh, and before his servants, and it became a serpent.

¹¹Then Pharaoh also called the wise men and the sorcerers: now the magicians of Egypt, they also did in like manner with their enchantments.

¹²For they cast down every man his rod, and they became serpents: but Aaron's rod swallowed up their rods.

¹³And he hardened Pharaoh's heart, that he hearkened not unto them; as the LORD had said.

¹⁴And the LORD said unto Moses, Pharaoh's heart is hardened, he refuseth to let the people go.

¹⁵Get thee unto Pharaoh in the morning; lo, he goeth out unto the water; and thou shalt stand by the river's brink against he come; and the rod which was turned to a serpent shalt thou take in thine hand.

¹⁶And thou shalt say unto him, The LORD God of the Hebrews hath sent me unto thee, saying, Let my people go, that they may serve me in the wilderness: and, behold, hitherto thou wouldest not hear.

¹⁷Thus saith the LORD, In this thou shalt know that I am the LORD: behold, I will smite with the rod that is in mine hand upon the waters which are in the river, and they shall be turned to blood.

¹⁸And the fish that is in the river shall die, and the river shall stink; and the Egyptians shall lothe to drink of the water of the river.

¹⁹And the LORD spake unto Moses, Say unto Aaron, Take thy rod, and stretch out thine hand upon the waters of Egypt, upon their streams, upon their rivers, and upon their ponds, and upon all their pools of water, that they may become blood; and that there may be blood throughout all the land of Egypt, both in vessels of wood, and in vessels of stone.

²⁰And Moses and Aaron did so, as the LORD commanded; and he lifted up the rod, and smote the waters that were in the river, in the sight of Pharaoh, and in the sight of his servants; and all the waters that were in the river were turned to blood.

²¹And the fish that was in the river died; and the river stank, and the Egyptians could not drink of the water of the river; and there was blood throughout all the land of Egypt.

²²And the magicians of Egypt did so with their enchantments: and Pharaoh's heart was hardened, neither did he hearken unto them; as the LORD had said.

²³And Pharaoh turned and went into his house, neither did he set his heart to this also.

²⁴And all the Egyptians digged round about the river for water to drink; for they could not drink of the water of the river.

²⁵And seven days were fulfilled, after that the LORD had smitten the river.

CHAPTER 8

¹And the LORD spake unto Moses, Go unto Pharaoh, and say unto him, Thus saith the LORD, Let my people go, that they may serve me.

²And if thou refuse to let them go, behold, I will smite all thy borders with frogs:

³And the river shall bring forth frogs abundantly, which shall go up and come into thine house, and into thy bedchamber, and upon thy bed, and into the house of thy servants, and upon thy people, and into thine ovens, and into thy kneadingtroughs:

⁴And the frogs shall come up both on thee, and upon thy people, and upon all thy servants.

⁵And the LORD spake unto Moses, Say unto Aaron, Stretch forth thine hand with thy rod over the streams, over the rivers, and over the ponds, and cause frogs to come up upon the land of Egypt.

⁶And Aaron stretched out his hand over the waters of Egypt; and the frogs came up, and covered the land of Egypt.

⁷And the magicians did so with their enchantments, and brought up frogs upon the land of Egypt.

⁸Then Pharaoh called for Moses and Aaron, and said, Intreat the LORD, that he may take away the frogs from me, and from my people; and I will let the people go, that they may do sacrifice unto the LORD.

⁹And Moses said unto Pharaoh, Glory over me: when shall I intreat for thee, and for thy servants, and for thy people, to destroy the frogs from thee and thy houses, that they may remain in the river only?

¹⁰And he said, To morrow. And he said, Be it according to thy word: that thou mayest know that there is none like unto the LORD our God.

¹¹And the frogs shall depart from thee, and from thy houses, and from thy servants, and from thy people; they shall remain in the river only.

¹²And Moses and Aaron went out from Pharaoh: and Moses cried unto the LORD because of the frogs which he had brought against Pharaoh.

¹³And the LORD did according to the word of Moses; and the frogs died out of the houses, out of the villages, and out of the fields.

¹⁴And they gathered them together upon heaps: and the land stank.

¹⁵But when Pharaoh saw that there was respite, he hardened his heart, and hearkened not unto them; as the LORD had said.

¹⁶And the LORD said unto Moses, Say unto Aaron, Stretch out thy rod,

and smite the dust of the land, that it may become lice throughout all the land of Egypt.

¹⁷And they did so; for Aaron stretched out his hand with his rod, and smote the dust of the earth, and it became lice in man, and in beast; all the dust of the land became lice throughout all the land of Egypt.

¹⁸And the magicians did so with their enchantments to bring forth lice, but they could not: so there were lice upon man, and upon beast.

¹⁹Then the magicians said unto Pharaoh, This is the finger of God: and Pharaoh's heart was hardened, and he hearkened not unto them; as the LORD had said.

²⁰And the LORD said unto Moses, Rise up early in the morning, and stand before Pharaoh; lo, he cometh forth to the water; and say unto him, Thus saith the LORD, Let my people go, that they may serve me.

²¹Else, if thou wilt not let my people go, behold, I will send swarms of flies upon thee, and upon thy servants, and upon thy people, and into thy houses: and the houses of the Egyptians shall be full of swarms of flies, and also the ground whereon they are.

²²And I will sever in that day the land of Goshen, in which my people dwell, that no swarms of flies shall be there; to the end thou mayest know that I am the LORD in the midst of the earth.

²³And I will put a division between my people and thy people: to morrow shall this sign be.

²⁴And the LORD did so; and there came a grievous swarm of flies into the house of Pharaoh, and into his servants' houses, and into all the land of Egypt: the land was corrupted by reason of the swarm of flies.

²⁵And Pharaoh called for Moses and for Aaron, and said, Go ye, sacrifice to your God in the land.

²⁶And Moses said, It is not meet so to do; for we shall sacrifice the abomination of the Egyptians to the LORD our God: lo, shall we sacrifice the abomination of the Egyptians before their eyes, and will they not stone us?

²⁷We will go three days' journey into the wilderness, and sacrifice to the LORD our God, as he shall command us.

²⁸And Pharaoh said, I will let you go, that ye may sacrifice to the LORD your God in the wilderness; only ye shall not go very far away: intreat for me.

²⁹And Moses said, Behold, I go out from thee, and I will intreat the LORD that the swarms of flies may depart from Pharaoh, from his

servants, and from his people, to morrow: but let not Pharaoh deal deceitfully any more in not letting the people go to sacrifice to the LORD.

³⁰And Moses went out from Pharaoh, and intreated the LORD.

³¹And the LORD did according to the word of Moses; and he removed the swarms of flies from Pharaoh, from his servants, and from his people; there remained not one.

³²And Pharaoh hardened his heart at this time also, neither would he let the people go.

CHAPTER 9

¹Then the LORD said unto Moses, Go in unto Pharaoh, and tell him, Thus saith the LORD God of the Hebrews, Let my people go, that they may serve me.

²For if thou refuse to let them go, and wilt hold them still,

³Behold, the hand of the LORD is upon thy cattle which is in the field, upon the horses, upon the asses, upon the camels, upon the oxen, and upon the sheep: there shall be a very grievous murrain.

⁴And the LORD shall sever between the cattle of Israel and the cattle of Egypt: and there shall nothing die of all that is the children's of Israel.

⁵And the LORD appointed a set time, saying, To morrow the LORD shall do this thing in the land.

⁶And the LORD did that thing on the morrow, and all the cattle of Egypt died: but of the cattle of the children of Israel died not one.

⁷And Pharaoh sent, and, behold, there was not one of the cattle of the Israelites dead. And the heart of Pharaoh was hardened, and he did not let the people go.

⁸And the LORD said unto Moses and unto Aaron, Take to you handfuls of ashes of the furnace, and let Moses sprinkle it toward the heaven in the sight of Pharaoh.

⁹And it shall become small dust in all the land of Egypt, and shall be a boil breaking forth with blains upon man, and upon beast, throughout all the land of Egypt.

¹⁰And they took ashes of the furnace, and stood before Pharaoh; and Moses sprinkled it up toward heaven; and it became a boil breaking forth with blains upon man, and upon beast.

¹¹And the magicians could not stand before Moses because of the boils; for the boil was upon the magicians, and upon all the Egyptians.

¹²And the LORD hardened the heart of Pharaoh, and he hearkened not unto them; as the LORD had spoken unto Moses.

¹³And the LORD said unto Moses, Rise up early in the morning, and stand before Pharaoh, and say unto him, Thus saith the LORD God of the Hebrews, Let my people go, that they may serve me.

¹⁴For I will at this time send all my plagues upon thine heart, and upon thy servants, and upon thy people; that thou mayest know that there is none like me in all the earth.

¹⁵For now I will stretch out my hand, that I may smite thee and thy people with pestilence; and thou shalt be cut off from the earth.

¹⁶And in very deed for this cause have I raised thee up, for to shew in thee my power; and that my name may be declared throughout all the earth.

¹⁷As yet exaltest thou thyself against my people, that thou wilt not let them go?

¹⁸Behold, to morrow about this time I will cause it to rain a very grievous hail, such as hath not been in Egypt since the foundation thereof even until now.

¹⁹Send therefore now, and gather thy cattle, and all that thou hast in the field; for upon every man and beast which shall be found in the field, and shall not be brought home, the hail shall come down upon them, and they shall die.

²⁰He that feared the word of the LORD among the servants of Pharaoh made his servants and his cattle flee into the houses:

²¹And he that regarded not the word of the LORD left his servants and his cattle in the field.

²²And the LORD said unto Moses, Stretch forth thine hand toward heaven, that there may be hail in all the land of Egypt, upon man, and upon beast, and upon every herb of the field, throughout the land of Egypt.

²³And Moses stretched forth his rod toward heaven: and the LORD sent thunder and hail, and the fire ran along upon the ground; and the LORD rained hail upon the land of Egypt.

²⁴So there was hail, and fire mingled with the hail, very grievous, such as there was none like it in all the land of Egypt since it became a nation.

²⁵And the hail smote throughout all the land of Egypt all that was in the field, both man and beast; and the hail smote every herb of the field, and brake every tree of the field.

²⁶Only in the land of Goshen, where the children of Israel were, was there no hail.

²⁷And Pharaoh sent, and called for Moses and Aaron, and said unto them, I have sinned this time: the LORD is righteous, and I and my people are wicked.

²⁸Intreat the LORD (for it is enough) that there be no more mighty thunderings and hail; and I will let you go, and ye shall stay no longer.

²⁹And Moses said unto him, As soon as I am gone out of the city, I will spread abroad my hands unto the LORD; and the thunder shall cease, neither shall there be any more hail; that thou mayest know how that the earth is the LORD's.

³⁰But as for thee and thy servants, I know that ye will not yet fear the LORD God.

³¹And the flax and the barley was smitten: for the barley was in the ear, and the flax was bolled.

³²But the wheat and the rie were not smitten: for they were not grown up.

³³And Moses went out of the city from Pharaoh, and spread abroad his hands unto the LORD: and the thunders and hail ceased, and the rain was not poured upon the earth.

³⁴And when Pharaoh saw that the rain and the hail and the thunders were ceased, he sinned yet more, and hardened his heart, he and his servants.

³⁵And the heart of Pharaoh was hardened, neither would he let the children of Israel go; as the LORD had spoken by Moses.

CHAPTER 10

¹And the LORD said unto Moses, Go in unto Pharaoh: for I have hardened his heart, and the heart of his servants, that I might shew these my signs before him:

²And that thou mayest tell in the ears of thy son, and of thy son's son, what things I have wrought in Egypt, and my signs which I have done among them; that ye may know how that I am the LORD.

³And Moses and Aaron came in unto Pharaoh, and said unto him, Thus saith the LORD God of the Hebrews, How long wilt thou refuse to humble thyself before me? let my people go, that they may serve me.

⁴Else, if thou refuse to let my people go, behold, to morrow will I bring the locusts into thy coast:

⁵And they shall cover the face of the earth, that one cannot be able to see the earth: and they shall eat the residue of that which is escaped, which remaineth unto you from the hail, and shall eat every tree which groweth for you out of the field:

⁶And they shall fill thy houses, and the houses of all thy servants, and the houses of all the Egyptians; which neither thy fathers, nor thy fathers' fathers have seen, since the day that they were upon the earth unto this day. And he turned himself, and went out from Pharaoh.

⁷And Pharaoh's servants said unto him, How long shall this man be a snare unto us? let the men go, that they may serve the LORD their God: knowest thou not yet that Egypt is destroyed?

⁸And Moses and Aaron were brought again unto Pharaoh: and he said unto them, Go, serve the LORD your God: but who are they that shall go?

⁹And Moses said, We will go with our young and with our old, with our sons and with our daughters, with our flocks and with our herds will we go; for we must hold a feast unto the LORD.

¹⁰And he said unto them, Let the LORD be so with you, as I will let you go, and your little ones: look to it; for evil is before you.

¹¹Not so: go now ye that are men, and serve the LORD; for that ye did desire. And they were driven out from Pharaoh's presence.

¹²And the LORD said unto Moses, Stretch out thine hand over the land of Egypt for the locusts, that they may come up upon the land of Egypt, and eat every herb of the land, even all that the hail hath left.

¹³And Moses stretched forth his rod over the land of Egypt, and the LORD brought an east wind upon the land all that day, and all that night; and when it was morning, the east wind brought the locusts.

¹⁴And the locust went up over all the land of Egypt, and rested in all the coasts of Egypt: very grievous were they; before them there were no such locusts as they, neither after them shall be such.

¹⁵For they covered the face of the whole earth, so that the land was darkened; and they did eat every herb of the land, and all the fruit of the trees which the hail had left: and there remained not any green thing in the trees, or in the herbs of the field, through all the land of Egypt.

¹⁶Then Pharaoh called for Moses and Aaron in haste; and he said, I have sinned against the LORD your God, and against you.

¹⁷Now therefore forgive, I pray thee, my sin only this once, and intreat the LORD your God, that he may take away from me this death only.

¹⁸And he went out from Pharaoh, and intreated the LORD.

¹⁹And the LORD turned a mighty strong west wind, which took away the locusts, and cast them into the Red sea; there remained not one locust in all the coasts of Egypt.

²⁰But the LORD hardened Pharaoh's heart, so that he would not let the children of Israel go.

²¹And the LORD said unto Moses, Stretch out thine hand toward heaven, that there may be darkness over the land of Egypt, even darkness which may be felt.

²²And Moses stretched forth his hand toward heaven; and there was a thick darkness in all the land of Egypt three days:

²³They saw not one another, neither rose any from his place for three days: but all the children of Israel had light in their dwellings.

²⁴And Pharaoh called unto Moses, and said, Go ye, serve the LORD; only let your flocks and your herds be stayed: let your little ones also go with you.

²⁵And Moses said, Thou must give us also sacrifices and burnt offerings, that we may sacrifice unto the LORD our God.

²⁶Our cattle also shall go with us; there shall not an hoof be left behind; for thereof must we take to serve the LORD our God; and we know not with what we must serve the LORD, until we come thither.

²⁷But the LORD hardened Pharaoh's heart, and he would not let them go.

²⁸And Pharaoh said unto him, Get thee from me, take heed to thyself, see my face no more; for in that day thou seest my face thou shalt die.

²⁹And Moses said, Thou hast spoken well, I will see thy face again no more.

CHAPTER 11

¹And the LORD said unto Moses, Yet will I bring one plague more upon Pharaoh, and upon Egypt; afterwards he will let you go hence: when he shall let you go, he shall surely thrust you out hence altogether.

²Speak now in the ears of the people, and let every man borrow of his neighbour, and every woman of her neighbour, jewels of silver and jewels of gold.

³And the LORD gave the people favour in the sight of the Egyptians. Moreover the man Moses was very great in the land of Egypt, in the sight of Pharaoh's servants, and in the sight of the people.

⁴And Moses said, Thus saith the LORD, About midnight will I go out into the midst of Egypt:

⁵And all the firstborn in the land of Egypt shall die, from the first born of Pharaoh that sitteth upon his throne, even unto the firstborn of the maidservant that is behind the mill; and all the firstborn of beasts.

⁶And there shall be a great cry throughout all the land of Egypt, such as there was none like it, nor shall be like it any more.

⁷But against any of the children of Israel shall not a dog move his tongue, against man or beast: that ye may know how that the LORD doth put a difference between the Egyptians and Israel.

⁸And all these thy servants shall come down unto me, and bow down themselves unto me, saying, Get thee out, and all the people that follow thee: and after that I will go out. And he went out from Pharaoh in a great anger.

⁹And the LORD said unto Moses, Pharaoh shall not hearken unto you; that my wonders may be multiplied in the land of Egypt.

¹⁰And Moses and Aaron did all these wonders before Pharaoh: and the LORD hardened Pharaoh's heart, so that he would not let the children of Israel go out of his land.

CHAPTER 12

¹And the LORD spake unto Moses and Aaron in the land of Egypt saying, ²This month shall be unto you the beginning of months: it shall be the first month of the year to you.

³Speak ye unto all the congregation of Israel, saying, In the tenth day of this month they shall take to them every man a lamb, according to the house of their fathers, a lamb for an house:

⁴And if the household be too little for the lamb, let him and his neighbour next unto his house take it according to the number of the souls; every man according to his eating shall make your count for the lamb.

⁵Your lamb shall be without blemish, a male of the first year: ye shall take it out from the sheep, or from the goats:

⁶And ye shall keep it up until the fourteenth day of the same month: and the whole assembly of the congregation of Israel shall kill it in the evening.

⁷And they shall take of the blood, and strike it on the two side posts and on the upper door post of the houses, wherein they shall eat it.

⁸And they shall eat the flesh

in that night, roast with fire, and unleavened bread; and with bitter herbs they shall eat it.

⁹Eat not of it raw, nor sodden at all with water, but roast with fire; his head with his legs, and with the purtenance thereof.

¹⁰And ye shall let nothing of it remain until the morning; and that which remaineth of it until the morning ye shall burn with fire.

¹¹And thus shall ye eat it; with your loins girded, your shoes on your feet, and your staff in your hand; and ye shall eat it in haste: it is the LORD's passover.

¹²For I will pass through the land of Egypt this night, and will smite all the firstborn in the land of Egypt, both man and beast; and against all the gods of Egypt I will execute judgment: I am the LORD.

¹³And the blood shall be to you for a token upon the houses where ye are: and when I see the blood, I will pass over you, and the plague shall not be upon you to destroy you, when I smite the land of Egypt.

¹⁴And this day shall be unto you for a memorial; and ye shall keep it a feast to the LORD throughout your generations; ye shall keep it a feast by an ordinance for ever.

¹⁵Seven days shall ye eat unleavened bread; even the first day ye shall put away leaven out of your houses: for whosoever eateth leavened bread from the first day until the seventh day, that soul shall be cut off from Israel.

¹⁶And in the first day there shall be an holy convocation, and in the seventh day there shall be an holy convocation to you; no manner of work shall be done in them, save that which every man must eat, that only may be done of you.

¹⁷And ye shall observe the feast of unleavened bread; for in this selfsame day have I brought your armies out of the land of Egypt: therefore shall ye observe this day in your generations by an ordinance for ever.

¹⁸In the first month, on the fourteenth day of the month at even, ye shall eat unleavened bread, until the one and twentieth day of the month at even.

¹⁹Seven days shall there be no leaven found in your houses: for whosoever eateth that which is leavened, even that soul shall be cut off from the congregation of Israel, whether he be a stranger, or born in the land.

²⁰Ye shall eat nothing leavened; in all your habitations shall ye eat unleavened bread.

²¹Then Moses called for all the elders of Israel, and said unto them, Draw out and take you a lamb

according to your families, and kill the passover.

²²And ye shall take a bunch of hyssop, and dip it in the blood that is in the bason, and strike the lintel and the two side posts with the blood that is in the bason; and none of you shall go out at the door of his house until the morning.

²³For the LORD will pass through to smite the Egyptians; and when he seeth the blood upon the lintel, and on the two side posts, the LORD will pass over the door, and will not suffer the destroyer to come in unto your houses to smite you.

²⁴And ye shall observe this thing for an ordinance to thee and to thy sons for ever.

²⁵And it shall come to pass, when ye be come to the land which the LORD will give you, according as he hath promised, that ye shall keep this service.

²⁶And it shall come to pass, when your children shall say unto you, What mean ye by this service?

²⁷That ye shall say, It is the sacrifice of the LORD's passover, who passed over the houses of the children of Israel in Egypt, when he smote the Egyptians, and delivered our houses. And the people bowed the head and worshipped.

²⁸And the children of Israel went away, and did as the LORD had commanded Moses and Aaron, so did they.

²⁹And it came to pass, that at midnight the LORD smote all the firstborn in the land of Egypt, from the firstborn of Pharaoh that sat on his throne unto the firstborn of the captive that was in the dungeon; and all the firstborn of cattle.

³⁰And Pharaoh rose up in the night, he, and all his servants, and all the Egyptians; and there was a great cry in Egypt; for there was not a house where there was not one dead.

³¹And he called for Moses and Aaron by night, and said, Rise up, and get you forth from among my people, both ye and the children of Israel; and go, serve the LORD, as ye have said.

³²Also take your flocks and your herds, as ye have said, and be gone; and bless me also.

³³And the Egyptians were urgent upon the people, that they might send them out of the land in haste; for they said, We be all dead men.

³⁴And the people took their dough before it was leavened, their kneadingtroughs being bound up in their clothes upon their shoulders.

³⁵And the children of Israel did according to the word of Moses; and they borrowed of the Egyptians

jewels of silver, and jewels of gold, and raiment:

³⁶And the LORD gave the people favour in the sight of the Egyptians, so that they lent unto them such things as they required. And they spoiled the Egyptians.

³⁷And the children of Israel journeyed from Rameses to Succoth, about six hundred thousand on foot that were men, beside children.

³⁸And a mixed multitude went up also with them; and flocks, and herds, even very much cattle.

³⁹And they baked unleavened cakes of the dough which they brought forth out of Egypt, for it was not leavened; because they were thrust out of Egypt, and could not tarry, neither had they prepared for themselves any victual.

⁴⁰Now the sojourning of the children of Israel, who dwelt in Egypt, was four hundred and thirty years.

⁴¹And it came to pass at the end of the four hundred and thirty years, even the selfsame day it came to pass, that all the hosts of the LORD went out from the land of Egypt.

⁴²It is a night to be much observed unto the LORD for bringing them out from the land of Egypt: this is that night of the LORD to be observed of all the children of Israel in their generations.

⁴³And the LORD said unto Moses and Aaron, This is the ordinance of the passover: There shall no stranger eat thereof:

⁴⁴But every man's servant that is bought for money, when thou hast circumcised him, then shall he eat thereof.

⁴⁵A foreigner and an hired servant shall not eat thereof.

⁴⁶In one house shall it be eaten; thou shalt not carry forth ought of the flesh abroad out of the house; neither shall ye break a bone thereof.

⁴⁷All the congregation of Israel shall keep it.

⁴⁸And when a stranger shall sojourn with thee, and will keep the passover to the LORD, let all his males be circumcised, and then let him come near and keep it; and he shall be as one that is born in the land: for no uncircumcised person shall eat thereof.

⁴⁹One law shall be to him that is homeborn, and unto the stranger that sojourneth among you.

⁵⁰Thus did all the children of Israel; as the LORD commanded Moses and Aaron, so did they.

⁵¹And it came to pass the selfsame day, that the LORD did bring the children of Israel out of the land of Egypt by their armies.

CHAPTER 13

¹And the LORD spake unto Moses, saying,

²Sanctify unto me all the firstborn, whatsoever openeth the womb among the children of Israel, both of man and of beast: it is mine.

³And Moses said unto the people, Remember this day, in which ye came out from Egypt, out of the house of bondage; for by strength of hand the LORD brought you out from this place: there shall no leavened bread be eaten.

⁴This day came ye out in the month Abib.

⁵And it shall be when the LORD shall bring thee into the land of the Canaanites, and the Hittites, and the Amorites, and the Hivites, and the Jebusites, which he sware unto thy fathers to give thee, a land flowing with milk and honey, that thou shalt keep this service in this month.

⁶Seven days thou shalt eat unleavened bread, and in the seventh day shall be a feast to the LORD.

⁷Unleavened bread shall be eaten seven days; and there shall no leavened bread be seen with thee, neither shall there be leaven seen with thee in all thy quarters.

⁸And thou shalt shew thy son in that day, saying, This is done because of that which the LORD did unto me when I came forth out of Egypt.

⁹And it shall be for a sign unto thee upon thine hand, and for a memorial between thine eyes, that the LORD's law may be in thy mouth: for with a strong hand hath the LORD brought thee out of Egypt.

¹⁰Thou shalt therefore keep this ordinance in his season from year to year.

¹¹And it shall be when the LORD shall bring thee into the land of the Canaanites, as he sware unto thee and to thy fathers, and shall give it thee,

¹²That thou shalt set apart unto the LORD all that openeth the matrix, and every firstling that cometh of a beast which thou hast; the males shall be the LORD's.

¹³And every firstling of an ass thou shalt redeem with a lamb; and if thou wilt not redeem it, then thou shalt break his neck: and all the firstborn of man among thy children shalt thou redeem.

¹⁴And it shall be when thy son asketh thee in time to come, saying, What is this? that thou shalt say unto him, By strength of hand the LORD brought us out from Egypt, from the house of bondage:

¹⁵And it came to pass, when

Pharaoh would hardly let us go, that the LORD slew all the firstborn in the land of Egypt, both the firstborn of man, and the firstborn of beast: therefore I sacrifice to the LORD all that openeth the matrix, being males; but all the firstborn of my children I redeem.

¹⁶And it shall be for a token upon thine hand, and for frontlets between thine eyes: for by strength of hand the LORD brought us forth out of Egypt.

¹⁷And it came to pass, when Pharaoh had let the people go, that God led them not through the way of the land of the Philistines, although that was near; for God said, Lest peradventure the people repent when they see war, and they return to Egypt:

¹⁸But God led the people about, through the way of the wilderness of the Red sea: and the children of Israel went up harnessed out of the land of Egypt.

¹⁹And Moses took the bones of Joseph with him: for he had straitly sworn the children of Israel, saying, God will surely visit you; and ye shall carry up my bones away hence with you.

²⁰And they took their journey from Succoth, and encamped in Etham, in the edge of the wilderness.

²¹And the LORD went before them by day in a pillar of a cloud, to lead them the way; and by night in a pillar of fire, to give them light; to go by day and night:

²²He took not away the pillar of the cloud by day, nor the pillar of fire by night, from before the people.

CHAPTER 14

¹And the LORD spake unto Moses, saying,

²Speak unto the children of Israel, that they turn and encamp before Pi-hahiroth, between Migdol and the sea, over against Baal-zephon: before it shall ye encamp by the sea.

³For Pharaoh will say of the children of Israel, They are entangled in the land, the wilderness hath shut them in.

⁴And I will harden Pharaoh's heart, that he shall follow after them; and I will be honoured upon Pharaoh, and upon all his host; that the Egyptians may know that I am the LORD. And they did so.

⁵And it was told the king of Egypt that the people fled: and the heart of Pharaoh and of his servants was turned against the people, and they said, Why have we

done this, that we have let Israel go from serving us?

⁶And he made ready his chariot, and took his people with him:

⁷And he took six hundred chosen chariots, and all the chariots of Egypt, and captains over every one of them.

⁸And the LORD hardened the heart of Pharaoh king of Egypt, and he pursued after the children of Israel: and the children of Israel went out with an high hand.

⁹But the Egyptians pursued after them, all the horses and chariots of Pharaoh, and his horsemen, and his army, and overtook them encamping by the sea, beside Pi-hahiroth, before Baal-zephon.

¹⁰And when Pharaoh drew nigh, the children of Israel lifted up their eyes, and, behold, the Egyptians marched after them; and they were sore afraid: and the children of Israel cried out unto the LORD.

¹¹And they said unto Moses, Because there were no graves in Egypt, hast thou taken us away to die in the wilderness? wherefore hast thou dealt thus with us, to carry us forth out of Egypt?

¹²Is not this the word that we did tell thee in Egypt, saying, Let us alone, that we may serve the Egyptians? For it had been better for us to serve the Egyptians, than that we should die in the wilderness.

¹³And Moses said unto the people, Fear ye not, stand still, and see the salvation of the LORD, which he will shew to you to day: for the Egyptians whom ye have seen to day, ye shall see them again no more for ever.

¹⁴The LORD shall fight for you, and ye shall hold your peace.

¹⁵And the LORD said unto Moses, Wherefore criest thou unto me? speak unto the children of Israel, that they go forward:

¹⁶But lift thou up thy rod, and stretch out thine hand over the sea, and divide it: and the children of Israel shall go on dry ground through the midst of the sea.

¹⁷And I, behold, I will harden the hearts of the Egyptians, and they shall follow them: and I will get me honour upon Pharaoh, and upon all his host, upon his chariots, and upon his horsemen.

¹⁸And the Egyptians shall know that I am the LORD, when I have gotten me honour upon Pharaoh, upon his chariots, and upon his horsemen.

¹⁹And the angel of God, which went before the camp of Israel, removed and went behind them; and the pillar of the cloud went from before their face, and stood behind them:

²⁰And it came between the camp of the Egyptians and the camp of Israel; and it was a cloud and darkness to them, but it gave light by night to these: so that the one came not near the other all the night.

²¹And Moses stretched out his hand over the sea; and the LORD caused the sea to go back by a strong east wind all that night, and made the sea dry land, and the waters were divided.

²²And the children of Israel went into the midst of the sea upon the dry ground: and the waters were a wall unto them on their right hand, and on their left.

²³And the Egyptians pursued, and went in after them to the midst of the sea, even all Pharaoh's horses, his chariots, and his horsemen.

²⁴And it came to pass, that in the morning watch the LORD looked unto the host of the Egyptians through the pillar of fire and of the cloud, and troubled the host of the Egyptians,

²⁵And took off their chariot wheels, that they drave them heavily: so that the Egyptians said, Let us flee from the face of Israel; for the LORD fighteth for them against the Egyptians.

²⁶And the LORD said unto Moses, Stretch out thine hand over the sea, that the waters may come again upon the Egyptians, upon their chariots, and upon their horsemen.

²⁷And Moses stretched forth his hand over the sea, and the sea returned to his strength when the morning appeared; and the Egyptians fled against it; and the LORD overthrew the Egyptians in the midst of the sea.

²⁸And the waters returned, and covered the chariots, and the horsemen, and all the host of Pharaoh that came into the sea after them; there remained not so much as one of them.

²⁹But the children of Israel walked upon dry land in the midst of the sea; and the waters were a wall unto them on their right hand, and on their left.

³⁰Thus the LORD saved Israel that day out of the hand of the Egyptians; and Israel saw the Egyptians dead upon the sea shore.

³¹And Israel saw that great work which the LORD did upon the Egyptians: and the people feared the LORD, and believed the LORD, and his servant Moses.

CHAPTER 15

¹Then sang Moses and the children of Israel this song unto the LORD, and spake, saying, I will sing unto the LORD, for he hath triumphed gloriously: the horse and his rider hath he thrown into the sea.

²The LORD is my strength and song, and he is become my salvation: he is my God, and I will prepare him an habitation; my father's God, and I will exalt him.

³The LORD is a man of war: the LORD is his name.

⁴Pharaoh's chariots and his host hath he cast into the sea: his chosen captains also are drowned in the Red sea.

⁵The depths have covered them: they sank into the bottom as a stone.

⁶Thy right hand, O LORD, is become glorious in power: thy right hand, O LORD, hath dashed in pieces the enemy.

⁷And in the greatness of thine excellency thou hast overthrown them that rose up against thee: thou sentest forth thy wrath, which consumed them as stubble.

⁸And with the blast of thy nostrils the waters were gathered together, the floods stood upright as an heap, and the depths were congealed in the heart of the sea.

⁹The enemy said, I will pursue, I will overtake, I will divide the spoil; my lust shall be satisfied upon them; I will draw my sword, my hand shall destroy them.

¹⁰Thou didst blow with thy wind, the sea covered them: they sank as lead in the mighty waters.

¹¹Who is like unto thee, O LORD, among the gods? who is like thee, glorious in holiness, fearful in praises, doing wonders?

¹²Thou stretchedst out thy right hand, the earth swallowed them.

¹³Thou in thy mercy hast led forth the people which thou hast redeemed: thou hast guided them in thy strength unto thy holy habitation.

¹⁴The people shall hear, and be afraid: sorrow shall take hold on the inhabitants of Palestina.

¹⁵Then the dukes of Edom shall be amazed; the mighty men of Moab, trembling shall take hold upon them; all the inhabitants of Canaan shall melt away.

¹⁶Fear and dread shall fall upon them; by the greatness of thine arm they shall be as still as a stone; till thy people pass over, O LORD, till the people pass over, which thou hast purchased.

¹⁷Thou shalt bring them in, and plant them in the mountain of thine inheritance, in the place, O LORD,

which thou hast made for thee to dwell in, in the Sanctuary, O LORD, which thy hands have established.

¹⁸The LORD shall reign for ever and ever.

¹⁹For the horse of Pharaoh went in with his chariots and with his horsemen into the sea, and the LORD brought again the waters of the sea upon them; but the children of Israel went on dry land in the midst of the sea.

²⁰And Miriam the prophetess, the sister of Aaron, took a timbrel in her hand; and all the women went out after her with timbrels and with dances.

²¹And Miriam answered them, Sing ye to the LORD, for he hath triumphed gloriously; the horse and his rider hath he thrown into the sea.

²²So Moses brought Israel from the Red sea, and they went out into the wilderness of Shur; and they went three days in the wilderness, and found no water.

²³And when they came to Marah, they could not drink of the waters of Marah, for they were bitter: therefore the name of it was called Marah.

²⁴And the people murmured against Moses, saying, What shall we drink?

²⁵And he cried unto the LORD; and the LORD shewed him a tree, which when he had cast into the waters, the waters were made sweet: there he made for them a statute and an ordinance, and there he proved them,

²⁶And said, If thou wilt diligently hearken to the voice of the LORD thy God, and wilt do that which is right in his sight, and wilt give ear to his commandments, and keep all his statutes, I will put none of these diseases upon thee, which I have brought upon the Egyptians: for I am the LORD that healeth thee.

²⁷And they came to Elim, where were twelve wells of water, and threescore and ten palm trees: and they encamped there by the waters.

CHAPTER 16

¹And they took their journey from Elim, and all the congregation of the children of Israel came unto the wilderness of Sin, which is between Elim and Sinai, on the fifteenth day of the second month after their departing out of the land of Egypt.

²And the whole congregation of the children of Israel murmured against Moses and Aaron in the wilderness:

³And the children of Israel said unto them, Would to God we had

died by the hand of the LORD in the land of Egypt, when we sat by the flesh pots, and when we did eat bread to the full; for ye have brought us forth into this wilderness, to kill this whole assembly with hunger.

⁴Then said the LORD unto Moses, Behold, I will rain bread from heaven for you; and the people shall go out and gather a certain rate every day, that I may prove them, whether they will walk in my law, or no.

⁵And it shall come to pass, that on the sixth day they shall prepare that which they bring in; and it shall be twice as much as they gather daily.

⁶And Moses and Aaron said unto all the children of Israel, At even, then ye shall know that the LORD hath brought you out from the land of Egypt:

⁷And in the morning, then ye shall see the glory of the LORD; for that he heareth your murmurings against the LORD: and what are we, that ye murmur against us?

⁸And Moses said, This shall be, when the LORD shall give you in the evening flesh to eat, and in the morning bread to the full; for that the LORD heareth your murmurings which ye murmur against him: and what are we? your murmurings are not against us, but against the LORD.

⁹And Moses spake unto Aaron, Say unto all the congregation of the children of Israel, Come near before the LORD: for he hath heard your murmurings.

¹⁰And it came to pass, as Aaron spake unto the whole congregation of the children of Israel, that they looked toward the wilderness, and, behold, the glory of the LORD appeared in the cloud.

¹¹And the LORD spake unto Moses, saying,

¹²I have heard the murmurings of the children of Israel: speak unto them, saying, At even ye shall eat flesh, and in the morning ye shall be filled with bread; and ye shall know that I am the LORD your God.

¹³And it came to pass, that at even the quails came up, and covered the camp: and in the morning the dew lay round about the host.

¹⁴And when the dew that lay was gone up, behold, upon the face of the wilderness there lay a small round thing, as small as the hoar frost on the ground.

¹⁵And when the children of Israel saw it, they said one to another, It is manna: for they wist not what it was. And Moses said unto them, This is the bread which the LORD hath given you to eat.

¹⁶This is the thing which the LORD hath commanded, Gather of it every man according to his

eating, an omer for every man, according to the number of your persons; take ye every man for them which are in his tents.

¹⁷And the children of Israel did so, and gathered, some more, some less.

¹⁸And when they did mete it with an omer, he that gathered much had nothing over, and he that gathered little had no lack; they gathered every man according to his eating.

¹⁹And Moses said, Let no man leave of it till the morning.

²⁰Notwithstanding they hearkened not unto Moses; but some of them left of it until the morning, and it bred worms, and stank: and Moses was wroth with them.

²¹And they gathered it every morning, every man according to his eating: and when the sun waxed hot, it melted.

²²And it came to pass, that on the sixth day they gathered twice as much bread, two omers for one man: and all the rulers of the congregation came and told Moses.

²³And he said unto them, This is that which the LORD hath said, To morrow is the rest of the holy sabbath unto the LORD: bake that which ye will bake to day, and seethe that ye will seethe; and that which remaineth over lay up for you to be kept until the morning.

²⁴And they laid it up till the morning, as Moses bade: and it did not stink, neither was there any worm therein.

²⁵And Moses said, Eat that to day; for to day is a sabbath unto the LORD: to day ye shall not find it in the field.

²⁶Six days ye shall gather it; but on the seventh day, which is the sabbath, in it there shall be none.

²⁷And it came to pass, that there went out some of the people on the seventh day for to gather, and they found none.

²⁸And the LORD said unto Moses, How long refuse ye to keep my commandments and my laws?

²⁹See, for that the LORD hath given you the sabbath, therefore he giveth you on the sixth day the bread of two days; abide ye every man in his place, let no man go out of his place on the seventh day.

³⁰So the people rested on the seventh day.

³¹And the house of Israel called the name thereof Manna: and it was like coriander seed, white; and the taste of it was like wafers made with honey.

³²And Moses said, This is the thing which the LORD commandeth, Fill an omer of it to be kept for your generations; that they may see the bread wherewith I have fed you in

the wilderness, when I brought you forth from the land of Egypt.

³³And Moses said unto Aaron, Take a pot, and put an omer full of manna therein, and lay it up before the LORD, to be kept for your generations.

³⁴As the LORD commanded Moses, so Aaron laid it up before the Testimony, to be kept.

³⁵And the children of Israel did eat manna forty years, until they came to a land inhabited; they did eat manna, until they came unto the borders of the land of Canaan.

³⁶Now an omer is the tenth part of an ephah.

CHAPTER 17

¹And all the congregation of the children of Israel journeyed from the wilderness of Sin, after their journeys, according to the commandment of the LORD, and pitched in Rephidim: and there was no water for the people to drink.

²Wherefore the people did chide with Moses, and said, Give us water that we may drink. And Moses said unto them, Why chide ye with me? wherefore do ye tempt the LORD?

³And the people thirsted there for water; and the people murmured against Moses, and said, Wherefore is this that thou hast brought us up out of Egypt, to kill us and our children and our cattle with thirst?

⁴And Moses cried unto the LORD, saying, What shall I do unto this people? they be almost ready to stone me.

⁵And the LORD said unto Moses, Go on before the people, and take with thee of the elders of Israel; and thy rod, wherewith thou smotest the river, take in thine hand, and go.

⁶Behold, I will stand before thee there upon the rock in Horeb; and thou shalt smite the rock, and there shall come water out of it, that the people may drink. And Moses did so in the sight of the elders of Israel.

⁷And he called the name of the place Massah, and Meribah, because of the chiding of the children of Israel, and because they tempted the LORD, saying, Is the LORD among us, or not?

⁸Then came Amalek, and fought with Israel in Rephidim.

⁹And Moses said unto Joshua, Choose us out men, and go out, fight with Amalek: to morrow I will stand on the top of the hill with the rod of God in mine hand.

¹⁰So Joshua did as Moses had said to him, and fought with Amalek: and Moses, Aaron, and Hur went up to the top of the hill.

[11]And it came to pass, when Moses held up his hand, that Israel prevailed: and when he let down his hand, Amalek prevailed.

[12]But Moses hands were heavy; and they took a stone, and put it under him, and he sat thereon; and Aaron and Hur stayed up his hands, the one on the one side, and the other on the other side; and his hands were steady until the going down of the sun.

[13]And Joshua discomfited Amalek and his people with the edge of the sword.

[14]And the LORD said unto Moses, Write this for a memorial in a book, and rehearse it in the ears of Joshua: for I will utterly put out the remembrance of Amalek from under heaven.

[15]And Moses built an altar, and called the name of it Jehovah-nissi:

[16]For he said, Because the LORD hath sworn that the LORD will have war with Amalek from generation to generation.

CHAPTER 18

[1]When Jethro, the priest of Midian, Moses' father in law, heard of all that God had done for Moses, and for Israel his people, and that the LORD had brought Israel out of Egypt;

[2]Then Jethro, Moses' father in law, took Zipporah, Moses' wife, after he had sent her back,

[3]And her two sons; of which the name of the one was Gershom; for he said, I have been an alien in a strange land:

[4]And the name of the other was Eliezer; for the God of my father, said he, was mine help, and delivered me from the sword of Pharaoh:

[5]And Jethro, Moses' father in law, came with his sons and his wife unto Moses into the wilderness, where he encamped at the mount of God:

[6]And he said unto Moses I thy father in law Jethro am come unto thee, and thy wife, and her two sons with her.

[7]And Moses went out to meet his father in law, and did obeisance, and kissed him; and they asked each other of their welfare; and they came into the tent.

[8]And Moses told his father in law all that the LORD had done unto Pharaoh and to the Egyptians for Israel's sake, and all the travail that had come upon them by the way, and how the LORD delivered them.

[9]And Jethro rejoiced for all the goodness which the LORD had done to Israel, whom he had

delivered out of the hand of the Egyptians.

¹⁰And Jethro said, Blessed be the LORD, who hath delivered you out of the hand of the Egyptians, and out of the hand of Pharaoh, who hath delivered the people from under the hand of the Egyptians.

¹¹Now I know that the LORD is greater than all gods: for in the thing wherein they dealt proudly he was above them.

¹²And Jethro, Moses' father in law, took a burnt offering and sacrifices for God: and Aaron came, and all the elders of Israel, to eat bread with Moses' father in law before God.

¹³And it came to pass on the morrow, that Moses sat to judge the people: and the people stood by Moses from the morning unto the evening.

¹⁴And when Moses' father in law saw all that he did to the people, he said, What is this thing that thou doest to the people? why sittest thou thyself alone, and all the people stand by thee from morning unto even?

¹⁵And Moses said unto his father in law, Because the people come unto me to enquire of God:

¹⁶When they have a matter, they come unto me; and I judge between one and another, and I do make them know the statutes of God, and his laws.

¹⁷And Moses' father in law said unto him, The thing that thou doest is not good.

¹⁸Thou wilt surely wear away, both thou, and this people that is with thee: for this thing is too heavy for thee; thou art not able to perform it thyself alone.

¹⁹Hearken now unto my voice, I will give thee counsel, and God shall be with thee: Be thou for the people to God-ward, that thou mayest bring the causes unto God:

²⁰And thou shalt teach them ordinances and laws, and shalt shew them the way wherein they must walk, and the work that they must do.

²¹Moreover thou shalt provide out of all the people able men, such as fear God, men of truth, hating covetousness; and place such over them, to be rulers of thousands, and rulers of hundreds, rulers of fifties, and rulers of tens:

²²And let them judge the people at all seasons: and it shall be, that every great matter they shall bring unto thee, but every small matter they shall judge: so shall it be easier for thyself, and they shall bear the burden with thee.

²³If thou shalt do this thing, and God command thee so, then thou

shalt be able to endure, and all this people shall also go to their place in peace.

²⁴So Moses hearkened to the voice of his father in law, and did all that he had said.

²⁵And Moses chose able men out of all Israel, and made them heads over the people, rulers of thousands, rulers of hundreds, rulers of fifties, and rulers of tens.

²⁶And they judged the people at all seasons: the hard causes they brought unto Moses, but every small matter they judged themselves.

²⁷And Moses let his father in law depart; and he went his way into his own land.

CHAPTER 19

¹In the third month, when the children of Israel were gone forth out of the land of Egypt, the same day came they into the wilderness of Sinai.

²For they were departed from Rephidim, and were come to the desert of Sinai, and had pitched in the wilderness; and there Israel camped before the mount.

³And Moses went up unto God, and the LORD called unto him out of the mountain, saying, Thus shalt thou say to the house of Jacob, and tell the children of Israel;

⁴Ye have seen what I did unto the Egyptians, and how I bare you on eagles' wings, and brought you unto myself.

⁵Now therefore, if ye will obey my voice indeed, and keep my covenant, then ye shall be a peculiar treasure unto me above all people: for all the earth is mine:

⁶And ye shall be unto me a kingdom of priests, and an holy nation. These are the words which thou shalt speak unto the children of Israel.

⁷And Moses came and called for the elders of the people, and laid before their faces all these words which the LORD commanded him.

⁸And all the people answered together, and said, All that the LORD hath spoken we will do. And Moses returned the words of the people unto the LORD.

⁹And the LORD said unto Moses, Lo, I come unto thee in a thick cloud, that the people may hear when I speak with thee, and believe thee for ever. And Moses told the words of the people unto the LORD.

¹⁰And the LORD said unto Moses, Go unto the people, and sanctify them to day and to morrow, and let them wash their clothes,

[11]And be ready against the third day: for the third day the LORD will come down in the sight of all the people upon mount Sinai.

[12]And thou shalt set bounds unto the people round about, saying, Take heed to yourselves, that ye go not up into the mount, or touch the border of it: whosoever toucheth the mount shall be surely put to death:

[13]There shall not an hand touch it, but he shall surely be stoned, or shot through; whether it be beast or man, it shall not live: when the trumpet soundeth long, they shall come up to the mount.

[14]And Moses went down from the mount unto the people, and sanctified the people; and they washed their clothes.

[15]And he said unto the people, Be ready against the third day: come not at your wives.

[16]And it came to pass on the third day in the morning, that there were thunders and lightnings, and a thick cloud upon the mount, and the voice of the trumpet exceeding loud; so that all the people that was in the camp trembled.

[17]And Moses brought forth the people out of the camp to meet with God; and they stood at the nether part of the mount.

[18]And mount Sinai was altogether on a smoke, because the LORD descended upon it in fire: and the smoke thereof ascended as the smoke of a furnace, and the whole mount quaked greatly.

[19]And when the voice of the trumpet sounded long, and waxed louder and louder, Moses spake, and God answered him by a voice.

[20]And the LORD came down upon mount Sinai, on the top of the mount: and the LORD called Moses up to the top of the mount; and Moses went up.

[21]And the LORD said unto Moses, Go down, charge the people, lest they break through unto the LORD to gaze, and many of them perish.

[22]And let the priests also, which come near to the LORD, sanctify themselves, lest the LORD break forth upon them.

[23]And Moses said unto the LORD, The people cannot come up to mount Sinai: for thou chargedst us, saying, Set bounds about the mount, and sanctify it.

[24]And the LORD said unto him, Away, get thee down, and thou shalt come up, thou, and Aaron with thee: but let not the priests and the people break through to come up unto the LORD, lest he break forth upon them.

[25]So Moses went down unto the people, and spake unto them.

CHAPTER 20

¹And God spake all these words, saying,

²I am the LORD thy God, which have brought thee out of the land of Egypt, out of the house of bondage.

³Thou shalt have no other gods before me.

⁴Thou shalt not make unto thee any graven image, or any likeness of any thing that is in heaven above, or that is in the earth beneath, or that is in the water under the earth.

⁵Thou shalt not bow down thyself to them, nor serve them: for I the LORD thy God am a jealous God, visiting the iniquity of the fathers upon the children unto the third and fourth generation of them that hate me;

⁶And shewing mercy unto thousands of them that love me, and keep my commandments.

⁷Thou shalt not take the name of the LORD thy God in vain; for the LORD will not hold him guiltless that taketh his name in vain.

⁸Remember the sabbath day, to keep it holy.

⁹Six days shalt thou labour, and do all thy work:

¹⁰But the seventh day is the sabbath of the LORD thy God: in it thou shalt not do any work, thou, nor thy son, nor thy daughter, thy manservant, nor thy maidservant, nor thy cattle, nor thy stranger that is within thy gates:

¹¹For in six days the LORD made heaven and earth, the sea, and all that in them is, and rested the seventh day: wherefore the LORD blessed the sabbath day, and hallowed it.

¹²Honour thy father and thy mother: that thy days may be long upon the land which the LORD thy God giveth thee.

¹³Thou shalt not kill.

¹⁴Thou shalt not commit adultery.

¹⁵Thou shalt not steal.

¹⁶Thou shalt not bear false witness against thy neighbour.

¹⁷Thou shalt not covet thy neighbour's house, thou shalt not covet thy neighbour's wife, nor his manservant, nor his maidservant, nor his ox, nor his ass, nor any thing that is thy neighbour's.

¹⁸And all the people saw the thunderings, and the lightnings, and the noise of the trumpet, and the mountain smoking: and when the people saw it, they removed, and stood afar off.

¹⁹And they said unto Moses, Speak thou with us, and we will hear: but let not God speak with us, lest we die.

²⁰And Moses said unto the people, Fear not: for God is come to prove you, and that his fear may be before your faces, that ye sin not.

²¹And the people stood afar off, and Moses drew near unto the thick darkness where God was.

²²And the LORD said unto Moses, Thus thou shalt say unto the children of Israel, Ye have seen that I have talked with you from heaven.

²³Ye shall not make with me gods of silver, neither shall ye make unto you gods of gold.

²⁴An altar of earth thou shalt make unto me, and shalt sacrifice thereon thy burnt offerings, and thy peace offerings, thy sheep, and thine oxen: in all places where I record my name I will come unto thee, and I will bless thee.

²⁵And if thou wilt make me an altar of stone, thou shalt not build it of hewn stone: for if thou lift up thy tool upon it, thou hast polluted it.

²⁶Neither shalt thou go up by steps unto mine altar, that thy nakedness be not discovered thereon.

CHAPTER 21

¹Now these are the judgments which thou shalt set before them.

²If thou buy an Hebrew servant, six years he shall serve: and in the seventh he shall go out free for nothing.

³If he came in by himself, he shall go out by himself: if he were married, then his wife shall go out with him.

⁴If his master have given him a wife, and she have born him sons or daughters; the wife and her children shall be her master's, and he shall go out by himself.

⁵And if the servant shall plainly say, I love my master, my wife, and my children; I will not go out free:

⁶Then his master shall bring him unto the judges; he shall also bring him to the door, or unto the door post; and his master shall bore his ear through with an aul; and he shall serve him for ever.

⁷And if a man sell his daughter to be a maidservant, she shall not go out as the menservants do.

⁸If she please not her master, who hath betrothed her to himself, then shall he let her be redeemed: to sell her unto a strange nation he shall have no power, seeing he hath dealt deceitfully with her.

⁹And if he have betrothed her unto his son, he shall deal with her after the manner of daughters.

¹⁰If he take him another wife; her food, her raiment, and her duty of marriage, shall he not diminish.

¹¹And if he do not these three unto her, then shall she go out free without money.

¹²He that smiteth a man, so that he die, shall be surely put to death.

¹³And if a man lie not in wait, but God deliver him into his hand; then I will appoint thee a place whither he shall flee.

¹⁴But if a man come presumptuously upon his neighbour, to slay him with guile; thou shalt take him from mine altar, that he may die.

¹⁵And he that smiteth his father, or his mother, shall be surely put to death.

¹⁶And he that stealeth a man, and selleth him, or if he be found in his hand, he shall surely be put to death.

¹⁷And he that curseth his father, or his mother, shall surely be put to death.

¹⁸And if men strive together, and one smite another with a stone, or with his fist, and he die not, but keepeth his bed:

¹⁹If he rise again, and walk abroad upon his staff, then shall he that smote him be quit: only he shall pay for the loss of his time, and shall cause him to be thoroughly healed.

²⁰And if a man smite his servant, or his maid, with a rod, and he die under his hand; he shall be surely punished.

²¹Notwithstanding, if he continue a day or two, he shall not be punished: for he is his money.

²²If men strive, and hurt a woman with child, so that her fruit depart from her, and yet no mischief follow: he shall be surely punished, according as the woman's husband will lay upon him; and he shall pay as the judges determine.

²³And if any mischief follow, then thou shalt give life for life,

²⁴Eye for eye, tooth for tooth, hand for hand, foot for foot,

²⁵Burning for burning, wound for wound, stripe for stripe.

²⁶And if a man smite the eye of his servant, or the eye of his maid, that it perish; he shall let him go free for his eye's sake.

²⁷And if he smite out his manservant's tooth, or his maidservant's tooth; he shall let him go free for his tooth's sake.

²⁸If an ox gore a man or a woman, that they die: then the ox shall be surely stoned, and his flesh shall not be eaten; but the owner of the ox shall be quit.

²⁹But if the ox were wont to push with his horn in time past, and it hath been testified to his owner, and he hath not kept him in, but that he hath killed a man or a woman; the ox shall be stoned, and his owner also shall be put to death.

³⁰If there be laid on him a sum of money, then he shall give for the ransom of his life whatsoever is laid upon him.

³¹Whether he have gored a son, or have gored a daughter, according to this judgment shall it be done unto him.

³²If the ox shall push a manservant or a maidservant; he shall give unto their master thirty shekels of silver, and the ox shall be stoned.

³³And if a man shall open a pit, or if a man shall dig a pit, and not cover it, and an ox or an ass fall therein;

³⁴The owner of the pit shall make it good, and give money unto the owner of them; and the dead beast shall be his.

³⁵And if one man's ox hurt another's, that he die; then they shall sell the live ox, and divide the money of it; and the dead ox also they shall divide.

³⁶Or if it be known that the ox hath used to push in time past, and his owner hath not kept him in; he shall surely pay ox for ox; and the dead shall be his own.

CHAPTER 22

¹If a man shall steal an ox, or a sheep, and kill it, or sell it; he shall restore five oxen for an ox, and four sheep for a sheep.

²If a thief be found breaking up, and be smitten that he die, there shall no blood be shed for him.

³If the sun be risen upon him, there shall be blood shed for him; for he should make full restitution; if he have nothing, then he shall be sold for his theft.

⁴If the theft be certainly found in his hand alive, whether it be ox, or ass, or sheep; he shall restore double.

⁵If a man shall cause a field or vineyard to be eaten, and shall put in his beast, and shall feed in another man's field; of the best of his own field, and of the best of his own vineyard, shall he make restitution.

⁶If fire break out, and catch in thorns, so that the stacks of corn, or the standing corn, or the field, be consumed therewith; he that kindled the fire shall surely make restitution.

⁷If a man shall deliver unto his neighbour money or stuff to keep, and it be stolen out of the man's house; if the thief be found, let him pay double.

⁸If the thief be not found, then the master of the house shall be brought unto the judges, to see whether he have put his hand unto his neighbour's goods.

⁹For all manner of trespass, whether it be for ox, for ass, for sheep, for raiment, or for any manner of lost thing which another challengeth to be his, the cause of both parties shall come before the judges; and whom the judges shall condemn, he shall pay double unto his neighbour.

¹⁰If a man deliver unto his neighbour an ass, or an ox, or a sheep, or any beast, to keep; and it die, or be hurt, or driven away, no man seeing it:

¹¹Then shall an oath of the LORD be between them both, that he hath not put his hand unto his neighbour's goods; and the owner of it shall accept thereof, and he shall not make it good.

¹²And if it be stolen from him, he shall make restitution unto the owner thereof.

¹³If it be torn in pieces, then let him bring it for witness, and he shall not make good that which was torn.

¹⁴And if a man borrow ought of his neighbour, and it be hurt, or die, the owner thereof being not with it, he shall surely make it good.

¹⁵But if the owner thereof be with it, he shall not make it good: if it be an hired thing, it came for his hire.

¹⁶And if a man entice a maid that is not betrothed, and lie with her, he shall surely endow her to be his wife.

¹⁷If her father utterly refuse to give her unto him, he shall pay money according to the dowry of virgins.

¹⁸Thou shalt not suffer a witch to live.

¹⁹Whosoever lieth with a beast shall surely be put to death.

²⁰He that sacrificeth unto any god, save unto the LORD only, he shall be utterly destroyed.

²¹Thou shalt neither vex a stranger, nor oppress him: for ye were strangers in the land of Egypt.

²²Ye shall not afflict any widow, or fatherless child.

²³If thou afflict them in any wise, and they cry at all unto me, I will surely hear their cry;

²⁴And my wrath shall wax hot, and I will kill you with the sword; and your wives shall be widows, and your children fatherless.

²⁵If thou lend money to any of my people that is poor by thee, thou shalt not be to him as an usurer, neither shalt thou lay upon him usury.

²⁶If thou at all take thy neighbour's raiment to pledge, thou shalt deliver it unto him by that the sun goeth down:

²⁷For that is his covering only, it is his raiment for his skin: wherein shall he sleep? and it shall come to pass, when he crieth unto me, that I will hear; for I am gracious.

²⁸Thou shalt not revile the gods, nor curse the ruler of thy people.

²⁹Thou shalt not delay to offer the first of thy ripe fruits, and of thy liquors: the firstborn of thy sons shalt thou give unto me.

³⁰Likewise shalt thou do with thine oxen, and with thy sheep: seven days it shall be with his dam; on the eighth day thou shalt give it me.

³¹And ye shall be holy men unto me: neither shall ye eat any flesh that is torn of beasts in the field; ye shall cast it to the dogs.

CHAPTER 23

¹Thou shalt not raise a false report: put not thine hand with the wicked to be an unrighteous witness.

²Thou shalt not follow a multitude to do evil; neither shalt thou speak in a cause to decline after many to wrest judgment:

³Neither shalt thou countenance a poor man in his cause.

⁴If thou meet thine enemy's ox or his ass going astray, thou shalt surely bring it back to him again.

⁵If thou see the ass of him that hateth thee lying under his burden, and wouldest forbear to help him, thou shalt surely help with him.

⁶Thou shalt not wrest the judgment of thy poor in his cause.

⁷Keep thee far from a false matter; and the innocent and righteous slay thou not: for I will not justify the wicked.

⁸And thou shalt take no gift: for the gift blindeth the wise, and perverteth the words of the righteous.

⁹Also thou shalt not oppress a stranger: for ye know the heart of a stranger, seeing ye were strangers in the land of Egypt.

¹⁰And six years thou shalt sow thy land, and shalt gather in the fruits thereof: ¹¹But the seventh year thou shalt let it rest and lie still; that the poor of thy people may eat: and what they leave the beasts of the field shall eat. In like manner thou shalt deal with thy vineyard, and with thy oliveyard.

¹²Six days thou shalt do thy work, and on the seventh day thou shalt rest: that thine ox and thine ass may rest, and the son of thy

handmaid, and the stranger, may be refreshed.

¹³And in all things that I have said unto you be circumspect: and make no mention of the name of other gods, neither let it be heard out of thy mouth.

¹⁴Three times thou shalt keep a feast unto me in the year.

¹⁵Thou shalt keep the feast of unleavened bread: (thou shalt eat unleavened bread seven days, as I commanded thee, in the time appointed of the month Abib; for in it thou camest out from Egypt: and none shall appear before me empty:)

¹⁶And the feast of harvest, the firstfruits of thy labours, which thou hast sown in the field: and the feast of ingathering, which is in the end of the year, when thou hast gathered in thy labours out of the field.

¹⁷Three items in the year all thy males shall appear before the LORD God.

¹⁸Thou shalt not offer the blood of my sacrifice with leavened bread; neither shall the fat of my sacrifice remain until the morning.

¹⁹The first of the firstfruits of thy land thou shalt bring into the house of the LORD thy God. Thou shalt not seethe a kid in his mother's milk.

²⁰Behold, I send an Angel before thee, to keep thee in the way, and to bring thee into the place which I have prepared.

²¹Beware of him, and obey his voice, provoke him not; for he will not pardon your transgressions: for my name is in him.

²²But if thou shalt indeed obey his voice, and do all that I speak; then I will be an enemy unto thine enemies, and an adversary unto thine adversaries.

²³For mine Angel shall go before thee, and bring thee in unto the Amorites, and the Hittites, and the Perizzites, and the Canaanites, the Hivites, and the Jebusites: and I will cut them off.

²⁴Thou shalt not bow down to their gods, nor serve them, nor do after their works: but thou shalt utterly overthrow them, and quite break down their images.

²⁵And ye shall serve the LORD your God, and he shall bless thy bread, and thy water; and I will take sickness away from the midst of thee.

²⁶There shall nothing cast their young, nor be barren, in thy land: the number of thy days I will fulfil.

²⁷I will send my fear before thee, and will destroy all the people to whom thou shalt come, and I will make all thine enemies turn their backs unto thee.

²⁸And I will send hornets before thee, which shall drive out the Hivite,

the Canaanite, and the Hittite, from before thee.

²⁹I will not drive them out from before thee in one year; lest the land become desolate, and the beast of the field multiply against thee.

³⁰By little and little I will drive them out from before thee, until thou be increased, and inherit the land.

³¹And I will set thy bounds from the Red sea even unto the sea of the Philistines, and from the desert unto the river: for I will deliver the inhabitants of the land into your hand; and thou shalt drive them out before thee.

³²Thou shalt make no covenant with them, nor with their gods.

³³They shall not dwell in thy land, lest they make thee sin against me: for if thou serve their gods, it will surely be a snare unto thee.

CHAPTER 24

¹And he said unto Moses, Come up unto the LORD, thou, and Aaron, Nadab, and Abihu, and seventy of the elders of Israel; and worship ye afar off.

²And Moses alone shall come near the LORD: but they shall not come nigh; neither shall the people go up with him.

³And Moses came and told the people all the words of the LORD, and all the judgments: and all the people answered with one voice, and said, All the words which the LORD hath said will we do.

⁴And Moses wrote all the words of the LORD, and rose up early in the morning, and builded an altar under the hill, and twelve pillars, according to the twelve tribes of Israel.

⁵And he sent young men of the children of Israel, which offered burnt offerings, and sacrificed peace offerings of oxen unto the LORD.

⁶And Moses took half of the blood, and put it in basons; and half of the blood he sprinkled on the altar.

⁷And he took the book of the covenant, and read in the audience of the people: and they said, All that the LORD hath said will we do, and be obedient.

⁸And Moses took the blood, and sprinkled it on the people, and said, Behold the blood of the covenant, which the LORD hath made with you concerning all these words.

⁹Then went up Moses, and Aaron, Nadab, and Abihu, and seventy of the elders of Israel:

¹⁰And they saw the God of Israel: and there was under his feet as it were a paved work of a sapphire

stone, and as it were the body of heaven in his clearness.

¹¹And upon the nobles of the children of Israel he laid not his hand: also they saw God, and did eat and drink.

¹²And the LORD said unto Moses, Come up to me into the mount, and be there: and I will give thee tables of stone, and a law, and commandments which I have written; that thou mayest teach them.

¹³And Moses rose up, and his minister Joshua: and Moses went up into the mount of God.

¹⁴And he said unto the elders, Tarry ye here for us, until we come again unto you: and, behold, Aaron and Hur are with you: if any man have any matters to do, let him come unto them.

¹⁵And Moses went up into the mount, and a cloud covered the mount.

¹⁶And the glory of the LORD abode upon mount Sinai, and the cloud covered it six days: and the seventh day he called unto Moses out of the midst of the cloud.

¹⁷And the sight of the glory of the LORD was like devouring fire on the top of the mount in the eyes of the children of Israel.

¹⁸And Moses went into the midst of the cloud, and gat him up into the mount: and Moses was in the mount forty days and forty nights.

CHAPTER 25

¹And the LORD spake unto Moses, saying,

²Speak unto the children of Israel, that they bring me an offering: of every man that giveth it willingly with his heart ye shall take my offering.

³And this is the offering which ye shall take of them; gold, and silver, and brass,

⁴And blue, and purple, and scarlet, and fine linen, and goats' hair,

⁵And rams' skins dyed red, and badgers' skins, and shittim wood,

⁶Oil for the light, spices for anointing oil, and for sweet incense,

⁷Onyx stones, and stones to be set in the ephod, and in the breastplate.

⁸And let them make me a sanctuary; that I may dwell among them.

⁹According to all that I shew thee, after the pattern of the tabernacle, and the pattern of all the instruments thereof, even so shall ye make it.

¹⁰And they shall make an ark of shittim wood: two cubits and a half shall be the length thereof, and a

cubit and a half the breadth thereof, and a cubit and a half the height thereof.

¹¹And thou shalt overlay it with pure gold, within and without shalt thou overlay it, and shalt make upon it a crown of gold round about.

¹²And thou shalt cast four rings of gold for it, and put them in the four corners thereof; and two rings shall be in the one side of it, and two rings in the other side of it.

¹³And thou shalt make staves of shittim wood, and overlay them with gold.

¹⁴And thou shalt put the staves into the rings by the sides of the ark, that the ark may be borne with them.

¹⁵The staves shall be in the rings of the ark: they shall not be taken from it.

¹⁶And thou shalt put into the ark the testimony which I shall give thee.

¹⁷And thou shalt make a mercy seat of pure gold: two cubits and a half shall be the length thereof, and a cubit and a half the breadth thereof.

¹⁸And thou shalt make two cherubims of gold, of beaten work shalt thou make them, in the two ends of the mercy seat.

¹⁹And make one cherub on the one end, and the other cherub on the other end: even of the mercy seat shall ye make the cherubims on the two ends thereof.

²⁰And the cherubims shall stretch forth their wings on high, covering the mercy seat with their wings, and their faces shall look one to another; toward the mercy seat shall the faces of the cherubims be.

²¹And thou shalt put the mercy seat above upon the ark; and in the ark thou shalt put the testimony that I shall give thee.

²²And there I will meet with thee, and I will commune with thee from above the mercy seat, from between the two cherubims which are upon the ark of the testimony, of all things which I will give thee in commandment unto the children of Israel.

²³Thou shalt also make a table of shittim wood: two cubits shall be the length thereof, and a cubit the breadth thereof, and a cubit and a half the height thereof.

²⁴And thou shalt overlay it with pure gold, and make thereto a crown of gold round about.

²⁵And thou shalt make unto it a border of an hand breadth round about, and thou shalt make a golden crown to the border thereof round about.

²⁶And thou shalt make for it four rings of gold, and put the rings in

the four corners that are on the four feet thereof.

²⁷Over against the border shall the rings be for places of the staves to bear the table.

²⁸And thou shalt make the staves of shittim wood, and overlay them with gold, that the table may be borne with them.

²⁹And thou shalt make the dishes thereof, and spoons thereof, and covers thereof, and bowls thereof, to cover withal: of pure gold shalt thou make them.

³⁰And thou shalt set upon the table shewbread before me alway.

³¹And thou shalt make a candlestick of pure gold: of beaten work shall the candlestick be made: his shaft, and his branches, his bowls, his knops, and his flowers, shall be of the same.

³²And six branches shall come out of the sides of it; three branches of the candlestick out of the one side, and three branches of the candlestick out of the other side:

³³Three bowls made like unto almonds, with a knop and a flower in one branch; and three bowls made like almonds in the other branch, with a knop and a flower: so in the six branches that come out of the candlestick.

³⁴And in the candlesticks shall be four bowls made like unto almonds, with their knops and their flowers.

³⁵And there shall be a knop under two branches of the same, and a knop under two branches of the same, and a knop under two branches of the same, according to the six branches that proceed out of the candlestick.

³⁶Their knops and their branches shall be of the same: all it shall be one beaten work of pure gold.

³⁷And thou shalt make the seven lamps thereof: and they shall light the lamps thereof, that they may give light over against it.

³⁸And the tongs thereof, and the snuffdishes thereof, shall be of pure gold.

³⁹Of a talent of pure gold shall he make it, with all these vessels.

⁴⁰And look that thou make them after their pattern, which was shewed thee in the mount.

CHAPTER 26

¹Moreover thou shalt make the tabernacle with ten curtains of fine twined linen, and blue, and purple, and scarlet: with cherubims of cunning work shalt thou make them.

²The length of one curtain shall be eight and twenty cubits, and the

breadth of one curtain four cubits: and every one of the curtains shall have one measure.

³The five curtains shall be coupled together one to another; and other five curtains shall be coupled one to another.

⁴And thou shalt make loops of blue upon the edge of the one curtain from the selvedge in the coupling; and likewise shalt thou make in the uttermost edge of another curtain, in the coupling of the second.

⁵Fifty loops shalt thou make in the one curtain, and fifty loops shalt thou make in the edge of the curtain that is in the coupling of the second; that the loops may take hold one of another.

⁶And thou shalt make fifty taches of gold, and couple the curtains together with the taches: and it shall be one tabernacle.

⁷And thou shalt make curtains of goats' hair to be a covering upon the tabernacle: eleven curtains shalt thou make.

⁸The length of one curtain shall be thirty cubits, and the breadth of one curtain four cubits: and the eleven curtains shall be all of one measure.

⁹And thou shalt couple five curtains by themselves, and six curtains by themselves, and shalt double the sixth curtain in the forefront of the tabernacle.

¹⁰And thou shalt make fifty loops on the edge of the one curtain that is outmost in the coupling, and fifty loops in the edge of the curtain which coupleth the second.

¹¹And thou shalt make fifty taches of brass, and put the taches into the loops, and couple the tent together, that it may be one.

¹²And the remnant that remaineth of the curtains of the tent, the half curtain that remaineth, shall hang over the backside of the tabernacle.

¹³And a cubit on the one side, and a cubit on the other side of that which remaineth in the length of the curtains of the tent, it shall hang over the sides of the tabernacle on this side and on that side, to cover it.

¹⁴And thou shalt make a covering for the tent of rams' skins dyed red, and a covering above of badgers' skins.

¹⁵And thou shalt make boards for the tabernacle of shittim wood standing up.

¹⁶Ten cubits shall be the length of a board, and a cubit and a half shall be the breadth of one board.

¹⁷Two tenons shall there be in one board, set in order one against another: thus shalt thou make for all the boards of the tabernacle.

¹⁸And thou shalt make the boards for the tabernacle, twenty boards on the south side southward.

¹⁹And thou shalt make forty sockets of silver under the twenty boards; two sockets under one board for his two tenons, and two sockets under another board for his two tenons.

²⁰And for the second side of the tabernacle on the north side there shall be twenty boards:

²¹And their forty sockets of silver; two sockets under one board, and two sockets under another board.

²²And for the sides of the tabernacle westward thou shalt make six boards.

²³And two boards shalt thou make for the corners of the tabernacle in the two sides.

²⁴And they shall be coupled together beneath, and they shall be coupled together above the head of it unto one ring: thus shall it be for them both; they shall be for the two corners.

²⁵And they shall be eight boards, and their sockets of silver, sixteen sockets; two sockets under one board, and two sockets under another board.

²⁶And thou shalt make bars of shittim wood; five for the boards of the one side of the tabernacle,

²⁷And five bars for the boards of the other side of the tabernacle, and five bars for the boards of the side of the tabernacle, for the two sides westward.

²⁸And the middle bar in the midst of the boards shall reach from end to end.

²⁹And thou shalt overlay the boards with gold, and make their rings of gold for places for the bars: and thou shalt overlay the bars with gold.

³⁰And thou shalt rear up the tabernacle according to the fashion thereof which was shewed thee in the mount.

³¹And thou shalt make a vail of blue, and purple, and scarlet, and fine twined linen of cunning work: with cherubims shall it be made:

³²And thou shalt hang it upon four pillars of shittim wood overlaid with gold: their hooks shall be of gold, upon the four sockets of silver.

³³And thou shalt hang up the vail under the taches, that thou mayest bring in thither within the vail the ark of the testimony: and the vail shall divide unto you between the holy place and the most holy.

³⁴And thou shalt put the mercy seat upon the ark of the testimony in the most holy place.

³⁵And thou shalt set the table without the vail, and the candlestick over against the table on the side

of the tabernacle toward the south: and thou shalt put the table on the north side.

³⁶And thou shalt make an hanging for the door of the tent, of blue, and purple, and scarlet, and fine twined linen, wrought with needlework.

³⁷And thou shalt make for the hanging five pillars of shittim wood, and overlay them with gold, and their hooks shall be of gold: and thou shalt cast five sockets of brass for them.

CHAPTER 27

¹And thou shalt make an altar of shittim wood, five cubits long, and five cubits broad; the altar shall be foursquare: and the height thereof shall be three cubits.

²And thou shalt make the horns of it upon the four corners thereof: his horns shall be of the same: and thou shalt overlay it with brass.

³And thou shalt make his pans to receive his ashes, and his shovels, and his basons, and his fleshhooks, and his firepans: all the vessels thereof thou shalt make of brass.

⁴And thou shalt make for it a grate of network of brass; and upon the net shalt thou make four brasen rings in the four corners thereof.

⁵And thou shalt put it under the compass of the altar beneath, that the net may be even to the midst of the altar.

⁶And thou shalt make staves for the altar, staves of shittim wood, and overlay them with brass.

⁷And the staves shall be put into the rings, and the staves shall be upon the two sides of the altar, to bear it.

⁸Hollow with boards shalt thou make it: as it was shewed thee in the mount, so shall they make it.

⁹And thou shalt make the court of the tabernacle: for the south side southward there shall be hangings for the court of fine twined linen of an hundred cubits long for one side:

¹⁰And the twenty pillars thereof and their twenty sockets shall be of brass; the hooks of the pillars and their fillets shall be of silver.

¹¹And likewise for the north side in length there shall be hangings of an hundred cubits long, and his twenty pillars and their twenty sockets of brass; the hooks of the pillars and their fillets of silver.

¹²And for the breadth of the court on the west side shall be hangings of fifty cubits: their pillars ten, and their sockets ten.

¹³And the breadth of the court on the east side eastward shall be fifty cubits.

14The hangings of one side of the gate shall be fifteen cubits: their pillars three, and their sockets three.

15And on the other side shall be hangings fifteen cubits: their pillars three, and their sockets three.

16And for the gate of the court shall be an hanging of twenty cubits, of blue, and purple, and scarlet, and fine twined linen, wrought with needlework: and their pillars shall be four, and their sockets four.

17All the pillars round about the court shall be filleted with silver; their hooks shall be of silver, and their sockets of brass.

18The length of the court shall be an hundred cubits, and the breadth fifty every where, and the height five cubits of fine twined linen, and their sockets of brass.

19All the vessels of the tabernacle in all the service thereof, and all the pins thereof, and all the pins of the court, shall be of brass.

20And thou shalt command the children of Israel, that they bring thee pure oil olive beaten for the light, to cause the lamp to burn always.

21In the tabernacle of the congregation without the vail, which is before the testimony, Aaron and his sons shall order it from evening to morning before the LORD: it shall be a statute for ever unto their generations on the behalf of the children of Israel.

CHAPTER 28

1And take thou unto thee Aaron thy brother, and his sons with him, from among the children of Israel, that he may minister unto me in the priest's office, even Aaron, Nadab and Abihu, Eleazar and Ithamar, Aaron's sons.

2And thou shalt make holy garments for Aaron thy brother for glory and for beauty.

3And thou shalt speak unto all that are wise hearted, whom I have filled with the spirit of wisdom, that they may make Aaron's garments to consecrate him, that he may minister unto me in the priest's office.

4And these are the garments which they shall make; a breastplate, and an ephod, and a robe, and a broidered coat, a mitre, and a girdle: and they shall make holy garments for Aaron thy brother, and his sons, that he may minister unto me in the priest's office.

5And they shall take gold, and blue, and purple, and scarlet, and fine linen.

6And they shall make the ephod of gold, of blue, and of purple, of scarlet, and fine twined linen, with cunning work.

[7]It shall have the two shoulder-pieces thereof joined at the two edges thereof; and so it shall be joined together.

[8]And the curious girdle of the ephod, which is upon it, shall be of the same, according to the work thereof; even of gold, of blue, and purple, and scarlet, and fine twined linen.

[9]And thou shalt take two onyx stones, and grave on them the names of the children of Israel:

[10]Six of their names on one stone, and the other six names of the rest on the other stone, according to their birth.

[11]With the work of an engraver in stone, like the engravings of a signet, shalt thou engrave the two stones with the names of the children of Israel: thou shalt make them to be set in ouches of gold.

[12]And thou shalt put the two stones upon the shoulders of the ephod for stones of memorial unto the children of Israel: and Aaron shall bear their names before the LORD upon his two shoulders for a memorial.

[13]And thou shalt make ouches of gold;

[14]And two chains of pure gold at the ends; of wreathen work shalt thou make them, and fasten the wreathen chains to the ouches.

[15]And thou shalt make the breastplate of judgment with cunning work; after the work of the ephod thou shalt make it; of gold, of blue, and of purple, and of scarlet, and of fine twined linen, shalt thou make it.

[16]Foursquare it shall be being doubled; a span shall be the length thereof, and a span shall be the breadth thereof.

[17]And thou shalt set in it settings of stones, even four rows of stones: the first row shall be a sardius, a topaz, and a carbuncle: this shall be the first row.

[18]And the second row shall be an emerald, a sapphire, and a diamond.

[19]And the third row a ligure, an agate, and an amethyst.

[20]And the fourth row a beryl, and an onyx, and a jasper: they shall be set in gold in their inclosings.

[21]And the stones shall be with the names of the children of Israel, twelve, according to their names, like the engravings of a signet; every one with his name shall they be according to the twelve tribes.

[22]And thou shalt make upon the breastplate chains at the ends of wreathen work of pure gold.

[23]And thou shalt make upon the breastplate two rings of gold, and

shalt put the two rings on the two ends of the breastplate.

²⁴And thou shalt put the two wreathen chains of gold in the two rings which are on the ends of the breastplate.

²⁵And the other two ends of the two wreathen chains thou shalt fasten in the two ouches, and put them on the shoulder-pieces of the ephod before it.

²⁶And thou shalt make two rings of gold, and thou shalt put them upon the two ends of the breastplate in the border thereof, which is in the side of the ephod inward.

²⁷And two other rings of gold thou shalt make, and shalt put them on the two sides of the ephod underneath, toward the forepart thereof, over against the other coupling thereof, above the curious girdle of the ephod.

²⁸And they shall bind the breastplate by the rings thereof unto the rings of the ephod with a lace of blue, that it may be above the curious girdle of the ephod, and that the breastplate be not loosed from the ephod.

²⁹And Aaron shall bear the names of the children of Israel in the breastplate of judgment upon his heart, when he goeth in unto the holy place, for a memorial before the LORD continually.

³⁰And thou shalt put in the breastplate of judgment the Urim and the Thummim; and they shall be upon Aaron's heart, when he goeth in before the LORD: and Aaron shall bear the judgment of the children of Israel upon his heart before the LORD continually.

³¹And thou shalt make the robe of the ephod all of blue.

³²And there shall be an hole in the top of it, in the midst thereof: it shall have a binding of woven work round about the hole of it, as it were the hole of an habergeon, that it be not rent.

³³And beneath upon the hem of it thou shalt make pomegranates of blue, and of purple, and of scarlet, round about the hem thereof; and bells of gold between them round about:

³⁴A golden bell and a pomegranate, a golden bell and a pomegranate, upon the hem of the robe round about.

³⁵And it shall be upon Aaron to minister: and his sound shall be heard when he goeth in unto the holy place before the LORD, and when he cometh out, that he die not.

³⁶And thou shalt make a plate of pure gold, and grave upon it, like the engravings of a signet, HOLINESS TO THE LORD.

³⁷And thou shalt put it on a blue lace, that it may be upon the mitre; upon the forefront of the mitre it shall be.

³⁸And it shall be upon Aaron's forehead, that Aaron may bear the iniquity of the holy things, which the children of Israel shall hallow in all their holy gifts; and it shall be always upon his forehead, that they may be accepted before the LORD.

³⁹And thou shalt embroider the coat of fine linen, and thou shalt make the mitre of fine linen, and thou shalt make the girdle of needlework.

⁴⁰And for Aaron's sons thou shalt make coats, and thou shalt make for them girdles, and bonnets shalt thou make for them, for glory and for beauty.

⁴¹And thou shalt put them upon Aaron thy brother, and his sons with him; and shalt anoint them, and consecrate them, and sanctify them, that they may minister unto me in the priest's office.

⁴²And thou shalt make them linen breeches to cover their nakedness; from the loins even unto the thighs they shall reach:

⁴³And they shall be upon Aaron, and upon his sons, when they come in unto the tabernacle of the congregation, or when they come near unto the altar to minister in the holy place; that they bear not iniquity, and die: it shall be a statute for ever unto him and his seed after him.

CHAPTER 29

¹And this is the thing that thou shalt do unto them to hallow them, to minister unto me in the priest's office: Take one young bullock, and two rams without blemish,

²And unleavened bread, and cakes unleavened tempered with oil, and wafers unleavened anointed with oil: of wheaten flour shalt thou make them.

³And thou shalt put them into one basket, and bring them in the basket, with the bullock and the two rams.

⁴And Aaron and his sons thou shalt bring unto the door of the tabernacle of the congregation, and shalt wash them with water.

⁵And thou shalt take the garments, and put upon Aaron the coat, and the robe of the ephod, and the ephod, and the breastplate, and gird him with the curious girdle of the ephod:

⁶And thou shalt put the mitre upon his head, and put the holy crown upon the mitre.

⁷Then shalt thou take the anointing oil, and pour it upon his head, and anoint him.

⁸And thou shalt bring his sons, and put coats upon them.

⁹And thou shalt gird them with girdles, Aaron and his sons, and put the bonnets on them: and the priest's office shall be theirs for a perpetual statute: and thou shalt consecrate Aaron and his sons.

¹⁰And thou shalt cause a bullock to be brought before the tabernacle of the congregation: and Aaron and his sons shall put their hands upon the head of the bullock.

¹¹And thou shalt kill the bullock before the LORD, by the door of the tabernacle of the congregation.

¹²And thou shalt take of the blood of the bullock, and put it upon the horns of the altar with thy finger, and pour all the blood beside the bottom of the altar.

¹³And thou shalt take all the fat that covereth the inwards, and the caul that is above the liver, and the two kidneys, and the fat that is upon them, and burn them upon the altar.

¹⁴But the flesh of the bullock, and his skin, and his dung, shalt thou burn with fire without the camp: it is a sin offering.

¹⁵Thou shalt also take one ram; and Aaron and his sons shall put their hands upon the head of the ram.

¹⁶And thou shalt slay the ram, and thou shalt take his blood, and sprinkle it round about upon the altar.

¹⁷And thou shalt cut the ram in pieces, and wash the inwards of him, and his legs, and put them unto his pieces, and unto his head.

¹⁸And thou shalt burn the whole ram upon the altar: it is a burnt offering unto the LORD: it is a sweet savour, an offering made by fire unto the LORD.

¹⁹And thou shalt take the other ram; and Aaron and his sons shall put their hands upon the head of the ram.

²⁰Then shalt thou kill the ram, and take of his blood, and put it upon the tip of the right ear of Aaron, and upon the tip of the right ear of his sons, and upon the thumb of their right hand, and upon the great toe of their right foot, and sprinkle the blood upon the altar round about.

²¹And thou shalt take of the blood that is upon the altar, and of the anointing oil, and sprinkle it upon Aaron, and upon his garments, and upon his sons, and upon the garments of his sons with him: and he shall be hallowed, and his garments, and his sons, and his sons' garments with him.

²²Also thou shalt take of the ram the fat and the rump, and the fat that

covereth the inwards, and the caul above the liver, and the two kidneys, and the fat that is upon them, and the right shoulder; for it is a ram of consecration:

²³And one loaf of bread, and one cake of oiled bread, and one wafer out of the basket of the unleavened bread that is before the LORD:

²⁴And thou shalt put all in the hands of Aaron, and in the hands of his sons; and shalt wave them for a wave offering before the LORD.

²⁵And thou shalt receive them of their hands, and burn them upon the altar for a burnt offering, for a sweet savour before the LORD: it is an offering made by fire unto the LORD.

²⁶And thou shalt take the breast of the ram of Aaron's consecration, and wave it for a wave offering before the LORD: and it shall be thy part.

²⁷And thou shalt sanctify the breast of the wave offering, and the shoulder of the heave offering, which is waved, and which is heaved up, of the ram of the consecration, even of that which is for Aaron, and of that which is for his sons:

²⁸And it shall be Aaron's and his sons' by a statute for ever from the children of Israel: for it is an heave offering: and it shall be an heave offering from the children of Israel of the sacrifice of their peace offerings, even their heave offering unto the LORD.

²⁹And the holy garments of Aaron shall be his sons' after him, to be anointed therein, and to be consecrated in them.

³⁰And that son that is priest in his stead shall put them on seven days, when he cometh into the tabernacle of the congregation to minister in the holy place.

³¹And thou shalt take the ram of the consecration, and seethe his flesh in the holy place.

³²And Aaron and his sons shall eat the flesh of the ram, and the bread that is in the basket by the door of the tabernacle of the congregation.

³³And they shall eat those things wherewith the atonement was made, to consecrate and to sanctify them: but a stranger shall not eat thereof, because they are holy.

³⁴And if ought of the flesh of the consecrations, or of the bread, remain unto the morning, then thou shalt burn the remainder with fire: it shall not be eaten, because it is holy.

³⁵And thus shalt thou do unto Aaron, and to his sons, according to all things which I have commanded thee: seven days shalt thou consecrate them.

³⁶And thou shalt offer every day a bullock for a sin offering for

atonement: and thou shalt cleanse the altar, when thou hast made an atonement for it, and thou shalt anoint it, to sanctify it.

37Seven days thou shalt make an atonement for the altar, and sanctify it; and it shall be an altar most holy: whatsoever toucheth the altar shall be holy.

38Now this is that which thou shalt offer upon the altar; two lambs of the first year day by day continually.

39The one lamb thou shalt offer in the morning; and the other lamb thou shalt offer at even:

40And with the one lamb a tenth deal of flour mingled with the fourth part of an hin of beaten oil; and the fourth part of an hin of wine for a drink offering.

41And the other lamb thou shalt offer at even, and shalt do thereto according to the meat offering of the morning, and according to the drink offering thereof, for a sweet savour, an offering made by fire unto the LORD.

42This shall be a continual burnt offering throughout your generations at the door of the tabernacle of the congregation before the LORD: where I will meet you, to speak there unto thee.

43And there I will meet with the children of Israel, and the tabernacle shall be sanctified by my glory.

44And I will sanctify the tabernacle of the congregation, and the altar: I will sanctify also both Aaron and his sons, to minister to me in the priest's office.

45And I will dwell among the children of Israel, and will be their God.

46And they shall know that I am the LORD their God, that brought them forth out of the land of Egypt, that I may dwell among them: I am the LORD their God.

CHAPTER 30

1And thou shalt make an altar to burn incense upon: of shittim wood shalt thou make it.

2A cubit shall be the length thereof, and a cubit the breadth thereof; foursquare shall it be: and two cubits shall be the height thereof: the horns thereof shall be of the same.

3And thou shalt overlay it with pure gold, the top thereof, and the sides thereof round about, and the horns thereof; and thou shalt make unto it a crown of gold round about.

4And two golden rings shalt thou make to it under the crown of it, by the two corners thereof, upon the two sides of it shalt thou make it;

and they shall be for places for the staves to bear it withal.

⁵And thou shalt make the staves of shittim wood, and overlay them with gold.

⁶And thou shalt put it before the vail that is by the ark of the testimony, before the mercy seat that is over the testimony, where I will meet with thee.

⁷And Aaron shall burn thereon sweet incense every morning: when he dresseth the lamps, he shall burn incense upon it.

⁸And when Aaron lighteth the lamps at even, he shall burn incense upon it, a perpetual incense before the LORD throughout your generations.

⁹Ye shall offer no strange incense thereon, nor burnt sacrifice, nor meat offering; neither shall ye pour drink offering thereon.

¹⁰And Aaron shall make an atonement upon the horns of it once in a year with the blood of the sin offering of atonements: once in the year shall he make atonement upon it throughout your generations: it is most holy unto the LORD.

¹¹And the LORD spake unto Moses, saying,

¹²When thou takest the sum of the children of Israel after their number, then shall they give every man a ransom for his soul unto the LORD, when thou numberest them; that there be no plague among them, when thou numberest them.

¹³This they shall give, every one that passeth among them that are numbered, half a shekel after the shekel of the sanctuary: (a shekel is twenty gerahs:) an half shekel shall be the offering of the LORD.

¹⁴Every one that passeth among them that are numbered, from twenty years old and above, shall give an offering unto the LORD.

¹⁵The rich shall not give more, and the poor shall not give less than half a shekel, when they give an offering unto the LORD, to make an atonement for your souls.

¹⁶And thou shalt take the atonement money of the children of Israel, and shalt appoint it for the service of the tabernacle of the congregation; that it may be a memorial unto the children of Israel before the LORD, to make an atonement for your souls.

¹⁷And the LORD spake unto Moses, saying,

¹⁸Thou shalt also make a laver of brass, and his foot also of brass, to wash withal: and thou shalt put it between the tabernacle of the congregation and the altar, and thou shalt put water therein.

¹⁹For Aaron and his sons shall wash their hands and their feet thereat:

²⁰When they go into the tabernacle of the congregation, they shall wash with water, that they die not; or when they come near to the altar to minister, to burn offering made by fire unto the LORD:

²¹So they shall wash their hands and their feet, that they die not: and it shall be a statute for ever to them, even to him and to his seed throughout their generations.

²²Moreover the LORD spake unto Moses, saying,

²³Take thou also unto thee principal spices, of pure myrrh five hundred shekels, and of sweet cinnamon half so much, even two hundred and fifty shekels, and of sweet calamus two hundred and fifty shekels,

²⁴And of cassia five hundred shekels, after the shekel of the sanctuary, and of oil olive an hin:

²⁵And thou shalt make it an oil of holy ointment, an ointment compound after the art of the apothecary: it shall be an holy anointing oil.

²⁶And thou shalt anoint the tabernacle of the congregation therewith, and the ark of the testimony,

²⁷And the table and all his vessels, and the candlestick and his vessels, and the altar of incense,

²⁸And the altar of burnt offering with all his vessels, and the laver and his foot.

²⁹And thou shalt sanctify them, that they may be most holy: whatsoever toucheth them shall be holy.

³⁰And thou shalt anoint Aaron and his sons, and consecrate them, that they may minister unto me in the priest's office.

³¹And thou shalt speak unto the children of Israel, saying, This shall be an holy anointing oil unto me throughout your generations.

³²Upon man's flesh shall it not be poured, neither shall ye make any other like it, after the composition of it: it is holy, and it shall be holy unto you.

³³Whosoever compoundeth any like it, or whosoever putteth any of it upon a stranger, shall even be cut off from his people.

³⁴And the LORD said unto Moses, Take unto thee sweet spices, stacte, and onycha, and galbanum; these sweet spices with pure frankincense: of each shall there be a like weight:

³⁵And thou shalt make it a perfume, a confection after the art of the apothecary, tempered together, pure and holy:

³⁶And thou shalt beat some of it very small, and put of it before the testimony in the tabernacle of the congregation, where I will meet with thee: it shall be unto you most holy.

³⁷And as for the perfume which thou shalt make, ye shall not make to yourselves according to the composition thereof: it shall be unto thee holy for the LORD.

³⁸Whosoever shall make like unto that, to smell thereto, shall even be cut off from his people.

CHAPTER 31

¹And the LORD spake unto Moses, saying,

²See, I have called by name Bezaleel the son of Uri, the son of Hur, of the tribe of Judah:

³And I have filled him with the spirit of God, in wisdom, and in understanding, and in knowledge, and in all manner of workmanship,

⁴To devise cunning works, to work in gold, and in silver, and in brass,

⁵And in cutting of stones, to set them, and in carving of timber, to work in all manner of workmanship.

⁶And I, behold, I have given with him Aholiab, the son of Ahisamach, of the tribe of Dan: and in the hearts of all that are wise hearted I have put wisdom, that they may make all that I have commanded thee;

⁷The tabernacle of the congregation, and the ark of the testimony, and the mercy seat that is thereupon, and all the furniture of the tabernacle,

⁸And the table and his furniture, and the pure candlestick with all his furniture, and the altar of incense,

⁹And the altar of burnt offering with all his furniture, and the laver and his foot,

¹⁰And the cloths of service, and the holy garments for Aaron the priest, and the garments of his sons, to minister in the priest's office,

¹¹And the anointing oil, and sweet incense for the holy place: according to all that I have commanded thee shall they do.

¹²And the LORD spake unto Moses, saying,

¹³Speak thou also unto the children of Israel, saying, Verily my sabbaths ye shall keep: for it is a sign between me and you throughout your generations; that ye may know that I am the LORD that doth sanctify you.

¹⁴Ye shall keep the sabbath therefore; for it is holy unto you: every one that defileth it shall surely

be put to death: for whosoever doeth any work therein, that soul shall be cut off from among his people.

¹⁵Six days may work be done; but in the seventh is the sabbath of rest, holy to the LORD: whosoever doeth any work in the sabbath day, he shall surely be put to death.

¹⁶Wherefore the children of Israel shall keep the sabbath, to observe the sabbath throughout their generations, for a perpetual covenant.

¹⁷It is a sign between me and the children of Israel for ever: for in six days the LORD made heaven and earth, and on the seventh day he rested, and was refreshed.

¹⁸And he gave unto Moses, when he had made an end of communing with him upon mount Sinai, two tables of testimony, tables of stone, written with the finger of God.

CHAPTER 32

¹And when the people saw that Moses delayed to come down out of the mount, the people gathered themselves together unto Aaron, and said unto him, Up, make us gods, which shall go before us; for as for this Moses, the man that brought us up out of the land of Egypt, we wot not what is become of him.

²And Aaron said unto them, Break off the golden earrings, which are in the ears of your wives, of your sons, and of your daughters, and bring them unto me.

³And all the people brake off the golden earrings which were in their ears, and brought them unto Aaron.

⁴And he received them at their hand, and fashioned it with a graving tool, after he had made it a molten calf: and they said, These be thy gods, O Israel, which brought thee up out of the land of Egypt.

⁵And when Aaron saw it, he built an altar before it; and Aaron made proclamation, and said, To morrow is a feast to the LORD.

⁶And they rose up early on the morrow, and offered burnt offerings, and brought peace offerings; and the people sat down to eat and to drink, and rose up to play.

⁷And the LORD said unto Moses, Go, get thee down; for thy people, which thou broughtest out of the land of Egypt, have corrupted themselves:

⁸They have turned aside quickly out of the way which I commanded them: they have made them a molten calf, and have worshipped it, and have sacrificed thereunto, and

said, These be thy gods, O Israel, which have brought thee up out of the land of Egypt.

⁹And the LORD said unto Moses, I have seen this people, and, behold, it is a stiffnecked people:

¹⁰Now therefore let me alone, that my wrath may wax hot against them, and that I may consume them: and I will make of thee a great nation.

¹¹And Moses besought the LORD his God, and said, LORD, why doth thy wrath wax hot against thy people, which thou hast brought forth out of the land of Egypt with great power, and with a mighty hand?

¹²Wherefore should the Egyptians speak, and say, For mischief did he bring them out, to slay them in the mountains, and to consume them from the face of the earth? Turn from thy fierce wrath, and repent of this evil against thy people.

¹³Remember Abraham, Isaac, and Israel, thy servants, to whom thou swarest by thine own self, and saidst unto them, I will multiply your seed as the stars of heaven, and all this land that I have spoken of will I give unto your seed, and they shall inherit it for ever.

¹⁴And the LORD repented of the evil which he thought to do unto his people.

¹⁵And Moses turned, and went down from the mount, and the two tables of the testimony were in his hand: the tables were written on both their sides; on the one side and on the other were they written.

¹⁶And the tables were the work of God, and the writing was the writing of God, graven upon the tables.

¹⁷And when Joshua heard the noise of the people as they shouted, he said unto Moses, There is a noise of war in the camp.

¹⁸And he said, It is not the voice of them that shout for mastery, neither is it the voice of them that cry for being overcome: but the noise of them that sing do I hear.

¹⁹And it came to pass, as soon as he came nigh unto the camp, that he saw the calf, and the dancing: and Moses' anger waxed hot, and he cast the tables out of his hands, and brake them beneath the mount.

²⁰And he took the calf which they had made, and burnt it in the fire, and ground it to powder, and strawed it upon the water, and made the children of Israel drink of it.

²¹And Moses said unto Aaron, What did this people unto thee, that thou hast brought so great a sin upon them?

²²And Aaron said, Let not the anger of my lord wax hot: thou knowest the people, that they are set on mischief.

²³For they said unto me, Make us gods, which shall go before us: for as for this Moses, the man that brought us up out of the land of Egypt, we wot not what is become of him.

²⁴And I said unto them, Whosoever hath any gold, let them break it off. So they gave it me: then I cast it into the fire, and there came out this calf.

²⁵And when Moses saw that the people were naked; (for Aaron had made them naked unto their shame among their enemies:)

²⁶Then Moses stood in the gate of the camp, and said, Who is on the LORD's side? let him come unto me. And all the sons of Levi gathered themselves together unto him.

²⁷And he said unto them, Thus saith the LORD God of Israel, Put every man his sword by his side, and go in and out from gate to gate throughout the camp, and slay every man his brother, and every man his companion, and every man his neighbour.

²⁸And the children of Levi did according to the word of Moses: and there fell of the people that day about three thousand men.

²⁹For Moses had said, Consecrate yourselves today to the LORD, even every man upon his son, and upon his brother; that he may bestow upon you a blessing this day.

³⁰And it came to pass on the morrow, that Moses said unto the people, Ye have sinned a great sin: and now I will go up unto the LORD; peradventure I shall make an atonement for your sin.

³¹And Moses returned unto the LORD, and said, Oh, this people have sinned a great sin, and have made them gods of gold.

³²Yet now, if thou wilt forgive their sin—; and if not, blot me, I pray thee, out of thy book which thou hast written.

³³And the LORD said unto Moses, Whosoever hath sinned against me, him will I blot out of my book.

³⁴Therefore now go, lead the people unto the place of which I have spoken unto thee: behold, mine Angel shall go before thee: nevertheless in the day when I visit I will visit their sin upon them.

³⁵And the LORD plagued the people, because they made the calf, which Aaron made.

CHAPTER 33

¹And the LORD said unto Moses, Depart, and go up hence, thou and

the people which thou hast brought up out of the land of Egypt, unto the land which I sware unto Abraham, to Isaac, and to Jacob, saying, Unto thy seed will I give it:

²And I will send an angel before thee; and I will drive out the Canaanite, the Amorite, and the Hittite, and the Perizzite, the Hivite, and the Jebusite:

³Unto a land flowing with milk and honey: for I will not go up in the midst of thee; for thou art a stiffnecked people: lest I consume thee in the way.

⁴And when the people heard these evil tidings, they mourned: and no man did put on him his ornaments.

⁵For the LORD had said unto Moses, Say unto the children of Israel, Ye are a stiffnecked people: I will come up into the midst of thee in a moment, and consume thee: therefore now put off thy ornaments from thee, that I may know what to do unto thee.

⁶And the children of Israel stripped themselves of their ornaments by the mount Horeb.

⁷And Moses took the tabernacle, and pitched it without the camp, afar off from the camp, and called it the Tabernacle of the congregation. And it came to pass, that every one which sought the LORD went out unto the tabernacle of the congregation, which was without the camp.

⁸And it came to pass, when Moses went out unto the tabernacle, that all the people rose up, and stood every man at his tent door, and looked after Moses, until he was gone into the tabernacle.

⁹And it came to pass, as Moses entered into the tabernacle, the cloudy pillar descended, and stood at the door of the tabernacle, and the Lord talked with Moses.

¹⁰And all the people saw the cloudy pillar stand at the tabernacle door: and all the people rose up and worshipped, every man in his tent door.

¹¹And the LORD spake unto Moses face to face, as a man speaketh unto his friend. And he turned again into the camp: but his servant Joshua, the son of Nun, a young man, departed not out of the tabernacle.

¹²And Moses said unto the LORD, See, thou sayest unto me, Bring up this people: and thou hast not let me know whom thou wilt send with me. Yet thou hast said, I know thee by name, and thou hast also found grace in my sight.

¹³Now therefore, I pray thee, if I have found grace in thy sight, shew me now thy way, that I may know thee, that I may find grace in thy

sight: and consider that this nation is thy people.

¹⁴And he said, My presence shall go with thee, and I will give thee rest.

¹⁵And he said unto him, If thy presence go not with me, carry us not up hence.

¹⁶For wherein shall it be known here that I and thy people have found grace in thy sight? is it not in that thou goest with us? so shall we be separated, I and thy people, from all the people that are upon the face of the earth.

¹⁷And the LORD said unto Moses, I will do this thing also that thou hast spoken: for thou hast found grace in my sight, and I know thee by name.

¹⁸And he said, I beseech thee, shew me thy glory.

¹⁹And he said, I will make all my goodness pass before thee, and I will proclaim the name of the LORD before thee; and will be gracious to whom I will be gracious, and will shew mercy on whom I will shew mercy.

²⁰And he said, Thou canst not see my face: for there shall no man see me, and live.

²¹And the LORD said, Behold, there is a place by me, and thou shalt stand upon a rock:

²²And it shall come to pass, while my glory passeth by, that I will put thee in a clift of the rock, and will cover thee with my hand while I pass by:

²³And I will take away mine hand, and thou shalt see my back parts: but my face shall not be seen.

CHAPTER 34

¹And the LORD said unto Moses, Hew thee two tables of stone like unto the first: and I will write upon these tables the words that were in the first tables, which thou brakest.

²And be ready in the morning, and come up in the morning unto mount Sinai, and present thyself there to me in the top of the mount.

³And no man shall come up with thee, neither let any man be seen throughout all the mount; neither let the flocks nor herds feed before that mount.

⁴And he hewed two tables of stone like unto the first; and Moses rose up early in the morning, and went up unto mount Sinai, as the LORD had commanded him, and took in his hand the two tables of stone.

⁵And the LORD descended in the cloud, and stood with him there, and proclaimed the name of the LORD.

⁶And the LORD passed by before him, and proclaimed, The LORD, The LORD God, merciful and gracious, longsuffering, and abundant in goodness and truth,

⁷Keeping mercy for thousands, forgiving iniquity and transgression and sin, and that will by no means clear the guilty; visiting the iniquity of the fathers upon the children, and upon the children's children, unto the third and to the fourth generation.

⁸And Moses made haste, and bowed his head toward the earth, and worshipped.

⁹And he said, If now I have found grace in thy sight, O LORD, let my LORD, I pray thee, go among us; for it is a stiffnecked people; and pardon our iniquity and our sin, and take us for thine inheritance.

¹⁰And he said, Behold, I make a covenant: before all thy people I will do marvels, such as have not been done in all the earth, nor in any nation: and all the people among which thou art shall see the work of the LORD: for it is a terrible thing that I will do with thee.

¹¹Observe thou that which I command thee this day: behold, I drive out before thee the Amorite, and the Canaanite, and the Hittite, and the Perizzite, and the Hivite, and the Jebusite.

¹²Take heed to thyself, lest thou make a covenant with the inhabitants of the land whither thou goest, lest it be for a snare in the midst of thee:

¹³But ye shall destroy their altars, break their images, and cut down their groves:

¹⁴For thou shalt worship no other god: for the LORD, whose name is Jealous, is a jealous God:

¹⁵Lest thou make a covenant with the inhabitants of the land, and they go a whoring after their gods, and do sacrifice unto their gods, and one call thee, and thou eat of his sacrifice;

¹⁶And thou take of their daughters unto thy sons, and their daughters go a whoring after their gods, and make thy sons go a whoring after their gods.

¹⁷Thou shalt make thee no molten gods.

¹⁸The feast of unleavened bread shalt thou keep. Seven days thou shalt eat unleavened bread, as I commanded thee, in the time of the month Abib: for in the month Abib thou camest out from Egypt.

¹⁹All that openeth the matrix is mine; and every firstling among thy cattle, whether ox or sheep, that is male.

²⁰But the firstling of an ass thou shalt redeem with a lamb: and if thou redeem him not, then

shalt thou break his neck. All the firstborn of thy sons thou shalt redeem. And none shall appear before me empty.

²¹Six days thou shalt work, but on the seventh day thou shalt rest: in earing time and in harvest thou shalt rest.

²²And thou shalt observe the feast of weeks, of the firstfruits of wheat harvest, and the feast of ingathering at the year's end.

²³Thrice in the year shall all your menchildren appear before the LORD God, the God of Israel.

²⁴For I will cast out the nations before thee, and enlarge thy borders: neither shall any man desire thy land, when thou shalt go up to appear before the LORD thy God thrice in the year.

²⁵Thou shalt not offer the blood of my sacrifice with leaven; neither shall the sacrifice of the feast of the passover be left unto the morning.

²⁶The first of the firstfruits of thy land thou shalt bring unto the house of the LORD thy God. Thou shalt not seethe a kid in his mother's milk.

²⁷And the LORD said unto Moses, Write thou these words: for after the tenor of these words I have made a covenant with thee and with Israel.

²⁸And he was there with the LORD forty days and forty nights; he did neither eat bread, nor drink water. And he wrote upon the tables the words of the covenant, the ten commandments.

²⁹And it came to pass, when Moses came down from mount Sinai with the two tables of testimony in Moses' hand, when he came down from the mount, that Moses wist not that the skin of his face shone while he talked with him.

³⁰And when Aaron and all the children of Israel saw Moses, behold, the skin of his face shone; and they were afraid to come nigh him.

³¹And Moses called unto them; and Aaron and all the rulers of the congregation returned unto him: and Moses talked with them.

³²And afterward all the children of Israel came nigh: and he gave them in commandment all that the LORD had spoken with him in mount Sinai.

³³And till Moses had done speaking with them, he put a vail on his face.

³⁴But when Moses went in before the LORD to speak with him, he took the vail off, until he came out. And he came out, and spake unto the children of Israel that which he was commanded.

³⁵And the children of Israel saw the face of Moses, that the skin of

Moses' face shone: and Moses put the vail upon his face again, until he went in to speak with him.

CHAPTER 35

¹And Moses gathered all the congregation of the children of Israel together, and said unto them, These are the words which the LORD hath commanded, that ye should do them.

²Six days shall work be done, but on the seventh day there shall be to you an holy day, a sabbath of rest to the LORD: whosoever doeth work therein shall be put to death.

³Ye shall kindle no fire throughout your habitations upon the sabbath day.

⁴And Moses spake unto all the congregation of the children of Israel, saying, This is the thing which the LORD commanded, saying,

⁵Take ye from among you an offering unto the LORD: whosoever is of a willing heart, let him bring it, an offering of the LORD; gold, and silver, and brass,

⁶And blue, and purple, and scarlet, and fine linen, and goats' hair,

⁷And rams' skins dyed red, and badgers' skins, and shittim wood,

⁸And oil for the light, and spices for anointing oil, and for the sweet incense,

⁹And onyx stones, and stones to be set for the ephod, and for the breastplate.

¹⁰And every wise hearted among you shall come, and make all that the LORD hath commanded;

¹¹The tabernacle, his tent, and his covering, his taches, and his boards, his bars, his pillars, and his sockets,

¹²The ark, and the staves thereof, with the mercy seat, and the vail of the covering,

¹³The table, and his staves, and all his vessels, and the shewbread,

¹⁴The candlestick also for the light, and his furniture, and his lamps, with the oil for the light,

¹⁵And the incense altar, and his staves, and the anointing oil, and the sweet incense, and the hanging for the door at the entering in of the tabernacle,

¹⁶The altar of burnt offering, with his brasen grate, his staves, and all his vessels, the laver and his foot,

¹⁷The hangings of the court, his pillars, and their sockets, and the hanging for the door of the court,

¹⁸The pins of the tabernacle, and the pins of the court, and their cords,

¹⁹The cloths of service, to do service in the holy place, the holy garments for Aaron the priest, and

the garments of his sons, to minister in the priest's office.

20 And all the congregation of the children of Israel departed from the presence of Moses.

21 And they came, every one whose heart stirred him up, and every one whom his spirit made willing, and they brought the LORD's offering to the work of the tabernacle of the congregation, and for all his service, and for the holy garments.

22 And they came, both men and women, as many as were willing hearted, and brought bracelets, and earrings, and rings, and tablets, all jewels of gold: and every man that offered offered an offering of gold unto the LORD.

23 And every man, with whom was found blue, and purple, and scarlet, and fine linen, and goats' hair, and red skins of rams, and badgers' skins, brought them.

24 Every one that did offer an offering of silver and brass brought the LORD's offering: and every man, with whom was found shittim wood for any work of the service, brought it.

25 And all the women that were wise hearted did spin with their hands, and brought that which they had spun, both of blue, and of purple, and of scarlet, and of fine linen.

26 And all the women whose heart stirred them up in wisdom spun goats' hair.

27 And the rulers brought onyx stones, and stones to be set, for the ephod, and for the breastplate;

28 And spice, and oil for the light, and for the anointing oil, and for the sweet incense.

29 The children of Israel brought a willing offering unto the LORD, every man and woman, whose heart made them willing to bring for all manner of work, which the LORD had commanded to be made by the hand of Moses.

30 And Moses said unto the children of Israel, See, the LORD hath called by name Bezaleel the son of Uri, the son of Hur, of the tribe of Judah;

31 And he hath filled him with the spirit of God, in wisdom, in understanding, and in knowledge, and in all manner of workmanship;

32 And to devise curious works, to work in gold, and in silver, and in brass,

33 And in the cutting of stones, to set them, and in carving of wood, to make any manner of cunning work.

34 And he hath put in his heart that he may teach, both he, and Aholiab, the son of Ahisamach, of the tribe of Dan.

³⁵Them hath he filled with wisdom of heart, to work all manner of work, of the engraver, and of the cunning workman, and of the embroiderer, in blue, and in purple, in scarlet, and in fine linen, and of the weaver, even of them that do any work, and of those that devise cunning work.

CHAPTER 36

¹Then wrought Bezaleel and Aholiab, and every wise hearted man, in whom the LORD put wisdom and understanding to know how to work all manner of work for the service of the sanctuary, according to all that the LORD had commanded.

²And Moses called Bezaleel and Aholiab, and every wise hearted man, in whose heart the LORD had put wisdom, even every one whose heart stirred him up to come unto the work to do it:

³And they received of Moses all the offering, which the children of Israel had brought for the work of the service of the sanctuary, to make it withal. And they brought yet unto him free offerings every morning.

⁴And all the wise men, that wrought all the work of the sanctuary, came every man from his work which they made;

⁵And they spake unto Moses, saying, The people bring much more than enough for the service of the work, which the LORD commanded to make.

⁶And Moses gave commandment, and they caused it to be proclaimed throughout the camp, saying, Let neither man nor woman make any more work for the offering of the sanctuary. So the people were restrained from bringing.

⁷For the stuff they had was sufficient for all the work to make it, and too much.

⁸And every wise hearted man among them that wrought the work of the tabernacle made ten curtains of fine twined linen, and blue, and purple, and scarlet: with cherubims of cunning work made he them.

⁹The length of one curtain was twenty and eight cubits, and the breadth of one curtain four cubits: the curtains were all of one size.

¹⁰And he coupled the five curtains one unto another: and the other five curtains he coupled one unto another.

¹¹And he made loops of blue on the edge of one curtain from the selvedge in the coupling: likewise he made in the uttermost side of

another curtain, in the coupling of the second.

¹²Fifty loops made he in one curtain, and fifty loops made he in the edge of the curtain which was in the coupling of the second: the loops held one curtain to another.

¹³And he made fifty taches of gold, and coupled the curtains one unto another with the taches: so it became one tabernacle.

¹⁴And he made curtains of goats' hair for the tent over the tabernacle: eleven curtains he made them.

¹⁵The length of one curtain was thirty cubits, and four cubits was the breadth of one curtain: the eleven curtains were of one size.

¹⁶And he coupled five curtains by themselves, and six curtains by themselves.

¹⁷And he made fifty loops upon the uttermost edge of the curtain in the coupling, and fifty loops made he upon the edge of the curtain which coupleth the second.

¹⁸And he made fifty taches of brass to couple the tent together, that it might be one.

¹⁹And he made a covering for the tent of rams' skins dyed red, and a covering of badgers' skins above that.

²⁰And he made boards for the tabernacle of shittim wood, standing up.

²¹The length of a board was ten cubits, and the breadth of a board one cubit and a half.

²²One board had two tenons, equally distant one from another: thus did he make for all the boards of the tabernacle.

²³And he made boards for the tabernacle; twenty boards for the south side southward:

²⁴And forty sockets of silver he made under the twenty boards; two sockets under one board for his two tenons, and two sockets under another board for his two tenons.

²⁵And for the other side of the tabernacle, which is toward the north corner, he made twenty boards,

²⁶And their forty sockets of silver; two sockets under one board, and two sockets under another board.

²⁷And for the sides of the tabernacle westward he made six boards.

²⁸And two boards made he for the corners of the tabernacle in the two sides.

²⁹And they were coupled beneath, and coupled together at the head thereof, to one ring: thus he did to both of them in both the corners.

³⁰And there were eight boards; and their sockets were sixteen sockets of silver, under every board two sockets.

³¹And he made bars of shittim wood; five for the boards of the one side of the tabernacle,

³²And five bars for the boards of the other side of the tabernacle, and five bars for the boards of the tabernacle for the sides westward.

³³And he made the middle bar to shoot through the boards from the one end to the other.

³⁴And he overlaid the boards with gold, and made their rings of gold to be places for the bars, and overlaid the bars with gold.

³⁵And he made a vail of blue, and purple, and scarlet, and fine twined linen: with cherubims made he it of cunning work.

³⁶And he made thereunto four pillars of shittim wood, and overlaid them with gold: their hooks were of gold; and he cast for them four sockets of silver.

³⁷And he made an hanging for the tabernacle door of blue, and purple, and scarlet, and fine twined linen, of needlework;

³⁸And the five pillars of it with their hooks: and he overlaid their chapiters and their fillets with gold: but their five sockets were of brass.

CHAPTER 37

¹And Bezaleel made the ark of shittim wood: two cubits and a half was the length of it, and a cubit and a half the breadth of it, and a cubit and a half the height of it:

²And he overlaid it with pure gold within and without, and made a crown of gold to it round about.

³And he cast for it four rings of gold, to be set by the four corners of it; even two rings upon the one side of it, and two rings upon the other side of it.

⁴And he made staves of shittim wood, and overlaid them with gold.

⁵And he put the staves into the rings by the sides of the ark, to bear the ark.

⁶And he made the mercy seat of pure gold: two cubits and a half was the length thereof, and one cubit and a half the breadth thereof.

⁷And he made two cherubims of gold, beaten out of one piece made he them, on the two ends of the mercy seat;

⁸One cherub on the end on this side, and another cherub on the other end on that side: out of the mercy seat made he the cherubims on the two ends thereof.

⁹And the cherubims spread out their wings on high, and covered

with their wings over the mercy seat, with their faces one to another; even to the mercy seatward were the faces of the cherubims.

¹⁰And he made the table of shittim wood: two cubits was the length thereof, and a cubit the breadth thereof, and a cubit and a half the height thereof:

¹¹And he overlaid it with pure gold, and made thereunto a crown of gold round about.

¹²Also he made thereunto a border of an handbreadth round about; and made a crown of gold for the border thereof round about.

¹³And he cast for it four rings of gold, and put the rings upon the four corners that were in the four feet thereof.

¹⁴Over against the border were the rings, the places for the staves to bear the table.

¹⁵And he made the staves of shittim wood, and overlaid them with gold, to bear the table.

¹⁶And he made the vessels which were upon the table, his dishes, and his spoons, and his bowls, and his covers to cover withal, of pure gold.

¹⁷And he made the candlestick of pure gold: of beaten work made he the candlestick; his shaft, and his branch, his bowls, his knops, and his flowers, were of the same:

¹⁸And six branches going out of the sides thereof; three branches of the candlestick out of the one side thereof, and three branches of the candlestick out of the other side thereof:

¹⁹Three bowls made after the fashion of almonds in one branch, a knop and a flower; and three bowls made like almonds in another branch, a knop and a flower: so throughout the six branches going out of the candlestick.

²⁰And in the candlestick were four bowls made like almonds, his knops, and his flowers:

²¹And a knop under two branches of the same, and a knop under two branches of the same, and a knop under two branches of the same, according to the six branches going out of it.

²²Their knops and their branches were of the same: all of it was one beaten work of pure gold.

²³And he made his seven lamps, and his snuffers, and his snuffdishes, of pure gold.

²⁴Of a talent of pure gold made he it, and all the vessels thereof.

²⁵And he made the incense altar of shittim wood: the length of it was a cubit, and the breadth of it a cubit; it was foursquare; and two cubits was the height of it; the horns thereof were of the same.

²⁶And he overlaid it with pure gold, both the top of it, and the sides thereof round about, and the horns of it: also he made unto it a crown of gold round about.

²⁷And he made two rings of gold for it under the crown thereof, by the two corners of it, upon the two sides thereof, to be places for the staves to bear it withal.

²⁸And he made the staves of shittim wood, and overlaid them with gold.

²⁹And he made the holy anointing oil, and the pure incense of sweet spices, according to the work of the apothecary.

CHAPTER 38

¹And he made the altar of burnt offering of shittim wood: five cubits was the length thereof, and five cubits the breadth thereof; it was foursquare; and three cubits the height thereof.

²And he made the horns thereof on the four corners of it; the horns thereof were of the same: and he overlaid it with brass.

³And he made all the vessels of the altar, the pots, and the shovels, and the basons, and the fleshhooks, and the firepans: all the vessels thereof made he of brass.

⁴And he made for the altar a brasen grate of network under the compass thereof beneath unto the midst of it.

⁵And he cast four rings for the four ends of the grate of brass, to be places for the staves.

⁶And he made the staves of shittim wood, and overlaid them with brass.

⁷And he put the staves into the rings on the sides of the altar, to bear it withal; he made the altar hollow with boards.

⁸And he made the laver of brass, and the foot of it of brass, of the lookingglasses of the women assembling, which assembled at the door of the tabernacle of the congregation.

⁹And he made the court: on the south side southward the hangings of the court were of fine twined linen, an hundred cubits:

¹⁰Their pillars were twenty, and their brasen sockets twenty; the hooks of the pillars and their fillets were of silver.

¹¹And for the north side the hangings were an hundred cubits, their pillars were twenty, and their sockets of brass twenty; the hooks of the pillars and their fillets of silver.

¹²And for the west side were hangings of fifty cubits, their pillars ten, and their sockets ten; the hooks of the pillars and their fillets of silver.

¹³And for the east side eastward fifty cubits.

¹⁴The hangings of the one side of the gate were fifteen cubits; their pillars three, and their sockets three.

¹⁵And for the other side of the court gate, on this hand and that hand, were hangings of fifteen cubits; their pillars three, and their sockets three.

¹⁶All the hangings of the court round about were of fine twined linen.

¹⁷And the sockets for the pillars were of brass; the hooks of the pillars and their fillets of silver; and the overlaying of their chapiters of silver; and all the pillars of the court were filleted with silver.

¹⁸And the hanging for the gate of the court was needlework, of blue, and purple, and scarlet, and fine twined linen: and twenty cubits was the length, and the height in the breadth was five cubits, answerable to the hangings of the court.

¹⁹And their pillars were four, and their sockets of brass four; their hooks of silver, and the overlaying of their chapiters and their fillets of silver.

²⁰And all the pins of the tabernacle, and of the court round about, were of brass.

²¹This is the sum of the tabernacle, even of the tabernacle of testimony, as it was counted, according to the commandment of Moses, for the service of the Levites, by the hand of Ithamar, son to Aaron the priest.

²²And Bezaleel the son Uri, the son of Hur, of the tribe of Judah, made all that the LORD commanded Moses.

²³And with him was Aholiab, son of Ahisamach, of the tribe of Dan, an engraver, and a cunning workman, and an embroiderer in blue, and in purple, and in scarlet, and fine linen.

²⁴All the gold that was occupied for the work in all the work of the holy place, even the gold of the offering, was twenty and nine talents, and seven hundred and thirty shekels, after the shekel of the sanctuary.

²⁵And the silver of them that were numbered of the congregation was an hundred talents, and a thousand seven hundred and threescore and fifteen shekels, after the shekel of the sanctuary:

²⁶A bekah for every man, that is, half a shekel, after the shekel of the sanctuary, for every one that went

to be numbered, from twenty years old and upward, for six hundred thousand and three thousand and five hundred and fifty men.

²⁷And of the hundred talents of silver were cast the sockets of the sanctuary, and the sockets of the vail; an hundred sockets of the hundred talents, a talent for a socket.

²⁸And of the thousand seven hundred seventy and five shekels he made hooks for the pillars, and overlaid their chapiters, and filleted them.

²⁹And the brass of the offering was seventy talents, and two thousand and four hundred shekels.

³⁰And therewith he made the sockets to the door of the tabernacle of the congregation, and the brasen altar, and the brasen grate for it, and all the vessels of the altar,

³¹And the sockets of the court round about, and the sockets of the court gate, and all the pins of the tabernacle, and all the pins of the court round about.

CHAPTER 39

¹And of the blue, and purple, and scarlet, they made cloths of service, to do service in the holy place, and made the holy garments for Aaron; as the LORD commanded Moses.

²And he made the ephod of gold, blue, and purple, and scarlet, and fine twined linen.

³And they did beat the gold into thin plates, and cut it into wires, to work it in the blue, and in the purple, and in the scarlet, and in the fine linen, with cunning work.

⁴They made shoulder-pieces for it, to couple it together: by the two edges was it coupled together.

⁵And the curious girdle of his ephod, that was upon it, was of the same, according to the work thereof; of gold, blue, and purple, and scarlet, and fine twined linen; as the LORD commanded Moses.

⁶And they wrought onyx stones inclosed in ouches of gold, graven, as signets are graven, with the names of the children of Israel.

⁷And he put them on the shoulders of the ephod, that they should be stones for a memorial to the children of Israel; as the LORD commanded Moses.

⁸And he made the breastplate of cunning work, like the work of the ephod; of gold, blue, and purple, and scarlet, and fine twined linen.

⁹It was foursquare; they made the breastplate double: a span was the length thereof, and a span the breadth thereof, being doubled.

¹⁰And they set in it four rows of stones: the first row was a sardius, a topaz, and a carbuncle: this was the first row.

¹¹And the second row, an emerald, a sapphire, and a diamond.

¹²And the third row, a ligure, an agate, and an amethyst.

¹³And the fourth row, a beryl, an onyx, and a jasper: they were inclosed in ouches of gold in their inclosings.

¹⁴And the stones were according to the names of the children of Israel, twelve, according to their names, like the engravings of a signet, every one with his name, according to the twelve tribes.

¹⁵And they made upon the breastplate chains at the ends, of wreathen work of pure gold.

¹⁶And they made two ouches of gold, and two gold rings; and put the two rings in the two ends of the breastplate.

¹⁷And they put the two wreathen chains of gold in the two rings on the ends of the breastplate.

¹⁸And the two ends of the two wreathen chains they fastened in the two ouches, and put them on the shoulder-pieces of the ephod, before it.

¹⁹And they made two rings of gold, and put them on the two ends of the breastplate, upon the border of it, which was on the side of the ephod inward.

²⁰And they made two other golden rings, and put them on the two sides of the ephod underneath, toward the forepart of it, over against the other coupling thereof, above the curious girdle of the ephod.

²¹And they did bind the breastplate by his rings unto the rings of the ephod with a lace of blue, that it might be above the curious girdle of the ephod, and that the breastplate might not be loosed from the ephod; as the LORD commanded Moses.

²²And he made the robe of the ephod of woven work, all of blue.

²³And there was an hole in the midst of the robe, as the hole of an habergeon, with a band round about the hole, that it should not rend.

²⁴And they made upon the hems of the robe pomegranates of blue, and purple, and scarlet, and twined linen.

²⁵And they made bells of pure gold, and put the bells between the pomegranates upon the hem of the robe, round about between the pomegranates;

²⁶A bell and a pomegranate, a bell and a pomegranate, round about the hem of the robe to minister in; as the LORD commanded Moses.

²⁷And they made coats of fine linen of woven work for Aaron, and for his sons,

²⁸And a mitre of fine linen, and goodly bonnets of fine linen, and linen breeches of fine twined linen,

²⁹And a girdle of fine twined linen, and blue, and purple, and scarlet, of needlework; as the LORD commanded Moses.

³⁰And they made the plate of the holy crown of pure gold, and wrote upon it a writing, like to the engravings of a signet, HOLINESS TO THE LORD.

³¹And they tied unto it a lace of blue, to fasten it on high upon the mitre; as the LORD commanded Moses.

³²Thus was all the work of the tabernacle of the tent of the congregation finished: and the children of Israel did according to all that the LORD commanded Moses, so did they.

³³And they brought the tabernacle unto Moses, the tent, and all his furniture, his taches, his boards, his bars, and his pillars, and his sockets,

³⁴And the covering of rams' skins dyed red, and the covering of badgers' skins, and the vail of the covering,

³⁵The ark of the testimony, and the staves thereof, and the mercy seat,

³⁶The table, and all the vessels thereof, and the shewbread,

³⁷The pure candlestick, with the lamps thereof, even with the lamps to be set in order, and all the vessels thereof, and the oil for light,

³⁸And the golden altar, and the anointing oil, and the sweet incense, and the hanging for the tabernacle door,

³⁹The brasen altar, and his grate of brass, his staves, and all his vessels, the laver and his foot,

⁴⁰The hangings of the court, his pillars, and his sockets, and the hanging for the court gate, his cords, and his pins, and all the vessels of the service of the tabernacle, for the tent of the congregation,

⁴¹The cloths of service to do service in the holy place, and the holy garments for Aaron the priest, and his sons' garments, to minister in the priest's office.

⁴²According to all that the LORD commanded Moses, so the children of Israel made all the work.

⁴³And Moses did look upon all the work, and, behold, they had done it as the LORD had commanded, even so had they done it: and Moses blessed them.

CHAPTER 40

¹And the LORD spake unto Moses, saying,

²On the first day of the first month shalt thou set up the tabernacle of the tent of the congregation.

³And thou shalt put therein the ark of the testimony, and cover the ark with the vail.

⁴And thou shalt bring in the table, and set in order the things that are to be set in order upon it; and thou shalt bring in the candlestick, and light the lamps thereof.

⁵And thou shalt set the altar of gold for the incense before the ark of the testimony, and put the hanging of the door to the tabernacle.

⁶And thou shalt set the altar of the burnt offering before the door of the tabernacle of the tent of the congregation.

⁷And thou shalt set the laver between the tent of the congregation and the altar, and shalt put water therein.

⁸And thou shalt set up the court round about, and hang up the hanging at the court gate.

⁹And thou shalt take the anointing oil, and anoint the tabernacle, and all that is therein, and shalt hallow it, and all the vessels thereof: and it shall be holy.

¹⁰And thou shalt anoint the altar of the burnt offering, and all his vessels, and sanctify the altar: and it shall be an altar most holy.

¹¹And thou shalt anoint the laver and his foot, and sanctify it.

¹²And thou shalt bring Aaron and his sons unto the door of the tabernacle of the congregation, and wash them with water.

¹³And thou shalt put upon Aaron the holy garments, and anoint him, and sanctify him; that he may minister unto me in the priest's office.

¹⁴And thou shalt bring his sons, and clothe them with coats:

¹⁵And thou shalt anoint them, as thou didst anoint their father, that they may minister unto me in the priest's office: for their anointing shall surely be an everlasting priesthood throughout their generations.

¹⁶Thus did Moses: according to all that the LORD commanded him, so did he.

¹⁷And it came to pass in the first month in the second year, on the first day of the month, that the tabernacle was reared up.

¹⁸And Moses reared up the tabernacle, and fastened his sockets, and set up the boards thereof, and put in the bars thereof, and reared up his pillars.

¹⁹And he spread abroad the tent over the tabernacle, and put the covering of the tent above upon it; as the LORD commanded Moses.

²⁰And he took and put the testimony into the ark, and set the staves on the ark, and put the mercy seat above upon the ark:

²¹And he brought the ark into the tabernacle, and set up the vail of the covering, and covered the ark of the testimony; as the LORD commanded Moses.

²²And he put the table in the tent of the congregation, upon the side of the tabernacle northward, without the vail.

²³And he set the bread in order upon it before the LORD; as the LORD had commanded Moses.

²⁴And he put the candlestick in the tent of the congregation, over against the table, on the side of the tabernacle southward.

²⁵And he lighted the lamps before the LORD; as the LORD commanded Moses.

²⁶And he put the golden altar in the tent of the congregation before the vail:

²⁷And he burnt sweet incense thereon; as the LORD commanded Moses.

²⁸And he set up the hanging at the door of the tabernacle.

²⁹And he put the altar of burnt offering by the door of the tabernacle of the tent of the congregation, and offered upon it the burnt offering and the meat offering; as the LORD commanded Moses.

³⁰And he set the laver between the tent of the congregation and the altar, and put water there, to wash withal.

³¹And Moses and Aaron and his sons washed their hands and their feet thereat:

³²When they went into the tent of the congregation, and when they came near unto the altar, they washed; as the LORD commanded Moses.

³³And he reared up the court round about the tabernacle and the altar, and set up the hanging of the court gate. So Moses finished the work.

³⁴Then a cloud covered the tent of the congregation, and the glory of the LORD filled the tabernacle.

³⁵And Moses was not able to enter into the tent of the congregation, because the cloud abode thereon, and the glory of the LORD filled the tabernacle.

³⁶And when the cloud was taken up from over the tabernacle, the children of Israel went onward in all their journeys:

37But if the cloud were not taken up, then they journeyed not till the day that it was taken up.

38For the cloud of the LORD was upon the tabernacle by day, and fire was on it by night, in the sight of all the house of Israel, throughout all their journeys.

LEVITICUS

ויקרא

CHAPTER 1

¹And the LORD called unto Moses, and spake unto him out of the tabernacle of the congregation, saying,

²Speak unto the children of Israel, and say unto them, If any man of you bring an offering unto the LORD, ye shall bring your offering of the cattle, even of the herd, and of the flock.

³If his offering be a burnt sacrifice of the herd, let him offer a male without blemish: he shall offer it of his own voluntary will at the door of the tabernacle of the congregation before the LORD.

⁴And he shall put his hand upon the head of the burnt offering; and it shall be accepted for him to make atonement for him.

⁵And he shall kill the bullock before the LORD: and the priests, Aaron's sons, shall bring the blood, and sprinkle the blood round about upon the altar that is by the door of the tabernacle of the congregation.

⁶And he shall flay the burnt offering, and cut it into his pieces.

⁷And the sons of Aaron the priest shall put fire upon the altar, and lay the wood in order upon the fire:

⁸And the priests, Aaron's sons, shall lay the parts, the head, and the fat, in order upon the wood that is on the fire which is upon the altar:

⁹But his inwards and his legs shall he wash in water: and the priest shall burn all on the altar, to be a burnt sacrifice, an offering made by fire, of a sweet savour unto the LORD.

¹⁰And if his offering be of the flocks, namely, of the sheep, or of the goats, for a burnt sacrifice; he shall bring it a male without blemish.

¹¹And he shall kill it on the side of the altar northward before the LORD: and the priests, Aaron's sons, shall sprinkle his blood round about upon the altar.

¹²And he shall cut it into his pieces, with his head and his fat: and the priest shall lay them in order on the wood that is on the fire which is upon the altar:

¹³But he shall wash the inwards and the legs with water: and the priest shall bring it all, and burn it upon the altar: it is a burnt sacrifice,

an offering made by fire, of a sweet savour unto the LORD.

¹⁴And if the burnt sacrifice for his offering to the LORD be of fowls, then he shall bring his offering of turtledoves, or of young pigeons.

¹⁵And the priest shall bring it unto the altar, and wring off his head, and burn it on the altar; and the blood thereof shall be wrung out at the side of the altar:

¹⁶And he shall pluck away his crop with his feathers, and cast it beside the altar on the east part, by the place of the ashes:

¹⁷And he shall cleave it with the wings thereof, but shall not divide it asunder: and the priest shall burn it upon the altar, upon the wood that is upon the fire: it is a burnt sacrifice, an offering made by fire, of a sweet savour unto the LORD.

CHAPTER 2

¹And when any will offer a meat offering unto the LORD, his offering shall be of fine flour; and he shall pour oil upon it, and put frankincense thereon:

²And he shall bring it to Aaron's sons the priests: and he shall take thereout his handful of the flour thereof, and of the oil thereof, with all the frankincense thereof; and the priest shall burn the memorial of it upon the altar, to be an offering made by fire, of a sweet savour unto the LORD:

³And the remnant of the meat offering shall be Aaron's and his sons': it is a thing most holy of the offerings of the LORD made by fire.

⁴And if thou bring an oblation of a meat offering baken in the oven, it shall be unleavened cakes of fine flour mingled with oil, or unleavened wafers anointed with oil.

⁵And if thy oblation be a meat offering baken in a pan, it shall be of fine flour unleavened, mingled with oil.

⁶Thou shalt part it in pieces, and pour oil thereon: it is a meat offering.

⁷And if thy oblation be a meat offering baken in the fryingpan, it shall be made of fine flour with oil.

⁸And thou shalt bring the meat offering that is made of these things unto the LORD: and when it is presented unto the priest, he shall bring it unto the altar.

⁹And the priest shall take from the meat offering a memorial thereof, and shall burn it upon the altar: it is an offering made by fire, of a sweet savour unto the LORD.

¹⁰And that which is left of the meat offering shall be Aaron's and his sons': it is a thing most holy of

the offerings of the LORD made by fire.

¹¹No meat offering, which ye shall bring unto the LORD, shall be made with leaven: for ye shall burn no leaven, nor any honey, in any offering of the LORD made by fire.

¹²As for the oblation of the firstfruits, ye shall offer them unto the LORD: but they shall not be burnt on the altar for a sweet savour.

¹³And every oblation of thy meat offering shalt thou season with salt; neither shalt thou suffer the salt of the covenant of thy God to be lacking from thy meat offering: with all thine offerings thou shalt offer salt.

¹⁴And if thou offer a meat offering of thy firstfruits unto the LORD, thou shalt offer for the meat offering of thy firstfruits green ears of corn dried by the fire, even corn beaten out of full ears.

¹⁵And thou shalt put oil upon it, and lay frankincense thereon: it is a meat offering.

¹⁶And the priest shall burn the memorial of it, part of the beaten corn thereof, and part of the oil thereof, with all the frankincense thereof: it is an offering made by fire unto the LORD.

CHAPTER 3

¹And if his oblation be a sacrifice of peace offering, if he offer it of the herd; whether it be a male or female, he shall offer it without blemish before the LORD.

²And he shall lay his hand upon the head of his offering, and kill it at the door of the tabernacle of the congregation: and Aaron's sons the priests shall sprinkle the blood upon the altar round about.

³And he shall offer of the sacrifice of the peace offering an offering made by fire unto the LORD; the fat that covereth the inwards, and all the fat that is upon the inwards,

⁴And the two kidneys, and the fat that is on them, which is by the flanks, and the caul above the liver, with the kidneys, it shall he take away.

⁵And Aaron's sons shall burn it on the altar upon the burnt sacrifice, which is upon the wood that is on the fire: it is an offering made by fire, of a sweet savour unto the LORD.

⁶And if his offering for a sacrifice of peace offering unto the LORD be of the flock; male or female, he shall offer it without blemish.

⁷If he offer a lamb for his offering, then shall he offer it before the LORD.

⁸And he shall lay his hand upon the head of his offering, and kill it before the tabernacle of the congregation: and Aaron's sons shall sprinkle the blood thereof round about upon the altar.

⁹And he shall offer of the sacrifice of the peace offering an offering made by fire unto the LORD; the fat thereof, and the whole rump, it shall he take off hard by the backbone; and the fat that covereth the inwards, and all the fat that is upon the inwards,

¹⁰And the two kidneys, and the fat that is upon them, which is by the flanks, and the caul above the liver, with the kidneys, it shall he take away.

¹¹And the priest shall burn it upon the altar: it is the food of the offering made by fire unto the LORD.

¹²And if his offering be a goat, then he shall offer it before the LORD.

¹³And he shall lay his hand upon the head of it, and kill it before the tabernacle of the congregation: and the sons of Aaron shall sprinkle the blood thereof upon the altar round about.

¹⁴And he shall offer thereof his offering, even an offering made by fire unto the LORD; the fat that covereth the inwards, and all the fat that is upon the inwards,

¹⁵And the two kidneys, and the fat that is upon them, which is by the flanks, and the caul above the liver, with the kidneys, it shall he take away.

¹⁶And the priest shall burn them upon the altar: it is the food of the offering made by fire for a sweet savour: all the fat is the LORD's.

¹⁷It shall be a perpetual statute for your generations throughout all your dwellings, that ye eat neither fat nor blood.

CHAPTER 4

¹And the LORD spake unto Moses, saying,

²Speak unto the children of Israel, saying, If a soul shall sin through ignorance against any of the commandments of the LORD concerning things which ought not to be done, and shall do against any of them:

³If the priest that is anointed do sin according to the sin of the people; then let him bring for his sin, which he hath sinned, a young bullock without blemish unto the LORD for a sin offering.

⁴And he shall bring the bullock unto the door of the tabernacle of the congregation before the LORD; and shall lay his hand upon the

bullock's head, and kill the bullock before the LORD.

⁵And the priest that is anointed shall take of the bullock's blood, and bring it to the tabernacle of the congregation:

⁶And the priest shall dip his finger in the blood, and sprinkle of the blood seven times before the LORD, before the vail of the sanctuary.

⁷And the priest shall put some of the blood upon the horns of the altar of sweet incense before the LORD, which is in the tabernacle of the congregation; and shall pour all the blood of the bullock at the bottom of the altar of the burnt offering, which is at the door of the tabernacle of the congregation.

⁸And he shall take off from it all the fat of the bullock for the sin offering; the fat that covereth the inwards, and all the fat that is upon the inwards,

⁹And the two kidneys, and the fat that is upon them, which is by the flanks, and the caul above the liver, with the kidneys, it shall he take away,

¹⁰As it was taken off from the bullock of the sacrifice of peace offerings: and the priest shall burn them upon the altar of the burnt offering.

¹¹And the skin of the bullock, and all his flesh, with his head, and with his legs, and his inwards, and his dung,

¹²Even the whole bullock shall he carry forth without the camp unto a clean place, where the ashes are poured out, and burn him on the wood with fire: where the ashes are poured out shall he be burnt.

¹³And if the whole congregation of Israel sin through ignorance, and the thing be hid from the eyes of the assembly, and they have done somewhat against any of the commandments of the LORD concerning things which should not be done, and are guilty;

¹⁴When the sin, which they have sinned against it, is known, then the congregation shall offer a young bullock for the sin, and bring him before the tabernacle of the congregation.

¹⁵And the elders of the congregation shall lay their hands upon the head of the bullock before the LORD: and the bullock shall be killed before the LORD.

¹⁶And the priest that is anointed shall bring of the bullock's blood to the tabernacle of the congregation:

¹⁷And the priest shall dip his finger in some of the blood, and sprinkle it seven times before the LORD, even before the vail.

¹⁸And he shall put some of the blood upon the horns of the altar

which is before the LORD, that is in the tabernacle of the congregation, and shall pour out all the blood at the bottom of the altar of the burnt offering, which is at the door of the tabernacle of the congregation.

19 And he shall take all his fat from him, and burn it upon the altar.

20 And he shall do with the bullock as he did with the bullock for a sin offering, so shall he do with this: and the priest shall make an atonement for them, and it shall be forgiven them.

21 And he shall carry forth the bullock without the camp, and burn him as he burned the first bullock: it is a sin offering for the congregation.

22 When a ruler hath sinned, and done somewhat through ignorance against any of the commandments of the LORD his God concerning things which should not be done, and is guilty;

23 Or if his sin, wherein he hath sinned, come to his knowledge; he shall bring his offering, a kid of the goats, a male without blemish:

24 And he shall lay his hand upon the head of the goat, and kill it in the place where they kill the burnt offering before the LORD: it is a sin offering.

25 And the priest shall take of the blood of the sin offering with his finger, and put it upon the horns of the altar of burnt offering, and shall pour out his blood at the bottom of the altar of burnt offering.

26 And he shall burn all his fat upon the altar, as the fat of the sacrifice of peace offerings: and the priest shall make an atonement for him as concerning his sin, and it shall be forgiven him.

27 And if any one of the common people sin through ignorance, while he doeth somewhat against any of the commandments of the LORD concerning things which ought not to be done, and be guilty;

28 Or if his sin, which he hath sinned, come to his knowledge: then he shall bring his offering, a kid of the goats, a female without blemish, for his sin which he hath sinned.

29 And he shall lay his hand upon the head of the sin offering, and slay the sin offering in the place of the burnt offering.

30 And the priest shall take of the blood thereof with his finger, and put it upon the horns of the altar of burnt offering, and shall pour out all the blood thereof at the bottom of the altar.

31 And he shall take away all the fat thereof, as the fat is taken away from off the sacrifice of peace offerings; and the priest shall burn it upon the altar for a sweet savour unto the LORD; and the priest shall make an

atonement for him, and it shall be forgiven him.

³²And if he bring a lamb for a sin offering, he shall bring it a female without blemish.

³³And he shall lay his hand upon the head of the sin offering, and slay it for a sin offering in the place where they kill the burnt offering.

³⁴And the priest shall take of the blood of the sin offering with his finger, and put it upon the horns of the altar of burnt offering, and shall pour out all the blood thereof at the bottom of the altar:

³⁵And he shall take away all the fat thereof, as the fat of the lamb is taken away from the sacrifice of the peace offerings; and the priest shall burn them upon the altar, according to the offerings made by fire unto the LORD: and the priest shall make an atonement for his sin that he hath committed, and it shall be forgiven him.

CHAPTER 5

¹And if a soul sin, and hear the voice of swearing, and is a witness, whether he hath seen or known of it; if he do not utter it, then he shall bear his iniquity.

²Or if a soul touch any unclean thing, whether it be a carcase of an unclean beast, or a carcase of unclean cattle, or the carcase of unclean creeping things, and if it be hidden from him; he also shall be unclean, and guilty.

³Or if he touch the uncleanness of man, whatsoever uncleanness it be that a man shall be defiled withal, and it be hid from him; when he knoweth of it, then he shall be guilty.

⁴Or if a soul swear, pronouncing with his lips to do evil, or to do good, whatsoever it be that a man shall pronounce with an oath, and it be hid from him; when he knoweth of it, then he shall be guilty in one of these.

⁵And it shall be, when he shall be guilty in one of these things, that he shall confess that he hath sinned in that thing:

⁶And he shall bring his trespass offering unto the LORD for his sin which he hath sinned, a female from the flock, a lamb or a kid of the goats, for a sin offering; and the priest shall make an atonement for him concerning his sin.

⁷And if he be not able to bring a lamb, then he shall bring for his trespass, which he hath committed, two turtledoves, or two young pigeons, unto the LORD; one for a sin offering, and the other for a burnt offering.

^{8}And he shall bring them unto the priest, who shall offer that which is for the sin offering first, and wring off his head from his neck, but shall not divide it asunder:

^{9}And he shall sprinkle of the blood of the sin offering upon the side of the altar; and the rest of the blood shall be wrung out at the bottom of the altar: it is a sin offering.

^{10}And he shall offer the second for a burnt offering, according to the manner: and the priest shall make an atonement for him for his sin which he hath sinned, and it shall be forgiven him.

^{11}But if he be not able to bring two turtledoves, or two young pigeons, then he that sinned shall bring for his offering the tenth part of an ephah of fine flour for a sin offering; he shall put no oil upon it, neither shall he put any frankincense thereon: for it is a sin offering.

^{12}Then shall he bring it to the priest, and the priest shall take his handful of it, even a memorial thereof, and burn it on the altar, according to the offerings made by fire unto the LORD: it is a sin offering.

^{13}And the priest shall make an atonement for him as touching his sin that he hath sinned in one of these, and it shall be forgiven him: and the remnant shall be the priest's, as a meat offering.

^{14}And the LORD spake unto Moses, saying,

^{15}If a soul commit a trespass, and sin through ignorance, in the holy things of the LORD; then he shall bring for his trespass unto the LORD a ram without blemish out of the flocks, with thy estimation by shekels of silver, after the shekel of the sanctuary, for a trespass offering.

^{16}And he shall make amends for the harm that he hath done in the holy thing, and shall add the fifth part thereto, and give it unto the priest: and the priest shall make an atonement for him with the ram of the trespass offering, and it shall be forgiven him.

^{17}And if a soul sin, and commit any of these things which are forbidden to be done by the commandments of the LORD; though he wist it not, yet is he guilty, and shall bear his iniquity.

^{18}And he shall bring a ram without blemish out of the flock, with thy estimation, for a trespass offering, unto the priest: and the priest shall make an atonement for him concerning his ignorance wherein he erred and wist it not, and it shall be forgiven him.

^{19}It is a trespass offering: he hath certainly trespassed against the LORD.

CHAPTER 6

¹And the LORD spake unto Moses, saying,

²If a soul sin, and commit a trespass against the LORD, and lie unto his neighbour in that which was delivered him to keep, or in fellowship, or in a thing taken away by violence, or hath deceived his neighbour;

³Or have found that which was lost, and lieth concerning it, and sweareth falsely; in any of all these that a man doeth, sinning therein:

⁴Then it shall be, because he hath sinned, and is guilty, that he shall restore that which he took violently away, or the thing which he hath deceitfully gotten, or that which was delivered him to keep, or the lost thing which he found,

⁵Or all that about which he hath sworn falsely; he shall even restore it in the principal, and shall add the fifth part more thereto, and give it unto him to whom it appertaineth, in the day of his trespass offering.

⁶And he shall bring his trespass offering unto the LORD, a ram without blemish out of the flock, with thy estimation, for a trespass offering, unto the priest:

⁷And the priest shall make an atonement for him before the LORD: and it shall be forgiven him for any thing of all that he hath done in trespassing therein.

⁸And the LORD spake unto Moses, saying,

⁹Command Aaron and his sons, saying, This is the law of the burnt offering: It is the burnt offering, because of the burning upon the altar all night unto the morning, and the fire of the altar shall be burning in it.

¹⁰And the priest shall put on his linen garment, and his linen breeches shall he put upon his flesh, and take up the ashes which the fire hath consumed with the burnt offering on the altar, and he shall put them beside the altar.

¹¹And he shall put off his garments, and put on other garments, and carry forth the ashes without the camp unto a clean place.

¹²And the fire upon the altar shall be burning in it; it shall not be put out: and the priest shall burn wood on it every morning, and lay the burnt offering in order upon it; and he shall burn thereon the fat of the peace offerings.

¹³The fire shall ever be burning upon the altar; it shall never go out.

¹⁴And this is the law of the meat offering: the sons of Aaron shall offer it before the LORD, before the altar.

¹⁵And he shall take of it his handful, of the flour of the meat offering, and of the oil thereof, and all the frankincense which is upon the meat offering, and shall burn it upon the altar for a sweet savour, even the memorial of it, unto the LORD.

¹⁶And the remainder thereof shall Aaron and his sons eat: with unleavened bread shall it be eaten in the holy place; in the court of the tabernacle of the congregation they shall eat it.

¹⁷It shall not be baken with leaven. I have given it unto them for their portion of my offerings made by fire; it is most holy, as is the sin offering, and as the trespass offering.

¹⁸All the males among the children of Aaron shall eat of it. It shall be a statute for ever in your generations concerning the offerings of the LORD made by fire: every one that toucheth them shall be holy.

¹⁹And the LORD spake unto Moses, saying,

²⁰This is the offering of Aaron and of his sons, which they shall offer unto the LORD in the day when he is anointed; the tenth part of an ephah of fine flour for a meat offering perpetual, half of it in the morning, and half thereof at night.

²¹In a pan it shall be made with oil; and when it is baken, thou shalt bring it in: and the baken pieces of the meat offering shalt thou offer for a sweet savour unto the LORD.

²²And the priest of his sons that is anointed in his stead shall offer it: it is a statute for ever unto the LORD; it shall be wholly burnt.

²³For every meat offering for the priest shall be wholly burnt: it shall not be eaten.

²⁴And the LORD spake unto Moses, saying,

²⁵Speak unto Aaron and to his sons, saying, This is the law of the sin offering: In the place where the burnt offering is killed shall the sin offering be killed before the LORD: it is most holy.

²⁶The priest that offereth it for sin shall eat it: in the holy place shall it be eaten, in the court of the tabernacle of the congregation.

²⁷Whatsoever shall touch the flesh thereof shall be holy: and when there is sprinkled of the blood thereof upon any garment, thou shalt wash that whereon it was sprinkled in the holy place.

²⁸But the earthen vessel wherein it is sodden shall be broken: and if it be sodden in a brasen pot, it shall be both scoured, and rinsed in water.

²⁹All the males among the priests shall eat thereof: it is most holy.

30And no sin offering, whereof any of the blood is brought into the tabernacle of the congregation to reconcile withal in the holy place, shall be eaten: it shall be burnt in the fire.

CHAPTER 7

1Likewise this is the law of the trespass offering: it is most holy.

2In the place where they kill the burnt offering shall they kill the trespass offering: and the blood thereof shall he sprinkle round about upon the altar.

3And he shall offer of it all the fat thereof; the rump, and the fat that covereth the inwards,

4And the two kidneys, and the fat that is on them, which is by the flanks, and the caul that is above the liver, with the kidneys, it shall he take away:

5And the priest shall burn them upon the altar for an offering made by fire unto the LORD: it is a trespass offering.

6Every male among the priests shall eat thereof: it shall be eaten in the holy place: it is most holy.

7As the sin offering is, so is the trespass offering: there is one law for them: the priest that maketh atonement therewith shall have it.

8And the priest that offereth any man's burnt offering, even the priest shall have to himself the skin of the burnt offering which he hath offered.

9And all the meat offering that is baken in the oven, and all that is dressed in the fryingpan, and in the pan, shall be the priest's that offereth it.

10And every meat offering, mingled with oil, and dry, shall all the sons of Aaron have, one as much as another.

11And this is the law of the sacrifice of peace offerings, which he shall offer unto the LORD.

12If he offer it for a thanksgiving, then he shall offer with the sacrifice of thanksgiving unleavened cakes mingled with oil, and unleavened wafers anointed with oil, and cakes mingled with oil, of fine flour, fried.

13Besides the cakes, he shall offer for his offering leavened bread with the sacrifice of thanksgiving of his peace offerings.

14And of it he shall offer one out of the whole oblation for an heave offering unto the LORD, and it shall be the priest's that sprinkleth the blood of the peace offerings.

15And the flesh of the sacrifice of his peace offerings for thanksgiving shall be eaten the same day that it is offered; he shall not leave any of it until the morning.

¹⁶But if the sacrifice of his offering be a vow, or a voluntary offering, it shall be eaten the same day that he offereth his sacrifice: and on the morrow also the remainder of it shall be eaten:

¹⁷But the remainder of the flesh of the sacrifice on the third day shall be burnt with fire.

¹⁸And if any of the flesh of the sacrifice of his peace offerings be eaten at all on the third day, it shall not be accepted, neither shall it be imputed unto him that offereth it: it shall be an abomination, and the soul that eateth of it shall bear his iniquity.

¹⁹And the flesh that toucheth any unclean thing shall not be eaten; it shall be burnt with fire: and as for the flesh, all that be clean shall eat thereof.

²⁰But the soul that eateth of the flesh of the sacrifice of peace offerings, that pertain unto the LORD, having his uncleanness upon him, even that soul shall be cut off from his people.

²¹Moreover the soul that shall touch any unclean thing, as the uncleanness of man, or any unclean beast, or any abominable unclean thing, and eat of the flesh of the sacrifice of peace offerings, which pertain unto the LORD, even that soul shall be cut off from his people.

²²And the LORD spake unto Moses, saying,

²³Speak unto the children of Israel, saying, Ye shall eat no manner of fat, of ox, or of sheep, or of goat.

²⁴And the fat of the beast that dieth of itself, and the fat of that which is torn with beasts, may be used in any other use: but ye shall in no wise eat of it.

²⁵For whosoever eateth the fat of the beast, of which men offer an offering made by fire unto the LORD, even the soul that eateth it shall be cut off from his people.

²⁶Moreover ye shall eat no manner of blood, whether it be of fowl or of beast, in any of your dwellings.

²⁷Whatsoever soul it be that eateth any manner of blood, even that soul shall be cut off from his people.

²⁸And the LORD spake unto Moses, saying,

²⁹Speak unto the children of Israel, saying, He that offereth the sacrifice of his peace offerings unto the LORD shall bring his oblation unto the LORD of the sacrifice of his peace offerings.

³⁰His own hands shall bring the offerings of the LORD made by fire, the fat with the breast, it shall he

bring, that the breast may be waved for a wave offering before the LORD.

³¹And the priest shall burn the fat upon the altar: but the breast shall be Aaron's and his sons'.

³²And the right shoulder shall ye give unto the priest for an heave offering of the sacrifices of your peace offerings.

³³He among the sons of Aaron, that offereth the blood of the peace offerings, and the fat, shall have the right shoulder for his part.

³⁴For the wave breast and the heave shoulder have I taken of the children of Israel from off the sacrifices of their peace offerings, and have given them unto Aaron the priest and unto his sons by a statute for ever from among the children of Israel.

³⁵This is the portion of the anointing of Aaron, and of the anointing of his sons, out of the offerings of the LORD made by fire, in the day when he presented them to minister unto the LORD in the priest's office;

³⁶Which the LORD commanded to be given them of the children of Israel, in the day that he anointed them, by a statute for ever throughout their generations.

³⁷This is the law of the burnt offering, of the meat offering, and of the sin offering, and of the trespass offering, and of the consecrations, and of the sacrifice of the peace offerings;

³⁸Which the LORD commanded Moses in mount Sinai, in the day that he commanded the children of Israel to offer their oblations unto the LORD, in the wilderness of Sinai.

CHAPTER 8

¹And the LORD spake unto Moses, saying,

²Take Aaron and his sons with him, and the garments, and the anointing oil, and a bullock for the sin offering, and two rams, and a basket of unleavened bread;

³And gather thou all the congregation together unto the door of the tabernacle of the congregation.

⁴And Moses did as the LORD commanded him; and the assembly was gathered together unto the door of the tabernacle of the congregation.

⁵And Moses said unto the congregation, This is the thing which the LORD commanded to be done.

⁶And Moses brought Aaron and his sons, and washed them with water.

⁷And he put upon him the coat, and girded him with the girdle, and clothed him with the robe, and put the ephod upon him, and he girded him with the curious girdle of the ephod, and bound it unto him therewith.

⁸And he put the breastplate upon him: also he put in the breastplate the Urim and the Thummim.

⁹And he put the mitre upon his head; also upon the mitre, even upon his forefront, did he put the golden plate, the holy crown; as the LORD commanded Moses.

¹⁰And Moses took the anointing oil, and anointed the tabernacle and all that was therein, and sanctified them.

¹¹And he sprinkled thereof upon the altar seven times, and anointed the altar and all his vessels, both the laver and his foot, to sanctify them.

¹²And he poured of the anointing oil upon Aaron's head, and anointed him, to sanctify him.

¹³And Moses brought Aaron's sons, and put coats upon them, and girded them with girdles, and put bonnets upon them; as the LORD commanded Moses.

¹⁴And he brought the bullock for the sin offering: and Aaron and his sons laid their hands upon the head of the bullock for the sin offering.

¹⁵And he slew it; and Moses took the blood, and put it upon the horns of the altar round about with his finger, and purified the altar, and poured the blood at the bottom of the altar, and sanctified it, to make reconciliation upon it.

¹⁶And he took all the fat that was upon the inwards, and the caul above the liver, and the two kidneys, and their fat, and Moses burned it upon the altar.

¹⁷But the bullock, and his hide, his flesh, and his dung, he burnt with fire without the camp; as the LORD commanded Moses.

¹⁸And he brought the ram for the burnt offering: and Aaron and his sons laid their hands upon the head of the ram.

¹⁹And he killed it; and Moses sprinkled the blood upon the altar round about.

²⁰And he cut the ram into pieces; and Moses burnt the head, and the pieces, and the fat.

²¹And he washed the inwards and the legs in water; and Moses burnt the whole ram upon the altar: it was a burnt sacrifice for a sweet savour, and an offering made by fire unto the LORD; as the LORD commanded Moses.

²²And he brought the other ram, the ram of consecration: and Aaron and his sons laid their hands upon the head of the ram.

²³And he slew it; and Moses took of the blood of it, and put it upon the tip of Aaron's right ear, and upon the thumb of his right hand, and upon the great toe of his right foot.

²⁴And he brought Aaron's sons, and Moses put of the blood upon the tip of their right ear, and upon the thumbs of their right hands, and upon the great toes of their right feet: and Moses sprinkled the blood upon the altar round about.

²⁵And he took the fat, and the rump, and all the fat that was upon the inwards, and the caul above the liver, and the two kidneys, and their fat, and the right shoulder:

²⁶And out of the basket of unleavened bread, that was before the LORD, he took one unleavened cake, and a cake of oiled bread, and one wafer, and put them on the fat, and upon the right shoulder:

²⁷And he put all upon Aaron's hands, and upon his sons' hands, and waved them for a wave offering before the LORD.

²⁸And Moses took them from off their hands, and burnt them on the altar upon the burnt offering: they were consecrations for a sweet savour: it is an offering made by fire unto the LORD.

²⁹And Moses took the breast, and waved it for a wave offering before the LORD: for of the ram of consecration it was Moses' part; as the LORD commanded Moses.

³⁰And Moses took of the anointing oil, and of the blood which was upon the altar, and sprinkled it upon Aaron, and upon his garments, and upon his sons, and upon his sons' garments with him; and sanctified Aaron, and his garments, and his sons, and his sons' garments with him.

³¹And Moses said unto Aaron and to his sons, Boil the flesh at the door of the tabernacle of the congregation: and there eat it with the bread that is in the basket of consecrations, as I commanded, saying, Aaron and his sons shall eat it.

³²And that which remaineth of the flesh and of the bread shall ye burn with fire.

³³And ye shall not go out of the door of the tabernacle of the congregation in seven days, until the days of your consecration be at an end: for seven days shall he consecrate you.

³⁴As he hath done this day, so the LORD hath commanded to do, to make an atonement for you.

³⁵Therefore shall ye abide at the door of the tabernacle of the congregation day and night seven days, and keep the charge of the

LORD, that ye die not: for so I am commanded.

³⁶So Aaron and his sons did all things which the LORD commanded by the hand of Moses.

CHAPTER 9

¹And it came to pass on the eighth day, that Moses called Aaron and his sons, and the elders of Israel;

²And he said unto Aaron, Take thee a young calf for a sin offering, and a ram for a burnt offering, without blemish, and offer them before the LORD.

³And unto the children of Israel thou shalt speak, saying, Take ye a kid of the goats for a sin offering; and a calf and a lamb, both of the first year, without blemish, for a burnt offering;

⁴Also a bullock and a ram for peace offerings, to sacrifice before the LORD; and a meat offering mingled with oil: for to day the LORD will appear unto you.

⁵And they brought that which Moses commanded before the tabernacle of the congregation: and all the congregation drew near and stood before the LORD.

⁶And Moses said, This is the thing which the LORD commanded that ye should do: and the glory of the LORD shall appear unto you.

⁷And Moses said unto Aaron, Go unto the altar, and offer thy sin offering, and thy burnt offering, and make an atonement for thyself, and for the people: and offer the offering of the people, and make an atonement for them; as the LORD commanded.

⁸Aaron therefore went unto the altar, and slew the calf of the sin offering, which was for himself.

⁹And the sons of Aaron brought the blood unto him: and he dipped his finger in the blood, and put it upon the horns of the altar, and poured out the blood at the bottom of the altar:

¹⁰But the fat, and the kidneys, and the caul above the liver of the sin offering, he burnt upon the altar; as the LORD commanded Moses.

¹¹And the flesh and the hide he burnt with fire without the camp.

¹²And he slew the burnt offering; and Aaron's sons presented unto him the blood, which he sprinkled round about upon the altar.

¹³And they presented the burnt offering unto him, with the pieces thereof, and the head: and he burnt them upon the altar.

¹⁴And he did wash the inwards and the legs, and burnt them upon the burnt offering on the altar.

¹⁵And he brought the people's offering, and took the goat, which was the sin offering for the people, and slew it, and offered it for sin, as the first.

¹⁶And he brought the burnt offering, and offered it according to the manner.

¹⁷And he brought the meat offering, and took an handful thereof, and burnt it upon the altar, beside the burnt sacrifice of the morning.

¹⁸He slew also the bullock and the ram for a sacrifice of peace offerings, which was for the people: and Aaron's sons presented unto him the blood, which he sprinkled upon the altar round about,

¹⁹And the fat of the bullock and of the ram, the rump, and that which covereth the inwards, and the kidneys, and the caul above the liver:

²⁰And they put the fat upon the breasts, and he burnt the fat upon the altar:

²¹And the breasts and the right shoulder Aaron waved for a wave offering before the LORD; as Moses commanded.

²²And Aaron lifted up his hand toward the people, and blessed them, and came down from offering of the sin offering, and the burnt offering, and peace offerings.

²³And Moses and Aaron went into the tabernacle of the congregation, and came out, and blessed the people: and the glory of the LORD appeared unto all the people.

²⁴And there came a fire out from before the LORD, and consumed upon the altar the burnt offering and the fat: which when all the people saw, they shouted, and fell on their faces.

CHAPTER 10

¹And Nadab and Abihu, the sons of Aaron, took either of them his censer, and put fire therein, and put incense thereon, and offered strange fire before the LORD, which he commanded them not.

²And there went out fire from the LORD, and devoured them, and they died before the LORD.

³Then Moses said unto Aaron, This is it that the LORD spake, saying, I will be sanctified in them that come nigh me, and before all the people I will be glorified. And Aaron held his peace.

⁴And Moses called Mishael and Elzaphan, the sons of Uzziel the uncle of Aaron, and said unto them, Come near, carry your brethren from before the sanctuary out of the camp.

⁵So they went near, and carried them in their coats out of the camp; as Moses had said.

⁶And Moses said unto Aaron, and unto Eleazar and unto Ithamar, his sons, Uncover not your heads, neither rend your clothes; lest ye die, and lest wrath come upon all the people: but let your brethren, the whole house of Israel, bewail the burning which the LORD hath kindled.

⁷And ye shall not go out from the door of the tabernacle of the congregation, lest ye die: for the anointing oil of the LORD is upon you. And they did according to the word of Moses.

⁸And the LORD spake unto Aaron, saying,

⁹Do not drink wine nor strong drink, thou, nor thy sons with thee, when ye go into the tabernacle of the congregation, lest ye die: it shall be a statute for ever throughout your generations:

¹⁰And that ye may put difference between holy and unholy, and between unclean and clean;

¹¹And that ye may teach the children of Israel all the statutes which the LORD hath spoken unto them by the hand of Moses.

¹²And Moses spake unto Aaron, and unto Eleazar and unto Ithamar, his sons that were left, Take the meat offering that remaineth of the offerings of the LORD made by fire, and eat it without leaven beside the altar: for it is most holy:

¹³And ye shall eat it in the holy place, because it is thy due, and thy sons' due, of the sacrifices of the LORD made by fire: for so I am commanded.

¹⁴And the wave breast and heave shoulder shall ye eat in a clean place; thou, and thy sons, and thy daughters with thee: for they be thy due, and thy sons' due, which are given out of the sacrifices of peace offerings of the children of Israel.

¹⁵The heave shoulder and the wave breast shall they bring with the offerings made by fire of the fat, to wave it for a wave offering before the LORD; and it shall be thine, and thy sons' with thee, by a statute for ever; as the LORD hath commanded.

¹⁶And Moses diligently sought the goat of the sin offering, and, behold, it was burnt: and he was angry with Eleazar and Ithamar, the sons of Aaron which were left alive, saying,

¹⁷Wherefore have ye not eaten the sin offering in the holy place, seeing it is most holy, and God hath given it you to bear the iniquity of the congregation, to make atonement for them before the LORD?

¹⁸Behold, the blood of it was not brought in within the holy place: ye should indeed have eaten it in the holy place, as I commanded.

¹⁹And Aaron said unto Moses, Behold, this day have they offered their sin offering and their burnt offering before the LORD; and such things have befallen me: and if I had eaten the sin offering to day, should it have been accepted in the sight of the LORD?

²⁰And when Moses heard that, he was content.

CHAPTER 11

¹And the LORD spake unto Moses and to Aaron, saying unto them,

²Speak unto the children of Israel, saying, These are the beasts which ye shall eat among all the beasts that are on the earth.

³Whatsoever parteth the hoof, and is clovenfooted, and cheweth the cud, among the beasts, that shall ye eat.

⁴Nevertheless these shall ye not eat of them that chew the cud, or of them that divide the hoof: as the camel, because he cheweth the cud, but divideth not the hoof; he is unclean unto you.

⁵And the coney, because he cheweth the cud, but divideth not the hoof; he is unclean unto you.

⁶And the hare, because he cheweth the cud, but divideth not the hoof; he is unclean unto you.

⁷And the swine, though he divide the hoof, and be clovenfooted, yet he cheweth not the cud; he is unclean to you.

⁸Of their flesh shall ye not eat, and their carcase shall ye not touch; they are unclean to you.

⁹These shall ye eat of all that are in the waters: whatsoever hath fins and scales in the waters, in the seas, and in the rivers, them shall ye eat.

¹⁰And all that have not fins and scales in the seas, and in the rivers, of all that move in the waters, and of any living thing which is in the waters, they shall be an abomination unto you:

¹¹They shall be even an abomination unto you; ye shall not eat of their flesh, but ye shall have their carcases in abomination.

¹²Whatsoever hath no fins nor scales in the waters, that shall be an abomination unto you.

¹³And these are they which ye shall have in abomination among the fowls; they shall not be eaten, they are an abomination: the eagle, and the ossifrage, and the ospray,

¹⁴And the vulture, and the kite after his kind;

¹⁵Every raven after his kind;

¹⁶And the owl, and the night hawk, and the cuckow, and the hawk after his kind,

¹⁷And the little owl, and the cormorant, and the great owl,

¹⁸And the swan, and the pelican, and the gier eagle,

¹⁹And the stork, the heron after her kind, and the lapwing, and the bat.

²⁰All fowls that creep, going upon all four, shall be an abomination unto you.

²¹Yet these may ye eat of every flying creeping thing that goeth upon all four, which have legs above their feet, to leap withal upon the earth;

²²Even these of them ye may eat; the locust after his kind, and the bald locust after his kind, and the beetle after his kind, and the grasshopper after his kind.

²³But all other flying creeping things, which have four feet, shall be an abomination unto you.

²⁴And for these ye shall be unclean: whosoever toucheth the carcase of them shall be unclean until the even.

²⁵And whosoever beareth ought of the carcase of them shall wash his clothes, and be unclean until the even.

²⁶The carcases of every beast which divideth the hoof, and is not clovenfooted, nor cheweth the cud, are unclean unto you: every one that toucheth them shall be unclean.

²⁷And whatsoever goeth upon his paws, among all manner of beasts that go on all four, those are unclean unto you: whoso toucheth their carcase shall be unclean until the even.

²⁸And he that beareth the carcase of them shall wash his clothes, and be unclean until the even: they are unclean unto you.

²⁹These also shall be unclean unto you among the creeping things that creep upon the earth; the weasel, and the mouse, and the tortoise after his kind,

³⁰And the ferret, and the chameleon, and the lizard, and the snail, and the mole.

³¹These are unclean to you among all that creep: whosoever doth touch them, when they be dead, shall be unclean until the even.

³²And upon whatsoever any of them, when they are dead, doth fall, it shall be unclean; whether it be any vessel of wood, or raiment, or skin, or sack, whatsoever vessel it be, wherein any work is done, it must be put into water, and it shall be unclean until the even; so it shall be cleansed.

³³And every earthen vessel, whereinto any of them falleth, whatsoever is in it shall be unclean; and ye shall break it.

³⁴Of all meat which may be eaten, that on which such water cometh shall be unclean: and all drink that may be drunk in every such vessel shall be unclean.

³⁵And every thing whereupon any part of their carcase falleth shall be unclean; whether it be oven, or ranges for pots, they shall be broken down: for they are unclean and shall be unclean unto you.

³⁶Nevertheless a fountain or pit, wherein there is plenty of water, shall be clean: but that which toucheth their carcase shall be unclean.

³⁷And if any part of their carcase fall upon any sowing seed which is to be sown, it shall be clean.

³⁸But if any water be put upon the seed, and any part of their carcase fall thereon, it shall be unclean unto you.

³⁹And if any beast, of which ye may eat, die; he that toucheth the carcase thereof shall be unclean until the even.

⁴⁰And he that eateth of the carcase of it shall wash his clothes, and be unclean until the even: he also that beareth the carcase of it shall wash his clothes, and be unclean until the even.

⁴¹And every creeping thing that creepeth upon the earth shall be an abomination; it shall not be eaten.

⁴²Whatsoever goeth upon the belly, and whatsoever goeth upon all four, or whatsoever hath more feet among all creeping things that creep upon the earth, them ye shall not eat; for they are an abomination.

⁴³Ye shall not make yourselves abominable with any creeping thing that creepeth, neither shall ye make yourselves unclean with them, that ye should be defiled thereby.

⁴⁴For I am the LORD your God: ye shall therefore sanctify yourselves, and ye shall be holy; for I am holy: neither shall ye defile yourselves with any manner of creeping thing that creepeth upon the earth.

⁴⁵For I am the LORD that bringeth you up out of the land of Egypt, to be your God: ye shall therefore be holy, for I am holy.

⁴⁶This is the law of the beasts, and of the fowl, and of every living creature that moveth in the waters, and of every creature that creepeth upon the earth:

⁴⁷To make a difference between the unclean and the clean, and between the beast that may be eaten and the beast that may not be eaten.

Chapter 12

¹And the LORD spake unto Moses, saying,

²Speak unto the children of Israel, saying, If a woman have conceived seed, and born a man child: then she shall be unclean seven days; according to the days of the separation for her infirmity shall she be unclean.

³And in the eighth day the flesh of his foreskin shall be circumcised.

⁴And she shall then continue in the blood of her purifying three and thirty days; she shall touch no hallowed thing, nor come into the sanctuary, until the days of her purifying be fulfilled.

⁵But if she bear a maid child, then she shall be unclean two weeks, as in her separation: and she shall continue in the blood of her purifying threescore and six days.

⁶And when the days of her purifying are fulfilled, for a son, or for a daughter, she shall bring a lamb of the first year for a burnt offering, and a young pigeon, or a turtledove, for a sin offering, unto the door of the tabernacle of the congregation, unto the priest:

⁷Who shall offer it before the LORD, and make an atonement for her; and she shall be cleansed from the issue of her blood. This is the law for her that hath born a male or a female.

⁸And if she be not able to bring a lamb, then she shall bring two turtles, or two young pigeons; the one for the burnt offering, and the other for a sin offering: and the priest shall make an atonement for her, and she shall be clean.

Chapter 13

¹And the LORD spake unto Moses and Aaron, saying,

²When a man shall have in the skin of his flesh a rising, a scab, or bright spot, and it be in the skin of his flesh like the plague of leprosy; then he shall be brought unto Aaron the priest, or unto one of his sons the priests:

³And the priest shall look on the plague in the skin of the flesh: and when the hair in the plague is turned white, and the plague in sight be deeper than the skin of his flesh, it is a plague of leprosy: and the priest shall look on him, and pronounce him unclean.

⁴If the bright spot be white in the skin of his flesh, and in sight be not deeper than the skin, and hair thereof be not turned white;

then the priest shall shut up him that hath the plague seven days:

⁵And the priest shall look on him the seventh day: and, behold, if the plague in his sight be at a stay, and the plague spread not in the skin; then the priest shall shut him up seven days more:

⁶And the priest shall look on him again the seventh day: and, behold, if the plague be somewhat dark, and the plague spread not in the skin, the priest shall pronounce him clean: it is but a scab: and he shall wash his clothes, and be clean.

⁷But if the scab spread much abroad in the skin, after that he hath been seen of the priest for his cleansing, he shall be seen of the priest again.

⁸And if the priest see that, behold, the scab spreadeth in the skin, then the priest shall pronounce him unclean: it is a leprosy.

⁹When the plague of leprosy is in a man, then he shall be brought unto the priest;

¹⁰And the priest shall see him: and, behold, if the rising be white in the skin, and it have turned the hair white, and there be quick raw flesh in the rising;

¹¹It is an old leprosy in the skin of his flesh, and the priest shall pronounce him unclean, and shall not shut him up: for he is unclean.

¹²And if a leprosy break out abroad in the skin, and the leprosy cover all the skin of him that hath the plague from his head even to his foot, wheresoever the priest looketh;

¹³Then the priest shall consider: and, behold, if the leprosy have covered all his flesh, he shall pronounce him clean that hath the plague: it is all turned white: he is clean.

¹⁴But when raw flesh appeareth in him, he shall be unclean.

¹⁵And the priest shall see the raw flesh, and pronounce him to be unclean: for the raw flesh is unclean: it is a leprosy.

¹⁶Or if the raw flesh turn again, and be changed unto white, he shall come unto the priest;

¹⁷And the priest shall see him: and, behold, if the plague be turned into white; then the priest shall pronounce him clean that hath the plague: he is clean.

¹⁸The flesh also, in which, even in the skin thereof, was a boil, and is healed,

¹⁹And in the place of the boil there be a white rising, or a bright spot, white, and somewhat reddish, and it be shewed to the priest;

²⁰And if, when the priest seeth it, behold, it be in sight lower than the skin, and the hair thereof be turned

white; the priest shall pronounce him unclean: it is a plague of leprosy broken out of the boil.

²¹But if the priest look on it, and, behold, there be no white hairs therein, and if it be not lower than the skin, but be somewhat dark; then the priest shall shut him up seven days:

²²And if it spread much abroad in the skin, then the priest shall pronounce him unclean: it is a plague.

²³But if the bright spot stay in his place, and spread not, it is a burning boil; and the priest shall pronounce him clean.

²⁴Or if there be any flesh, in the skin whereof there is a hot burning, and the quick flesh that burneth have a white bright spot, somewhat reddish, or white;

²⁵Then the priest shall look upon it: and, behold, if the hair in the bright spot be turned white, and it be in sight deeper than the skin; it is a leprosy broken out of the burning: wherefore the priest shall pronounce him unclean: it is the plague of leprosy.

²⁶But if the priest look on it, and, behold, there be no white hair in the bright spot, and it be no lower than the other skin, but be somewhat dark; then the priest shall shut him up seven days:

²⁷And the priest shall look upon him the seventh day: and if it be spread much abroad in the skin, then the priest shall pronounce him unclean: it is the plague of leprosy.

²⁸And if the bright spot stay in his place, and spread not in the skin, but it be somewhat dark; it is a rising of the burning, and the priest shall pronounce him clean: for it is an inflammation of the burning.

²⁹If a man or woman have a plague upon the head or the beard;

³⁰Then the priest shall see the plague: and, behold, if it be in sight deeper than the skin; and there be in it a yellow thin hair; then the priest shall pronounce him unclean: it is a dry scall, even a leprosy upon the head or beard.

³¹And if the priest look on the plague of the scall, and, behold, it be not in sight deeper than the skin, and that there is no black hair in it; then the priest shall shut up him that hath the plague of the scall seven days:

³²And in the seventh day the priest shall look on the plague: and, behold, if the scall spread not, and there be in it no yellow hair, and the scall be not in sight deeper than the skin;

³³He shall be shaven, but the scall shall he not shave; and the priest shall shut up him that hath the scall seven days more:

³⁴And in the seventh day the priest shall look on the scall: and, behold, if the scall be not spread in the skin, nor be in sight deeper than the skin; then the priest shall pronounce him clean: and he shall wash his clothes, and be clean.

³⁵But if the scall spread much in the skin after his cleansing;

³⁶Then the priest shall look on him: and, behold, if the scall be spread in the skin, the priest shall not seek for yellow hair; he is unclean.

³⁷But if the scall be in his sight at a stay, and that there is black hair grown up therein; the scall is healed, he is clean: and the priest shall pronounce him clean.

³⁸If a man also or a woman have in the skin of their flesh bright spots, even white bright spots;

³⁹Then the priest shall look: and, behold, if the bright spots in the skin of their flesh be darkish white; it is a freckled spot that groweth in the skin; he is clean.

⁴⁰And the man whose hair is fallen off his head, he is bald; yet is he clean.

⁴¹And he that hath his hair fallen off from the part of his head toward his face, he is forehead bald: yet is he clean.

⁴²And if there be in the bald head, or bald forehead, a white reddish sore; it is a leprosy sprung up in his bald head, or his bald forehead.

⁴³Then the priest shall look upon it: and, behold, if the rising of the sore be white reddish in his bald head, or in his bald forehead, as the leprosy appeareth in the skin of the flesh;

⁴⁴He is a leprous man, he is unclean: the priest shall pronounce him utterly unclean; his plague is in his head.

⁴⁵And the leper in whom the plague is, his clothes shall be rent, and his head bare, and he shall put a covering upon his upper lip, and shall cry, Unclean, unclean.

⁴⁶All the days wherein the plague shall be in him he shall be defiled; he is unclean: he shall dwell alone; without the camp shall his habitation be.

⁴⁷The garment also that the plague of leprosy is in, whether it be a woollen garment, or a linen garment;

⁴⁸Whether it be in the warp, or woof; of linen, or of woollen; whether in a skin, or in any thing made of skin;

⁴⁹And if the plague be greenish or reddish in the garment, or in the skin, either in the warp, or in the woof, or in any thing of skin; it is a plague of leprosy, and shall be shewed unto the priest:

⁵⁰And the priest shall look upon the plague, and shut up it that hath the plague seven days:

⁵¹And he shall look on the plague on the seventh day: if the plague be spread in the garment, either in the warp, or in the woof, or in a skin, or in any work that is made of skin; the plague is a fretting leprosy; it is unclean.

⁵²He shall therefore burn that garment, whether warp or woof, in woollen or in linen, or any thing of skin, wherein the plague is: for it is a fretting leprosy; it shall be burnt in the fire.

⁵³And if the priest shall look, and, behold, the plague be not spread in the garment, either in the warp, or in the woof, or in any thing of skin;

⁵⁴Then the priest shall command that they wash the thing wherein the plague is, and he shall shut it up seven days more:

⁵⁵And the priest shall look on the plague, after that it is washed: and, behold, if the plague have not changed his colour, and the plague be not spread; it is unclean; thou shalt burn it in the fire; it is fret inward, whether it be bare within or without.

⁵⁶And if the priest look, and, behold, the plague be somewhat dark after the washing of it; then he shall rend it out of the garment, or out of the skin, or out of the warp, or out of the woof:

⁵⁷And if it appear still in the garment, either in the warp, or in the woof, or in any thing of skin; it is a spreading plague: thou shalt burn that wherein the plague is with fire.

⁵⁸And the garment, either warp, or woof, or whatsoever thing of skin it be, which thou shalt wash, if the plague be departed from them, then it shall be washed the second time, and shall be clean.

⁵⁹This is the law of the plague of leprosy in a garment of woollen or linen, either in the warp, or woof, or any thing of skins, to pronounce it clean, or to pronounce it unclean.

CHAPTER 14

¹And the LORD spake unto Moses, saying,

²This shall be the law of the leper in the day of his cleansing: He shall be brought unto the priest:

³And the priest shall go forth out of the camp; and the priest shall look, and, behold, if the plague of leprosy be healed in the leper;

⁴Then shall the priest command to take for him that is to be cleansed two birds alive and clean, and cedar wood, and scarlet, and hyssop:

⁵And the priest shall command that one of the birds be killed in an earthen vessel over running water:

⁶As for the living bird, he shall take it, and the cedar wood, and the scarlet, and the hyssop, and shall dip them and the living bird in the blood of the bird that was killed over the running water:

⁷And he shall sprinkle upon him that is to be cleansed from the leprosy seven times, and shall pronounce him clean, and shall let the living bird loose into the open field.

⁸And he that is to be cleansed shall wash his clothes, and shave off all his hair, and wash himself in water, that he may be clean: and after that he shall come into the camp, and shall tarry abroad out of his tent seven days.

⁹But it shall be on the seventh day, that he shall shave all his hair off his head and his beard and his eyebrows, even all his hair he shall shave off: and he shall wash his clothes, also he shall wash his flesh in water, and he shall be clean.

¹⁰And on the eighth day he shall take two he lambs without blemish, and one ewe lamb of the first year without blemish, and three tenth deals of fine flour for a meat offering, mingled with oil, and one log of oil.

¹¹And the priest that maketh him clean shall present the man that is to be made clean, and those things, before the LORD, at the door of the tabernacle of the congregation:

¹²And the priest shall take one he lamb, and offer him for a trespass offering, and the log of oil, and wave them for a wave offering before the LORD:

¹³And he shall slay the lamb in the place where he shall kill the sin offering and the burnt offering, in the holy place: for as the sin offering is the priest's, so is the trespass offering: it is most holy:

¹⁴And the priest shall take some of the blood of the trespass offering, and the priest shall put it upon the tip of the right ear of him that is to be cleansed, and upon the thumb of his right hand, and upon the great toe of his right foot:

¹⁵And the priest shall take some of the log of oil, and pour it into the palm of his own left hand:

¹⁶And the priest shall dip his right finger in the oil that is in his left hand, and shall sprinkle of the oil with his finger seven times before the LORD:

¹⁷And of the rest of the oil that is in his hand shall the priest put upon the tip of the right ear of him that is to be cleansed, and upon the thumb of his right hand, and upon

the great toe of his right foot, upon the blood of the trespass offering:

¹⁸And the remnant of the oil that is in the priest's hand he shall pour upon the head of him that is to be cleansed: and the priest shall make an atonement for him before the LORD.

¹⁹And the priest shall offer the sin offering, and make an atonement for him that is to be cleansed from his uncleanness; and afterward he shall kill the burnt offering:

²⁰And the priest shall offer the burnt offering and the meat offering upon the altar: and the priest shall make an atonement for him, and he shall be clean.

²¹And if he be poor, and cannot get so much; then he shall take one lamb for a trespass offering to be waved, to make an atonement for him, and one tenth deal of fine flour mingled with oil for a meat offering, and a log of oil;

²²And two turtledoves, or two young pigeons, such as he is able to get; and the one shall be a sin offering, and the other a burnt offering.

²³And he shall bring them on the eighth day for his cleansing unto the priest, unto the door of the tabernacle of the congregation, before the LORD.

²⁴And the priest shall take the lamb of the trespass offering, and

the log of oil, and the priest shall wave them for a wave offering before the LORD:

²⁵And he shall kill the lamb of the trespass offering, and the priest shall take some of the blood of the trespass offering, and put it upon the tip of the right ear of him that is to be cleansed, and upon the thumb of his right hand, and upon the great toe of his right foot:

²⁶And the priest shall pour of the oil into the palm of his own left hand:

²⁷And the priest shall sprinkle with his right finger some of the oil that is in his left hand seven times before the LORD:

²⁸And the priest shall put of the oil that is in his hand upon the tip of the right ear of him that is to be cleansed, and upon the thumb of his right hand, and upon the great toe of his right foot, upon the place of the blood of the trespass offering:

²⁹And the rest of the oil that is in the priest's hand he shall put upon the head of him that is to be cleansed, to make an atonement for him before the LORD.

³⁰And he shall offer the one of the turtledoves, or of the young pigeons, such as he can get;

³¹Even such as he is able to get, the one for a sin offering, and the other for a burnt offering, with the

meat offering: and the priest shall make an atonement for him that is to be cleansed before the LORD.

³²This is the law of him in whom is the plague of leprosy, whose hand is not able to get that which pertaineth to his cleansing.

³³And the LORD spake unto Moses and unto Aaron, saying,

³⁴When ye be come into the land of Canaan, which I give to you for a possession, and I put the plague of leprosy in a house of the land of your possession;

³⁵And he that owneth the house shall come and tell the priest, saying, It seemeth to me there is as it were a plague in the house:

³⁶Then the priest shall command that they empty the house, before the priest go into it to see the plague, that all that is in the house be not made unclean: and afterward the priest shall go in to see the house:

³⁷And he shall look on the plague, and, behold, if the plague be in the walls of the house with hollow strakes, greenish or reddish, which in sight are lower than the wall;

³⁸Then the priest shall go out of the house to the door of the house, and shut up the house seven days:

³⁹And the priest shall come again the seventh day, and shall look: and, behold, if the plague be spread in the walls of the house;

⁴⁰Then the priest shall command that they take away the stones in which the plague is, and they shall cast them into an unclean place without the city:

⁴¹And he shall cause the house to be scraped within round about, and they shall pour out the dust that they scrape off without the city into an unclean place:

⁴²And they shall take other stones, and put them in the place of those stones; and he shall take other morter, and shall plaister the house.

⁴³And if the plague come again, and break out in the house, after that he hath taken away the stones, and after he hath scraped the house, and after it is plaistered;

⁴⁴Then the priest shall come and look, and, behold, if the plague be spread in the house, it is a fretting leprosy in the house; it is unclean.

⁴⁵And he shall break down the house, the stones of it, and the timber thereof, and all the morter of the house; and he shall carry them forth out of the city into an unclean place.

⁴⁶Moreover he that goeth into the house all the while that it is shut up shall be unclean until the even.

⁴⁷And he that lieth in the house shall wash his clothes; and he that eateth in the house shall wash his clothes.

⁴⁸And if the priest shall come in, and look upon it, and, behold, the plague hath not spread in the house, after the house was plaistered: then the priest shall pronounce the house clean, because the plague is healed.

⁴⁹And he shall take to cleanse the house two birds, and cedar wood, and scarlet, and hyssop:

⁵⁰And he shall kill the one of the birds in an earthen vessel over running water:

⁵¹And he shall take the cedar wood, and the hyssop, and the scarlet, and the living bird, and dip them in the blood of the slain bird, and in the running water, and sprinkle the house seven times:

⁵²And he shall cleanse the house with the blood of the bird, and with the running water, and with the living bird, and with the cedar wood, and with the hyssop, and with the scarlet:

⁵³But he shall let go the living bird out of the city into the open fields, and make an atonement for the house: and it shall be clean.

⁵⁴This is the law for all manner of plague of leprosy, and scall,

⁵⁵And for the leprosy of a garment, and of a house,

⁵⁶And for a rising, and for a scab, and for a bright spot:

⁵⁷To teach when it is unclean, and when it is clean: this is the law of leprosy.

CHAPTER 15

¹And the LORD spake unto Moses and to Aaron, saying,

²Speak unto the children of Israel, and say unto them, When any man hath a running issue out of his flesh, because of his issue he is unclean.

³And this shall be his uncleanness in his issue: whether his flesh run with his issue, or his flesh be stopped from his issue, it is his uncleanness.

⁴Every bed, whereon he lieth that hath the issue, is unclean: and every thing, whereon he sitteth, shall be unclean.

⁵And whosoever toucheth his bed shall wash his clothes, and bathe himself in water, and be unclean until the even.

⁶And he that sitteth on any thing whereon he sat that hath the issue shall wash his clothes, and bathe himself in water, and be unclean until the even.

⁷And he that toucheth the flesh of him that hath the issue shall wash his clothes, and bathe himself in water, and be unclean until the even.

⁸And if he that hath the issue spit upon him that is clean; then he shall wash his clothes, and bathe himself in water, and be unclean until the even.

⁹And what saddle soever he rideth upon that hath the issue shall be unclean.

¹⁰And whosoever toucheth any thing that was under him shall be unclean until the even: and he that beareth any of those things shall wash his clothes, and bathe himself in water, and be unclean until the even.

¹¹And whomsoever he toucheth that hath the issue, and hath not rinsed his hands in water, he shall wash his clothes, and bathe himself in water, and be unclean until the even.

¹²And the vessel of earth, that he toucheth which hath the issue, shall be broken: and every vessel of wood shall be rinsed in water.

¹³And when he that hath an issue is cleansed of his issue; then he shall number to himself seven days for his cleansing, and wash his clothes, and bathe his flesh in running water, and shall be clean.

¹⁴And on the eighth day he shall take to him two turtledoves, or two young pigeons, and come before the LORD unto the door of the tabernacle of the congregation, and give them unto the priest:

¹⁵And the priest shall offer them, the one for a sin offering, and the other for a burnt offering; and the priest shall make an atonement for him before the LORD for his issue.

¹⁶And if any man's seed of copulation go out from him, then he shall wash all his flesh in water, and be unclean until the even.

¹⁷And every garment, and every skin, whereon is the seed of copulation, shall be washed with water, and be unclean until the even.

¹⁸The woman also with whom man shall lie with seed of copulation, they shall both bathe themselves in water, and be unclean until the even.

¹⁹And if a woman have an issue, and her issue in her flesh be blood, she shall be put apart seven days: and whosoever toucheth her shall be unclean until the even.

²⁰And every thing that she lieth upon in her separation shall be unclean: every thing also that she sitteth upon shall be unclean.

²¹And whosoever toucheth her bed shall wash his clothes, and bathe himself in water, and be unclean until the even.

²²And whosoever toucheth any thing that she sat upon shall wash his clothes, and bathe himself in water, and be unclean until the even.

²³And if it be on her bed, or on any thing whereon she sitteth, when he toucheth it, he shall be unclean until the even.

²⁴And if any man lie with her at all, and her flowers be upon him, he shall be unclean seven days; and all

the bed whereon he lieth shall be unclean.

²⁵And if a woman have an issue of her blood many days out of the time of her separation, or if it run beyond the time of her separation; all the days of the issue of her uncleanness shall be as the days of her separation: she shall be unclean.

²⁶Every bed whereon she lieth all the days of her issue shall be unto her as the bed of her separation: and whatsoever she sitteth upon shall be unclean, as the uncleanness of her separation.

²⁷And whosoever toucheth those things shall be unclean, and shall wash his clothes, and bathe himself in water, and be unclean until the even.

²⁸But if she be cleansed of her issue, then she shall number to herself seven days, and after that she shall be clean.

²⁹And on the eighth day she shall take unto her two turtles, or two young pigeons, and bring them unto the priest, to the door of the tabernacle of the congregation.

³⁰And the priest shall offer the one for a sin offering, and the other for a burnt offering; and the priest shall make an atonement for her before the LORD for the issue of her uncleanness.

³¹Thus shall ye separate the children of Israel from their uncleanness; that they die not in their uncleanness, when they defile my tabernacle that is among them.

³²This is the law of him that hath an issue, and of him whose seed goeth from him, and is defiled therewith;

³³And of her that is sick of her flowers, and of him that hath an issue, of the man, and of the woman, and of him that lieth with her that is unclean.

CHAPTER 16

¹And the LORD spake unto Moses after the death of the two sons of Aaron, when they offered before the LORD, and died;

²And the LORD said unto Moses, Speak unto Aaron thy brother, that he come not at all times into the holy place within the vail before the mercy seat, which is upon the ark; that he die not: for I will appear in the cloud upon the mercy seat.

³Thus shall Aaron come into the holy place: with a young bullock for a sin offering, and a ram for a burnt offering.

⁴He shall put on the holy linen coat, and he shall have the linen breeches upon his flesh, and shall be girded with a linen girdle, and with

the linen mitre shall he be attired: these are holy garments; therefore shall he wash his flesh in water, and so put them on.

⁵And he shall take of the congregation of the children of Israel two kids of the goats for a sin offering, and one ram for a burnt offering.

⁶And Aaron shall offer his bullock of the sin offering, which is for himself, and make an atonement for himself, and for his house.

⁷And he shall take the two goats, and present them before the LORD at the door of the tabernacle of the congregation.

⁸And Aaron shall cast lots upon the two goats; one lot for the LORD, and the other lot for the scapegoat.

⁹And Aaron shall bring the goat upon which the LORD's lot fell, and offer him for a sin offering.

¹⁰But the goat, on which the lot fell to be the scapegoat, shall be presented alive before the LORD, to make an atonement with him, and to let him go for a scapegoat into the wilderness.

¹¹And Aaron shall bring the bullock of the sin offering, which is for himself, and shall make an atonement for himself, and for his house, and shall kill the bullock of the sin offering which is for himself:

¹²And he shall take a censer full of burning coals of fire from off the altar before the LORD, and his hands full of sweet incense beaten small, and bring it within the vail:

¹³And he shall put the incense upon the fire before the LORD, that the cloud of the incense may cover the mercy seat that is upon the testimony, that he die not:

¹⁴And he shall take of the blood of the bullock, and sprinkle it with his finger upon the mercy seat eastward; and before the mercy seat shall he sprinkle of the blood with his finger seven times.

¹⁵Then shall he kill the goat of the sin offering, that is for the people, and bring his blood within the vail, and do with that blood as he did with the blood of the bullock, and sprinkle it upon the mercy seat, and before the mercy seat:

¹⁶And he shall make an atonement for the holy place, because of the uncleanness of the children of Israel, and because of their transgressions in all their sins: and so shall he do for the tabernacle of the congregation, that remaineth among them in the midst of their uncleanness.

¹⁷And there shall be no man in the tabernacle of the congregation when he goeth in to make an atonement in the holy place, until

he come out, and have made an atonement for himself, and for his household, and for all the congregation of Israel.

18 And he shall go out unto the altar that is before the LORD, and make an atonement for it; and shall take of the blood of the bullock, and of the blood of the goat, and put it upon the horns of the altar round about.

19 And he shall sprinkle of the blood upon it with his finger seven times, and cleanse it, and hallow it from the uncleanness of the children of Israel.

20 And when he hath made an end of reconciling the holy place, and the tabernacle of the congregation, and the altar, he shall bring the live goat:

21 And Aaron shall lay both his hands upon the head of the live goat, and confess over him all the iniquities of the children of Israel, and all their transgressions in all their sins, putting them upon the head of the goat, and shall send him away by the hand of a fit man into the wilderness:

22 And the goat shall bear upon him all their iniquities unto a land not inhabited: and he shall let go the goat in the wilderness.

23 And Aaron shall come into the tabernacle of the congregation, and shall put off the linen garments, which he put on when he went into the holy place, and shall leave them there:

24 And he shall wash his flesh with water in the holy place, and put on his garments, and come forth, and offer his burnt offering, and the burnt offering of the people, and make an atonement for himself, and for the people.

25 And the fat of the sin offering shall he burn upon the altar.

26 And he that let go the goat for the scapegoat shall wash his clothes, and bathe his flesh in water, and afterward come into the camp.

27 And the bullock for the sin offering, and the goat for the sin offering, whose blood was brought in to make atonement in the holy place, shall one carry forth without the camp; and they shall burn in the fire their skins, and their flesh, and their dung.

28 And he that burneth them shall wash his clothes, and bathe his flesh in water, and afterward he shall come into the camp.

29 And this shall be a statute for ever unto you: that in the seventh month, on the tenth day of the month, ye shall afflict your souls, and do no work at all, whether it be one of your own country, or a stranger that sojourneth among you:

³⁰For on that day shall the priest make an atonement for you, to cleanse you, that ye may be clean from all your sins before the LORD.

³¹It shall be a sabbath of rest unto you, and ye shall afflict your souls, by a statute for ever.

³²And the priest, whom he shall anoint, and whom he shall consecrate to minister in the priest's office in his father's stead, shall make the atonement, and shall put on the linen clothes, even the holy garments:

³³And he shall make an atonement for the holy sanctuary, and he shall make an atonement for the tabernacle of the congregation, and for the altar, and he shall make an atonement for the priests, and for all the people of the congregation.

³⁴And this shall be an everlasting statute unto you, to make an atonement for the children of Israel for all their sins once a year. And he did as the LORD commanded Moses.

CHAPTER 17

¹And the LORD spake unto Moses, saying,

²Speak unto Aaron, and unto his sons, and unto all the children of Israel, and say unto them; This is the thing which the LORD hath commanded, saying,

³What man soever there be of the house of Israel, that killeth an ox, or lamb, or goat, in the camp, or that killeth it out of the camp,

⁴And bringeth it not unto the door of the tabernacle of the congregation, to offer an offering unto the LORD before the tabernacle of the LORD; blood shall be imputed unto that man; he hath shed blood; and that man shall be cut off from among his people:

⁵To the end that the children of Israel may bring their sacrifices, which they offer in the open field, even that they may bring them unto the LORD, unto the door of the tabernacle of the congregation, unto the priest, and offer them for peace offerings unto the LORD.

⁶And the priest shall sprinkle the blood upon the altar of the LORD at the door of the tabernacle of the congregation, and burn the fat for a sweet savour unto the LORD.

⁷And they shall no more offer their sacrifices unto devils, after whom they have gone a whoring. This shall be a statute for ever unto them throughout their generations.

⁸And thou shalt say unto them, Whatsoever man there be of the house of Israel, or of the strangers

which sojourn among you, that offereth a burnt offering or sacrifice,

⁹And bringeth it not unto the door of the tabernacle of the congregation, to offer it unto the LORD; even that man shall be cut off from among his people.

¹⁰And whatsoever man there be of the house of Israel, or of the strangers that sojourn among you, that eateth any manner of blood; I will even set my face against that soul that eateth blood, and will cut him off from among his people.

¹¹For the life of the flesh is in the blood: and I have given it to you upon the altar to make an atonement for your souls: for it is the blood that maketh an atonement for the soul.

¹²Therefore I said unto the children of Israel, No soul of you shall eat blood, neither shall any stranger that sojourneth among you eat blood.

¹³And whatsoever man there be of the children of Israel, or of the strangers that sojourn among you, which hunteth and catcheth any beast or fowl that may be eaten; he shall even pour out the blood thereof, and cover it with dust.

¹⁴For it is the life of all flesh; the blood of it is for the life thereof: therefore I said unto the children of Israel, Ye shall eat the blood

of no manner of flesh: for the life of all flesh is the blood thereof: whosoever eateth it shall be cut off.

¹⁵And every soul that eateth that which died of itself, or that which was torn with beasts, whether it be one of your own country, or a stranger, he shall both wash his clothes, and bathe himself in water, and be unclean until the even: then shall he be clean.

¹⁶But if he wash them not, nor bathe his flesh; then he shall bear his iniquity.

CHAPTER 18

¹And the LORD spake unto Moses, saying,

²Speak unto the children of Israel, and say unto them, I am the LORD your God.

³After the doings of the land of Egypt, wherein ye dwelt, shall ye not do: and after the doings of the land of Canaan, whither I bring you, shall ye not do: neither shall ye walk in their ordinances.

⁴Ye shall do my judgments, and keep mine ordinances, to walk therein: I am the LORD your God.

⁵Ye shall therefore keep my statutes, and my judgments: which

if a man do, he shall live in them: I am the LORD.

⁶None of you shall approach to any that is near of kin to him, to uncover their nakedness: I am the LORD.

⁷The nakedness of thy father, or the nakedness of thy mother, shalt thou not uncover: she is thy mother; thou shalt not uncover her nakedness.

⁸The nakedness of thy father's wife shalt thou not uncover: it is thy father's nakedness.

⁹The nakedness of thy sister, the daughter of thy father, or daughter of thy mother, whether she be born at home, or born abroad, even their nakedness thou shalt not uncover.

¹⁰The nakedness of thy son's daughter, or of thy daughter's daughter, even their nakedness thou shalt not uncover: for theirs is thine own nakedness.

¹¹The nakedness of thy father's wife's daughter, begotten of thy father, she is thy sister, thou shalt not uncover her nakedness.

¹²Thou shalt not uncover the nakedness of thy father's sister: she is thy father's near kinswoman.

¹³Thou shalt not uncover the nakedness of thy mother's sister: for she is thy mother's near kinswoman.

¹⁴Thou shalt not uncover the nakedness of thy father's brother, thou shalt not approach to his wife: she is thine aunt.

¹⁵Thou shalt not uncover the nakedness of thy daughter in law: she is thy son's wife; thou shalt not uncover her nakedness.

¹⁶Thou shalt not uncover the nakedness of thy brother's wife: it is thy brother's nakedness.

¹⁷Thou shalt not uncover the nakedness of a woman and her daughter, neither shalt thou take her son's daughter, or her daughter's daughter, to uncover her nakedness; for they are her near kinswomen: it is wickedness.

¹⁸Neither shalt thou take a wife to her sister, to vex her, to uncover her nakedness, beside the other in her life time.

¹⁹Also thou shalt not approach unto a woman to uncover her nakedness, as long as she is put apart for her uncleanness.

²⁰Moreover thou shalt not lie carnally with thy neighbour's wife, to defile thyself with her.

²¹And thou shalt not let any of thy seed pass through the fire to Molech, neither shalt thou profane the name of thy God: I am the LORD.

²²Thou shalt not lie with mankind, as with womankind: it is abomination.

²³Neither shalt thou lie with any beast to defile thyself therewith: neither shall any woman stand before a beast to lie down thereto: it is confusion.

²⁴Defile not ye yourselves in any of these things: for in all these the nations are defiled which I cast out before you:

²⁵And the land is defiled: therefore I do visit the iniquity thereof upon it, and the land itself vomiteth out her inhabitants.

²⁶Ye shall therefore keep my statutes and my judgments, and shall not commit any of these abominations; neither any of your own nation, nor any stranger that sojourneth among you:

²⁷(For all these abominations have the men of the land done, which were before you, and the land is defiled;)

²⁸That the land spue not you out also, when ye defile it, as it spued out the nations that were before you.

²⁹For whosoever shall commit any of these abominations, even the souls that commit them shall be cut off from among their people.

³⁰Therefore shall ye keep mine ordinance, that ye commit not any one of these abominable customs, which were committed before you, and that ye defile not yourselves therein: I am the LORD your God.

CHAPTER 19

¹And the LORD spake unto Moses, saying,

²Speak unto all the congregation of the children of Israel, and say unto them, Ye shall be holy: for I the LORD your God am holy.

³Ye shall fear every man his mother, and his father, and keep my sabbaths: I am the LORD your God.

⁴Turn ye not unto idols, nor make to yourselves molten gods: I am the LORD your God.

⁵And if ye offer a sacrifice of peace offerings unto the LORD, ye shall offer it at your own will.

⁶It shall be eaten the same day ye offer it, and on the morrow: and if ought remain until the third day, it shall be burnt in the fire.

⁷And if it be eaten at all on the third day, it is abominable; it shall not be accepted.

⁸Therefore every one that eateth it shall bear his iniquity, because he hath profaned the hallowed thing of the LORD: and that soul shall be cut off from among his people.

⁹And when ye reap the harvest of your land, thou shalt not wholly reap the corners of thy field, neither shalt thou gather the gleanings of thy harvest.

¹⁰And thou shalt not glean thy vineyard, neither shalt thou gather every grape of thy vineyard; thou shalt leave them for the poor and stranger: I am the LORD your God.

¹¹Ye shall not steal, neither deal falsely, neither lie one to another.

¹²And ye shall not swear by my name falsely, neither shalt thou profane the name of thy God: I am the LORD.

¹³Thou shalt not defraud thy neighbour, neither rob him: the wages of him that is hired shall not abide with thee all night until the morning.

¹⁴Thou shalt not curse the deaf, nor put a stumblingblock before the blind, but shalt fear thy God: I am the LORD.

¹⁵Ye shall do no unrighteousness in judgment: thou shalt not respect the person of the poor, nor honor the person of the mighty: but in righteousness shalt thou judge thy neighbour.

¹⁶Thou shalt not go up and down as a talebearer among thy people: neither shalt thou stand against the blood of thy neighbour; I am the LORD.

¹⁷Thou shalt not hate thy brother in thine heart: thou shalt in any wise rebuke thy neighbour, and not suffer sin upon him.

¹⁸Thou shalt not avenge, nor bear any grudge against the children of thy people, but thou shalt love thy neighbour as thyself: I am the LORD.

¹⁹Ye shall keep my statutes. Thou shalt not let thy cattle gender with a diverse kind: thou shalt not sow thy field with mingled seed: neither shall a garment mingled of linen and woollen come upon thee.

²⁰And whosoever lieth carnally with a woman, that is a bondmaid, betrothed to an husband, and not at all redeemed, nor freedom given her; she shall be scourged; they shall not be put to death, because she was not free.

²¹And he shall bring his trespass offering unto the LORD, unto the door of the tabernacle of the congregation, even a ram for a trespass offering.

²²And the priest shall make an atonement for him with the ram of the trespass offering before the LORD for his sin which he hath done: and the sin which he hath done shall be forgiven him.

²³And when ye shall come into the land, and shall have planted all manner of trees for food, then ye shall count the fruit thereof as uncircumcised: three years shall it be as uncircumcised unto you: it shall not be eaten of.

²⁴But in the fourth year all the fruit thereof shall be holy to praise the LORD withal.

²⁵And in the fifth year shall ye eat of the fruit thereof, that it may yield unto you the increase thereof: I am the LORD your God.

²⁶Ye shall not eat any thing with the blood: neither shall ye use enchantment, nor observe times.

²⁷Ye shall not round the corners of your heads, neither shalt thou mar the corners of thy beard.

²⁸Ye shall not make any cuttings in your flesh for the dead, nor print any marks upon you: I am the LORD.

²⁹Do not prostitute thy daughter, to cause her to be a whore; lest the land fall to whoredom, and the land become full of wickedness.

³⁰Ye shall keep my sabbaths, and reverence my sanctuary: I am the LORD.

³¹Regard not them that have familiar spirits, neither seek after wizards, to be defiled by them: I am the LORD your God.

³²Thou shalt rise up before the hoary head, and honour the face of the old man, and fear thy God: I am the LORD.

³³And if a stranger sojourn with thee in your land, ye shall not vex him.

³⁴But the stranger that dwelleth with you shall be unto you as one born among you, and thou shalt love him as thyself; for ye were strangers in the land of Egypt: I am the LORD your God.

³⁵Ye shall do no unrighteousness in judgment, in meteyard, in weight, or in measure.

³⁶Just balances, just weights, a just ephah, and a just hin, shall ye have: I am the LORD your God, which brought you out of the land of Egypt.

³⁷Therefore shall ye observe all my statutes, and all my judgments, and do them: I am the LORD.

CHAPTER 20

¹And the LORD spake unto Moses, saying,

²Again, thou shalt say to the children of Israel, Whosoever he be of the children of Israel, or of the strangers that sojourn in Israel, that giveth any of his seed unto Molech; he shall surely be put to death: the people of the land shall stone him with stones.

³And I will set my face against that man, and will cut him off from among his people; because he hath given of his seed unto Molech, to

defile my sanctuary, and to profane my holy name.

⁴And if the people of the land do any ways hide their eyes from the man, when he giveth of his seed unto Molech, and kill him not:

⁵Then I will set my face against that man, and against his family, and will cut him off, and all that go a whoring after him, to commit whoredom with Molech, from among their people.

⁶And the soul that turneth after such as have familiar spirits, and after wizards, to go a whoring after them, I will even set my face against that soul, and will cut him off from among his people.

⁷Sanctify yourselves therefore, and be ye holy: for I am the LORD your God.

⁸And ye shall keep my statutes, and do them: I am the LORD which sanctify you.

⁹For every one that curseth his father or his mother shall be surely put to death: he hath cursed his father or his mother; his blood shall be upon him.

¹⁰And the man that committeth adultery with another man's wife, even he that committeth adultery with his neighbour's wife, the adulterer and the adulteress shall surely be put to death.

¹¹And the man that lieth with his father's wife hath uncovered his father's nakedness: both of them shall surely be put to death; their blood shall be upon them.

¹²And if a man lie with his daughter in law, both of them shall surely be put to death: they have wrought confusion; their blood shall be upon them.

¹³If a man also lie with mankind, as he lieth with a woman, both of them have committed an abomination: they shall surely be put to death; their blood shall be upon them.

¹⁴And if a man take a wife and her mother, it is wickedness: they shall be burnt with fire, both he and they; that there be no wickedness among you,

¹⁵And if a man lie with a beast, he shall surely be put to death: and ye shall slay the beast.

¹⁶And if a woman approach unto any beast, and lie down thereto, thou shalt kill the woman, and the beast: they shall surely be put to death; their blood shall be upon them.

¹⁷And if a man shall take his sister, his father's daughter, or his mother's daughter, and see her nakedness, and she see his nakedness; it is a wicked thing; and they shall be cut off in the sight of their people: he hath uncovered his sister's nakedness; he shall bear his iniquity.

18And if a man shall lie with a woman having her sickness, and shall uncover her nakedness; he hath discovered her fountain, and she hath uncovered the fountain of her blood: and both of them shall be cut off from among their people.

19And thou shalt not uncover the nakedness of thy mother's sister, nor of thy father's sister: for he uncovereth his near kin: they shall bear their iniquity.

20And if a man shall lie with his uncle's wife, he hath uncovered his uncle's nakedness: they shall bear their sin; they shall die childless.

21And if a man shall take his brother's wife, it is an unclean thing: he hath uncovered his brother's nakedness; they shall be childless.

22Ye shall therefore keep all my statutes, and all my judgments, and do them: that the land, whither I bring you to dwell therein, spue you not out.

23And ye shall not walk in the manners of the nation, which I cast out before you: for they committed all these things, and therefore I abhorred them.

24But I have said unto you, Ye shall inherit their land, and I will give it unto you to possess it, a land that floweth with milk and honey: I am the LORD your God, which have separated you from other people.

25Ye shall therefore put difference between clean beasts and unclean, and between unclean fowls and clean: and ye shall not make your souls abominable by beast, or by fowl, or by any manner of living thing that creepeth on the ground, which I have separated from you as unclean.

26And ye shall be holy unto me: for I the LORD am holy, and have severed you from other people, that ye should be mine.

27A man also or woman that hath a familiar spirit, or that is a wizard, shall surely be put to death: they shall stone them with stones: their blood shall be upon them.

CHAPTER 21

1And the LORD said unto Moses, Speak unto the priests the sons of Aaron, and say unto them, There shall none be defiled for the dead among his people:

2But for his kin, that is near unto him, that is, for his mother, and for his father, and for his son, and for his daughter, and for his brother.

3And for his sister a virgin, that is nigh unto him, which hath had no husband; for her may he be defiled.

[4]But he shall not defile himself, being a chief man among his people, to profane himself.

[5]They shall not make baldness upon their head, neither shall they shave off the corner of their beard, nor make any cuttings in their flesh.

[6]They shall be holy unto their God, and not profane the name of their God: for the offerings of the LORD made by fire, and the bread of their God, they do offer: therefore they shall be holy.

[7]They shall not take a wife that is a whore, or profane; neither shall they take a woman put away from her husband: for he is holy unto his God.

[8]Thou shalt sanctify him therefore; for he offereth the bread of thy God: he shall be holy unto thee: for I the LORD, which sanctify you, am holy.

[9]And the daughter of any priest, if she profane herself by playing the whore, she profaneth her father: she shall be burnt with fire.

[10]And he that is the high priest among his brethren, upon whose head the anointing oil was poured, and that is consecrated to put on the garments, shall not uncover his head, nor rend his clothes;

[11]Neither shall he go in to any dead body, nor defile himself for his father, or for his mother;

[12]Neither shall he go out of the sanctuary, nor profane the sanctuary of his God; for the crown of the anointing oil of his God is upon him: I am the LORD.

[13]And he shall take a wife in her virginity.

[14]A widow, or a divorced woman, or profane, or an harlot, these shall he not take: but he shall take a virgin of his own people to wife.

[15]Neither shall he profane his seed among his people: for I the LORD do sanctify him.

[16]And the LORD spake unto Moses, saying,

[17]Speak unto Aaron, saying, Whosoever he be of thy seed in their generations that hath any blemish, let him not approach to offer the bread of his God.

[18]For whatsoever man he be that hath a blemish, he shall not approach: a blind man, or a lame, or he that hath a flat nose, or any thing superfluous,

[19]Or a man that is brokenfooted, or brokenhanded,

[20]Or crookbackt, or a dwarf, or that hath a blemish in his eye, or be scurvy, or scabbed, or hath his stones broken;

[21]No man that hath a blemish of the seed of Aaron the priest shall come nigh to offer the offerings of the LORD made by fire: he hath a

blemish; he shall not come nigh to offer the bread of his God.

²²He shall eat the bread of his God, both of the most holy, and of the holy.

²³Only he shall not go in unto the vail, nor come nigh unto the altar, because he hath a blemish; that he profane not my sanctuaries: for I the LORD do sanctify them.

²⁴And Moses told it unto Aaron, and to his sons, and unto all the children of Israel.

CHAPTER 22

¹And the LORD spake unto Moses, saying,

²Speak unto Aaron and to his sons, that they separate themselves from the holy things of the children of Israel, and that they profane not my holy name in those things which they hallow unto me: I am the LORD.

³Say unto them, Whosoever he be of all your seed among your generations, that goeth unto the holy things, which the children of Israel hallow unto the LORD, having his uncleanness upon him, that soul shall be cut off from my presence: I am the LORD.

⁴What man soever of the seed of Aaron is a leper, or hath a running issue; he shall not eat of the holy things, until he be clean. And whoso toucheth any thing that is unclean by the dead, or a man whose seed goeth from him;

⁵Or whosoever toucheth any creeping thing, whereby he may be made unclean, or a man of whom he may take uncleanness, whatsoever uncleanness he hath;

⁶The soul which hath touched any such shall be unclean until even, and shall not eat of the holy things, unless he wash his flesh with water.

⁷And when the sun is down, he shall be clean, and shall afterward eat of the holy things; because it is his food.

⁸That which dieth of itself, or is torn with beasts, he shall not eat to defile himself therewith; I am the LORD.

⁹They shall therefore keep mine ordinance, lest they bear sin for it, and die therefore, if they profane it: I the LORD do sanctify them.

¹⁰There shall no stranger eat of the holy thing: a sojourner of the priest, or an hired servant, shall not eat of the holy thing.

¹¹But if the priest buy any soul with his money, he shall eat of it, and he that is born in his house: they shall eat of his meat.

¹²If the priest's daughter also be married unto a stranger, she may not eat of an offering of the holy things.

¹³But if the priest's daughter be a widow, or divorced, and have no child, and is returned unto her father's house, as in her youth, she shall eat of her father's meat: but there shall be no stranger eat thereof.

¹⁴And if a man eat of the holy thing unwittingly, then he shall put the fifth part thereof unto it, and shall give it unto the priest with the holy thing.

¹⁵And they shall not profane the holy things of the children of Israel, which they offer unto the LORD;

¹⁶Or suffer them to bear the iniquity of trespass, when they eat their holy things: for I the LORD do sanctify them.

¹⁷And the LORD spake unto Moses, saying,

¹⁸Speak unto Aaron, and to his sons, and unto all the children of Israel, and say unto them, Whatsoever he be of the house of Israel, or of the strangers in Israel, that will offer his oblation for all his vows, and for all his freewill offerings, which they will offer unto the LORD for a burnt offering;

¹⁹Ye shall offer at your own will a male without blemish, of the beeves, of the sheep, or of the goats.

²⁰But whatsoever hath a blemish, that shall ye not offer: for it shall not be acceptable for you.

²¹And whosoever offereth a sacrifice of peace offerings unto the LORD to accomplish his vow, or a freewill offering in beeves or sheep, it shall be perfect to be accepted; there shall be no blemish therein.

²²Blind, or broken, or maimed, or having a wen, or scurvy, or scabbed, ye shall not offer these unto the LORD, nor make an offering by fire of them upon the altar unto the LORD.

²³Either a bullock or a lamb that hath any thing superfluous or lacking in his parts, that mayest thou offer for a freewill offering; but for a vow it shall not be accepted.

²⁴Ye shall not offer unto the LORD that which is bruised, or crushed, or broken, or cut; neither shall ye make any offering thereof in your land.

²⁵Neither from a stranger's hand shall ye offer the bread of your God of any of these; because their corruption is in them, and blemishes be in them: they shall not be accepted for you.

²⁶And the LORD spake unto Moses, saying,

²⁷When a bullock, or a sheep, or a goat, is brought forth, then it shall be seven days under the dam; and

from the eighth day and thenceforth it shall be accepted for an offering made by fire unto the LORD.

²⁸And whether it be cow, or ewe, ye shall not kill it and her young both in one day.

²⁹And when ye will offer a sacrifice of thanksgiving unto the LORD, offer it at your own will.

³⁰On the same day it shall be eaten up; ye shall leave none of it until the morrow: I am the LORD.

³¹Therefore shall ye keep my commandments, and do them: I am the LORD.

³²Neither shall ye profane my holy name; but I will be hallowed among the children of Israel: I am the LORD which hallow you,

³³That brought you out of the land of Egypt, to be your God: I am the LORD.

CHAPTER 23

¹And the LORD spake unto Moses, saying,

²Speak unto the children of Israel, and say unto them, Concerning the feasts of the LORD, which ye shall proclaim to be holy convocations, even these are my feasts.

³Six days shall work be done: but the seventh day is the sabbath of rest, an holy convocation; ye shall do no work therein: it is the sabbath of the LORD in all your dwellings.

⁴These are the feasts of the LORD, even holy convocations, which ye shall proclaim in their seasons.

⁵In the fourteenth day of the first month at even is the LORD's passover.

⁶And on the fifteenth day of the same month is the feast of unleavened bread unto the LORD: seven days ye must eat unleavened bread.

⁷In the first day ye shall have an holy convocation: ye shall do no servile work therein.

⁸But ye shall offer an offering made by fire unto the LORD seven days: in the seventh day is an holy convocation: ye shall do no servile work therein.

⁹And the LORD spake unto Moses, saying,

¹⁰Speak unto the children of Israel, and say unto them, When ye be come into the land which I give unto you, and shall reap the harvest thereof, then ye shall bring a sheaf of the firstfruits of your harvest unto the priest:

¹¹And he shall wave the sheaf before the LORD, to be accepted for you: on the morrow after the sabbath the priest shall wave it.

¹²And ye shall offer that day when ye wave the sheaf an he lamb without blemish of the first year for a burnt offering unto the LORD.

¹³And the meat offering thereof shall be two tenth deals of fine flour mingled with oil, an offering made by fire unto the LORD for a sweet savour: and the drink offering thereof shall be of wine, the fourth part of an hin.

¹⁴And ye shall eat neither bread, nor parched corn, nor green ears, until the selfsame day that ye have brought an offering unto your God: it shall be a statute for ever throughout your generations in all your dwellings.

¹⁵And ye shall count unto you from the morrow after the sabbath, from the day that ye brought the sheaf of the wave offering; seven sabbaths shall be complete:

¹⁶Even unto the morrow after the seventh sabbath shall ye number fifty days; and ye shall offer a new meat offering unto the LORD.

¹⁷Ye shall bring out of your habitations two wave loaves of two tenth deals; they shall be of fine flour; they shall be baken with leaven; they are the firstfruits unto the LORD.

¹⁸And ye shall offer with the bread seven lambs without blemish of the first year, and one young bullock, and two rams: they shall be for a burnt offering unto the LORD, with their meat offering, and their drink offerings, even an offering made by fire, of sweet savour unto the LORD.

¹⁹Then ye shall sacrifice one kid of the goats for a sin offering, and two lambs of the first year for a sacrifice of peace offerings.

²⁰And the priest shall wave them with the bread of the firstfruits for a wave offering before the LORD, with the two lambs: they shall be holy to the LORD for the priest.

²¹And ye shall proclaim on the selfsame day, that it may be an holy convocation unto you: ye shall do no servile work therein: it shall be a statute for ever in all your dwellings throughout your generations.

²²And when ye reap the harvest of your land, thou shalt not make clean riddance of the corners of thy field when thou reapest, neither shalt thou gather any gleaning of thy harvest: thou shalt leave them unto the poor, and to the stranger: I am the LORD your God.

²³And the LORD spake unto Moses, saying,

²⁴Speak unto the children of Israel, saying, In the seventh month, in the first day of the month, shall ye have a sabbath, a memorial

of blowing of trumpets, an holy convocation.

²⁵Ye shall do no servile work therein: but ye shall offer an offering made by fire unto the LORD.

²⁶And the LORD spake unto Moses, saying,

²⁷Also on the tenth day of this seventh month there shall be a day of atonement: it shall be an holy convocation unto you; and ye shall afflict your souls, and offer an offering made by fire unto the LORD.

²⁸And ye shall do no work in that same day: for it is a day of atonement, to make an atonement for you before the LORD your God.

²⁹For whatsoever soul it be that shall not be afflicted in that same day, he shall be cut off from among his people.

³⁰And whatsoever soul it be that doeth any work in that same day, the same soul will I destroy from among his people.

³¹Ye shall do no manner of work: it shall be a statute for ever throughout your generations in all your dwellings.

³²It shall be unto you a sabbath of rest, and ye shall afflict your souls: in the ninth day of the month at even, from even unto even, shall ye celebrate your sabbath.

³³And the LORD spake unto Moses, saying,

³⁴Speak unto the children of Israel, saying, The fifteenth day of this seventh month shall be the feast of tabernacles for seven days unto the LORD.

³⁵On the first day shall be an holy convocation: ye shall do no servile work therein.

³⁶Seven days ye shall offer an offering made by fire unto the LORD: on the eighth day shall be an holy convocation unto you; and ye shall offer an offering made by fire unto the LORD: it is a solemn assembly; and ye shall do no servile work therein.

³⁷These are the feasts of the LORD, which ye shall proclaim to be holy convocations, to offer an offering made by fire unto the LORD, a burnt offering, and a meat offering, a sacrifice, and drink offerings, every thing upon his day:

³⁸Beside the sabbaths of the LORD, and beside your gifts, and beside all your vows, and beside all your freewill offerings, which ye give unto the LORD.

³⁹Also in the fifteenth day of the seventh month, when ye have gathered in the fruit of the land, ye shall keep a feast unto the LORD seven days: on the first day shall be a

sabbath, and on the eighth day shall be a sabbath.

⁴⁰And ye shall take you on the first day the boughs of goodly trees, branches of palm trees, and the boughs of thick trees, and willows of the brook; and ye shall rejoice before the LORD your God seven days.

⁴¹And ye shall keep it a feast unto the LORD seven days in the year. It shall be a statute for ever in your generations: ye shall celebrate it in the seventh month.

⁴²Ye shall dwell in booths seven days; all that are Israelites born shall dwell in booths:

⁴³That your generations may know that I made the children of Israel to dwell in booths, when I brought them out of the land of Egypt: I am the LORD your God.

⁴⁴And Moses declared unto the children of Israel the feasts of the LORD.

CHAPTER 24

¹And the LORD spake unto Moses, saying,

²Command the children of Israel, that they bring unto thee pure oil olive beaten for the light, to cause the lamps to burn continually.

³Without the vail of the testimony, in the tabernacle of the congregation, shall Aaron order it from the evening unto the morning before the LORD continually: it shall be a statute for ever in your generations.

⁴He shall order the lamps upon the pure candlestick before the LORD continually.

⁵And thou shalt take fine flour, and bake twelve cakes thereof: two tenth deals shall be in one cake.

⁶And thou shalt set them in two rows, six on a row, upon the pure table before the LORD.

⁷And thou shalt put pure frankincense upon each row, that it may be on the bread for a memorial, even an offering made by fire unto the LORD.

⁸Every sabbath he shall set it in order before the LORD continually, being taken from the children of Israel by an everlasting covenant.

⁹And it shall be Aaron's and his sons'; and they shall eat it in the holy place: for it is most holy unto him of the offerings of the LORD made by fire by a perpetual statute.

¹⁰And the son of an Israelitish woman, whose father was an Egyptian, went out among the children of Israel: and this son of the Israelitish woman and a man of Israel strove together in the camp;

¹¹And the Israelitish woman's son blasphemed the name of the Lord, and cursed. And they brought him unto Moses: (and his mother's name was Shelomith, the daughter of Dibri, of the tribe of Dan:)

¹²And they put him in ward, that the mind of the LORD might be shewed them.

¹³And the LORD spake unto Moses, saying,

¹⁴Bring forth him that hath cursed without the camp; and let all that heard him lay their hands upon his head, and let all the congregation stone him.

¹⁵And thou shalt speak unto the children of Israel, saying, Whosoever curseth his God shall bear his sin.

¹⁶And he that blasphemeth the name of the LORD, he shall surely be put to death, and all the congregation shall certainly stone him: as well the stranger, as he that is born in the land, when he blasphemeth the name of the Lord, shall be put to death.

¹⁷And he that killeth any man shall surely be put to death.

¹⁸And he that killeth a beast shall make it good; beast for beast.

¹⁹And if a man cause a blemish in his neighbour; as he hath done, so shall it be done to him;

²⁰Breach for breach, eye for eye, tooth for tooth: as he hath caused a blemish in a man, so shall it be done to him again.

²¹And he that killeth a beast, he shall restore it: and he that killeth a man, he shall be put to death.

²²Ye shall have one manner of law, as well for the stranger, as for one of your own country: for I am the LORD your God.

²³And Moses spake to the children of Israel, that they should bring forth him that had cursed out of the camp, and stone him with stones. And the children of Israel did as the LORD commanded Moses.

CHAPTER 25

¹And the LORD spake unto Moses in mount Sinai, saying,

²Speak unto the children of Israel, and say unto them, When ye come into the land which I give you, then shall the land keep a sabbath unto the LORD.

³Six years thou shalt sow thy field, and six years thou shalt prune thy vineyard, and gather in the fruit thereof;

⁴But in the seventh year shall be a sabbath of rest unto the land, a sabbath for the LORD: thou shalt neither sow thy field, nor prune thy vineyard.

⁵That which groweth of its own accord of thy harvest thou shalt not reap, neither gather the grapes of thy vine undressed: for it is a year of rest unto the land.

⁶And the sabbath of the land shall be meat for you; for thee, and for thy servant, and for thy maid, and for thy hired servant, and for thy stranger that sojourneth with thee.

⁷And for thy cattle, and for the beast that are in thy land, shall all the increase thereof be meat.

⁸And thou shalt number seven sabbaths of years unto thee, seven times seven years; and the space of the seven sabbaths of years shall be unto thee forty and nine years.

⁹Then shalt thou cause the trumpet of the jubile to sound on the tenth day of the seventh month, in the day of atonement shall ye make the trumpet sound throughout all your land.

¹⁰And ye shall hallow the fiftieth year, and proclaim liberty throughout all the land unto all the inhabitants thereof: it shall be a jubile unto you; and ye shall return every man unto his possession, and ye shall return every man unto his family.

¹¹A jubile shall that fiftieth year be unto you: ye shall not sow, neither reap that which groweth of itself in it, nor gather the grapes in it of thy vine undressed.

¹²For it is the jubile; it shall be holy unto you: ye shall eat the increase thereof out of the field.

¹³In the year of this jubile ye shall return every man unto his possession.

¹⁴And if thou sell ought unto thy neighbour, or buyest ought of thy neighbour's hand, ye shall not oppress one another:

¹⁵According to the number of years after the jubile thou shalt buy of thy neighbour, and according unto the number of years of the fruits he shall sell unto thee:

¹⁶According to the multitude of years thou shalt increase the price thereof, and according to the fewness of years thou shalt diminish the price of it: for according to the number of the years of the fruits doth he sell unto thee.

¹⁷Ye shall not therefore oppress one another; but thou shalt fear thy God: for I am the LORD your God.

¹⁸Wherefore ye shall do my statutes, and keep my judgments, and do them; and ye shall dwell in the land in safety.

¹⁹And the land shall yield her fruit, and ye shall eat your fill, and dwell therein in safety.

²⁰And if ye shall say, What shall we eat the seventh year? behold, we shall not sow, nor gather in our increase:

²¹Then I will command my blessing upon you in the sixth year, and it shall bring forth fruit for three years.

²²And ye shall sow the eighth year, and eat yet of old fruit until the ninth year; until her fruits come in ye shall eat of the old store.

²³The land shall not be sold for ever: for the land is mine, for ye are strangers and sojourners with me.

²⁴And in all the land of your possession ye shall grant a redemption for the land.

²⁵If thy brother be waxen poor, and hath sold away some of his possession, and if any of his kin come to redeem it, then shall he redeem that which his brother sold.

²⁶And if the man have none to redeem it, and himself be able to redeem it;

²⁷Then let him count the years of the sale thereof, and restore the overplus unto the man to whom he sold it; that he may return unto his possession.

²⁸But if he be not able to restore it to him, then that which is sold shall remain in the hand of him that hath bought it until the year of jubile: and in the jubile it shall go out, and he shall return unto his possession.

²⁹And if a man sell a dwelling house in a walled city, then he may redeem it within a whole year after it is sold; within a full year may he redeem it.

³⁰And if it be not redeemed within the space of a full year, then the house that is in the walled city shall be established for ever to him that bought it throughout his generations: it shall not go out in the jubile.

³¹But the houses of the villages which have no wall round about them shall be counted as the fields of the country: they may be redeemed, and they shall go out in the jubile.

³²Notwithstanding the cities of the Levites, and the houses of the cities of their possession, may the Levites redeem at any time.

³³And if a man purchase of the Levites, then the house that was sold, and the city of his possession, shall go out in the year of jubile: for the houses of the cities of the Levites are their possession among the children of Israel.

³⁴But the field of the suburbs of their cities may not be sold; for it is their perpetual possession.

³⁵And if thy brother be waxen poor, and fallen in decay with thee; then thou shalt relieve him: yea, though he be a stranger, or a sojourner; that he may live with thee.

³⁶Take thou no usury of him, or increase: but fear thy God; that thy brother may live with thee.

³⁷Thou shalt not give him thy money upon usury, nor lend him thy victuals for increase.

³⁸I am the LORD your God, which brought you forth out of the land of Egypt, to give you the land of Canaan, and to be your God.

³⁹And if thy brother that dwelleth by thee be waxen poor, and be sold unto thee; thou shalt not compel him to serve as a bondservant:

⁴⁰But as an hired servant, and as a sojourner, he shall be with thee, and shall serve thee unto the year of jubile.

⁴¹And then shall he depart from thee, both he and his children with him, and shall return unto his own family, and unto the possession of his fathers shall he return.

⁴²For they are my servants, which I brought forth out of the land of Egypt: they shall not be sold as bondmen.

⁴³Thou shalt not rule over him with rigour; but shalt fear thy God.

⁴⁴Both thy bondmen, and thy bondmaids, which thou shalt have, shall be of the heathen that are round about you; of them shall ye buy bondmen and bondmaids.

⁴⁵Moreover of the children of the strangers that do sojourn among you, of them shall ye buy, and of their families that are with you, which they begat in your land: and they shall be your possession.

⁴⁶And ye shall take them as an inheritance for your children after you, to inherit them for a possession; they shall be your bondmen for ever: but over your brethren the children of Israel, ye shall not rule one over another with rigour.

⁴⁷And if a sojourner or stranger wax rich by thee, and thy brother that dwelleth by him wax poor, and sell himself unto the stranger or sojourner by thee, or to the stock of the stranger's family:

⁴⁸After that he is sold he may be redeemed again; one of his brethren may redeem him:

⁴⁹Either his uncle, or his uncle's son, may redeem him, or any that is nigh of kin unto him of his family may redeem him; or if he be able, he may redeem himself.

⁵⁰And he shall reckon with him that bought him from the year that he was sold to him unto the year of jubile: and the price of his sale shall be according unto the number of years, according to the time of an hired servant shall it be with him.

⁵¹If there be yet many years behind, according unto them he shall give again the price of his redemption out of the money that he was bought for.

⁵²And if there remain but few years unto the year of jubile, then he shall count with him, and according unto his years shall he give him again the price of his redemption.

⁵³And as a yearly hired servant shall he be with him: and the other shall not rule with rigour over him in thy sight.

⁵⁴And if he be not redeemed in these years, then he shall go out in the year of jubile, both he, and his children with him.

⁵⁵For unto me the children of Israel are servants; they are my servants whom I brought forth out of the land of Egypt: I am the LORD your God.

CHAPTER 26

¹Ye shall make you no idols nor graven image, neither rear you up a standing image, neither shall ye set up any image of stone in your land, to bow down unto it: for I am the LORD your God.

²Ye shall keep my sabbaths, and reverence my sanctuary: I am the LORD.

³If ye walk in my statutes, and keep my commandments, and do them;

⁴Then I will give you rain in due season, and the land shall yield her increase, and the trees of the field shall yield their fruit.

⁵And your threshing shall reach unto the vintage, and the vintage shall reach unto the sowing time: and ye shall eat your bread to the full, and dwell in your land safely.

⁶And I will give peace in the land, and ye shall lie down, and none shall make you afraid: and I will rid evil beasts out of the land, neither shall the sword go through your land.

⁷And ye shall chase your enemies, and they shall fall before you by the sword.

⁸And five of you shall chase an hundred, and an hundred of you shall put ten thousand to flight: and your enemies shall fall before you by the sword.

⁹For I will have respect unto you, and make you fruitful, and multiply you, and establish my covenant with you.

¹⁰And ye shall eat old store, and bring forth the old because of the new.

¹¹And I set my tabernacle among you: and my soul shall not abhor you.

¹²And I will walk among you, and will be your God, and ye shall be my people.

¹³I am the LORD your God, which brought you forth out of the

land of Egypt, that ye should not be their bondmen; and I have broken the bands of your yoke, and made you go upright.

¹⁴But if ye will not hearken unto me, and will not do all these commandments;

¹⁵And if ye shall despise my statutes, or if your soul abhor my judgments, so that ye will not do all my commandments, but that ye break my covenant:

¹⁶I also will do this unto you; I will even appoint over you terror, consumption, and the burning ague, that shall consume the eyes, and cause sorrow of heart: and ye shall sow your seed in vain, for your enemies shall eat it.

¹⁷And I will set my face against you, and ye shall be slain before your enemies: they that hate you shall reign over you; and ye shall flee when none pursueth you.

¹⁸And if ye will not yet for all this hearken unto me, then I will punish you seven times more for your sins.

¹⁹And I will break the pride of your power; and I will make your heaven as iron, and your earth as brass:

²⁰And your strength shall be spent in vain: for your land shall not yield her increase, neither shall the trees of the land yield their fruits.

²¹And if ye walk contrary unto me, and will not hearken unto me; I will bring seven times more plagues upon you according to your sins.

²²I will also send wild beasts among you, which shall rob you of your children, and destroy your cattle, and make you few in number; and your high ways shall be desolate.

²³And if ye will not be reformed by me by these things, but will walk contrary unto me;

²⁴Then will I also walk contrary unto you, and will punish you yet seven times for your sins.

²⁵And I will bring a sword upon you, that shall avenge the quarrel of my covenant: and when ye are gathered together within your cities, I will send the pestilence among you; and ye shall be delivered into the hand of the enemy.

²⁶And when I have broken the staff of your bread, ten women shall bake your bread in one oven, and they shall deliver you your bread again by weight: and ye shall eat, and not be satisfied.

²⁷And if ye will not for all this hearken unto me, but walk contrary unto me;

²⁸Then I will walk contrary unto you also in fury; and I, even I, will chastise you seven times for your sins.

²⁹And ye shall eat the flesh of your sons, and the flesh of your daughters shall ye eat.

³⁰And I will destroy your high places, and cut down your images, and cast your carcases upon the carcases of your idols, and my soul shall abhor you.

³¹And I will make your cities waste, and bring your sanctuaries unto desolation, and I will not smell the savour of your sweet odours.

³²And I will bring the land into desolation: and your enemies which dwell therein shall be astonished at it.

³³And I will scatter you among the heathen, and will draw out a sword after you: and your land shall be desolate, and your cities waste.

³⁴Then shall the land enjoy her sabbaths, as long as it lieth desolate, and ye be in your enemies' land; even then shall the land rest, and enjoy her sabbaths.

³⁵As long as it lieth desolate it shall rest; because it did not rest in your sabbaths, when ye dwelt upon it.

³⁶And upon them that are left alive of you I will send a faintness into their hearts in the lands of their enemies; and the sound of a shaken leaf shall chase them; and they shall flee, as fleeing from a sword; and they shall fall when none pursueth.

³⁷And they shall fall one upon another, as it were before a sword, when none pursueth: and ye shall have no power to stand before your enemies.

³⁸And ye shall perish among the heathen, and the land of your enemies shall eat you up.

³⁹And they that are left of you shall pine away in their iniquity in your enemies' lands; and also in the iniquities of their fathers shall they pine away with them.

⁴⁰If they shall confess their iniquity, and the iniquity of their fathers, with their trespass which they trespassed against me, and that also they have walked contrary unto me;

⁴¹And that I also have walked contrary unto them, and have brought them into the land of their enemies; if then their uncircumcised hearts be humbled, and they then accept of the punishment of their iniquity:

⁴²Then will I remember my covenant with Jacob, and also my covenant with Isaac, and also my covenant with Abraham will I remember; and I will remember the land.

⁴³The land also shall be left of them, and shall enjoy her sabbaths, while she lieth desolate without them: and they shall accept of the punishment of their iniquity: because, even because they despised my judgments, and because their soul abhorred my statutes.

44And yet for all that, when they be in the land of their enemies, I will not cast them away, neither will I abhor them, to destroy them utterly, and to break my covenant with them: for I am the LORD their God.

45But I will for their sakes remember the covenant of their ancestors, whom I brought forth out of the land of Egypt in the sight of the heathen, that I might be their God: I am the LORD.

46These are the statutes and judgments and laws, which the LORD made between him and the children of Israel in mount Sinai by the hand of Moses.

CHAPTER 27

1And the LORD spake unto Moses, saying,

2Speak unto the children of Israel, and say unto them, When a man shall make a singular vow, the persons shall be for the LORD by thy estimation.

3And thy estimation shall be of the male from twenty years old even unto sixty years old, even thy estimation shall be fifty shekels of silver, after the shekel of the sanctuary.

4And if it be a female, then thy estimation shall be thirty shekels.

5And if it be from five years old even unto twenty years old, then thy estimation shall be of the male twenty shekels, and for the female ten shekels.

6And if it be from a month old even unto five years old, then thy estimation shall be of the male five shekels of silver, and for the female thy estimation shall be three shekels of silver.

7And if it be from sixty years old and above; if it be a male, then thy estimation shall be fifteen shekels, and for the female ten shekels.

8But if he be poorer than thy estimation, then he shall present himself before the priest, and the priest shall value him; according to his ability that vowed shall the priest value him.

9And if it be a beast, whereof men bring an offering unto the LORD, all that any man giveth of such unto the LORD shall be holy.

10He shall not alter it, nor change it, a good for a bad, or a bad for a good: and if he shall at all change beast for beast, then it and the exchange thereof shall be holy.

11And if it be any unclean beast, of which they do not offer a sacrifice unto the LORD, then he shall present the beast before the priest:

¹²And the priest shall value it, whether it be good or bad: as thou valuest it, who art the priest, so shall it be.

¹³But if he will at all redeem it, then he shall add a fifth part thereof unto thy estimation.

¹⁴And when a man shall sanctify his house to be holy unto the LORD, then the priest shall estimate it, whether it be good or bad: as the priest shall estimate it, so shall it stand.

¹⁵And if he that sanctified it will redeem his house, then he shall add the fifth part of the money of thy estimation unto it, and it shall be his.

¹⁶And if a man shall sanctify unto the LORD some part of a field of his possession, then thy estimation shall be according to the seed thereof: an homer of barley seed shall be valued at fifty shekels of silver.

¹⁷If he sanctify his field from the year of jubile, according to thy estimation it shall stand.

¹⁸But if he sanctify his field after the jubile, then the priest shall reckon unto him the money according to the years that remain, even unto the year of the jubile, and it shall be abated from thy estimation.

¹⁹And if he that sanctified the field will in any wise redeem it, then he shall add the fifth part of the money of thy estimation unto it, and it shall be assured to him.

²⁰And if he will not redeem the field, or if he have sold the field to another man, it shall not be redeemed any more.

²¹But the field, when it goeth out in the jubile, shall be holy unto the LORD, as a field devoted; the possession thereof shall be the priest's.

²²And if a man sanctify unto the LORD a field which he hath bought, which is not of the fields of his possession;

²³Then the priest shall reckon unto him the worth of thy estimation, even unto the year of the jubile: and he shall give thine estimation in that day, as a holy thing unto the LORD.

²⁴In the year of the jubile the field shall return unto him of whom it was bought, even to him to whom the possession of the land did belong.

²⁵And all thy estimations shall be according to the shekel of the sanctuary: twenty gerahs shall be the shekel.

²⁶Only the firstling of the beasts, which should be the LORD's firstling, no man shall sanctify it; whether it be ox, or sheep: it is the LORD's.

²⁷And if it be of an unclean beast, then he shall redeem it according

to thine estimation, and shall add a fifth part of it thereto: or if it be not redeemed, then it shall be sold according to thy estimation.

²⁸Notwithstanding no devoted thing, that a man shall devote unto the LORD of all that he hath, both of man and beast, and of the field of his possession, shall be sold or redeemed: every devoted thing is most holy unto the LORD.

²⁹None devoted, which shall be devoted of men, shall be redeemed; but shall surely be put to death.

³⁰And all the tithe of the land, whether of the seed of the land, or of the fruit of the tree, is the LORD's: it is holy unto the LORD.

³¹And if a man will at all redeem ought of his tithes, he shall add thereto the fifth part thereof.

³²And concerning the tithe of the herd, or of the flock, even of whatsoever passeth under the rod, the tenth shall be holy unto the LORD.

³³He shall not search whether it be good or bad, neither shall he change it: and if he change it at all, then both it and the change thereof shall be holy; it shall not be redeemed.

³⁴These are the commandments, which the LORD commanded Moses for the children of Israel in mount Sinai.

NUMBERS

במדבר

CHAPTER 1

¹And the LORD spake unto Moses in the wilderness of Sinai, in the tabernacle of the congregation, on the first day of the second month, in the second year after they were come out of the land of Egypt, saying,

²Take ye the sum of all the congregation of the children of Israel, after their families, by the house of their fathers, with the number of their names, every male by their polls;

³From twenty years old and upward, all that are able to go forth to war in Israel: thou and Aaron shall number them by their armies.

⁴And with you there shall be a man of every tribe; every one head of the house of his fathers.

⁵And these are the names of the men that shall stand with you: of the tribe of Reuben; Elizur the son of Shedeur.

⁶Of Simeon; Shelumiel the son of Zurishaddai.

⁷Of Judah; Nahshon the son of Amminadab.

⁸Of Issachar; Nethaneel the son of Zuar.

⁹Of Zebulun; Eliab the son of Helon.

¹⁰Of the children of Joseph: of Ephraim; Elishama the son of Ammihud: of Manasseh; Gamaliel the son of Pedahzur.

¹¹Of Ben-jamin; Abidan the son of Gideoni.

¹²Of Dan; Ahiezer the son of Ammishaddai.

¹³Of Asher; Pagiel the son of Ocran.

¹⁴Of Gad; Eliasaph the son of Deuel.

¹⁵Of Naphtali; Ahira the son of Enan.

¹⁶These were the renowned of the congregation, princes of the tribes of their fathers, heads of thousands in Israel.

¹⁷And Moses and Aaron took these men which are expressed by their names:

¹⁸And they assembled all the congregation together on the first day of the second month, and they declared their pedigrees after their families, by the house of their fathers, according to the number of the names, from twenty years old and upward, by their polls.

¹⁹As the LORD commanded Moses, so he numbered them in the wilderness of Sinai.

²⁰And the children of Reuben, Israel's eldest son, by their generations, after their families, by the house of their fathers, according to the number of the names, by their polls, every male from twenty years old and upward, all that were able to go forth to war;

²¹Those that were numbered of them, even of the tribe of Reuben, were forty and six thousand and five hundred.

²²Of the children of Simeon, by their generations, after their families, by the house of their fathers, those that were numbered of them, according to the number of the names, by their polls, every male from twenty years old and upward, all that were able to go forth to war;

²³Those that were numbered of them, even of the tribe of Simeon, were fifty and nine thousand and three hundred.

²⁴Of the children of Gad, by their generations, after their families, by the house of their fathers, according to the number of the names, from twenty years old and upward, all that were able to go forth to war;

²⁵Those that were numbered of them, even of the tribe of Gad, were forty and five thousand six hundred and fifty.

²⁶Of the children of Judah, by their generations, after their families, by the house of their fathers, according to the number of the names, from twenty years old and upward, all that were able to go forth to war;

²⁷Those that were numbered of them, even of the tribe of Judah, were threescore and fourteen thousand and six hundred.

²⁸Of the children of Issachar, by their generations, after their families, by the house of their fathers, according to the number of the names, from twenty years old and upward, all that were able to go forth to war;

²⁹Those that were numbered of them, even of the tribe of Issachar, were fifty and four thousand and four hundred.

³⁰Of the children of Zebulun, by their generations, after their families, by the house of their fathers, according to the number of the names, from twenty years old and upward, all that were able to go forth to war;

³¹Those that were numbered of them, even of the tribe of Zebulun, were fifty and seven thousand and four hundred.

³²Of the children of Joseph, namely, of the children of Ephraim,

by their generations, after their families, by the house of their fathers, according to the number of the names, from twenty years old and upward, all that were able to go forth to war;

³³Those that were numbered of them, even of the tribe of Ephraim, were forty thousand and five hundred.

³⁴Of the children of Manasseh, by their generations, after their families, by the house of their fathers, according to the number of the names, from twenty years old and upward, all that were able to go forth to war;

³⁵Those that were numbered of them, even of the tribe of Manasseh, were thirty and two thousand and two hundred.

³⁶Of the children of Ben-jamin, by their generations, after their families, by the house of their fathers, according to the number of the names, from twenty years old and upward, all that were able to go forth to war;

³⁷Those that were numbered of them, even of the tribe of Ben-jamin, were thirty and five thousand and four hundred.

³⁸Of the children of Dan, by their generations, after their families, by the house of their fathers, according to the number of

the names, from twenty years old and upward, all that were able to go forth to war;

³⁹Those that were numbered of them, even of the tribe of Dan, were threescore and two thousand and seven hundred.

⁴⁰Of the children of Asher, by their generations, after their families, by the house of their fathers, according to the number of the names, from twenty years old and upward, all that were able to go forth to war;

⁴¹Those that were numbered of them, even of the tribe of Asher, were forty and one thousand and five hundred.

⁴²Of the children of Naphtali, throughout their generations, after their families, by the house of their fathers, according to the number of the names, from twenty years old and upward, all that were able to go forth to war;

⁴³Those that were numbered of them, even of the tribe of Naphtali, were fifty and three thousand and four hundred.

⁴⁴These are those that were numbered, which Moses and Aaron numbered, and the princes of Israel, being twelve men: each one was for the house of his fathers.

⁴⁵So were all those that were numbered of the children of Israel,

by the house of their fathers, from twenty years old and upward, all that were able to go forth to war in Israel;

⁴⁶Even all they that were numbered were six hundred thousand and three thousand and five hundred and fifty.

⁴⁷But the Levites after the tribe of their fathers were not numbered among them.

⁴⁸For the LORD had spoken unto Moses, saying,

⁴⁹Only thou shalt not number the tribe of Levi, neither take the sum of them among the children of Israel:

⁵⁰But thou shalt appoint the Levites over the tabernacle of testimony, and over all the vessels thereof, and over all things that belong to it: they shall bear the tabernacle, and all the vessels thereof; and they shall minister unto it, and shall encamp round about the tabernacle.

⁵¹And when the tabernacle setteth forward, the Levites shall take it down: and when the tabernacle is to be pitched, the Levites shall set it up: and the stranger that cometh nigh shall be put to death.

⁵²And the children of Israel shall pitch their tents, every man by his own camp, and every man by his own standard, throughout their hosts.

⁵³But the Levites shall pitch round about the tabernacle of testimony, that there be no wrath upon the congregation of the children of Israel: and the Levites shall keep the charge of the tabernacle of testimony.

⁵⁴And the children of Israel did according to all that the LORD commanded Moses, so did they.

CHAPTER 2

¹And the LORD spake unto Moses and unto Aaron, saying,

²Every man of the children of Israel shall pitch by his own standard, with the ensign of their father's house: far off about the tabernacle of the congregation shall they pitch.

³And on the east side toward the rising of the sun shall they of the standard of the camp of Judah pitch throughout their armies: and Nahshon the son of Amminadab shall be captain of the children of Judah.

⁴And his host, and those that were numbered of them, were threescore and fourteen thousand and six hundred.

⁵And those that do pitch next unto him shall be the tribe of

Issachar: and Nethaneel the son of Zuar shall be captain of the children of Issachar.

⁶And his host, and those that were numbered thereof, were fifty and four thousand and four hundred.

⁷Then the tribe of Zebulun: and Eliab the son of Helon shall be captain of the children of Zebulun.

⁸And his host, and those that were numbered thereof, were fifty and seven thousand and four hundred.

⁹All that were numbered in the camp of Judah were an hundred thousand and fourscore thousand and six thousand and four hundred, throughout their armies. These shall first set forth.

¹⁰On the south side shall be the standard of the camp of Reuben according to their armies: and the captain of the children of Reuben shall be Elizur the son of Shedeur.

¹¹And his host, and those that were numbered thereof, were forty and six thousand and five hundred.

¹²And those which pitch by him shall be the tribe of Simeon: and the captain of the children of Simeon shall be Shelumiel the son of Zurishaddai.

¹³And his host, and those that were numbered of them, were fifty and nine thousand and three hundred.

¹⁴Then the tribe of Gad: and the captain of the sons of Gad shall be Eliasaph the son of Reuel.

¹⁵And his host, and those that were numbered of them, were forty and five thousand and six hundred and fifty.

¹⁶All that were numbered in the camp of Reuben were an hundred thousand and fifty and one thousand and four hundred and fifty, throughout their armies. And they shall set forth in the second rank.

¹⁷Then the tabernacle of the congregation shall set forward with the camp of the Levites in the midst of the camp: as they encamp, so shall they set forward, every man in his place by their standards.

¹⁸On the west side shall be the standard of the camp of Ephraim according to their armies: and the captain of the sons of Ephraim shall be Elishama the son of Ammihud.

¹⁹And his host, and those that were numbered of them, were forty thousand and five hundred.

²⁰And by him shall be the tribe of Manasseh: and the captain of the children of Manasseh shall be Gamaliel the son of Pedahzur.

²¹And his host, and those that were numbered of them, were thirty and two thousand and two hundred.

²²Then the tribe of Ben-jamin: and the captain of the sons of Ben-

jamin shall be Abidan the son of Gideoni.

²³And his host, and those that were numbered of them, were thirty and five thousand and four hundred.

²⁴All that were numbered of the camp of Ephraim were an hundred thousand and eight thousand and an hundred, throughout their armies. And they shall go forward in the third rank.

²⁵The standard of the camp of Dan shall be on the north side by their armies: and the captain of the children of Dan shall be Ahiezer the son of Ammishaddai.

²⁶And his host, and those that were numbered of them, were threescore and two thousand and seven hundred.

²⁷And those that encamp by him shall be the tribe of Asher: and the captain of the children of Asher shall be Pagiel the son of Ocran.

²⁸And his host, and those that were numbered of them, were forty and one thousand and five hundred.

²⁹Then the tribe of Naphtali: and the captain of the children of Naphtali shall be Ahira the son of Enan.

³⁰And his host, and those that were numbered of them, were fifty and three thousand and four hundred.

³¹All they that were numbered in the camp of Dan were an hundred thousand and fifty and seven thousand and six hundred. They shall go hindmost with their standards.

³²These are those which were numbered of the children of Israel by the house of their fathers: all those that were numbered of the camps throughout their hosts were six hundred thousand and three thousand and five hundred and fifty.

³³But the Levites were not numbered among the children of Israel; as the LORD commanded Moses.

³⁴And the children of Israel did according to all that the LORD commanded Moses: so they pitched by their standards, and so they set forward, every one after their families, according to the house of their fathers.

CHAPTER 3

¹These also are the generations of Aaron and Moses in the day that the LORD spake with Moses in mount Sinai.

²And these are the names of the sons of Aaron; Nadab the firstborn, and Abihu, Eleazar, and Ithamar.

³These are the names of the sons of Aaron, the priests which were

anointed, whom he consecrated to minister in the priest's office.

⁴And Nadab and Abihu died before the LORD, when they offered strange fire before the LORD, in the wilderness of Sinai, and they had no children: and Eleazar and Ithamar ministered in the priest's office in the sight of Aaron their father.

⁵And the LORD spake unto Moses, saying,

⁶Bring the tribe of Levi near, and present them before Aaron the priest, that they may minister unto him.

⁷And they shall keep his charge, and the charge of the whole congregation before the tabernacle of the congregation, to do the service of the tabernacle.

⁸And they shall keep all the instruments of the tabernacle of the congregation, and the charge of the children of Israel, to do the service of the tabernacle.

⁹And thou shalt give the Levites unto Aaron and to his sons: they are wholly given unto him out of the children of Israel.

¹⁰And thou shalt appoint Aaron and his sons, and they shall wait on their priest's office: and the stranger that cometh nigh shall be put to death.

¹¹And the LORD spake unto Moses, saying,

¹²And I, behold, I have taken the Levites from among the children of Israel instead of all the firstborn that openeth the matrix among the children of Israel: therefore the Levites shall be mine;

¹³Because all the firstborn are mine; for on the day that I smote all the firstborn in the land of Egypt I hallowed unto me all the firstborn in Israel, both man and beast: mine shall they be: I am the LORD.

¹⁴And the LORD spake unto Moses in the wilderness of Sinai, saying,

¹⁵Number the children of Levi after the house of their fathers, by their families: every male from a month old and upward shalt thou number them.

¹⁶And Moses numbered them according to the word of the LORD, as he was commanded.

¹⁷And these were the sons of Levi by their names; Gershon, and Kohath, and Merari.

¹⁸And these are the names of the sons of Gershon by their families; Libni, and Shimei.

¹⁹And the sons of Kohath by their families; Amram, and Izehar, Hebron, and Uzziel.

²⁰And the sons of Merari by their families; Mahli, and Mushi. These are the families of the Levites

according to the house of their fathers.

²¹Of Gershon was the family of the Libnites, and the family of the Shimites: these are the families of the Gershonites.

²²Those that were numbered of them, according to the number of all the males, from a month old and upward, even those that were numbered of them were seven thousand and five hundred.

²³The families of the Gershonites shall pitch behind the tabernacle westward.

²⁴And the chief of the house of the father of the Gershonites shall be Eliasaph the son of Lael.

²⁵And the charge of the sons of Gershon in the tabernacle of the congregation shall be the tabernacle, and the tent, the covering thereof, and the hanging for the door of the tabernacle of the congregation,

²⁶And the hangings of the court, and the curtain for the door of the court, which is by the tabernacle, and by the altar round about, and the cords of it for all the service thereof.

²⁷And of Kohath was the family of the Amramites, and the family of the Izeharites, and the family of the Hebronites, and the family of the Uzzielites: these are the families of the Kohathites.

²⁸In the number of all the males, from a month old and upward, were eight thousand and six hundred, keeping the charge of the sanctuary.

²⁹The families of the sons of Kohath shall pitch on the side of the tabernacle southward.

³⁰And the chief of the house of the father of the families of the Kohathites shall be Elizaphan the son of Uzziel.

³¹And their charge shall be the ark, and the table, and the candlestick, and the altars, and the vessels of the sanctuary wherewith they minister, and the hanging, and all the service thereof.

³²And Eleazar the son of Aaron the priest shall be chief over the chief of the Levites, and have the oversight of them that keep the charge of the sanctuary.

³³Of Merari was the family of the Mahlites, and the family of the Mushites: these are the families of Merari.

³⁴And those that were numbered of them, according to the number of all the males, from a month old and upward, were six thousand and two hundred.

³⁵And the chief of the house of the father of the families of Merari was Zuriel the son of Abihail: these shall pitch on the side of the tabernacle northward.

³⁶And under the custody and charge of the sons of Merari shall be the boards of the tabernacle, and the bars thereof, and the pillars thereof, and the sockets thereof, and all the vessels thereof, and all that serveth thereto,

³⁷And the pillars of the court round about, and their sockets, and their pins, and their cords.

³⁸But those that encamp before the tabernacle toward the east, even before the tabernacle of the congregation eastward, shall be Moses, and Aaron and his sons, keeping the charge of the sanctuary for the charge of the children of Israel; and the stranger that cometh nigh shall be put to death.

³⁹All that were numbered of the Levites, which Moses and Aaron numbered at the commandment of the LORD, throughout their families, all the males from a month old and upward, were twenty and two thousand.

⁴⁰And the LORD said unto Moses, Number all the firstborn of the males of the children of Israel from a month old and upward, and take the number of their names.

⁴¹And thou shalt take the Levites for me (I am the LORD) instead of all the firstborn among the children of Israel; and the cattle of the Levites instead of all the firstlings among the cattle of the children of Israel.

⁴²And Moses numbered, as the LORD commanded him, all the firstborn among the children of Israel.

⁴³And all the firstborn males by the number of names, from a month old and upward, of those that were numbered of them, were twenty and two thousand two hundred and threescore and thirteen.

⁴⁴And the LORD spake unto Moses, saying,

⁴⁵Take the Levites instead of all the firstborn among the children of Israel, and the cattle of the Levites instead of their cattle; and the Levites shall be mine: I am the LORD.

⁴⁶And for those that are to be redeemed of the two hundred and threescore and thirteen of the firstborn of the children of Israel, which are more than the Levites;

⁴⁷Thou shalt even take five shekels apiece by the poll, after the shekel of the sanctuary shalt thou take them: (the shekel is twenty gerahs:)

⁴⁸And thou shalt give the money, wherewith the odd number of them is to be redeemed, unto Aaron and to his sons.

⁴⁹And Moses took the redemption money of them that were over and above them that were redeemed by the Levites:

^{50}Of the firstborn of the children of Israel took he the money; a thousand three hundred and threescore and five shekels, after the shekel of the sanctuary:

^{51}And Moses gave the money of them that were redeemed unto Aaron and to his sons, according to the word of the LORD, as the LORD commanded Moses.

CHAPTER 4

^{1}And the LORD spake unto Moses and unto Aaron, saying,

^{2}Take the sum of the sons of Kohath from among the sons of Levi, after their families, by the house of their fathers,

^{3}From thirty years old and upward even until fifty years old, all that enter into the host, to do the work in the tabernacle of the congregation.

^{4}This shall be the service of the sons of Kohath in the tabernacle of the congregation, about the most holy things:

^{5}And when the camp setteth forward, Aaron shall come, and his sons, and they shall take down the covering vail, and cover the ark of testimony with it:

^{6}And shall put thereon the covering of badgers' skins, and shall spread over it a cloth wholly of blue, and shall put in the staves thereof.

^{7}And upon the table of shewbread they shall spread a cloth of blue, and put thereon the dishes, and the spoons, and the bowls, and covers to cover withal: and the continual bread shall be thereon:

^{8}And they shall spread upon them a cloth of scarlet, and cover the same with a covering of badgers' skins, and shall put in the staves thereof.

^{9}And they shall take a cloth of blue, and cover the candlestick of the light, and his lamps, and his tongs, and his snuffdishes, and all the oil vessels thereof, wherewith they minister unto it:

^{10}And they shall put it and all the vessels thereof within a covering of badgers' skins, and shall put it upon a bar.

^{11}And upon the golden altar they shall spread a cloth of blue, and cover it with a covering of badgers' skins, and shall put to the staves thereof:

^{12}And they shall take all the instruments of ministry, wherewith they minister in the sanctuary, and put them in a cloth of blue, and cover them with a covering of badgers' skins, and shall put them on a bar:

^{13}And they shall take away the ashes from the altar, and spread a purple cloth thereon:

¹⁴And they shall put upon it all the vessels thereof, wherewith they minister about it, even the censers, the fleshhooks, and the shovels, and the basons, all the vessels of the altar; and they shall spread upon it a covering of badgers' skins, and put to the staves of it.

¹⁵And when Aaron and his sons have made an end of covering the sanctuary, and all the vessels of the sanctuary, as the camp is to set forward; after that, the sons of Kohath shall come to bear it: but they shall not touch any holy thing, lest they die. These things are the burden of the sons of Kohath in the tabernacle of the congregation.

¹⁶And to the office of Eleazar the son of Aaron the priest pertaineth the oil for the light, and the sweet incense, and the daily meat offering, and the anointing oil, and the oversight of all the tabernacle, and of all that therein is, in the sanctuary, and in the vessels thereof.

¹⁷And the LORD spake unto Moses and unto Aaron saying,

¹⁸Cut ye not off the tribe of the families of the Kohathites from among the Levites:

¹⁹But thus do unto them, that they may live, and not die, when they approach unto the most holy things: Aaron and his sons shall go in, and appoint them every one to his service and to his burden:

²⁰But they shall not go in to see when the holy things are covered, lest they die.

²¹And the LORD spake unto Moses, saying,

²²Take also the sum of the sons of Gershon, throughout the houses of their fathers, by their families;

²³From thirty years old and upward until fifty years old shalt thou number them; all that enter in to perform the service, to do the work in the tabernacle of the congregation.

²⁴This is the service of the families of the Gershonites, to serve, and for burdens:

²⁵And they shall bear the curtains of the tabernacle, and the tabernacle of the congregation, his covering, and the covering of the badgers' skins that is above upon it, and the hanging for the door of the tabernacle of the congregation,

²⁶And the hangings of the court, and the hanging for the door of the gate of the court, which is by the tabernacle and by the altar round about, and their cords, and all the instruments of their service, and all that is made for them: so shall they serve.

²⁷At the appointment of Aaron and his sons shall be all the service of the sons of the Gershonites, in

all their burdens, and in all their service: and ye shall appoint unto them in charge all their burdens.

²⁸This is the service of the families of the sons of Gershon in the tabernacle of the congregation: and their charge shall be under the hand of Ithamar the son of Aaron the priest.

²⁹As for the sons of Merari, thou shalt number them after their families, by the house of their fathers;

³⁰From thirty years old and upward even unto fifty years old shalt thou number them, every one that entereth into the service, to do the work of the tabernacle of the congregation.

³¹And this is the charge of their burden, according to all their service in the tabernacle of the congregation; the boards of the tabernacle, and the bars thereof, and the pillars thereof, and sockets thereof,

³²And the pillars of the court round about, and their sockets, and their pins, and their cords, with all their instruments, and with all their service: and by name ye shall reckon the instruments of the charge of their burden.

³³This is the service of the families of the sons of Merari, according to all their service, in the tabernacle of the congregation, under the hand of Ithamar the son of Aaron the priest.

³⁴And Moses and Aaron and the chief of the congregation numbered the sons of the Kohathites after their families, and after the house of their fathers,

³⁵From thirty years old and upward even unto fifty years old, every one that entereth into the service, for the work in the tabernacle of the congregation:

³⁶And those that were numbered of them by their families were two thousand seven hundred and fifty.

³⁷These were they that were numbered of the families of the Kohathites, all that might do service in the tabernacle of the congregation, which Moses and Aaron did number according to the commandment of the LORD by the hand of Moses.

³⁸And those that were numbered of the sons of Gershon, throughout their families, and by the house of their fathers,

³⁹From thirty years old and upward even unto fifty years old, every one that entereth into the service, for the work in the tabernacle of the congregation,

⁴⁰Even those that were numbered of them, throughout their families, by the house of their fathers, were

two thousand and six hundred and thirty.

[41]These are they that were numbered of the families of the sons of Gershon, of all that might do service in the tabernacle of the congregation, whom Moses and Aaron did number according to the commandment of the LORD.

[42]And those that were numbered of the families of the sons of Merari, throughout their families, by the house of their fathers,

[43]From thirty years old and upward even unto fifty years old, every one that entereth into the service, for the work in the tabernacle of the congregation,

[44]Even those that were numbered of them after their families, were three thousand and two hundred.

[45]These be those that were numbered of the families of the sons of Merari, whom Moses and Aaron numbered according to the word of the LORD by the hand of Moses.

[46]All those that were numbered of the Levites, whom Moses and Aaron and the chief of Israel numbered, after their families, and after the house of their fathers,

[47]From thirty years old and upward even unto fifty years old, every one that came to do the service of the ministry, and the service of the burden in the tabernacle of the congregation.

[48]Even those that were numbered of them, were eight thousand and five hundred and fourscore,

[49]According to the commandment of the LORD they were numbered by the hand of Moses, every one according to his service, and according to his burden: thus were they numbered of him, as the LORD commanded Moses.

CHAPTER 5

[1]And the LORD spake unto Moses, saying,

[2]Command the children of Israel, that they put out of the camp every leper, and every one that hath an issue, and whosoever is defiled by the dead:

[3]Both male and female shall ye put out, without the camp shall ye put them; that they defile not their camps, in the midst whereof I dwell.

[4]And the children of Israel did so, and put them out without the camp: as the LORD spake unto Moses, so did the children of Israel.

[5]And the LORD spake unto Moses, saying,

[6]Speak unto the children of Israel, When a man or woman shall

commit any sin that men commit, to do a trespass against the LORD, and that person be guilty;

⁷Then they shall confess their sin which they have done: and he shall recompense his trespass with the principal thereof, and add unto it the fifth part thereof, and give it unto him against whom he hath trespassed.

⁸But if the man have no kinsman to recompense the trespass unto, let the trespass be recompensed unto the LORD, even to the priest; beside the ram of the atonement, whereby an atonement shall be made for him.

⁹And every offering of all the holy things of the children of Israel, which they bring unto the priest, shall be his.

¹⁰And every man's hallowed things shall be his: whatsoever any man giveth the priest, it shall be his.

¹¹And the LORD spake unto Moses, saying,

¹²Speak unto the children of Israel, and say unto them, If any man's wife go aside, and commit a trespass against him,

¹³And a man lie with her carnally, and it be hid from the eyes of her husband, and be kept close, and she be defiled, and there be no witness against her, neither she be taken with the manner;

¹⁴And the spirit of jealousy come upon him, and he be jealous of his wife, and she be defiled: or if the spirit of jealousy come upon him, and he be jealous of his wife, and she be not defiled:

¹⁵Then shall the man bring his wife unto the priest, and he shall bring her offering for her, the tenth part of an ephah of barley meal; he shall pour no oil upon it, nor put frankincense thereon; for it is an offering of jealousy, an offering of memorial, bringing iniquity to remembrance.

¹⁶And the priest shall bring her near, and set her before the LORD:

¹⁷And the priest shall take holy water in an earthen vessel; and of the dust that is in the floor of the tabernacle the priest shall take, and put it into the water:

¹⁸And the priest shall set the woman before the LORD, and uncover the woman's head, and put the offering of memorial in her hands, which is the jealousy offering: and the priest shall have in his hand the bitter water that causeth the curse:

¹⁹And the priest shall charge her by an oath, and say unto the woman, If no man have lain with thee, and if thou hast not gone aside to uncleanness with another instead of thy husband, be thou free from this bitter water that causeth the curse:

20But if thou hast gone aside to another instead of thy husband, and if thou be defiled, and some man have lain with thee beside thine husband:

21Then the priest shall charge the woman with an oath of cursing, and the priest shall say unto the woman, The LORD make thee a curse and an oath among thy people, when the LORD doth make thy thigh to rot, and thy belly to swell;

22And this water that causeth the curse shall go into thy bowels, to make thy belly to swell, and thy thigh to rot: And the woman shall say, Amen, amen.

23And the priest shall write these curses in a book, and he shall blot them out with the bitter water:

24And he shall cause the woman to drink the bitter water that causeth the curse: and the water that causeth the curse shall enter into her, and become bitter.

25Then the priest shall take the jealousy offering out of the woman's hand, and shall wave the offering before the LORD, and offer it upon the altar:

26And the priest shall take an handful of the offering, even the memorial thereof, and burn it upon the altar, and afterward shall cause the woman to drink the water.

27And when he hath made her to drink the water, then it shall come to pass, that, if she be defiled, and have done trespass against her husband, that the water that causeth the curse shall enter into her, and become bitter, and her belly shall swell, and her thigh shall rot: and the woman shall be a curse among her people.

28And if the woman be not defiled, but be clean; then she shall be free, and shall conceive seed.

29This is the law of jealousies, when a wife goeth aside to another instead of her husband, and is defiled;

30Or when the spirit of jealousy cometh upon him, and he be jealous over his wife, and shall set the woman before the LORD, and the priest shall execute upon her all this law.

31Then shall the man be guiltless from iniquity, and this woman shall bear her iniquity.

CHAPTER 6

1And the LORD spake unto Moses, saying,

2Speak unto the children of Israel, and say unto them, When either man or woman shall separate themselves to vow a vow of a

Nazarite, to separate themselves unto the LORD:

³He shall separate himself from wine and strong drink, and shall drink no vinegar of wine, or vinegar of strong drink, neither shall he drink any liquor of grapes, nor eat moist grapes, or dried.

⁴All the days of his separation shall he eat nothing that is made of the vine tree, from the kernels even to the husk.

⁵All the days of the vow of his separation there shall no razor come upon his head: until the days be fulfilled, in the which he separateth himself unto the LORD, he shall be holy, and shall let the locks of the hair of his head grow.

⁶All the days that he separateth himself unto the LORD he shall come at no dead body.

⁷He shall not make himself unclean for his father, or for his mother, for his brother, or for his sister, when they die: because the consecration of his God is upon his head.

⁸All the days of his separation he is holy unto the LORD.

⁹And if any man die very suddenly by him, and he hath defiled the head of his consecration; then he shall shave his head in the day of his cleansing, on the seventh day shall he shave it.

¹⁰And on the eighth day he shall bring two turtles, or two young pigeons, to the priest, to the door of the tabernacle of the congregation:

¹¹And the priest shall offer the one for a sin offering, and the other for a burnt offering, and make an atonement for him, for that he sinned by the dead, and shall hallow his head that same day.

¹²And he shall consecrate unto the LORD the days of his separation, and shall bring a lamb of the first year for a trespass offering: but the days that were before shall be lost, because his separation was defiled.

¹³And this is the law of the Nazarite, when the days of his separation are fulfilled: he shall be brought unto the door of the tabernacle of the congregation:

¹⁴And he shall offer his offering unto the LORD, one he lamb of the first year without blemish for a burnt offering, and one ewe lamb of the first year without blemish for a sin offering, and one ram without blemish for peace offerings,

¹⁵And a basket of unleavened bread, cakes of fine flour mingled with oil, and wafers of unleavened bread anointed with oil, and their meat offering, and their drink offerings.

¹⁶And the priest shall bring them before the LORD, and shall offer

his sin offering, and his burnt offering:

¹⁷And he shall offer the ram for a sacrifice of peace offerings unto the LORD, with the basket of unleavened bread: the priest shall offer also his meat offering, and his drink offering.

¹⁸And the Nazarite shall shave the head of his separation at the door of the tabernacle of the congregation, and shall take the hair of the head of his separation, and put it in the fire which is under the sacrifice of the peace offerings.

¹⁹And the priest shall take the sodden shoulder of the ram, and one unleavened cake out of the basket, and one unleavened wafer, and shall put them upon the hands of the Nazarite, after the hair of his separation is shaven:

²⁰And the priest shall wave them for a wave offering before the LORD: this is holy for the priest, with the wave breast and heave shoulder: and after that the Nazarite may drink wine.

²¹This is the law of the Nazarite who hath vowed, and of his offering unto the LORD for his separation, beside that that his hand shall get: according to the vow which he vowed, so he must do after the law of his separation.

²²And the LORD spake unto Moses, saying,

²³Speak unto Aaron and unto his sons, saying, On this wise ye shall bless the children of Israel, saying unto them,

²⁴The LORD bless thee, and keep thee:

²⁵The LORD make his face shine upon thee, and be gracious unto thee:

²⁶The LORD lift up his countenance upon thee, and give thee peace.

²⁷And they shall put my name upon the children of Israel, and I will bless them.

CHAPTER 7

¹And it came to pass on the day that Moses had fully set up the tabernacle, and had anointed it, and sanctified it, and all the instruments thereof, both the altar and all the vessels thereof, and had anointed them, and sanctified them;

²That the princes of Israel, heads of the house of their fathers, who were the princes of the tribes, and were over them that were numbered, offered:

³And they brought their offering before the LORD, six covered wagons, and twelve oxen; a wagon for two of the princes, and for each

one an ox: and they brought them before the tabernacle.

⁴And the LORD spake unto Moses, saying,

⁵Take it of them, that they may be to do the service of the tabernacle of the congregation; and thou shalt give them unto the Levites, to every man according to his service.

⁶And Moses took the wagons and the oxen, and gave them unto the Levites.

⁷Two wagons and four oxen he gave unto the sons of Gershon, according to their service:

⁸And four wagons and eight oxen he gave unto the sons of Merari, according unto their service, under the hand of Ithamar the son of Aaron the priest.

⁹But unto the sons of Kohath he gave none: because the service of the sanctuary belonging unto them was that they should bear upon their shoulders.

¹⁰And the princes offered for dedicating of the altar in the day that it was anointed, even the princes offered their offering before the altar.

¹¹And the LORD said unto Moses, They shall offer their offering, each prince on his day, for the dedicating of the altar.

¹²And he that offered his offering the first day was Nahshon the son of Amminadab, of the tribe of Judah:

¹³And his offering was one silver charger, the weight thereof was an hundred and thirty shekels, one silver bowl of seventy shekels, after the shekel of the sanctuary; both of them were full of fine flour mingled with oil for a meat offering:

¹⁴One spoon of ten shekels of gold, full of incense:

¹⁵One young bullock, one ram, one lamb of the first year, for a burnt offering:

¹⁶One kid of the goats for a sin offering:

¹⁷And for a sacrifice of peace offerings, two oxen, five rams, five he goats, five lambs of the first year: this was the offering of Nahshon the son of Amminadab.

¹⁸On the second day Nethaneel the son of Zuar, prince of Issachar, did offer:

¹⁹He offered for his offering one silver charger, the weight whereof was an hundred and thirty shekels, one silver bowl of seventy shekels, after the shekel of the sanctuary; both of them full of fine flour mingled with oil for a meat offering:

²⁰One spoon of gold of ten shekels, full of incense:

²¹One young bullock, one ram, one lamb of the first year, for a burnt offering:

²²One kid of the goats for a sin offering:

²³And for a sacrifice of peace offerings, two oxen, five rams, five he goats, five lambs of the first year: this was the offering of Nethaneel the son of Zuar.

²⁴On the third day Eliab the son of Helon, prince of the children of Zebulun, did offer:

²⁵His offering was one silver charger, the weight whereof was an hundred and thirty shekels, one silver bowl of seventy shekels, after the shekel of the sanctuary; both of them full of fine flour mingled with oil for a meat offering:

²⁶One golden spoon of ten shekels, full of incense:

²⁷One young bullock, one ram, one lamb of the first year, for a burnt offering:

²⁸One kid of the goats for a sin offering:

²⁹And for a sacrifice of peace offerings, two oxen, five rams, five he goats, five lambs of the first year: this was the offering of Eliab the son of Helon.

³⁰On the fourth day Elizur the son of Shedeur, prince of the children of Reuben, did offer:

³¹His offering was one silver charger of the weight of an hundred and thirty shekels, one silver bowl of seventy shekels, after the shekel of the sanctuary; both of them full of fine flour mingled with oil for a meat offering:

³²One golden spoon of ten shekels, full of incense:

³³One young bullock, one ram, one lamb of the first year, for a burnt offering:

³⁴One kid of the goats for a sin offering:

³⁵And for a sacrifice of peace offerings, two oxen, five rams, five he goats, five lambs of the first year: this was the offering of Elizur the son of Shedeur.

³⁶On the fifth day Shelumiel the son of Zurishaddai, prince of the children of Simeon, did offer:

³⁷His offering was one silver charger, the weight whereof was an hundred and thirty shekels, one silver bowl of seventy shekels, after the shekel of the sanctuary; both of them full of fine flour mingled with oil for a meat offering:

³⁸One golden spoon of ten shekels, full of incense:

³⁹One young bullock, one ram, one lamb of the first year, for a burnt offering:

⁴⁰One kid of the goats for a sin offering:

⁴¹And for a sacrifice of peace offerings, two oxen, five rams, five he goats, five lambs of the first year:

this was the offering of Shelumiel the son of Zurishaddai.

⁴²On the sixth day Eliasaph the son of Deuel, prince of the children of Gad, offered:

⁴³His offering was one silver charger of the weight of an hundred and thirty shekels, a silver bowl of seventy shekels, after the shekel of the sanctuary; both of them full of fine flour mingled with oil for a meat offering:

⁴⁴One golden spoon of ten shekels, full of incense:

⁴⁵One young bullock, one ram, one lamb of the first year, for a burnt offering:

⁴⁶One kid of the goats for a sin offering:

⁴⁷And for a sacrifice of peace offerings, two oxen, five rams, five he goats, five lambs of the first year: this was the offering of Eliasaph the son of Deuel.

⁴⁸On the seventh day Elishama the son of Ammihud, prince of the children of Ephraim, offered:

⁴⁹His offering was one silver charger, the weight whereof was an hundred and thirty shekels, one silver bowl of seventy shekels, after the shekel of the sanctuary; both of them full of fine flour mingled with oil for a meat offering:

⁵⁰One golden spoon of ten shekels, full of incense:

⁵¹One young bullock, one ram, one lamb of the first year, for a burnt offering:

⁵²One kid of the goats for a sin offering:

⁵³And for a sacrifice of peace offerings, two oxen, five rams, five he goats, five lambs of the first year: this was the offering of Elishama the son of Ammihud.

⁵⁴On the eighth day offered Gamaliel the son of Pedahzur, prince of the children of Manasseh:

⁵⁵His offering was one silver charger of the weight of an hundred and thirty shekels, one silver bowl of seventy shekels, after the shekel of the sanctuary; both of them full of fine flour mingled with oil for a meat offering:

⁵⁶One golden spoon of ten shekels, full of incense:

⁵⁷One young bullock, one ram, one lamb of the first year, for a burnt offering:

⁵⁸One kid of the goats for a sin offering:

⁵⁹And for a sacrifice of peace offerings, two oxen, five rams, five he goats, five lambs of the first year: this was the offering of Gamaliel the son of Pedahzur.

⁶⁰On the ninth day Abidan the son of Gideoni, prince of the children of Ben-jamin, offered:

⁶¹His offering was one silver

charger, the weight whereof was an hundred and thirty shekels, one silver bowl of seventy shekels, after the shekel of the sanctuary; both of them full of fine flour mingled with oil for a meat offering:

⁶²One golden spoon of ten shekels, full of incense:

⁶³One young bullock, one ram, one lamb of the first year, for a burnt offering:

⁶⁴One kid of the goats for a sin offering:

⁶⁵And for a sacrifice of peace offerings, two oxen, five rams, five he goats, five lambs of the first year: this was the offering of Abidan the son of Gideoni.

⁶⁶On the tenth day Ahiezer the son of Ammishaddai, prince of the children of Dan, offered:

⁶⁷His offering was one silver charger, the weight whereof was an hundred and thirty shekels, one silver bowl of seventy shekels, after the shekel of the sanctuary; both of them full of fine flour mingled with oil for a meat offering:

⁶⁸One golden spoon of ten shekels, full of incense:

⁶⁹One young bullock, one ram, one lamb of the first year, for a burnt offering:

⁷⁰One kid of the goats for a sin offering:

⁷¹And for a sacrifice of peace offerings, two oxen, five rams, five he goats, five lambs of the first year: this was the offering of Ahiezer the son of Ammishaddai.

⁷²On the eleventh day Pagiel the son of Ocran, prince of the children of Asher, offered:

⁷³His offering was one silver charger, the weight whereof was an hundred and thirty shekels, one silver bowl of seventy shekels, after the shekel of the sanctuary; both of them full of fine flour mingled with oil for a meat offering:

⁷⁴One golden spoon of ten shekels, full of incense:

⁷⁵One young bullock, one ram, one lamb of the first year, for a burnt offering:

⁷⁶One kid of the goats for a sin offering:

⁷⁷And for a sacrifice of peace offerings, two oxen, five rams, five he goats, five lambs of the first year: this was the offering of Pagiel the son of Ocran.

⁷⁸On the twelfth day Ahira the son of Enan, prince of the children of Naphtali, offered:

⁷⁹His offering was one silver charger, the weight whereof was an hundred and thirty shekels, one silver bowl of seventy shekels, after the shekel of the sanctuary; both of them full of fine flour mingled with oil for a meat offering:

80 One golden spoon of ten shekels, full of incense:

81 One young bullock, one ram, one lamb of the first year, for a burnt offering:

82 One kid of the goats for a sin offering:

83 And for a sacrifice of peace offerings, two oxen, five rams, five he goats, five lambs of the first year: this was the offering of Ahira the son of Enan.

84 This was the dedication of the altar, in the day when it was anointed, by the princes of Israel: twelve chargers of silver, twelve silver bowls, twelve spoons of gold:

85 Each charger of silver weighing an hundred and thirty shekels, each bowl seventy: all the silver vessels weighed two thousand and four hundred shekels, after the shekel of the sanctuary:

86 The golden spoons were twelve, full of incense, weighing ten shekels apiece, after the shekel of the sanctuary: all the gold of the spoons was an hundred and twenty shekels.

87 All the oxen for the burnt offering were twelve bullocks, the rams twelve, the lambs of the first year twelve, with their meat offering: and the kids of the goats for sin offering twelve.

88 And all the oxen for the sacrifice of the peace offerings were twenty and four bullocks, the rams sixty, the he goats sixty, the lambs of the first year sixty. This was the dedication of the altar, after that it was anointed.

89 And when Moses was gone into the tabernacle of the congregation to speak with him, then he heard the voice of one speaking unto him from off the mercy seat that was upon the ark of testimony, from between the two cherubims: and he spake unto him.

CHAPTER 8

1 And the LORD spake unto Moses, saying,

2 Speak unto Aaron and say unto him, When thou lightest the lamps, the seven lamps shall give light over against the candlestick.

3 And Aaron did so; he lighted the lamps thereof over against the candlestick, as the LORD commanded Moses.

4 And this work of the candlestick was of beaten gold, unto the shaft thereof, unto the flowers thereof, was beaten work: according unto the pattern which the LORD had shewed Moses, so he made the candlestick.

5 And the LORD spake unto Moses, saying,

⁶Take the Levites from among the children of Israel, and cleanse them.

⁷And thus shalt thou do unto them, to cleanse them: Sprinkle water of purifying upon them, and let them shave all their flesh, and let them wash their clothes, and so make themselves clean.

⁸Then let them take a young bullock with his meat offering, even fine flour mingled with oil, and another young bullock shalt thou take for a sin offering.

⁹And thou shalt bring the Levites before the tabernacle of the congregation: and thou shalt gather the whole assembly of the children of Israel together:

¹⁰And thou shalt bring the Levites before the LORD: and the children of Israel shall put their hands upon the Levites:

¹¹And Aaron shall offer the Levites before the LORD for an offering of the children of Israel, that they may execute the service of the LORD.

¹²And the Levites shall lay their hands upon the heads of the bullocks: and thou shalt offer the one for a sin offering, and the other for a burnt offering, unto the LORD, to make an atonement for the Levites.

¹³And thou shalt set the Levites before Aaron, and before his sons, and offer them for an offering unto the LORD.

¹⁴Thus shalt thou separate the Levites from among the children of Israel: and the Levites shall be mine.

¹⁵And after that shall the Levites go in to do the service of the tabernacle of the congregation: and thou shalt cleanse them, and offer them for an offering.

¹⁶For they are wholly given unto me from among the children of Israel; instead of such as open every womb, even instead of the firstborn of all the children of Israel, have I taken them unto me.

¹⁷For all the firstborn of the children of Israel are mine, both man and beast: on the day that I smote every firstborn in the land of Egypt I sanctified them for myself.

¹⁸And I have taken the Levites for all the firstborn of the children of Israel.

¹⁹And I have given the Levites as a gift to Aaron and to his sons from among the children of Israel, to do the service of the children of Israel in the tabernacle of the congregation, and to make an atonement for the children of Israel: that there be no plague among the children of Israel, when the children of Israel come nigh unto the sanctuary.

²⁰And Moses, and Aaron, and all the congregation of the children

of Israel, did to the Levites according unto all that the LORD commanded Moses concerning the Levites, so did the children of Israel unto them.

21 And the Levites were purified, and they washed their clothes; and Aaron offered them as an offering before the LORD; and Aaron made an atonement for them to cleanse them.

22 And after that went the Levites in to do their service in the tabernacle of the congregation before Aaron, and before his sons: as the LORD had commanded Moses concerning the Levites, so did they unto them.

23 And the LORD spake unto Moses, saying,

24 This is it that belongeth unto the Levites: from twenty and five years old and upward they shall go in to wait upon the service of the tabernacle of the congregation:

25 And from the age of fifty years they shall cease waiting upon the service thereof, and shall serve no more:

26 But shall minister with their brethren in the tabernacle of the congregation, to keep the charge, and shall do no service. Thus shalt thou do unto the Levites touching their charge.

CHAPTER 9

1 And the LORD spake unto Moses in the wilderness of Sinai, in the first month of the second year after they were come out of the land of Egypt, saying,

2 Let the children of Israel also keep the passover at his appointed season.

3 In the fourteenth day of this month, at even, ye shall keep it in his appointed season: according to all the rites of it, and according to all the ceremonies thereof, shall ye keep it.

4 And Moses spake unto the children of Israel, that they should keep the passover.

5 And they kept the passover on the fourteenth day of the first month at even in the wilderness of Sinai: according to all that the LORD commanded Moses, so did the children of Israel.

6 And there were certain men, who were defiled by the dead body of a man, that they could not keep the passover on that day: and they came before Moses and before Aaron on that day:

7 And those men said unto him, We are defiled by the dead body of a man: wherefore are we kept back, that we may not offer an offering of

the LORD in his appointed season among the children of Israel?

⁸And Moses said unto them, Stand still, and I will hear what the LORD will command concerning you.

⁹And the LORD spake unto Moses, saying,

¹⁰Speak unto the children of Israel, saying, If any man of you or of your posterity shall be unclean by reason of a dead body, or be in a journey afar off, yet he shall keep the passover unto the LORD.

¹¹The fourteenth day of the second month at even they shall keep it, and eat it with unleavened bread and bitter herbs.

¹²They shall leave none of it unto the morning, nor break any bone of it: according to all the ordinances of the passover they shall keep it.

¹³But the man that is clean, and is not in a journey, and forbeareth to keep the passover, even the same soul shall be cut off from among his people: because he brought not the offering of the LORD in his appointed season, that man shall bear his sin.

¹⁴And if a stranger shall sojourn among you, and will keep the passover unto the LORD; according to the ordinance of the passover, and according to the manner thereof, so shall he do: ye shall

have one ordinance, both for the stranger, and for him that was born in the land.

¹⁵And on the day that the tabernacle was reared up the cloud covered the tabernacle, namely, the tent of the testimony: and at even there was upon the tabernacle as it were the appearance of fire, until the morning.

¹⁶So it was alway: the cloud covered it by day, and the appearance of fire by night.

¹⁷And when the cloud was taken up from the tabernacle, then after that the children of Israel journeyed: and in the place where the cloud abode, there the children of Israel pitched their tents.

¹⁸At the commandment of the LORD the children of Israel journeyed, and at the commandment of the LORD they pitched: as long as the cloud abode upon the tabernacle they rested in their tents.

¹⁹And when the cloud tarried long upon the tabernacle many days, then the children of Israel kept the charge of the LORD, and journeyed not.

²⁰And so it was, when the cloud was a few days upon the tabernacle; according to the commandment of the LORD they abode in their tents, and according to the commandment of the LORD they journeyed.

²¹And so it was, when the cloud abode from even unto the morning, and that the cloud was taken up in the morning, then they journeyed: whether it was by day or by night that the cloud was taken up, they journeyed.

²²Or whether it were two days, or a month, or a year, that the cloud tarried upon the tabernacle, remaining thereon, the children of Israel abode in their tents, and journeyed not: but when it was taken up, they journeyed.

²³At the commandment of the LORD they rested in the tents, and at the commandment of the LORD they journeyed: they kept the charge of the LORD, at the commandment of the LORD by the hand of Moses.

CHAPTER 10

¹And the LORD spake unto Moses, saying,

²Make thee two trumpets of silver; of a whole piece shalt thou make them: that thou mayest use them for the calling of the assembly, and for the journeying of the camps.

³And when they shall blow with them, all the assembly shall assemble themselves to thee at the door of the tabernacle of the congregation.

⁴And if they blow but with one trumpet, then the princes, which are heads of the thousands of Israel, shall gather themselves unto thee.

⁵When ye blow an alarm, then the camps that lie on the east parts shall go forward.

⁶When ye blow an alarm the second time, then the camps that lie on the south side shall take their journey: they shall blow an alarm for their journeys.

⁷But when the congregation is to be gathered together, ye shall blow, but ye shall not sound an alarm.

⁸And the sons of Aaron, the priests, shall blow with the trumpets; and they shall be to you for an ordinance for ever throughout your generations.

⁹And if ye go to war in your land against the enemy that oppresseth you, then ye shall blow an alarm with the trumpets; and ye shall be remembered before the LORD your God, and ye shall be saved from your enemies.

¹⁰Also in the day of your gladness, and in your solemn days, and in the beginnings of your months, ye shall blow with the trumpets over your burnt offerings, and over the sacrifices of your peace offerings; that they may be to you for a memorial before your God: I am the LORD your God.

¹¹And it came to pass on the twentieth day of the second month, in the second year, that the cloud was taken up from off the tabernacle of the testimony.

¹²And the children of Israel took their journeys out of the wilderness of Sinai; and the cloud rested in the wilderness of Paran.

¹³And they first took their journey according to the commandment of the LORD by the hand of Moses.

¹⁴In the first place went the standard of the camp of the children of Judah according to their armies: and over his host was Nahshon the son of Amminadab.

¹⁵And over the host of the tribe of the children of Issachar was Nethaneel the son of Zuar.

¹⁶And over the host of the tribe of the children of Zebulun was Eliab the son of Helon.

¹⁷And the tabernacle was taken down; and the sons of Gershon and the sons of Merari set forward, bearing the tabernacle.

¹⁸And the standard of the camp of Reuben set forward according to their armies: and over his host was Elizur the son of Shedeur.

¹⁹And over the host of the tribe of the children of Simeon was Shelumiel the son of Zurishaddai.

²⁰And over the host of the tribe of the children of Gad was Eliasaph the son of Deuel.

²¹And the Kohathites set forward, bearing the sanctuary: and the other did set up the tabernacle against they came.

²²And the standard of the camp of the children of Ephraim set forward according to their armies: and over his host was Elishama the son of Ammihud.

²³And over the host of the tribe of the children of Manasseh was Gamaliel the son of Pedahzur.

²⁴And over the host of the tribe of the children of Ben-jamin was Abidan the son of Gideoni.

²⁵And the standard of the camp of the children of Dan set forward, which was the rereward of all the camps throughout their hosts: and over his host was Ahiezer the son of Ammishaddai.

²⁶And over the host of the tribe of the children of Asher was Pagiel the son of Ocran.

²⁷And over the host of the tribe of the children of Naphtali was Ahira the son of Enan.

²⁸Thus were the journeyings of the children of Israel according to their armies, when they set forward.

²⁹And Moses said unto Hobab, the son of Raguel the Midianite, Moses' father in law, We are journeying unto the place of which the LORD

said, I will give it you: come thou with us, and we will do thee good: for the LORD hath spoken good concerning Israel.

³⁰And he said unto him, I will not go; but I will depart to mine own land, and to my kindred.

³¹And he said, Leave us not, I pray thee; forasmuch as thou knowest how we are to encamp in the wilderness, and thou mayest be to us instead of eyes.

³²And it shall be, if thou go with us, yea, it shall be, that what goodness the LORD shall do unto us, the same will we do unto thee.

³³And they departed from the mount of the LORD three days' journey: and the ark of the covenant of the LORD went before them in the three days' journey, to search out a resting place for them.

³⁴And the cloud of the LORD was upon them by day, when they went out of the camp.

³⁵And it came to pass, when the ark set forward, that Moses said, Rise up, LORD, and let thine enemies be scattered; and let them that hate thee flee before thee.

³⁶And when it rested, he said, Return, O LORD, unto the many thousands of Israel.

CHAPTER 11

¹And when the people complained, it displeased the LORD: and the LORD heard it; and his anger was kindled; and the fire of the LORD burnt among them, and consumed them that were in the uttermost parts of the camp.

²And the people cried unto Moses; and when Moses prayed unto the LORD, the fire was quenched.

³And he called the name of the place Taberah: because the fire of the LORD burnt among them.

⁴And the mixt multitude that was among them fell a lusting: and the children of Israel also wept again, and said, Who shall give us flesh to eat?

⁵We remember the fish, which we did eat in Egypt freely; the cucumbers, and the melons, and the leeks, and the onions, and the garlick:

⁶But now our soul is dried away: there is nothing at all, beside this manna, before our eyes.

⁷And the manna was as coriander seed, and the colour thereof as the colour of bdellium.

⁸And the people went about, and gathered it, and ground it in mills, or beat it in a mortar, and baked it in pans, and made cakes of it: and

the taste of it was as the taste of fresh oil.

⁹And when the dew fell upon the camp in the night, the manna fell upon it.

¹⁰Then Moses heard the people weep throughout their families, every man in the door of his tent: and the anger of the LORD was kindled greatly; Moses also was displeased.

¹¹And Moses said unto the LORD, Wherefore hast thou afflicted thy servant? and wherefore have I not found favour in thy sight, that thou layest the burden of all this people upon me?

¹²Have I conceived all this people? have I begotten them, that thou shouldest say unto me, Carry them in thy bosom, as a nursing father beareth the sucking child, unto the land which thou swarest unto their fathers?

¹³Whence should I have flesh to give unto all this people? for they weep unto me, saying, Give us flesh, that we may eat.

¹⁴I am not able to bear all this people alone, because it is too heavy for me.

¹⁵And if thou deal thus with me, kill me, I pray thee, out of hand, if I have found favour in thy sight; and let me not see my wretchedness.

¹⁶And the LORD said unto Moses, Gather unto me seventy men of the elders of Israel, whom thou knowest to be the elders of the people, and officers over them; and bring them unto the tabernacle of the congregation, that they may stand there with thee.

¹⁷And I will come down and talk with thee there: and I will take of the spirit which is upon thee, and will put it upon them; and they shall bear the burden of the people with thee, that thou bear it not thyself alone.

¹⁸And say thou unto the people, Sanctify yourselves against to morrow, and ye shall eat flesh: for ye have wept in the ears of the LORD, saying, Who shall give us flesh to eat? for it was well with us in Egypt: therefore the LORD will give you flesh, and ye shall eat.

¹⁹Ye shall not eat one day, nor two days, nor five days, neither ten days, nor twenty days;

²⁰But even a whole month, until it come out at your nostrils, and it be loathsome unto you: because that ye have despised the LORD which is among you, and have wept before him, saying, Why came we forth out of Egypt?

²¹And Moses said, The people, among whom I am, are six hundred thousand footmen; and thou hast said, I will give them flesh, that they may eat a whole month.

²²Shall the flocks and the herds be slain for them, to suffice them? or shall all the fish of the sea be gathered together for them, to suffice them?

²³And the LORD said unto Moses, Is the LORD's hand waxed short? thou shalt see now whether my word shall come to pass unto thee or not.

²⁴And Moses went out, and told the people the words of the LORD, and gathered the seventy men of the elders of the people, and set them round about the tabernacle.

²⁵And the LORD came down in a cloud, and spake unto him, and took of the spirit that was upon him, and gave it unto the seventy elders: and it came to pass, that, when the spirit rested upon them, they prophesied, and did not cease.

²⁶But there remained two of the men in the camp, the name of the one was Eldad, and the name of the other Medad: and the spirit rested upon them; and they were of them that were written, but went not out unto the tabernacle: and they prophesied in the camp.

²⁷And there ran a young man, and told Moses, and said, Eldad and Medad do prophesy in the camp.

²⁸And Joshua the son of Nun, the servant of Moses, one of his young men, answered and said, My lord Moses, forbid them.

²⁹And Moses said unto him, Enviest thou for my sake? would God that all the LORD's people were prophets, and that the LORD would put his spirit upon them!

³⁰And Moses gat him into the camp, he and the elders of Israel.

³¹And there went forth a wind from the LORD, and brought quails from the sea, and let them fall by the camp, as it were a day's journey on this side, and as it were a day's journey on the other side, round about the camp, and as it were two cubits high upon the face of the earth.

³²And the people stood up all that day, and all that night, and all the next day, and they gathered the quails: he that gathered least gathered ten homers: and they spread them all abroad for themselves round about the camp.

³³And while the flesh was yet between their teeth, ere it was chewed, the wrath of the LORD was kindled against the people, and the LORD smote the people with a very great plague.

³⁴And he called the name of that place Kibroth-hattaavah: because there they buried the people that lusted.

³⁵And the people journeyed from Kibroth-hattaavah unto Hazeroth; and abode at Hazeroth.

CHAPTER 12

¹And Miriam and Aaron spake against Moses because of the Ethiopian woman whom he had married: for he had married an Ethiopian woman.

²And they said, Hath the LORD indeed spoken only by Moses? hath he not spoken also by us? And the LORD heard it.

³(Now the man Moses was very meek, above all the men which were upon the face of the earth.)

⁴And the LORD spake suddenly unto Moses, and unto Aaron, and unto Miriam, Come out ye three unto the tabernacle of the congregation. And they three came out.

⁵And the LORD came down in the pillar of the cloud, and stood in the door of the tabernacle, and called Aaron and Miriam: and they both came forth.

⁶And he said, Hear now my words: If there be a prophet among you, I the LORD will make myself known unto him in a vision, and will speak unto him in a dream.

⁷My servant Moses is not so, who is faithful in all mine house.

⁸With him will I speak mouth to mouth, even apparently, and not in dark speeches; and the similitude of the LORD shall he behold: wherefore then were ye not afraid to speak against my servant Moses?

⁹And the anger of the LORD was kindled against them; and he departed.

¹⁰And the cloud departed from off the tabernacle; and, behold, Miriam became leprous, white as snow: and Aaron looked upon Miriam, and, behold, she was leprous.

¹¹And Aaron said unto Moses, Alas, my lord, I beseech thee, lay not the sin upon us, wherein we have done foolishly, and wherein we have sinned.

¹²Let her not be as one dead, of whom the flesh is half consumed when he cometh out of his mother's womb.

¹³And Moses cried unto the LORD, saying, Heal her now, O God, I beseech thee.

¹⁴And the LORD said unto Moses, If her father had but spit in her face, should she not be ashamed seven days? let her be shut out from the camp seven days, and after that let her be received in again.

¹⁵And Miriam was shut out from the camp seven days: and the people journeyed not till Miriam was brought in again.

¹⁶And afterward the people removed from Hazeroth, and pitched in the wilderness of Paran.

CHAPTER 13

¹And the LORD spake unto Moses, saying,

²Send thou men, that they may search the land of Canaan, which I give unto the children of Israel: of every tribe of their fathers shall ye send a man, every one a ruler among them.

³And Moses by the commandment of the LORD sent them from the wilderness of Paran: all those men were heads of the children of Israel.

⁴And these were their names: of the tribe of Reuben, Shammua the son of Zaccur.

⁵Of the tribe of Simeon, Shaphat the son of Hori.

⁶Of the tribe of Judah, Caleb the son of Jephunneh.

⁷Of the tribe of Issachar, Igal the son of Joseph.

⁸Of the tribe of Ephraim, Oshea the son of Nun.

⁹Of the tribe of Ben-jamin, Palti the son of Raphu.

¹⁰Of the tribe of Zebulun, Gaddiel the son of Sodi.

¹¹Of the tribe of Joseph, namely, of the tribe of Manasseh, Gaddi the son of Susi.

¹²Of the tribe of Dan, Ammiel the son of Gemalli.

¹³Of the tribe of Asher, Sethur the son of Michael.

¹⁴Of the tribe of Naphtali, Nahbi the son of Vophsi.

¹⁵Of the tribe of Gad, Geuel the son of Machi.

¹⁶These are the names of the men which Moses sent to spy out the land. And Moses called Oshea the son of Nun Jehoshua.

¹⁷And Moses sent them to spy out the land of Canaan, and said unto them, Get you up this way southward, and go up into the mountain:

¹⁸And see the land, what it is, and the people that dwelleth therein, whether they be strong or weak, few or many;

¹⁹And what the land is that they dwell in, whether it be good or bad; and what cities they be that they dwell in, whether in tents, or in strong holds;

²⁰And what the land is, whether it be fat or lean, whether there be wood therein, or not. And be ye of good courage, and bring of the fruit of the land. Now the time was the time of the firstripe grapes.

²¹So they went up, and searched the land from the wilderness of Zin unto Rehob, as men come to Hamath.

²²And they ascended by the south, and came unto Hebron; where Ahiman, Sheshai, and Talmai,

the children of Anak, were. (Now Hebron was built seven years before Zoan in Egypt.)

²³And they came unto the brook of Eshcol, and cut down from thence a branch with one cluster of grapes, and they bare it between two upon a staff; and they brought of the pomegranates, and of the figs.

²⁴The place was called the brook Eshcol, because of the cluster of grapes which the children of Israel cut down from thence.

²⁵And they returned from searching of the land after forty days.

²⁶And they went and came to Moses, and to Aaron, and to all the congregation of the children of Israel, unto the wilderness of Paran, to Kadesh; and brought back word unto them, and unto all the congregation, and shewed them the fruit of the land.

²⁷And they told him, and said, We came unto the land whither thou sentest us, and surely it floweth with milk and honey; and this is the fruit of it.

²⁸Nevertheless the people be strong that dwell in the land, and the cities are walled, and very great: and moreover we saw the children of Anak there.

²⁹The Amalekites dwell in the land of the south: and the Hittites, and the Jebusites, and the Amorites, dwell in the mountains: and the Canaanites dwell by the sea, and by the coast of Jordan.

³⁰And Caleb stilled the people before Moses, and said, Let us go up at once, and possess it; for we are well able to overcome it.

³¹But the men that went up with him said, We be not able to go up against the people; for they are stronger than we.

³²And they brought up an evil report of the land which they had searched unto the children of Israel, saying, The land, through which we have gone to search it, is a land that eateth up the inhabitants thereof; and all the people that we saw in it are men of a great stature.

³³And there we saw the giants, the sons of Anak, which come of the giants: and we were in our own sight as grasshoppers, and so we were in their sight.

CHAPTER 14

¹And all the congregation lifted up their voice, and cried; and the people wept that night.

²And all the children of Israel murmured against Moses and against Aaron: and the whole

congregation said unto them, Would God that we had died in the land of Egypt! or would God we had died in this wilderness!

³And wherefore hath the LORD brought us unto this land, to fall by the sword, that our wives and our children should be a prey? were it not better for us to return into Egypt?

⁴And they said one to another, Let us make a captain, and let us return into Egypt.

⁵Then Moses and Aaron fell on their faces before all the assembly of the congregation of the children of Israel.

⁶And Joshua the son of Nun, and Caleb the son of Jephunneh, which were of them that searched the land, rent their clothes:

⁷And they spake unto all the company of the children of Israel, saying, The land, which we passed through to search it, is an exceeding good land.

⁸If the LORD delight in us, then he will bring us into this land, and give it us; a land which floweth with milk and honey.

⁹Only rebel not ye against the LORD, neither fear ye the people of the land; for they are bread for us: their defence is departed from them, and the LORD is with us: fear them not.

¹⁰But all the congregation bade stone them with stones. And the glory of the LORD appeared in the tabernacle of the congregation before all the children of Israel.

¹¹And the LORD said unto Moses, How long will this people provoke me? and how long will it be ere they believe me, for all the signs which I have shewed among them?

¹²I will smite them with the pestilence, and disinherit them, and will make of thee a greater nation and mightier than they.

¹³And Moses said unto the LORD, Then the Egyptians shall hear it, (for thou broughtest up this people in thy might from among them;)

¹⁴And they will tell it to the inhabitants of this land: for they have heard that thou LORD art among this people, that thou LORD art seen face to face, and that thy cloud standeth over them, and that thou goest before them, by day time in a pillar of a cloud, and in a pillar of fire by night.

¹⁵Now if thou shalt kill all this people as one man, then the nations which have heard the fame of thee will speak, saying,

¹⁶Because the LORD was not able to bring this people into the land which he sware unto them, therefore he hath slain them in the wilderness.

¹⁷And now, I beseech thee, let the power of my LORD be great, according as thou hast spoken, saying,

¹⁸The LORD is longsuffering, and of great mercy, forgiving iniquity and transgression, and by no means clearing the guilty, visiting the iniquity of the fathers upon the children unto the third and fourth generation.

¹⁹Pardon, I beseech thee, the iniquity of this people according unto the greatness of thy mercy, and as thou hast forgiven this people, from Egypt even until now.

²⁰And the LORD said, I have pardoned according to thy word:

²¹But as truly as I live, all the earth shall be filled with the glory of the LORD.

²²Because all those men which have seen my glory, and my miracles, which I did in Egypt and in the wilderness, and have tempted me now these ten times, and have not hearkened to my voice;

²³Surely they shall not see the land which I sware unto their fathers, neither shall any of them that provoked me see it:

²⁴But my servant Caleb, because he had another spirit with him, and hath followed me fully, him will I bring into the land whereinto he went; and his seed shall possess it.

²⁵(Now the Amalekites and the Canaanites dwelt in the valley.) Tomorrow turn you, and get you into the wilderness by the way of the Red sea.

²⁶And the LORD spake unto Moses and unto Aaron, saying,

²⁷How long shall I bear with this evil congregation, which murmur against me? I have heard the murmurings of the children of Israel, which they murmur against me.

²⁸Say unto them, As truly as I live, saith the LORD, as ye have spoken in mine ears, so will I do to you:

²⁹Your carcases shall fall in this wilderness; and all that were numbered of you, according to your whole number, from twenty years old and upward which have murmured against me.

³⁰Doubtless ye shall not come into the land, concerning which I sware to make you dwell therein, save Caleb the son of Jephunneh, and Joshua the son of Nun.

³¹But your little ones, which ye said should be a prey, them will I bring in, and they shall know the land which ye have despised.

³²But as for you, your carcases, they shall fall in this wilderness.

³³And your children shall wander in the wilderness forty years, and bear your whoredoms, until your carcases be wasted in the wilderness.

³⁴After the number of the days in which ye searched the land, even forty days, each day for a year, shall ye bear your iniquities, even forty years, and ye shall know my breach of promise.

³⁵I the LORD have said, I will surely do it unto all this evil congregation, that are gathered together against me: in this wilderness they shall be consumed, and there they shall die.

³⁶And the men, which Moses sent to search the land, who returned, and made all the congregation to murmur against him, by bringing up a slander upon the land,

³⁷Even those men that did bring up the evil report upon the land, died by the plague before the LORD.

³⁸But Joshua the son of Nun, and Caleb the son of Jephunneh, which were of the men that went to search the land, lived still.

³⁹And Moses told these sayings unto all the children of Israel: and the people mourned greatly.

⁴⁰And they rose up early in the morning, and gat them up into the top of the mountain, saying, Lo, we be here, and will go up unto the place which the LORD hath promised: for we have sinned.

⁴¹And Moses said, Wherefore now do ye transgress the commandment of the LORD? but it shall not prosper.

⁴²Go not up, for the LORD is not among you; that ye be not smitten before your enemies.

⁴³For the Amalekites and the Canaanites are there before you, and ye shall fall by the sword: because ye are turned away from the LORD, therefore the LORD will not be with you.

⁴⁴But they presumed to go up unto the hill top: nevertheless the ark of the covenant of the LORD, and Moses, departed not out of the camp.

⁴⁵Then the Amalekites came down, and the Canaanites which dwelt in that hill, and smote them, and discomfited them, even unto Hormah.

CHAPTER 15

¹And the LORD spake unto Moses, saying,

²Speak unto the children of Israel, and say unto them, When ye be come into the land of your habitations, which I give unto you,

³And will make an offering by fire unto the LORD, a burnt offering, or a sacrifice in performing a vow, or in a freewill offering, or in your

solemn feasts, to make a sweet savour unto the LORD, of the herd or of the flock:

⁴Then shall he that offereth his offering unto the LORD bring a meat offering of a tenth deal of flour mingled with the fourth part of an hin of oil.

⁵And the fourth part of an hin of wine for a drink offering shalt thou prepare with the burnt offering or sacrifice, for one lamb.

⁶Or for a ram, thou shalt prepare for a meat offering two tenth deals of flour mingled with the third part of an hin of oil.

⁷And for a drink offering thou shalt offer the third part of an hin of wine, for a sweet savour unto the LORD.

⁸And when thou preparest a bullock for a burnt offering, or for a sacrifice in performing a vow, or peace offerings unto the LORD:

⁹Then shall he bring with a bullock a meat offering of three tenth deals of flour mingled with half an hin of oil.

¹⁰And thou shalt bring for a drink offering half an hin of wine, for an offering made by fire, of a sweet savour unto the LORD.

¹¹Thus shall it be done for one bullock, or for one ram, or for a lamb, or a kid.

¹²According to the number that ye shall prepare, so shall ye do to every one according to their number.

¹³All that are born of the country shall do these things after this manner, in offering an offering made by fire, of a sweet savour unto the LORD.

¹⁴And if a stranger sojourn with you, or whosoever be among you in your generations, and will offer an offering made by fire, of a sweet savour unto the LORD; as ye do, so he shall do.

¹⁵One ordinance shall be both for you of the congregation, and also for the stranger that sojourneth with you, an ordinance for ever in your generations: as ye are, so shall the stranger be before the LORD.

¹⁶One law and one manner shall be for you, and for the stranger that sojourneth with you.

¹⁷And the LORD spake unto Moses, saying,

¹⁸Speak unto the children of Israel, and say unto them, When ye come into the land whither I bring you,

¹⁹Then it shall be, that, when ye eat of the bread of the land, ye shall offer up an heave offering unto the LORD.

²⁰Ye shall offer up a cake of the first of your dough for an heave offering: as ye do the heave offering

of the threshingfloor, so shall ye heave it.

²¹Of the first of your dough ye shall give unto the LORD an heave offering in your generations.

²²And if ye have erred, and not observed all these commandments, which the LORD hath spoken unto Moses,

²³Even all that the LORD hath commanded you by the hand of Moses, from the day that the LORD commanded Moses, and henceforward among your generations;

²⁴Then it shall be, if ought be committed by ignorance without the knowledge of the congregation, that all the congregation shall offer one young bullock for a burnt offering, for a sweet savour unto the LORD, with his meat offering, and his drink offering, according to the manner, and one kid of the goats for a sin offering.

²⁵And the priest shall make an atonement for all the congregation of the children of Israel, and it shall be forgiven them; for it is ignorance: and they shall bring their offering, a sacrifice made by fire unto the LORD, and their sin offering before the LORD, for their ignorance:

²⁶And it shall be forgiven all the congregation of the children of Israel, and the stranger that sojourneth among them; seeing all the people were in ignorance.

²⁷And if any soul sin through ignorance, then he shall bring a she goat of the first year for a sin offering.

²⁸And the priest shall make an atonement for the soul that sinneth ignorantly, when he sinneth by ignorance before the LORD, to make an atonement for him; and it shall be forgiven him.

²⁹Ye shall have one law for him that sinneth through ignorance, both for him that is born among the children of Israel, and for the stranger that sojourneth among them.

³⁰But the soul that doeth ought presumptuously, whether he be born in the land, or a stranger, the same reproacheth the LORD; and that soul shall be cut off from among his people.

³¹Because he hath despised the word of the LORD, and hath broken his commandment, that soul shall utterly be cut off; his iniquity shall be upon him.

³²And while the children of Israel were in the wilderness, they found a man that gathered sticks upon the sabbath day.

³³And they that found him gathering sticks brought him unto Moses and Aaron, and unto all the congregation.

³⁴And they put him in ward, because it was not declared what should be done to him.

³⁵And the LORD said unto Moses, The man shall be surely put to death: all the congregation shall stone him with stones without the camp.

³⁶And all the congregation brought him without the camp, and stoned him with stones, and he died; as the LORD commanded Moses.

³⁷And the LORD spake unto Moses, saying,

³⁸Speak unto the children of Israel, and bid them that they make them fringes in the borders of their garments throughout their generations, and that they put upon the fringe of the borders a ribband of blue:

³⁹And it shall be unto you for a fringe, that ye may look upon it, and remember all the commandments of the LORD, and do them; and that ye seek not after your own heart and your own eyes, after which ye use to go a whoring:

⁴⁰That ye may remember, and do all my commandments, and be holy unto your God.

⁴¹I am the LORD your God, which brought you out of the land of Egypt, to be your God: I am the LORD your God.

CHAPTER 16

¹Now Korah, the son of Izhar, the son of Kohath, the son of Levi, and Dathan and Abiram, the sons of Eliab, and On, the son of Peleth, sons of Reuben, took men:

²And they rose up before Moses, with certain of the children of Israel, two hundred and fifty princes of the assembly, famous in the congregation, men of renown:

³And they gathered themselves together against Moses and against Aaron, and said unto them, Ye take too much upon you, seeing all the congregation are holy, every one of them, and the LORD is among them: wherefore then lift ye up yourselves above the congregation of the LORD?

⁴And when Moses heard it, he fell upon his face:

⁵And he spake unto Korah and unto all his company, saying, Even to morrow the LORD will shew who are his, and who is holy; and will cause him to come near unto him: even him whom he hath chosen will he cause to come near unto him.

⁶This do; Take you censers, Korah, and all his company;

⁷And put fire therein, and put incense in them before the LORD

to morrow: and it shall be that the man whom the LORD doth choose, he shall be holy: ye take too much upon you, ye sons of Levi.

⁸And Moses said unto Korah, Hear, I pray you, ye sons of Levi:

⁹Seemeth it but a small thing unto you, that the God of Israel hath separated you from the congregation of Israel, to bring you near to himself to do the service of the tabernacle of the LORD, and to stand before the congregation to minister unto them?

¹⁰And he hath brought thee near to him, and all thy brethren the sons of Levi with thee: and seek ye the priesthood also?

¹¹For which cause both thou and all thy company are gathered together against the LORD: and what is Aaron, that ye murmur against him?

¹²And Moses sent to call Dathan and Abiram, the sons of Eliab: which said, We will not come up:

¹³Is it a small thing that thou hast brought us up out of a land that floweth with milk and honey, to kill us in the wilderness, except thou make thyself altogether a prince over us?

¹⁴Moreover thou hast not brought us into a land that floweth with milk and honey, or given us inheritance of fields and vineyards: wilt thou put out the eyes of these men? we will not come up.

¹⁵And Moses was very wroth, and said unto the LORD, Respect not thou their offering: I have not taken one ass from them, neither have I hurt one of them.

¹⁶And Moses said unto Korah, Be thou and all thy company before the LORD, thou, and they, and Aaron, to morrow:

¹⁷And take every man his censer, and put incense in them, and bring ye before the LORD every man his censer, two hundred and fifty censers; thou also, and Aaron, each of you his censer.

¹⁸And they took every man his censer, and put fire in them, and laid incense thereon, and stood in the door of the tabernacle of the congregation with Moses and Aaron.

¹⁹And Korah gathered all the congregation against them unto the door of the tabernacle of the congregation: and the glory of the LORD appeared unto all the congregation.

²⁰And the LORD spake unto Moses and unto Aaron, saying,

²¹Separate yourselves from among this congregation, that I may consume them in a moment.

²²And they fell upon their faces, and said, O God, the God of the

spirits of all flesh, shall one man sin, and wilt thou be wroth with all the congregation?

²³And the LORD spake unto Moses, saying,

²⁴Speak unto the congregation, saying, Get you up from about the tabernacle of Korah, Dathan, and Abiram.

²⁵And Moses rose up and went unto Dathan and Abiram; and the elders of Israel followed him.

²⁶And he spake unto the congregation, saying, Depart, I pray you, from the tents of these wicked men, and touch nothing of theirs, lest ye be consumed in all their sins.

²⁷So they gat up from the tabernacle of Korah, Dathan, and Abiram, on every side: and Dathan and Abiram came out, and stood in the door of their tents, and their wives, and their sons, and their little children.

²⁸And Moses said, Hereby ye shall know that the LORD hath sent me to do all these works; for I have not done them of mine own mind.

²⁹If these men die the common death of all men, or if they be visited after the visitation of all men; then the LORD hath not sent me.

³⁰But if the LORD make a new thing, and the earth open her mouth, and swallow them up, with all that appertain unto them, and they go down quick into the pit; then ye shall understand that these men have provoked the LORD.

³¹And it came to pass, as he had made an end of speaking all these words, that the ground clave asunder that was under them:

³²And the earth opened her mouth, and swallowed them up, and their houses, and all the men that appertained unto Korah, and all their goods.

³³They, and all that appertained to them, went down alive into the pit, and the earth closed upon them: and they perished from among the congregation.

³⁴And all Israel that were round about them fled at the cry of them: for they said, Lest the earth swallow us up also.

³⁵And there came out a fire from the LORD, and consumed the two hundred and fifty men that offered incense.

³⁶And the LORD spake unto Moses, saying,

³⁷Speak unto Eleazar the son of Aaron the priest, that he take up the censers out of the burning, and scatter thou the fire yonder; for they are hallowed.

³⁸The censers of these sinners against their own souls, let them make them broad plates for a covering of the altar: for they offered

them before the LORD, therefore they are hallowed: and they shall be a sign unto the children of Israel.

³⁹And Eleazar the priest took the brasen censers, wherewith they that were burnt had offered; and they were made broad plates for a covering of the altar:

⁴⁰To be a memorial unto the children of Israel, that no stranger, which is not of the seed of Aaron, come near to offer incense before the LORD; that he be not as Korah, and as his company: as the LORD said to him by the hand of Moses.

⁴¹But on the morrow all the congregation of the children of Israel murmured against Moses and against Aaron, saying, Ye have killed the people of the LORD.

⁴²And it came to pass, when the congregation was gathered against Moses and against Aaron, that they looked toward the tabernacle of the congregation: and, behold, the cloud covered it, and the glory of the LORD appeared.

⁴³And Moses and Aaron came before the tabernacle of the congregation.

⁴⁴And the LORD spake unto Moses, saying,

⁴⁵Get you up from among this congregation, that I may consume them as in a moment. And they fell upon their faces.

⁴⁶And Moses said unto Aaron, Take a censer, and put fire therein from off the altar, and put on incense, and go quickly unto the congregation, and make an atonement for them: for there is wrath gone out from the LORD; the plague is begun.

⁴⁷And Aaron took as Moses commanded, and ran into the midst of the congregation; and, behold, the plague was begun among the people: and he put on incense, and made an atonement for the people.

⁴⁸And he stood between the dead and the living; and the plague was stayed.

⁴⁹Now they that died in the plague were fourteen thousand and seven hundred, beside them that died about the matter of Korah.

⁵⁰And Aaron returned unto Moses unto the door of the tabernacle of the congregation: and the plague was stayed.

CHAPTER 17

¹And the LORD spake unto Moses, saying,

²Speak unto the children of Israel, and take of every one of them a rod according to the house of their fathers, of all their princes according

to the house of their fathers twelve rods: write thou every man's name upon his rod.

³And thou shalt write Aaron's name upon the rod of Levi: for one rod shall be for the head of the house of their fathers.

⁴And thou shalt lay them up in the tabernacle of the congregation before the testimony, where I will meet with you.

⁵And it shall come to pass, that the man's rod, whom I shall choose, shall blossom: and I will make to cease from me the murmurings of the children of Israel, whereby they murmur against you.

⁶And Moses spake unto the children of Israel, and every one of their princes gave him a rod apiece for each prince one, according to their fathers' houses, even twelve rods: and the rod of Aaron was among their rods.

⁷And Moses laid up the rods before the LORD in the tabernacle of witness.

⁸And it came to pass, that on the morrow Moses went into the tabernacle of witness; and, behold, the rod of Aaron for the house of Levi was budded, and brought forth buds, and bloomed blossoms, and yielded almonds.

⁹And Moses brought out all the rods from before the LORD unto all the children of Israel: and they looked, and took every man his rod.

¹⁰And the LORD said unto Moses, Bring Aaron's rod again before the testimony, to be kept for a token against the rebels; and thou shalt quite take away their murmurings from me, that they die not.

¹¹And Moses did so: as the LORD commanded him, so did he.

¹²And the children of Israel spake unto Moses, saying, Behold, we die, we perish, we all perish.

¹³Whosoever cometh any thing near unto the tabernacle of the LORD shall die: shall we be consumed with dying?

CHAPTER 18

¹And the LORD said unto Aaron, Thou and thy sons and thy father's house with thee shall bear the iniquity of the sanctuary: and thou and thy sons with thee shall bear the iniquity of your priesthood.

²And thy brethren also of the tribe of Levi, the tribe of thy father, bring thou with thee, that they may be joined unto thee, and minister unto thee: but thou and thy sons with thee shall minister before the tabernacle of witness.

³And they shall keep thy charge, and the charge of all the tabernacle: only they shall not come nigh the vessels of the sanctuary and the altar, that neither they, nor ye also, die.

⁴And they shall be joined unto thee, and keep the charge of the tabernacle of the congregation, for all the service of the tabernacle: and a stranger shall not come nigh unto you.

⁵And ye shall keep the charge of the sanctuary, and the charge of the altar: that there be no wrath any more upon the children of Israel.

⁶And I, behold, I have taken your brethren the Levites from among the children of Israel: to you they are given as a gift for the LORD, to do the service of the tabernacle of the congregation.

⁷Therefore thou and thy sons with thee shall keep your priest's office for everything of the altar, and within the vail; and ye shall serve: I have given your priest's office unto you as a service of gift: and the stranger that cometh nigh shall be put to death.

⁸And the LORD spake unto Aaron, Behold, I also have given thee the charge of mine heave offerings of all the hallowed things of the children of Israel; unto thee have I given them by reason of the anointing, and to thy sons, by an ordinance for ever.

⁹This shall be thine of the most holy things, reserved from the fire: every oblation of theirs, every meat offering of theirs, and every sin offering of theirs, and every trespass offering of theirs which they shall render unto me, shall be most holy for thee and for thy sons.

¹⁰In the most holy place shalt thou eat it; every male shall eat it: it shall be holy unto thee.

¹¹And this is thine; the heave offering of their gift, with all the wave offerings of the children of Israel: I have given them unto thee, and to thy sons and to thy daughters with thee, by a statute for ever: every one that is clean in thy house shall eat of it.

¹²All the best of the oil, and all the best of the wine, and of the wheat, the firstfruits of them which they shall offer unto the LORD, them have I given thee.

¹³And whatsoever is first ripe in the land, which they shall bring unto the LORD, shall be thine; every one that is clean in thine house shall eat of it.

¹⁴Every thing devoted in Israel shall be thine.

¹⁵Every thing that openeth the matrix in all flesh, which they bring unto the LORD, whether it be

of men or beasts, shall be thine: nevertheless the firstborn of man shalt thou surely redeem, and the firstling of unclean beasts shalt thou redeem.

¹⁶And those that are to be redeemed from a month old shalt thou redeem, according to thine estimation, for the money of five shekels, after the shekel of the sanctuary, which is twenty gerahs.

¹⁷But the firstling of a cow, or the firstling of a sheep, or the firstling of a goat, thou shalt not redeem; they are holy: thou shalt sprinkle their blood upon the altar, and shalt burn their fat for an offering made by fire, for a sweet savour unto the LORD.

¹⁸And the flesh of them shall be thine, as the wave breast and as the right shoulder are thine.

¹⁹All the heave offerings of the holy things, which the children of Israel offer unto the LORD, have I given thee, and thy sons and thy daughters with thee, by a statute for ever: it is a covenant of salt for ever before the LORD unto thee and to thy seed with thee.

²⁰And the LORD spake unto Aaron, Thou shalt have no inheritance in their land, neither shalt thou have any part among them: I am thy part and thine inheritance among the children of Israel.

²¹And, behold, I have given the children of Levi all the tenth in Israel for an inheritance, for their service which they serve, even the service of the tabernacle of the congregation.

²²Neither must the children of Israel henceforth come nigh the tabernacle of the congregation, lest they bear sin, and die.

²³But the Levites shall do the service of the tabernacle of the congregation, and they shall bear their iniquity: it shall be a statute for ever throughout your generations, that among the children of Israel they have no inheritance.

²⁴But the tithes of the children of Israel, which they offer as an heave offering unto the LORD, I have given to the Levites to inherit: therefore I have said unto them, Among the children of Israel they shall have no inheritance.

²⁵And the LORD spake unto Moses, saying,

²⁶Thus speak unto the Levites, and say unto them, When ye take of the children of Israel the tithes which I have given you from them for your inheritance, then ye shall offer up an heave offering of it for the LORD, even a tenth part of the tithe.

²⁷And this your heave offering shall be reckoned unto you, as

though it were the corn of the threshingfloor, and as the fulness of the winepress.

²⁸Thus ye also shall offer an heave offering unto the LORD of all your tithes, which ye receive of the children of Israel; and ye shall give thereof the LORD's heave offering to Aaron the priest.

²⁹Out of all your gifts ye shall offer every heave offering of the LORD, of all the best thereof, even the hallowed part thereof out of it.

³⁰Therefore thou shalt say unto them, When ye have heaved the best thereof from it, then it shall be counted unto the Levites as the increase of the threshingfloor, and as the increase of the winepress.

³¹And ye shall eat it in every place, ye and your households: for it is your reward for your service in the tabernacle of the congregation.

³²And ye shall bear no sin by reason of it, when ye have heaved from it the best of it: neither shall ye pollute the holy things of the children of Israel, lest ye die.

CHAPTER 19

¹And the LORD spake unto Moses and unto Aaron, saying,

²This is the ordinance of the law which the LORD hath commanded, saying, Speak unto the children of Israel, that they bring thee a red heifer without spot, wherein is no blemish, and upon which never came yoke:

³And ye shall give her unto Eleazar the priest, that he may bring her forth without the camp, and one shall slay her before his face:

⁴And Eleazar the priest shall take of her blood with his finger, and sprinkle of her blood directly before the tabernacle of the congregation seven times:

⁵And one shall burn the heifer in his sight; her skin, and her flesh, and her blood, with her dung, shall he burn:

⁶And the priest shall take cedar wood, and hyssop, and scarlet, and cast it into the midst of the burning of the heifer.

⁷Then the priest shall wash his clothes, and he shall bathe his flesh in water, and afterward he shall come into the camp, and the priest shall be unclean until the even.

⁸And he that burneth her shall wash his clothes in water, and bathe his flesh in water, and shall be unclean until the even.

⁹And a man that is clean shall gather up the ashes of the heifer, and lay them up without the camp in a clean place, and it shall be kept

for the congregation of the children of Israel for a water of separation: it is a purification for sin.

¹⁰And he that gathereth the ashes of the heifer shall wash his clothes, and be unclean until the even: and it shall be unto the children of Israel, and unto the stranger that sojourneth among them, for a statute for ever.

¹¹He that toucheth the dead body of any man shall be unclean seven days.

¹²He shall purify himself with it on the third day, and on the seventh day he shall be clean: but if he purify not himself the third day, then the seventh day he shall not be clean.

¹³Whosoever toucheth the dead body of any man that is dead, and purifieth not himself, defileth the tabernacle of the LORD; and that soul shall be cut off from Israel: because the water of separation was not sprinkled upon him, he shall be unclean; his uncleanness is yet upon him.

¹⁴This is the law, when a man dieth in a tent: all that come into the tent, and all that is in the tent, shall be unclean seven days.

¹⁵And every open vessel, which hath no covering bound upon it, is unclean.

¹⁶And whosoever toucheth one that is slain with a sword in the open fields, or a dead body, or a bone of a man, or a grave, shall be unclean seven days.

¹⁷And for an unclean person they shall take of the ashes of the burnt heifer of purification for sin, and running water shall be put thereto in a vessel:

¹⁸And a clean person shall take hyssop, and dip it in the water, and sprinkle it upon the tent, and upon all the vessels, and upon the persons that were there, and upon him that touched a bone, or one slain, or one dead, or a grave:

¹⁹And the clean person shall sprinkle upon the unclean on the third day, and on the seventh day: and on the seventh day he shall purify himself, and wash his clothes, and bathe himself in water, and shall be clean at even.

²⁰But the man that shall be unclean, and shall not purify himself, that soul shall be cut off from among the congregation, because he hath defiled the sanctuary of the LORD: the water of separation hath not been sprinkled upon him; he is unclean.

²¹And it shall be a perpetual statute unto them, that he that sprinkleth the water of separation shall wash his clothes; and he that toucheth the water of separation shall be unclean until even.

²²And whatsoever the unclean person toucheth shall be unclean; and the soul that toucheth it shall be unclean until even.

CHAPTER 20

¹Then came the children of Israel, even the whole congregation, into the desert of Zin in the first month: and the people abode in Kadesh; and Miriam died there, and was buried there.

²And there was no water for the congregation: and they gathered themselves together against Moses and against Aaron.

³And the people chode with Moses, and spake, saying, Would God that we had died when our brethren died before the LORD!

⁴And why have ye brought up the congregation of the LORD into this wilderness, that we and our cattle should die there?

⁵And wherefore have ye made us to come up out of Egypt, to bring us in unto this evil place? it is no place of seed, or of figs, or of vines, or of pomegranates; neither is there any water to drink.

⁶And Moses and Aaron went from the presence of the assembly unto the door of the tabernacle of the congregation, and they fell upon their faces: and the glory of the LORD appeared unto them.

⁷And the LORD spake unto Moses, saying,

⁸Take the rod, and gather thou the assembly together, thou, and Aaron thy brother, and speak ye unto the rock before their eyes; and it shall give forth his water, and thou shalt bring forth to them water out of the rock: so thou shalt give the congregation and their beasts drink.

⁹And Moses took the rod from before the LORD, as he commanded him.

¹⁰And Moses and Aaron gathered the congregation together before the rock, and he said unto them, Hear now, ye rebels; must we fetch you water out of this rock?

¹¹And Moses lifted up his hand, and with his rod he smote the rock twice: and the water came out abundantly, and the congregation drank, and their beasts also.

¹²And the LORD spake unto Moses and Aaron, Because ye believed me not, to sanctify me in the eyes of the children of Israel, therefore ye shall not bring this congregation into the land which I have given them.

¹³This is the water of Meribah; because the children of Israel

strove with the LORD, and he was sanctified in them.

14And Moses sent messengers from Kadesh unto the king of Edom, Thus saith thy brother Israel, Thou knowest all the travail that hath befallen us:

15How our fathers went down into Egypt, and we have dwelt in Egypt a long time; and the Egyptians vexed us, and our fathers:

16And when we cried unto the LORD, he heard our voice, and sent an angel, and hath brought us forth out of Egypt: and, behold, we are in Kadesh, a city in the uttermost of thy border:

17Let us pass, I pray thee, through thy country: we will not pass through the fields, or through the vineyards, neither will we drink of the water of the wells: we will go by the king's high way, we will not turn to the right hand nor to the left, until we have passed thy borders.

18And Edom said unto him, Thou shalt not pass by me, lest I come out against thee with the sword.

19And the children of Israel said unto him, We will go by the high way: and if I and my cattle drink of thy water, then I will pay for it: I will only, without doing anything else, go through on my feet.

20And he said, Thou shalt not go through. And Edom came out against him with much people, and with a strong hand.

21Thus Edom refused to give Israel passage through his border: wherefore Israel turned away from him.

22And the children of Israel, even the whole congregation, journeyed from Kadesh, and came unto mount Hor.

23And the LORD spake unto Moses and Aaron in mount Hor, by the coast of the land of Edom, saying,

24Aaron shall be gathered unto his people: for he shall not enter into the land which I have given unto the children of Israel, because ye rebelled against my word at the water of Meribah.

25Take Aaron and Eleazar his son, and bring them up unto mount Hor:

26And strip Aaron of his garments, and put them upon Eleazar his son: and Aaron shall be gathered unto his people, and shall die there.

27And Moses did as the LORD commanded: and they went up into mount Hor in the sight of all the congregation.

28And Moses stripped Aaron of his garments, and put them upon Eleazar his son; and Aaron died there in the top of the mount: and Moses and Eleazar came down from the mount.

²⁹And when all the congregation saw that Aaron was dead, they mourned for Aaron thirty days, even all the house of Israel.

CHAPTER 21

¹And when king Arad the Canaanite, which dwelt in the south, heard tell that Israel came by the way of the spies; then he fought against Israel, and took some of them prisoners.

²And Israel vowed a vow unto the LORD, and said, If thou wilt indeed deliver this people into my hand, then I will utterly destroy their cities.

³And the LORD hearkened to the voice of Israel, and delivered up the Canaanites; and they utterly destroyed them and their cities: and he called the name of the place Hormah.

⁴And they journeyed from mount Hor by the way of the Red sea, to compass the land of Edom: and the soul of the people was much discouraged because of the way.

⁵And the people spake against God, and against Moses, Wherefore have ye brought us up out of Egypt to die in the wilderness? for there is no bread, neither is there any water; and our soul loatheth this light bread.

⁶And the LORD sent fiery serpents among the people, and they bit the people; and much people of Israel died.

⁷Therefore the people came to Moses, and said, We have sinned, for we have spoken against the LORD, and against thee; pray unto the LORD, that he take away the serpents from us. And Moses prayed for the people.

⁸And the LORD said unto Moses, Make thee a fiery serpent, and set it upon a pole: and it shall come to pass, that every one that is bitten, when he looketh upon it, shall live.

⁹And Moses made a serpent of brass, and put it upon a pole, and it came to pass, that if a serpent had bitten any man, when he beheld the serpent of brass, he lived.

¹⁰And the children of Israel set forward, and pitched in Oboth.

¹¹And they journeyed from Oboth, and pitched at Ije-abarim, in the wilderness which is before Moab, toward the sunrising.

¹²From thence they removed, and pitched in the valley of Zared.

¹³From thence they removed, and pitched on the other side of Arnon, which is in the wilderness that cometh out of the coasts of the Amorites: for Arnon is the border

of Moab, between Moab and the Amorites.

¹⁴Wherefore it is said in the book of the wars of the LORD, What he did in the Red sea, and in the brooks of Arnon,

¹⁵And at the stream of the brooks that goeth down to the dwelling of Ar, and lieth upon the border of Moab.

¹⁶And from thence they went to Beer: that is the well whereof the LORD spake unto Moses, Gather the people together, and I will give them water.

¹⁷Then Israel sang this song, Spring up, O well; sing ye unto it:

¹⁸The princes digged the well, the nobles of the people digged it, by the direction of the lawgiver, with their staves. And from the wilderness they went to Mattanah:

¹⁹And from Mattanah to Nahaliel: and from Nahaliel to Bamoth:

²⁰And from Bamoth in the valley, that is in the country of Moab, to the top of Pisgah, which looketh toward Jeshimon.

²¹And Israel sent messengers unto Sihon king of the Amorites, saying,

²²Let me pass through thy land: we will not turn into the fields, or into the vineyards; we will not drink of the waters of the well: but we will go along by the king's high way, until we be past thy borders.

²³And Sihon would not suffer Israel to pass through his border: but Sihon gathered all his people together, and went out against Israel into the wilderness: and he came to Jahaz, and fought against Israel.

²⁴And Israel smote him with the edge of the sword, and possessed his land from Arnon unto Jabbok, even unto the children of Ammon: for the border of the children of Ammon was strong.

²⁵And Israel took all these cities: and Israel dwelt in all the cities of the Amorites, in Heshbon, and in all the villages thereof.

²⁶For Heshbon was the city of Sihon the king of the Amorites, who had fought against the former king of Moab, and taken all his land out of his hand, even unto Arnon.

²⁷Wherefore they that speak in proverbs say, Come into Heshbon, let the city of Sihon be built and prepared:

²⁸For there is a fire gone out of Heshbon, a flame from the city of Sihon: it hath consumed Ar of Moab, and the lords of the high places of Arnon.

²⁹Woe to thee, Moab! thou art undone, O people of Chemosh: he hath given his sons that escaped, and his daughters, into captivity unto Sihon king of the Amorites.

30We have shot at them; Heshbon is perished even unto Dibon, and we have laid them waste even unto Nophah, which reacheth unto Medeba.

31Thus Israel dwelt in the land of the Amorites.

32And Moses sent to spy out Jaazer, and they took the villages thereof, and drove out the Amorites that were there.

33And they turned and went up by the way of Bashan: and Og the king of Bashan went out against them, he, and all his people, to the battle at Edrei.

34And the LORD said unto Moses, Fear him not: for I have delivered him into thy hand, and all his people, and his land; and thou shalt do to him as thou didst unto Sihon king of the Amorites, which dwelt at Heshbon.

35So they smote him, and his sons, and all his people, until there was none left him alive: and they possessed his land.

CHAPTER 22

1And the children of Israel set forward, and pitched in the plains of Moab on this side Jordan by Jericho.

2And Balak the son of Zippor saw all that Israel had done to the Amorites.

3And Moab was sore afraid of the people, because they were many: and Moab was distressed because of the children of Israel.

4And Moab said unto the elders of Midian, Now shall this company lick up all that are round about us, as the ox licketh up the grass of the field. And Balak the son of Zippor was king of the Moabites at that time.

5He sent messengers therefore unto Balaam the son of Beor to Pethor, which is by the river of the land of the children of his people, to call him, saying, Behold, there is a people come out from Egypt: behold, they cover the face of the earth, and they abide over against me:

6Come now therefore, I pray thee, curse me this people; for they are too mighty for me: peradventure I shall prevail, that we may smite them, and that I may drive them out of the land: for I wot that he whom thou blessest is blessed, and he whom thou cursest is cursed.

7And the elders of Moab and the elders of Midian departed with the rewards of divination in their hand; and they came unto Balaam, and spake unto him the words of Balak.

8And he said unto them, Lodge here this night, and I will bring you word again, as the LORD shall speak unto me: and the princes of Moab abode with Balaam.

⁹And God came unto Balaam, and said, What men are these with thee?

¹⁰And Balaam said unto God, Balak the son of Zippor, king of Moab, hath sent unto me, saying,

¹¹Behold, there is a people come out of Egypt, which covereth the face of the earth: come now, curse me them; peradventure I shall be able to overcome them, and drive them out.

¹²And God said unto Balaam, Thou shalt not go with them; thou shalt not curse the people: for they are blessed.

¹³And Balaam rose up in the morning, and said unto the princes of Balak, Get you into your land: for the LORD refuseth to give me leave to go with you.

¹⁴And the princes of Moab rose up, and they went unto Balak, and said, Balaam refuseth to come with us.

¹⁵And Balak sent yet again princes, more, and more honourable than they.

¹⁶And they came to Balaam, and said to him, Thus saith Balak the son of Zippor, Let nothing, I pray thee, hinder thee from coming unto me:

¹⁷For I will promote thee unto very great honour, and I will do whatsoever thou sayest unto me: come therefore, I pray thee, curse me this people.

¹⁸And Balaam answered and said unto the servants of Balak, If Balak would give me his house full of silver and gold, I cannot go beyond the word of the LORD my God, to do less or more.

¹⁹Now therefore, I pray you, tarry ye also here this night, that I may know what the LORD will say unto me more.

²⁰And God came unto Balaam at night, and said unto him, If the men come to call thee, rise up, and go with them; but yet the word which I shall say unto thee, that shalt thou do.

²¹And Balaam rose up in the morning, and saddled his ass, and went with the princes of Moab.

²²And God's anger was kindled because he went: and the angel of the LORD stood in the way for an adversary against him. Now he was riding upon his ass, and his two servants were with him.

²³And the ass saw the angel of the LORD standing in the way, and his sword drawn in his hand: and the ass turned aside out of the way, and went into the field: and Balaam smote the ass, to turn her into the way.

²⁴But the angel of the LORD stood in a path of the vineyards, a

wall being on this side, and a wall on that side.

²⁵And when the ass saw the angel of the LORD, she thrust herself unto the wall, and crushed Balaam's foot against the wall: and he smote her again.

²⁶And the angel of the LORD went further, and stood in a narrow place, where was no way to turn either to the right hand or to the left.

²⁷And when the ass saw the angel of the LORD, she fell down under Balaam: and Balaam's anger was kindled, and he smote the ass with a staff.

²⁸And the LORD opened the mouth of the ass, and she said unto Balaam, What have I done unto thee, that thou hast smitten me these three times?

²⁹And Balaam said unto the ass, Because thou hast mocked me: I would there were a sword in mine hand, for now would I kill thee.

³⁰And the ass said unto Balaam, Am not I thine ass, upon which thou hast ridden ever since I was thine unto this day? was I ever wont to do so unto thee? And he said, Nay.

³¹Then the LORD opened the eyes of Balaam, and he saw the angel of the LORD standing in the way, and his sword drawn in his hand: and he bowed down his head, and fell flat on his face.

³²And the angel of the LORD said unto him, Wherefore hast thou smitten thine ass these three times? behold, I went out to withstand thee, because thy way is perverse before me:

³³And the ass saw me, and turned from me these three times: unless she had turned from me, surely now also I had slain thee, and saved her alive.

³⁴And Balaam said unto the angel of the LORD, I have sinned; for I knew not that thou stoodest in the way against me: now therefore, if it displease thee, I will get me back again.

³⁵And the angel of the LORD said unto Balaam, Go with the men: but only the word that I shall speak unto thee, that thou shalt speak. So Balaam went with the princes of Balak.

³⁶And when Balak heard that Balaam was come, he went out to meet him unto a city of Moab, which is in the border of Arnon, which is in the utmost coast.

³⁷And Balak said unto Balaam, Did I not earnestly send unto thee to call thee? wherefore camest thou not unto me? am I not able indeed to promote thee to honour?

³⁸And Balaam said unto Balak, Lo, I am come unto thee: have I now any power at all to say any

thing? the word that God putteth in my mouth, that shall I speak.

³⁹And Balaam went with Balak, and they came unto Kirjathhuzoth.

⁴⁰And Balak offered oxen and sheep, and sent to Balaam, and to the princes that were with him.

⁴¹And it came to pass on the morrow, that Balak took Balaam, and brought him up into the high places of Baal, that thence he might see the utmost part of the people.

CHAPTER 23

¹And Balaam said unto Balak, Build me here seven altars, and prepare me here seven oxen and seven rams.

²And Balak did as Balaam had spoken; and Balak and Balaam offered on every altar a bullock and a ram.

³And Balaam said unto Balak, Stand by thy burnt offering, and I will go: peradventure the LORD will come to meet me: and whatsoever he sheweth me I will tell thee. And he went to an high place.

⁴And God met Balaam: and he said unto him, I have prepared seven altars, and I have offered upon every altar a bullock and a ram.

⁵And the LORD put a word in Balaam's mouth, and said, Return unto Balak, and thus thou shalt speak.

⁶And he returned unto him, and, lo, he stood by his burnt sacrifice, he, and all the princes of Moab.

⁷And he took up his parable, and said, Balak the king of Moab hath brought me from Aram, out of the mountains of the east, saying, Come, curse me Jacob, and come, defy Israel.

⁸How shall I curse, whom God hath not cursed? or how shall I defy, whom the LORD hath not defied?

⁹For from the top of the rocks I see him, and from the hills I behold him: lo, the people shall dwell alone, and shall not be reckoned among the nations.

¹⁰Who can count the dust of Jacob, and the number of the fourth part of Israel? Let me die the death of the righteous, and let my last end be like his!

¹¹And Balak said unto Balaam, What hast thou done unto me? I took thee to curse mine enemies, and, behold, thou hast blessed them altogether.

¹²And he answered and said, Must I not take heed to speak that which the LORD hath put in my mouth?

¹³And Balak said unto him, Come, I pray thee, with me unto another place, from whence thou mayest see

them: thou shalt see but the utmost part of them, and shalt not see them all: and curse me them from thence.

¹⁴And he brought him into the field of Zophim, to the top of Pisgah, and built seven altars, and offered a bullock and a ram on every altar.

¹⁵And he said unto Balak, Stand here by thy burnt offering, while I meet the LORD yonder.

¹⁶And the LORD met Balaam, and put a word in his mouth, and said, Go again unto Balak, and say thus.

¹⁷And when he came to him, behold, he stood by his burnt offering, and the princes of Moab with him. And Balak said unto him, What hath the LORD spoken?

¹⁸And he took up his parable, and said, Rise up, Balak, and hear; hearken unto me, thou son of Zippor:

¹⁹God is not a man, that he should lie; neither the son of man, that he should repent: hath he said, and shall he not do it? or hath he spoken, and shall he not make it good?

²⁰Behold, I have received commandment to bless: and he hath blessed; and I cannot reverse it.

²¹He hath not beheld iniquity in Jacob, neither hath he seen perverseness in Israel: the LORD his God is with him, and the shout of a king is among them.

²²God brought them out of Egypt; he hath as it were the strength of an unicorn.

²³Surely there is no enchantment against Jacob, neither is there any divination against Israel: according to this time it shall be said of Jacob and of Israel, What hath God wrought!

²⁴Behold, the people shall rise up as a great lion, and lift up himself as a young lion: he shall not lie down until he eat of the prey, and drink the blood of the slain.

²⁵And Balak said unto Balaam, Neither curse them at all, nor bless them at all.

²⁶But Balaam answered and said unto Balak, Told not I thee, saying, All that the LORD speaketh, that I must do?

²⁷And Balak said unto Balaam, Come, I pray thee, I will bring thee unto another place; peradventure it will please God that thou mayest curse me them from thence.

²⁸And Balak brought Balaam unto the top of Peor, that looketh toward Jeshimon.

²⁹And Balaam said unto Balak, Build me here seven altars, and prepare me here seven bullocks and seven rams.

³⁰And Balak did as Balaam had said, and offered a bullock and a ram on every altar.

CHAPTER 24

¹And when Balaam saw that it pleased the LORD to bless Israel, he went not, as at other times, to seek for enchantments, but he set his face toward the wilderness.

²And Balaam lifted up his eyes, and he saw Israel abiding in his tents according to their tribes; and the spirit of God came upon him.

³And he took up his parable, and said, Balaam the son of Beor hath said, and the man whose eyes are open hath said:

⁴He hath said, which heard the words of God, which saw the vision of the Almighty, falling into a trance, but having his eyes open:

⁵How goodly are thy tents, O Jacob, and thy tabernacles, O Israel!

⁶As the valleys are they spread forth, as gardens by the river's side, as the trees of lign aloes which the LORD hath planted, and as cedar trees beside the waters.

⁷He shall pour the water out of his buckets, and his seed shall be in many waters, and his king shall be higher than Agag, and his kingdom shall be exalted.

⁸God brought him forth out of Egypt; he hath as it were the strength of an unicorn: he shall eat up the nations his enemies, and shall break their bones, and pierce them through with his arrows.

⁹He couched, he lay down as a lion, and as a great lion: who shall stir him up? Blessed is he that blesseth thee, and cursed is he that curseth thee.

¹⁰And Balak's anger was kindled against Balaam, and he smote his hands together: and Balak said unto Balaam, I called thee to curse mine enemies, and, behold, thou hast altogether blessed them these three times.

¹¹Therefore now flee thou to thy place: I thought to promote thee unto great honour; but, lo, the LORD hath kept thee back from honour.

¹²And Balaam said unto Balak, Spake I not also to thy messengers which thou sentest unto me, saying,

¹³If Balak would give me his house full of silver and gold, I cannot go beyond the commandment of the LORD, to do either good or bad of mine own mind; but what the LORD saith, that will I speak?

¹⁴And now, behold, I go unto my people: come therefore, and I will advertise thee what this people shall do to thy people in the latter days.

¹⁵And he took up his parable, and said, Balaam the son of Beor hath said, and the man whose eyes are open hath said:

¹⁶He hath said, which heard the words of God, and knew the knowledge of the most High, which saw the vision of the Almighty, falling into a trance, but having his eyes open:

¹⁷I shall see him, but not now: I shall behold him, but not nigh: there shall come a Star out of Jacob, and a Sceptre shall rise out of Israel, and shall smite the corners of Moab, and destroy all the children of Sheth.

¹⁸And Edom shall be a possession, Seir also shall be a possession for his enemies; and Israel shall do valiantly.

¹⁹Out of Jacob shall come he that shall have dominion, and shall destroy him that remaineth of the city.

²⁰And when he looked on Amalek, he took up his parable, and said, Amalek was the first of the nations; but his latter end shall be that he perish for ever.

²¹And he looked on the Kenites, and took up his parable, and said, Strong is thy dwellingplace, and thou puttest thy nest in a rock.

²²Nevertheless the Kenite shall be wasted, until Asshur shall carry thee away captive.

²³And he took up his parable, and said, Alas, who shall live when God doeth this!

²⁴And ships shall come from the coast of Chittim, and shall afflict Asshur, and shall afflict Eber, and he also shall perish for ever.

²⁵And Balaam rose up, and went and returned to his place: and Balak also went his way.

CHAPTER 25

¹And Israel abode in Shittim, and the people began to commit whoredom with the daughters of Moab.

²And they called the people unto the sacrifices of their gods: and the people did eat, and bowed down to their gods.

³And Israel joined himself unto Baal-peor: and the anger of the LORD was kindled against Israel.

⁴And the LORD said unto Moses, Take all the heads of the people, and hang them up before the LORD against the sun, that the fierce anger of the LORD may be turned away from Israel.

⁵And Moses said unto the judges of Israel, Slay ye every one his men that were joined unto Baal-peor.

⁶And, behold, one of the children of Israel came and brought unto his brethren a Midianitish woman in the sight of Moses, and in the sight of all the congregation of the children of Israel, who were weeping before

the door of the tabernacle of the congregation.

⁷And when Phinehas, the son of Eleazar, the son of Aaron the priest, saw it, he rose up from among the congregation, and took a javelin in his hand;

⁸And he went after the man of Israel into the tent, and thrust both of them through, the man of Israel, and the woman through her belly. So the plague was stayed from the children of Israel.

⁹And those that died in the plague were twenty and four thousand.

¹⁰And the LORD spake unto Moses, saying,

¹¹Phinehas, the son of Eleazar, the son of Aaron the priest, hath turned my wrath away from the children of Israel, while he was zealous for my sake among them, that I consumed not the children of Israel in my jealousy.

¹²Wherefore say, Behold, I give unto him my covenant of peace:

¹³And he shall have it, and his seed after him, even the covenant of an everlasting priesthood; because he was zealous for his God, and made an atonement for the children of Israel.

¹⁴Now the name of the Israelite that was slain, even that was slain with the Midianitish woman, was Zimri, the son of Salu, a prince of a chief house among the Simeonites.

¹⁵And the name of the Midianitish woman that was slain was Cozbi, the daughter of Zur; he was head over a people, and of a chief house in Midian.

¹⁶And the LORD spake unto Moses, saying,

¹⁷Vex the Midianites, and smite them:

¹⁸For they vex you with their wiles, wherewith they have beguiled you in the matter of Peor, and in the matter of Cozbi, the daughter of a prince of Midian, their sister, which was slain in the day of the plague for Peor's sake.

CHAPTER 26

¹And it came to pass after the plague, that the LORD spake unto Moses and unto Eleazar the son of Aaron the priest, saying,

²Take the sum of all the congregation of the children of Israel, from twenty years old and upward, throughout their fathers' house, all that are able to go to war in Israel.

³And Moses and Eleazar the priest spake with them in the plains of Moab by Jordan near Jericho, saying,

⁴Take the sum of the people, from twenty years old and upward; as the

LORD commanded Moses and the children of Israel, which went forth out of the land of Egypt.

⁵Reuben, the eldest son of Israel: the children of Reuben; Hanoch, of whom cometh the family of the Hanochites: of Pallu, the family of the Palluites:

⁶Of Hezron, the family of the Hezronites: of Carmi, the family of the Carmites.

⁷These are the families of the Reubenites: and they that were numbered of them were forty and three thousand and seven hundred and thirty.

⁸And the sons of Pallu; Eliab.

⁹And the sons of Eliab; Nemuel, and Dathan, and Abiram. This is that Dathan and Abiram, which were famous in the congregation, who strove against Moses and against Aaron in the company of Korah, when they strove against the LORD:

¹⁰And the earth opened her mouth, and swallowed them up together with Korah, when that company died, what time the fire devoured two hundred and fifty men: and they became a sign.

¹¹Notwithstanding the children of Korah died not.

¹²The sons of Simeon after their families: of Nemuel, the family of the Nemuelites: of Jamin, the family of the Jaminites: of Jachin, the family of the Jachinites:

¹³Of Zerah, the family of the Zarhites: of Shaul, the family of the Shaulites.

¹⁴These are the families of the Simeonites, twenty and two thousand and two hundred.

¹⁵The children of Gad after their families: of Zephon, the family of the Zephonites: of Haggi, the family of the Haggites: of Shuni, the family of the Shunites:

¹⁶Of Ozni, the family of the Oznites: of Eri, the family of the Erites:

¹⁷Of Arod, the family of the Arodites: of Areli, the family of the Arelites.

¹⁸These are the families of the children of Gad according to those that were numbered of them, forty thousand and five hundred.

¹⁹The sons of Judah were Er and Onan: and Er and Onan died in the land of Canaan.

²⁰And the sons of Judah after their families were; of Shelah, the family of the Shelanites: of Pharez, the family of the Pharzites: of Zerah, the family of the Zarhites.

²¹And the sons of Pharez were; of Hezron, the family of the Hezronites: of Hamul, the family of the Hamulites.

²²These are the families of Judah according to those that were numbered of them, threescore and sixteen thousand and five hundred.

²³Of the sons of Issachar after their families: of Tola, the family of the Tolaites: of Pua, the family of the Punites:

²⁴Of Jashub, the family of the Jashubites: of Shimron, the family of the Shimronites.

²⁵These are the families of Issachar according to those that were numbered of them, threescore and four thousand and three hundred.

²⁶Of the sons of Zebulun after their families: of Sered, the family of the Sardites: of Elon, the family of the Elonites: of Jahleel, the family of the Jahleelites.

²⁷These are the families of the Zebulunites according to those that were numbered of them, threescore thousand and five hundred.

²⁸The sons of Joseph after their families were Manasseh and Ephraim.

²⁹Of the sons of Manasseh: of Machir, the family of the Machirites: and Machir begat Gilead: of Gilead come the family of the Gileadites.

³⁰These are the sons of Gilead: of Jeezer, the family of the Jeezerites: of Helek, the family of the Helekites:

³¹And of Asriel, the family of the Asrielites: and of Shechem, the family of the Shechemites:

³²And of Shemida, the family of the Shemidaites: and of Hepher, the family of the Hepherites.

³³And Zelophehad the son of Hepher had no sons, but daughters: and the names of the daughters of Zelophehad were Mahlah, and Noah, Hoglah, Milcah, and Tirzah.

³⁴These are the families of Manasseh, and those that were numbered of them, fifty and two thousand and seven hundred.

³⁵These are the sons of Ephraim after their families: of Shuthelah, the family of the Shuthalhites: of Becher, the family of the Bachrites: of Tahan, the family of the Tahanites.

³⁶And these are the sons of Shuthelah: of Eran, the family of the Eranites.

³⁷These are the families of the sons of Ephraim according to those that were numbered of them, thirty and two thousand and five hundred. These are the sons of Joseph after their families.

³⁸The sons of Ben-jamin after their families: of Bela, the family of the Belaites: of Ashbel, the family of the Ashbelites: of Ahiram, the family of the Ahiramites:

³⁹Of Shupham, the family of the Shuphamites: of Hupham, the family of the Huphamites.

⁴⁰And the sons of Bela were Ard and Naaman: of Ard, the family of the Ardites: and of Naaman, the family of the Naamites.

⁴¹These are the sons of Ben-jamin after their families: and they that were numbered of them were forty and five thousand and six hundred.

⁴²These are the sons of Dan after their families: of Shuham, the family of the Shuhamites. These are the families of Dan after their families.

⁴³All the families of the Shuhamites, according to those that were numbered of them, were threescore and four thousand and four hundred.

⁴⁴Of the children of Asher after their families: of Jimna, the family of the Jimnites: of Jesui, the family of the Jesuites: of Beriah, the family of the Beriites.

⁴⁵Of the sons of Beriah: of Heber, the family of the Heberites: of Malchiel, the family of the Malchielites.

⁴⁶And the name of the daughter of Asher was Sarah.

⁴⁷These are the families of the sons of Asher according to those that were numbered of them; who were fifty and three thousand and four hundred.

⁴⁸Of the sons of Naphtali after their families: of Jahzeel, the family of the Jahzeelites: of Guni, the family of the Gunites:

⁴⁹Of Jezer, the family of the Jezerites: of Shillem, the family of the Shillemites.

⁵⁰These are the families of Naphtali according to their families: and they that were numbered of them were forty and five thousand and four hundred.

⁵¹These were the numbered of the children of Israel, six hundred thousand and a thousand seven hundred and thirty.

⁵²And the LORD spake unto Moses, saying,

⁵³Unto these the land shall be divided for an inheritance according to the number of names.

⁵⁴To many thou shalt give the more inheritance, and to few thou shalt give the less inheritance: to every one shall his inheritance be given according to those that were numbered of him.

⁵⁵Notwithstanding the land shall be divided by lot: according to the names of the tribes of their fathers they shall inherit.

⁵⁶According to the lot shall the possession thereof be divided between many and few.

⁵⁷And these are they that were numbered of the Levites after their

families: of Gershon, the family of the Gershonites: of Kohath, the family of the Kohathites: of Merari, the family of the Merarites.

⁵⁸These are the families of the Levites: the family of the Libnites, the family of the Hebronites, the family of the Mahlites, the family of the Mushites, the family of the Korathites. And Kohath begat Amram.

⁵⁹And the name of Amram's wife was Jochebed, the daughter of Levi, whom her mother bare to Levi in Egypt: and she bare unto Amram Aaron and Moses, and Miriam their sister.

⁶⁰And unto Aaron was born Nadab, and Abihu, Eleazar, and Ithamar.

⁶¹And Nadab and Abihu died, when they offered strange fire before the LORD.

⁶²And those that were numbered of them were twenty and three thousand, all males from a month old and upward: for they were not numbered among the children of Israel, because there was no inheritance given them among the children of Israel.

⁶³These are they that were numbered by Moses and Eleazar the priest, who numbered the children of Israel in the plains of Moab by Jordan near Jericho.

⁶⁴But among these there was not a man of them whom Moses and Aaron the priest numbered, when they numbered the children of Israel in the wilderness of Sinai.

⁶⁵For the LORD had said of them, They shall surely die in the wilderness. And there was not left a man of them, save Caleb the son of Jephunneh, and Joshua the son of Nun.

CHAPTER 27

¹Then came the daughters of Zelophehad, the son of Hepher, the son of Gilead, the son of Machir, the son of Manasseh, of the families of Manasseh the son of Joseph: and these are the names of his daughters; Mahlah, Noah, and Hoglah, and Milcah, and Tirzah.

²And they stood before Moses, and before Eleazar the priest, and before the princes and all the congregation, by the door of the tabernacle of the congregation, saying,

³Our father died in the wilderness, and he was not in the company of them that gathered themselves together against the LORD in the company of Korah; but died in his own sin, and had no sons.

⁴Why should the name of our father be done away from among his family, because he hath no son? Give unto us therefore a possession among the brethren of our father.

⁵And Moses brought their cause before the LORD.

⁶And the LORD spake unto Moses, saying,

⁷The daughters of Zelophehad speak right: thou shalt surely give them a possession of an inheritance among their father's brethren; and thou shalt cause the inheritance of their father to pass unto them.

⁸And thou shalt speak unto the children of Israel, saying, If a man die, and have no son, then ye shall cause his inheritance to pass unto his daughter.

⁹And if he have no daughter, then ye shall give his inheritance unto his brethren.

¹⁰And if he have no brethren, then ye shall give his inheritance unto his father's brethren.

¹¹And if his father have no brethren, then ye shall give his inheritance unto his kinsman that is next to him of his family, and he shall possess it: and it shall be unto the children of Israel a statute of judgment, as the LORD commanded Moses.

¹²And the LORD said unto Moses, Get thee up into this mount Abarim, and see the land which I have given unto the children of Israel.

¹³And when thou hast seen it, thou also shalt be gathered unto thy people, as Aaron thy brother was gathered.

¹⁴For ye rebelled against my commandment in the desert of Zin, in the strife of the congregation, to sanctify me at the water before their eyes: that is the water of Meribah in Kadesh in the wilderness of Zin.

¹⁵And Moses spake unto the LORD, saying,

¹⁶Let the LORD, the God of the spirits of all flesh, set a man over the congregation,

¹⁷Which may go out before them, and which may go in before them, and which may lead them out, and which may bring them in; that the congregation of the LORD be not as sheep which have no shepherd.

¹⁸And the LORD said unto Moses, Take thee Joshua the son of Nun, a man in whom is the spirit, and lay thine hand upon him;

¹⁹And set him before Eleazar the priest, and before all the congregation; and give him a charge in their sight.

²⁰And thou shalt put some of thine honour upon him, that all the congregation of the children of Israel may be obedient.

²¹And he shall stand before Eleazar the priest, who shall ask counsel for him after the judgment of Urim before the LORD: at his word shall they go out, and at his word they shall come in, both he, and all the children of Israel with him, even all the congregation.

²²And Moses did as the LORD commanded him: and he took Joshua, and set him before Eleazar the priest, and before all the congregation:

²³And he laid his hands upon him, and gave him a charge, as the LORD commanded by the hand of Moses.

CHAPTER 28

¹And the LORD spake unto Moses, saying,

²Command the children of Israel, and say unto them, My offering, and my bread for my sacrifices made by fire, for a sweet savour unto me, shall ye observe to offer unto me in their due season.

³And thou shalt say unto them, This is the offering made by fire which ye shall offer unto the LORD; two lambs of the first year without spot day by day, for a continual burnt offering.

⁴The one lamb shalt thou offer in the morning, and the other lamb shalt thou offer at even;

⁵And a tenth part of an ephah of flour for a meat offering, mingled with the fourth part of an hin of beaten oil.

⁶It is a continual burnt offering, which was ordained in mount Sinai for a sweet savour, a sacrifice made by fire unto the LORD.

⁷And the drink offering thereof shall be the fourth part of an hin for the one lamb: in the holy place shalt thou cause the strong wine to be poured unto the LORD for a drink offering.

⁸And the other lamb shalt thou offer at even: as the meat offering of the morning, and as the drink offering thereof, thou shalt offer it, a sacrifice made by fire, of a sweet savour unto the LORD.

⁹And on the sabbath day two lambs of the first year without spot, and two tenth deals of flour for a meat offering, mingled with oil, and the drink offering thereof:

¹⁰This is the burnt offering of every sabbath, beside the continual burnt offering, and his drink offering.

¹¹And in the beginnings of your months ye shall offer a burnt offering unto the LORD; two young bullocks, and one ram, seven lambs of the first year without spot;

¹²And three tenth deals of flour for a meat offering, mingled with oil, for one bullock; and two tenth deals of flour for a meat offering, mingled with oil, for one ram;

¹³And a several tenth deal of flour mingled with oil for a meat offering unto one lamb; for a burnt offering of a sweet savour, a sacrifice made by fire unto the LORD.

¹⁴And their drink offerings shall be half an hin of wine unto a bullock, and the third part of an hin unto a ram, and a fourth part of an hin unto a lamb: this is the burnt offering of every month throughout the months of the year.

¹⁵And one kid of the goats for a sin offering unto the LORD shall be offered, beside the continual burnt offering, and his drink offering.

¹⁶And in the fourteenth day of the first month is the passover of the LORD.

¹⁷And in the fifteenth day of this month is the feast: seven days shall unleavened bread be eaten.

¹⁸In the first day shall be an holy convocation; ye shall do no manner of servile work therein:

¹⁹But ye shall offer a sacrifice made by fire for a burnt offering unto the LORD; two young bullocks, and one ram, and seven lambs of the first year: they shall be unto you without blemish:

²⁰And their meat offering shall be of flour mingled with oil: three tenth deals shall ye offer for a bullock, and two tenth deals for a ram;

²¹A several tenth deal shalt thou offer for every lamb, throughout the seven lambs:

²²And one goat for a sin offering, to make an atonement for you.

²³Ye shall offer these beside the burnt offering in the morning, which is for a continual burnt offering.

²⁴After this manner ye shall offer daily, throughout the seven days, the meat of the sacrifice made by fire, of a sweet savour unto the LORD: it shall be offered beside the continual burnt offering, and his drink offering.

²⁵And on the seventh day ye shall have an holy convocation; ye shall do no servile work.

²⁶Also in the day of the firstfruits, when ye bring a new meat offering unto the LORD, after your weeks be out, ye shall have an holy convocation; ye shall do no servile work:

²⁷But ye shall offer the burnt offering for a sweet savour unto the LORD; two young bullocks, one ram, seven lambs of the first year;

²⁸And their meat offering of flour mingled with oil, three tenth deals unto one bullock, two tenth deals unto one ram,

²⁹A several tenth deal unto one lamb, throughout the seven lambs;

³⁰And one kid of the goats, to make an atonement for you.

³¹Ye shall offer them beside the continual burnt offering, and his meat offering, (they shall be unto you without blemish) and their drink offerings.

CHAPTER 29

¹And in the seventh month, on the first day of the month, ye shall have an holy convocation; ye shall do no servile work: it is a day of blowing the trumpets unto you.

²And ye shall offer a burnt offering for a sweet savour unto the LORD; one young bullock, one ram, and seven lambs of the first year without blemish:

³And their meat offering shall be of flour mingled with oil, three tenth deals for a bullock, and two tenth deals for a ram,

⁴And one tenth deal for one lamb, throughout the seven lambs:

⁵And one kid of the goats for a sin offering, to make an atonement for you:

⁶Beside the burnt offering of the month, and his meat offering, and the daily burnt offering, and his meat offering, and their drink offerings, according unto their manner, for a sweet savour, a sacrifice made by fire unto the LORD.

⁷And ye shall have on the tenth day of this seventh month an holy convocation; and ye shall afflict your souls: ye shall not do any work therein:

⁸But ye shall offer a burnt offering unto the LORD for a sweet savour; one young bullock, one ram, and seven lambs of the first year; they shall be unto you without blemish:

⁹And their meat offering shall be of flour mingled with oil, three tenth deals to a bullock, and two tenth deals to one ram,

¹⁰A several tenth deal for one lamb, throughout the seven lambs:

¹¹One kid of the goats for a sin offering; beside the sin offering of atonement, and the continual burnt offering, and the meat offering of it, and their drink offerings.

¹²And on the fifteenth day of the seventh month ye shall have an holy convocation; ye shall do no servile work, and ye shall keep a feast unto the LORD seven days:

¹³And ye shall offer a burnt offering, a sacrifice made by fire, of a sweet savour unto the LORD; thirteen young bullocks, two rams, and fourteen lambs of the first year; they shall be without blemish:

¹⁴And their meat offering shall be of flour mingled with oil, three tenth deals unto every bullock of the thirteen bullocks, two tenth deals to each ram of the two rams,

¹⁵And a several tenth deal to each lamb of the fourteen lambs:

¹⁶And one kid of the goats for a sin offering; beside the continual burnt offering, his meat offering, and his drink offering.

¹⁷And on the second day ye shall offer twelve young bullocks, two rams, fourteen lambs of the first year without spot:

¹⁸And their meat offering and their drink offerings for the bullocks, for the rams, and for the lambs, shall be according to their number, after the manner:

¹⁹And one kid of the goats for a sin offering; beside the continual burnt offering, and the meat offering thereof, and their drink offerings.

²⁰And on the third day eleven bullocks, two rams, fourteen lambs of the first year without blemish;

²¹And their meat offering and their drink offerings for the bullocks, for the rams, and for the lambs, shall be according to their number, after the manner:

²²And one goat for a sin offering; beside the continual burnt offering, and his meat offering, and his drink offering.

²³And on the fourth day ten bullocks, two rams, and fourteen lambs of the first year without blemish:

²⁴Their meat offering and their drink offerings for the bullocks, for the rams, and for the lambs, shall be according to their number, after the manner:

²⁵And one kid of the goats for a sin offering; beside the continual burnt offering, his meat offering, and his drink offering.

²⁶And on the fifth day nine bullocks, two rams, and fourteen lambs of the first year without spot:

²⁷And their meat offering and their drink offerings for the bullocks, for the rams, and for the lambs, shall be according to their number, after the manner:

²⁸And one goat for a sin offering; beside the continual burnt offering, and his meat offering, and his drink offering.

²⁹And on the sixth day eight bullocks, two rams, and fourteen lambs of the first year without blemish:

³⁰And their meat offering and their drink offerings for the bullocks, for the rams, and for the lambs, shall be according to their number, after the manner:

³¹And one goat for a sin offering; beside the continual burnt offering,

his meat offering, and his drink offering.

³²And on the seventh day seven bullocks, two rams, and fourteen lambs of the first year without blemish:

³³And their meat offering and their drink offerings for the bullocks, for the rams, and for the lambs, shall be according to their number, after the manner:

³⁴And one goat for a sin offering; beside the continual burnt offering, his meat offering, and his drink offering.

³⁵On the eighth day ye shall have a solemn assembly: ye shall do no servile work therein:

³⁶But ye shall offer a burnt offering, a sacrifice made by fire, of a sweet savour unto the LORD: one bullock, one ram, seven lambs of the first year without blemish:

³⁷Their meat offering and their drink offerings for the bullock, for the ram, and for the lambs, shall be according to their number, after the manner:

³⁸And one goat for a sin offering; beside the continual burnt offering, and his meat offering, and his drink offering.

³⁹These things ye shall do unto the LORD in your set feasts, beside your vows, and your freewill offerings, for your burnt offerings, and for your meat offerings, and for your drink offerings, and for your peace offerings.

⁴⁰And Moses told the children of Israel according to all that the LORD commanded Moses.

CHAPTER 30

¹And Moses spake unto the heads of the tribes concerning the children of Israel, saying, This is the thing which the LORD hath commanded.

²If a man vow a vow unto the LORD, or swear an oath to bind his soul with a bond; he shall not break his word, he shall do according to all that proceedeth out of his mouth.

³If a woman also vow a vow unto the LORD, and bind herself by a bond, being in her father's house in her youth;

⁴And her father hear her vow, and her bond wherewith she hath bound her soul, and her father shall hold his peace at her; then all her vows shall stand, and every bond wherewith she hath bound her soul shall stand.

⁵But if her father disallow her in the day that he heareth; not any of her vows, or of her bonds wherewith she hath bound her soul, shall stand:

and the LORD shall forgive her, because her father disallowed her.

⁶And if she had at all an husband, when she vowed, or uttered ought out of her lips, wherewith she bound her soul;

⁷And her husband heard it, and held his peace at her in the day that he heard it: then her vows shall stand, and her bonds wherewith she bound her soul shall stand.

⁸But if her husband disallowed her on the day that he heard it; then he shall make her vow which she vowed, and that which she uttered with her lips, wherewith she bound her soul, of none effect: and the LORD shall forgive her.

⁹But every vow of a widow, and of her that is divorced, wherewith they have bound their souls, shall stand against her.

¹⁰And if she vowed in her husband's house, or bound her soul by a bond with an oath;

¹¹And her husband heard it, and held his peace at her, and disallowed her not: then all her vows shall stand, and every bond wherewith she bound her soul shall stand.

¹²But if her husband hath utterly made them void on the day he heard them; then whatsoever proceeded out of her lips concerning her vows, or concerning the bond of her soul, shall not stand: her husband hath made them void; and the LORD shall forgive her.

¹³Every vow, and every binding oath to afflict the soul, her husband may establish it, or her husband may make it void.

¹⁴But if her husband altogether hold his peace at her from day to day; then he establisheth all her vows, or all her bonds, which are upon her: he confirmeth them, because he held his peace at her in the day that he heard them.

¹⁵But if he shall any ways make them void after that he hath heard them; then he shall bear her iniquity.

¹⁶These are the statutes, which the LORD commanded Moses, between a man and his wife, between the father and his daughter, being yet in her youth in her father's house.

CHAPTER 31

¹And the LORD spake unto Moses, saying,

²Avenge the children of Israel of the Midianites: afterward shalt thou be gathered unto thy people.

³And Moses spake unto the people, saying, Arm some of yourselves unto the war, and let them go against the Midianites, and avenge the LORD of Midian.

⁴Of every tribe a thousand, throughout all the tribes of Israel, shall ye send to the war.

⁵So there were delivered out of the thousands of Israel, a thousand of every tribe, twelve thousand armed for war.

⁶And Moses sent them to the war, a thousand of every tribe, them and Phinehas the son of Eleazar the priest, to the war, with the holy instruments, and the trumpets to blow in his hand.

⁷And they warred against the Midianites, as the LORD commanded Moses; and they slew all the males.

⁸And they slew the kings of Midian, beside the rest of them that were slain; namely, Evi, and Rekem, and Zur, and Hur, and Reba, five kings of Midian: Balaam also the son of Beor they slew with the sword.

⁹And the children of Israel took all the women of Midian captives, and their little ones, and took the spoil of all their cattle, and all their flocks, and all their goods.

¹⁰And they burnt all their cities wherein they dwelt, and all their goodly castles, with fire.

¹¹And they took all the spoil, and all the prey, both of men and of beasts.

¹²And they brought the captives, and the prey, and the spoil, unto Moses, and Eleazar the priest, and unto the congregation of the children of Israel, unto the camp at the plains of Moab, which are by Jordan near Jericho.

¹³And Moses, and Eleazar the priest, and all the princes of the congregation, went forth to meet them without the camp.

¹⁴And Moses was wroth with the officers of the host, with the captains over thousands, and captains over hundreds, which came from the battle.

¹⁵And Moses said unto them, Have ye saved all the women alive?

¹⁶Behold, these caused the children of Israel, through the counsel of Balaam, to commit trespass against the LORD in the matter of Peor, and there was a plague among the congregation of the LORD.

¹⁷Now therefore kill every male among the little ones, and kill every woman that hath known man by lying with him.

¹⁸But all the women children, that have not known a man by lying with him, keep alive for yourselves.

¹⁹And do ye abide without the camp seven days: whosoever hath killed any person, and whosoever hath touched any slain, purify both yourselves and your captives on the third day, and on the seventh day.

²⁰And purify all your raiment, and all that is made of skins, and all work of goats' hair, and all things made of wood.

²¹And Eleazar the priest said unto the men of war which went to the battle, This is the ordinance of the law which the LORD commanded Moses;

²²Only the gold, and the silver, the brass, the iron, the tin, and the lead,

²³Every thing that may abide the fire, ye shall make it go through the fire, and it shall be clean: nevertheless it shall be purified with the water of separation: and all that abideth not the fire ye shall make go through the water.

²⁴And ye shall wash your clothes on the seventh day, and ye shall be clean, and afterward ye shall come into the camp.

²⁵And the LORD spake unto Moses, saying,

²⁶Take the sum of the prey that was taken, both of man and of beast, thou, and Eleazar the priest, and the chief fathers of the congregation:

²⁷And divide the prey into two parts; between them that took the war upon them, who went out to battle, and between all the congregation:

²⁸And levy a tribute unto the Lord of the men of war which went out to battle: one soul of five hundred, both of the persons, and of the beeves, and of the asses, and of the sheep:

²⁹Take it of their half, and give it unto Eleazar the priest, for an heave offering of the LORD.

³⁰And of the children of Israel's half, thou shalt take one portion of fifty, of the persons, of the beeves, of the asses, and of the flocks, of all manner of beasts, and give them unto the Levites, which keep the charge of the tabernacle of the LORD.

³¹And Moses and Eleazar the priest did as the LORD commanded Moses.

³²And the booty, being the rest of the prey which the men of war had caught, was six hundred thousand and seventy thousand and five thousand sheep,

³³And threescore and twelve thousand beeves,

³⁴And threescore and one thousand asses,

³⁵And thirty and two thousand persons in all, of women that had not known man by lying with him.

³⁶And the half, which was the portion of them that went out to war, was in number three hundred thousand and seven and thirty thousand and five hundred sheep:

³⁷And the LORD's tribute of the sheep was six hundred and threescore and fifteen.

³⁸And the beeves were thirty and six thousand; of which the LORD's tribute was threescore and twelve.

³⁹And the asses were thirty thousand and five hundred; of which the LORD's tribute was threescore and one.

⁴⁰And the persons were sixteen thousand; of which the LORD's tribute was thirty and two persons.

⁴¹And Moses gave the tribute, which was the LORD's heave offering, unto Eleazar the priest, as the LORD commanded Moses.

⁴²And of the children of Israel's half, which Moses divided from the men that warred,

⁴³(Now the half that pertained unto the congregation was three hundred thousand and thirty thousand and seven thousand and five hundred sheep,

⁴⁴And thirty and six thousand beeves,

⁴⁵And thirty thousand asses and five hundred,

⁴⁶And sixteen thousand persons;)

⁴⁷Even of the children of Israel's half, Moses took one portion of fifty, both of man and of beast, and gave them unto the Levites, which kept the charge of the tabernacle of the LORD; as the LORD commanded Moses.

⁴⁸And the officers which were over thousands of the host, the captains of thousands, and captains of hundreds, came near unto Moses:

⁴⁹And they said unto Moses, Thy servants have taken the sum of the men of war which are under our charge, and there lacketh not one man of us.

⁵⁰We have therefore brought an oblation for the LORD, what every man hath gotten, of jewels of gold, chains, and bracelets, rings, earrings, and tablets, to make an atonement for our souls before the LORD.

⁵¹And Moses and Eleazar the priest took the gold of them, even all wrought jewels.

⁵²And all the gold of the offering that they offered up to the LORD, of the captains of thousands, and of the captains of hundreds, was sixteen thousand seven hundred and fifty shekels.

⁵³(For the men of war had taken spoil, every man for himself.)

⁵⁴And Moses and Eleazar the priest took the gold of the captains of thousands and of hundreds, and brought it into the tabernacle of the congregation, for a memorial for the children of Israel before the LORD.

CHAPTER 32

¹Now the children of Reuben and the children of Gad had a very great multitude of cattle: and when they saw the land of Jazer, and the land of Gilead, that, behold, the place was a place for cattle;

²The children of Gad and the children of Reuben came and spake unto Moses, and to Eleazar the priest, and unto the princes of the congregation, saying,

³Ataroth, and Dibon, and Jazer, and Nimrah, and Heshbon, and Elealeh, and Shebam, and Nebo, and Beon,

⁴Even the country which the LORD smote before the congregation of Israel, is a land for cattle, and thy servants have cattle:

⁵Wherefore, said they, if we have found grace in thy sight, let this land be given unto thy servants for a possession, and bring us not over Jordan.

⁶And Moses said unto the children of Gad and to the children of Reuben, Shall your brethren go to war, and shall ye sit here?

⁷And wherefore discourage ye the heart of the children of Israel from going over into the land which the LORD hath given them?

⁸Thus did your fathers, when I sent them from Kadesh-barnea to see the land.

⁹For when they went up unto the valley of Eshcol, and saw the land, they discouraged the heart of the children of Israel, that they should not go into the land which the LORD had given them.

¹⁰And the LORD's anger was kindled the same time, and he sware, saying,

¹¹Surely none of the men that came up out of Egypt, from twenty years old and upward, shall see the land which I sware unto Abraham, unto Isaac, and unto Jacob; because they have not wholly followed me:

¹²Save Caleb the son of Jephunneh the Kenezite, and Joshua the son of Nun: for they have wholly followed the LORD.

¹³And the LORD's anger was kindled against Israel, and he made them wander in the wilderness forty years, until all the generation, that had done evil in the sight of the LORD, was consumed.

¹⁴And, behold, ye are risen up in your fathers' stead, an increase of sinful men, to augment yet the fierce anger of the LORD toward Israel.

¹⁵For if ye turn away from after him, he will yet again leave them in the wilderness; and ye shall destroy all this people.

16And they came near unto him, and said, We will build sheepfolds here for our cattle, and cities for our little ones:

17But we ourselves will go ready armed before the children of Israel, until we have brought them unto their place: and our little ones shall dwell in the fenced cities because of the inhabitants of the land.

18We will not return unto our houses, until the children of Israel have inherited every man his inheritance.

19For we will not inherit with them on yonder side Jordan, or forward; because our inheritance is fallen to us on this side Jordan eastward.

20And Moses said unto them, If ye will do this thing, if ye will go armed before the LORD to war,

21And will go all of you armed over Jordan before the LORD, until he hath driven out his enemies from before him,

22And the land be subdued before the LORD: then afterward ye shall return, and be guiltless before the LORD, and before Israel; and this land shall be your possession before the LORD.

23But if ye will not do so, behold, ye have sinned against the LORD: and be sure your sin will find you out.

24Build you cities for your little ones, and folds for your sheep; and do that which hath proceeded out of your mouth.

25And the children of Gad and the children of Reuben spake unto Moses, saying, Thy servants will do as my lord commandeth.

26Our little ones, our wives, our flocks, and all our cattle, shall be there in the cities of Gilead:

27But thy servants will pass over, every man armed for war, before the LORD to battle, as my lord saith.

28So concerning them Moses commanded Eleazar the priest, and Joshua the son of Nun, and the chief fathers of the tribes of the children of Israel:

29And Moses said unto them, If the children of Gad and the children of Reuben will pass with you over Jordan, every man armed to battle, before the LORD, and the land shall be subdued before you; then ye shall give them the land of Gilead for a possession:

30But if they will not pass over with you armed, they shall have possessions among you in the land of Canaan.

31And the children of Gad and the children of Reuben answered, saying, As the LORD hath said unto thy servants, so will we do.

³²We will pass over armed before the LORD into the land of Canaan, that the possession of our inheritance on this side Jordan may be ours.

³³And Moses gave unto them, even to the children of Gad, and to the children of Reuben, and unto half the tribe of Manasseh the son of Joseph, the kingdom of Sihon king of the Amorites, and the kingdom of Og king of Bashan, the land, with the cities thereof in the coasts, even the cities of the country round about.

³⁴And the children of Gad built Dibon, and Ataroth, and Aroer,

³⁵And Atroth, Shophan, and Jaazer, and Jogbehah,

³⁶And Beth-nimrah, and Bethharan, fenced cities: and folds for sheep.

³⁷And the children of Reuben built Heshbon, and Elealeh, and Kirjathaim,

³⁸And Nebo, and Baal-meon, (their names being changed,) and Shibmah: and gave other names unto the cities which they builded.

³⁹And the children of Machir the son of Manasseh went to Gilead, and took it, and dispossessed the Amorite which was in it.

⁴⁰And Moses gave Gilead unto Machir the son of Manasseh; and he dwelt therein.

⁴¹And Jair the son of Manasseh went and took the small towns thereof, and called them Havoth-jair.

⁴²And Nobah went and took Kenath, and the villages thereof, and called it Nobah, after his own name.

CHAPTER 33

¹These are the journeys of the children of Israel, which went forth out of the land of Egypt with their armies under the hand of Moses and Aaron.

²And Moses wrote their goings out according to their journeys by the commandment of the LORD: and these are their journeys according to their goings out.

³And they departed from Rameses in the first month, on the fifteenth day of the first month; on the morrow after the passover the children of Israel went out with an high hand in the sight of all the Egyptians.

⁴For the Egyptians buried all their firstborn, which the LORD had smitten among them: upon their gods also the LORD executed judgments.

⁵And the children of Israel removed from Rameses, and pitched in Succoth.

⁶And they departed from Succoth, and pitched in Etham, which is in the edge of the wilderness.

⁷And they removed from Etham, and turned again unto Pi-hahiroth, which is before Baal-zephon: and they pitched before Migdol.

⁸And they departed from before Pi-hahiroth, and passed through the midst of the sea into the wilderness, and went three days' journey in the wilderness of Etham, and pitched in Marah.

⁹And they removed from Marah, and came unto Elim: and in Elim were twelve fountains of water, and threescore and ten palm trees; and they pitched there.

¹⁰And they removed from Elim, and encamped by the Red sea.

¹¹And they removed from the Red sea, and encamped in the wilderness of Sin.

¹²And they took their journey out of the wilderness of Sin, and encamped in Dophkah.

¹³And they departed from Dophkah, and encamped in Alush.

¹⁴And they removed from Alush, and encamped at Rephidim, where was no water for the people to drink.

¹⁵And they departed from Rephidim, and pitched in the wilderness of Sinai.

¹⁶And they removed from the desert of Sinai, and pitched at Kibroth-hattaavah.

¹⁷And they departed from Kibroth-hattaavah, and encamped at Hazeroth.

¹⁸And they departed from Hazeroth, and pitched in Rithmah.

¹⁹And they departed from Rithmah, and pitched at Rimmon-parez.

²⁰And they departed from Rimmon-parez, and pitched in Libnah.

²¹And they removed from Libnah, and pitched at Rissah.

²²And they journeyed from Rissah, and pitched in Kehelathah.

²³And they went from Kehelathah, and pitched in mount Shapher.

²⁴And they removed from mount Shapher, and encamped in Haradah.

²⁵And they removed from Haradah, and pitched in Makheloth.

²⁶And they removed from Makheloth, and encamped at Tahath.

²⁷And they departed from Tahath, and pitched at Tarah.

²⁸And they removed from Tarah, and pitched in Mithcah.

²⁹And they went from Mithcah, and pitched in Hashmonah.

³⁰And they departed from Hashmonah, and encamped at Moseroth.

³¹And they departed from Moseroth, and pitched in Benejaakan.

³²And they removed from Benejaakan, and encamped at Horhagidgad.

³³And they went from Horhagidgad, and pitched in Jotbathah.

³⁴And they removed from Jotbathah, and encamped at Ebronah.

³⁵And they departed from Ebronah, and encamped at Eziongaber.

³⁶And they removed from Eziongaber, and pitched in the wilderness of Zin, which is Kadesh.

³⁷And they removed from Kadesh, and pitched in mount Hor, in the edge of the land of Edom.

³⁸And Aaron the priest went up into mount Hor at the commandment of the LORD, and died there, in the fortieth year after the children of Israel were come out of the land of Egypt, in the first day of the fifth month.

³⁹And Aaron was an hundred and twenty and three years old when he died in mount Hor.

⁴⁰And king Arad the Canaanite, which dwelt in the south in the land of Canaan, heard of the coming of the children of Israel.

⁴¹And they departed from mount Hor, and pitched in Zalmonah.

⁴²And they departed from Zalmonah, and pitched in Punon.

⁴³And they departed from Punon, and pitched in Oboth.

⁴⁴And they departed from Oboth, and pitched in Ije-abarim, in the border of Moab.

⁴⁵And they departed from Iim, and pitched in Dibon-gad.

⁴⁶And they removed from Dibon-gad, and encamped in Almon-diblathaim.

⁴⁷And they removed from Almon-diblathaim, and pitched in the mountains of Abarim, before Nebo.

⁴⁸And they departed from the mountains of Abarim, and pitched in the plains of Moab by Jordan near Jericho.

⁴⁹And they pitched by Jordan, from Beth-jesimoth even unto Abel-shittim in the plains of Moab.

⁵⁰And the LORD spake unto Moses in the plains of Moab by Jordan near Jericho, saying,

⁵¹Speak unto the children of Israel, and say unto them, When ye are passed over Jordan into the land of Canaan;

⁵²Then ye shall drive out all the inhabitants of the land from before you, and destroy all their pictures, and destroy all their molten images, and quite pluck down all their high places:

⁵³And ye shall dispossess the inhabitants of the land, and dwell therein: for I have given you the land to possess it.

⁵⁴And ye shall divide the land by lot for an inheritance among your families: and to the more ye shall give the more inheritance, and to the fewer ye shall give the less inheritance: every man's inheritance shall be in the place where his lot falleth; according to the tribes of your fathers ye shall inherit.

⁵⁵But if ye will not drive out the inhabitants of the land from before you; then it shall come to pass, that those which ye let remain of them shall be pricks in your eyes, and thorns in your sides, and shall vex you in the land wherein ye dwell.

⁵⁶Moreover it shall come to pass, that I shall do unto you, as I thought to do unto them.

CHAPTER 34

¹And the LORD spake unto Moses, saying,

²Command the children of Israel, and say unto them, When ye come into the land of Canaan; (this is the land that shall fall unto you for an inheritance, even the land of Canaan with the coasts thereof:)

³Then your south quarter shall be from the wilderness of Zin along by the coast of Edom, and your south border shall be the outmost coast of the salt sea eastward:

⁴And your border shall turn from the south to the ascent of Akrabbim, and pass on to Zin: and the going forth thereof shall be from the south to Kadesh-barnea, and shall go on to Hazar-addar, and pass on to Azmon:

⁵And the border shall fetch a compass from Azmon unto the river of Egypt, and the goings out of it shall be at the sea.

⁶And as for the western border, ye shall even have the great sea for a border: this shall be your west border.

⁷And this shall be your north border: from the great sea ye shall point out for you mount Hor:

⁸From mount Hor ye shall point out your border unto the entrance of Hamath; and the goings forth of the border shall be to Zedad:

⁹And the border shall go on to Ziphron, and the goings out of it shall be at Hazar-enan: this shall be your north border.

¹⁰And ye shall point out your east border from Hazar-enan to Shepham:

¹¹And the coast shall go down from Shepham to Riblah, on the

east side of Ain; and the border shall descend, and shall reach unto the side of the sea of Chinnereth eastward:

¹²And the border shall go down to Jordan, and the goings out of it shall be at the salt sea: this shall be your land with the coasts thereof round about.

¹³And Moses commanded the children of Israel, saying, This is the land which ye shall inherit by lot, which the LORD commanded to give unto the nine tribes, and to the half tribe:

¹⁴For the tribe of the children of Reuben according to the house of their fathers, and the tribe of the children of Gad according to the house of their fathers, have received their inheritance; and half the tribe of Manasseh have received their inheritance:

¹⁵The two tribes and the half tribe have received their inheritance on this side Jordan near Jericho eastward, toward the sunrising.

¹⁶And the LORD spake unto Moses, saying,

¹⁷These are the names of the men which shall divide the land unto you: Eleazar the priest, and Joshua the son of Nun.

¹⁸And ye shall take one prince of every tribe, to divide the land by inheritance.

¹⁹And the names of the men are these: Of the tribe of Judah, Caleb the son of Jephunneh.

²⁰And of the tribe of the children of Simeon, Shemuel the son of Ammihud.

²¹Of the tribe of Ben-jamin, Elidad the son of Chislon.

²²And the prince of the tribe of the children of Dan, Bukki the son of Jogli.

²³The prince of the children of Joseph, for the tribe of the children of Manasseh, Hanniel the son of Ephod.

²⁴And the prince of the tribe of the children of Ephraim, Kemuel the son of Shiphtan.

²⁵And the prince of the tribe of the children of Zebulun, Elizaphan the son of Parnach.

²⁶And the prince of the tribe of the children of Issachar, Paltiel the son of Azzan.

²⁷And the prince of the tribe of the children of Asher, Ahihud the son of Shelomi.

²⁸And the prince of the tribe of the children of Naphtali, Pedahel the son of Ammihud.

²⁹These are they whom the LORD commanded to divide the inheritance unto the children of Israel in the land of Canaan.

CHAPTER 35

¹And the LORD spake unto Moses in the plains of Moab by Jordan near Jericho, saying,

²Command the children of Israel, that they give unto the Levites of the inheritance of their possession cities to dwell in; and ye shall give also unto the Levites suburbs for the cities round about them.

³And the cities shall they have to dwell in; and the suburbs of them shall be for their cattle, and for their goods, and for all their beasts.

⁴And the suburbs of the cities, which ye shall give unto the Levites, shall reach from the wall of the city and outward a thousand cubits round about.

⁵And ye shall measure from without the city on the east side two thousand cubits, and on the south side two thousand cubits, and on the west side two thousand cubits, and on the north side two thousand cubits; and the city shall be in the midst: this shall be to them the suburbs of the cities.

⁶And among the cities which ye shall give unto the Levites there shall be six cities for refuge, which ye shall appoint for the manslayer, that he may flee thither: and to them ye shall add forty and two cities.

⁷So all the cities which ye shall give to the Levites shall be forty and eight cities: them shall ye give with their suburbs.

⁸And the cities which ye shall give shall be of the possession of the children of Israel: from them that have many ye shall give many; but from them that have few ye shall give few: every one shall give of his cities unto the Levites according to his inheritance which he inheriteth.

⁹And the LORD spake unto Moses, saying,

¹⁰Speak unto the children of Israel, and say unto them, When ye be come over Jordan into the land of Canaan;

¹¹Then ye shall appoint you cities to be cities of refuge for you; that the slayer may flee thither, which killeth any person at unawares.

¹²And they shall be unto you cities for refuge from the avenger; that the manslayer die not, until he stand before the congregation in judgment.

¹³And of these cities which ye shall give six cities shall ye have for refuge.

¹⁴Ye shall give three cities on this side Jordan, and three cities shall ye give in the land of Canaan, which shall be cities of refuge.

¹⁵These six cities shall be a refuge, both for the children of Israel,

and for the stranger, and for the sojourner among them: that every one that killeth any person unawares may flee thither.

¹⁶And if he smite him with an instrument of iron, so that he die, he is a murderer: the murderer shall surely be put to death.

¹⁷And if he smite him with throwing a stone, wherewith he may die, and he die, he is a murderer: the murderer shall surely be put to death.

¹⁸Or if he smite him with an hand weapon of wood, wherewith he may die, and he die, he is a murderer: the murderer shall surely be put to death.

¹⁹The revenger of blood himself shall slay the murderer: when he meeteth him, he shall slay him.

²⁰But if he thrust him of hatred, or hurl at him by laying of wait, that he die;

²¹Or in enmity smite him with his hand, that he die: he that smote him shall surely be put to death; for he is a murderer: the revenger of blood shall slay the murderer, when he meeteth him.

²²But if he thrust him suddenly without enmity, or have cast upon him any thing without laying of wait,

²³Or with any stone, wherewith a man may die, seeing him not, and cast it upon him, that he die, and was not his enemy, neither sought his harm:

²⁴Then the congregation shall judge between the slayer and the revenger of blood according to these judgments:

²⁵And the congregation shall deliver the slayer out of the hand of the revenger of blood, and the congregation shall restore him to the city of his refuge, whither he was fled: and he shall abide in it unto the death of the high priest, which was anointed with the holy oil.

²⁶But if the slayer shall at any time come without the border of the city of his refuge, whither he was fled;

²⁷And the revenger of blood find him without the borders of the city of his refuge, and the revenger of blood kill the slayer; he shall not be guilty of blood:

²⁸Because he should have remained in the city of his refuge until the death of the high priest: but after the death of the high priest the slayer shall return into the land of his possession.

²⁹So these things shall be for a statute of judgment unto you throughout your generations in all your dwellings.

³⁰Whoso killeth any person, the murderer shall be put to death by the mouth of witnesses: but one

witness shall not testify against any person to cause him to die.

³¹Moreover ye shall take no satisfaction for the life of a murderer, which is guilty of death: but he shall be surely put to death.

³²And ye shall take no satisfaction for him that is fled to the city of his refuge, that he should come again to dwell in the land, until the death of the priest.

³³So ye shall not pollute the land wherein ye are: for blood it defileth the land: and the land cannot be cleansed of the blood that is shed therein, but by the blood of him that shed it.

³⁴Defile not therefore the land which ye shall inhabit, wherein I dwell: for I the LORD dwell among the children of Israel.

CHAPTER 36

¹And the chief fathers of the families of the children of Gilead, the son of Machir, the son of Manasseh, of the families of the sons of Joseph, came near, and spake before Moses, and before the princes, the chief fathers of the children of Israel:

²And they said, The LORD commanded my lord to give the land for an inheritance by lot to the children of Israel: and my lord was commanded by the LORD to give the inheritance of Zelophehad our brother unto his daughters.

³And if they be married to any of the sons of the other tribes of the children of Israel, then shall their inheritance be taken from the inheritance of our fathers, and shall be put to the inheritance of the tribe whereunto they are received: so shall it be taken from the lot of our inheritance.

⁴And when the jubile of the children of Israel shall be, then shall their inheritance be put unto the inheritance of the tribe whereunto they are received: so shall their inheritance be taken away from the inheritance of the tribe of our fathers.

⁵And Moses commanded the children of Israel according to the word of the LORD, saying, The tribe of the sons of Joseph hath said well.

⁶This is the thing which the LORD doth command concerning the daughters of Zelophehad, saying, Let them marry to whom they think best; only to the family of the tribe of their father shall they marry.

⁷So shall not the inheritance of the children of Israel remove from

tribe to tribe: for every one of the children of Israel shall keep himself to the inheritance of the tribe of his fathers.

8And every daughter, that possesseth an inheritance in any tribe of the children of Israel, shall be wife unto one of the family of the tribe of her father, that the children of Israel may enjoy every man the inheritance of his fathers.

9Neither shall the inheritance remove from one tribe to another tribe; but every one of the tribes of the children of Israel shall keep himself to his own inheritance.

10Even as the LORD commanded Moses, so did the daughters of Zelophehad:

11For Mahlah, Tirzah, and Hoglah, and Milcah, and Noah, the daughters of Zelophehad, were married unto their father's brothers' sons:

12And they were married into the families of the sons of Manasseh the son of Joseph, and their inheritance remained in the tribe of the family of their father.

13These are the commandments and the judgments, which the LORD commanded by the hand of Moses unto the children of Israel in the plains of Moab by Jordan near Jericho.

DEUTERONOMY

דברים

CHAPTER 1

¹These be the words which Moses spake unto all Israel on this side Jordan in the wilderness, in the plain over against the Red sea, between Paran, and Tophel, and Laban, and Hazeroth, and Dizahab.

²(There are eleven days' journey from Horeb by the way of mount Seir unto Kadesh-barnea.)

³And it came to pass in the fortieth year, in the eleventh month, on the first day of the month, that Moses spake unto the children of Israel, according unto all that the LORD had given him in commandment unto them;

⁴After he had slain Sihon the king of the Amorites, which dwelt in Heshbon, and Og the king of Bashan, which dwelt at Astaroth in Edrei:

⁵On this side Jordan, in the land of Moab, began Moses to declare this law, saying,

⁶The LORD our God spake unto us in Horeb, saying, Ye have dwelt long enough in this mount:

⁷Turn you, and take your journey, and go to the mount of the Amorites, and unto all the places nigh thereunto, in the plain, in the hills, and in the vale, and in the south, and by the sea side, to the land of the Canaanites, and unto Lebanon, unto the great river, the river Euphrates.

⁸Behold, I have set the land before you: go in and possess the land which the LORD sware unto your fathers, Abraham, Isaac, and Jacob, to give unto them and to their seed after them.

⁹And I spake unto you at that time, saying, I am not able to bear you myself alone:

¹⁰The LORD your God hath multiplied you, and, behold, ye are this day as the stars of heaven for multitude.

¹¹(The LORD God of your fathers make you a thousand times so many more as ye are, and bless you, as he hath promised you!)

¹²How can I myself alone bear your cumbrance, and your burden, and your strife?

¹³Take you wise men, and understanding, and known among your tribes, and I will make them rulers over you.

¹⁴And ye answered me, and said, The thing which thou hast spoken is good for us to do.

¹⁵So I took the chief of your tribes, wise men, and known, and made them heads over you, captains over thousands, and captains over hundreds, and captains over fifties, and captains over tens, and officers among your tribes.

¹⁶And I charged your judges at that time, saying, Hear the causes between your brethren, and judge righteously between every man and his brother, and the stranger that is with him.

¹⁷Ye shall not respect persons in judgment; but ye shall hear the small as well as the great; ye shall not be afraid of the face of man; for the judgment is God's: and the cause that is too hard for you, bring it unto me, and I will hear it.

¹⁸And I commanded you at that time all the things which ye should do.

¹⁹And when we departed from Horeb, we went through all that great and terrible wilderness, which ye saw by the way of the mountain of the Amorites, as the LORD our God commanded us; and we came to Kadesh-barnea.

²⁰And I said unto you, Ye are come unto the mountain of the Amorites, which the LORD our God doth give unto us.

²¹Behold, the LORD thy God hath set the land before thee: go up and possess it, as the LORD God of thy fathers hath said unto thee; fear not, neither be discouraged.

²²And ye came near unto me every one of you, and said, We will send men before us, and they shall search us out the land, and bring us word again by what way we must go up, and into what cities we shall come.

²³And the saying pleased me well: and I took twelve men of you, one of a tribe:

²⁴And they turned and went up into the mountain, and came unto the valley of Eshcol, and searched it out.

²⁵And they took of the fruit of the land in their hands, and brought it down unto us, and brought us word again, and said, It is a good land which the LORD our God doth give us.

²⁶Notwithstanding ye would not go up, but rebelled against the commandment of the LORD your God:

²⁷And ye murmured in your tents, and said, Because the LORD hated us, he hath brought us forth out of the land of Egypt, to deliver us into the hand of the Amorites, to destroy us.

²⁸Whither shall we go up? our brethren have discouraged our

heart, saying, The people is greater and taller than we; the cities are great and walled up to heaven; and moreover we have seen the sons of the Anakims there.

²⁹Then I said unto you, Dread not, neither be afraid of them.

³⁰The LORD your God which goeth before you, he shall fight for you, according to all that he did for you in Egypt before your eyes;

³¹And in the wilderness, where thou hast seen how that the LORD thy God bare thee, as a man doth bear his son, in all the way that ye went, until ye came into this place.

³²Yet in this thing ye did not believe the LORD your God,

³³Who went in the way before you, to search you out a place to pitch your tents in, in fire by night, to shew you by what way ye should go, and in a cloud by day.

³⁴And the LORD heard the voice of your words, and was wroth, and sware, saying,

³⁵Surely there shall not one of these men of this evil generation see that good land, which I sware to give unto your fathers.

³⁶Save Caleb the son of Jephunneh; he shall see it, and to him will I give the land that he hath trodden upon, and to his children, because he hath wholly followed the LORD.

³⁷Also the LORD was angry with me for your sakes, saying, Thou also shalt not go in thither.

³⁸But Joshua the son of Nun, which standeth before thee, he shall go in thither: encourage him: for he shall cause Israel to inherit it.

³⁹Moreover your little ones, which ye said should be a prey, and your children, which in that day had no knowledge between good and evil, they shall go in thither, and unto them will I give it, and they shall possess it.

⁴⁰But as for you, turn you, and take your journey into the wilderness by the way of the Red sea.

⁴¹Then ye answered and said unto me, We have sinned against the LORD, we will go up and fight, according to all that the LORD our God commanded us. And when ye had girded on every man his weapons of war, ye were ready to go up into the hill.

⁴²And the LORD said unto me, Say unto them. Go not up, neither fight; for I am not among you; lest ye be smitten before your enemies.

⁴³So I spake unto you; and ye would not hear, but rebelled against the commandment of the LORD, and went presumptuously up into the hill.

⁴⁴And the Amorites, which dwelt in that mountain, came out against

you, and chased you, as bees do, and destroyed you in Seir, even unto Hormah.

⁴⁵And ye returned and wept before the LORD; but the LORD would not hearken to your voice, nor give ear unto you.

⁴⁶So ye abode in Kadesh many days, according unto the days that ye abode there.

CHAPTER 2

¹Then we turned, and took our journey into the wilderness by the way of the Red sea, as the LORD spake unto me: and we compassed mount Seir many days.

²And the LORD spake unto me, saying,

³Ye have compassed this mountain long enough: turn you northward.

⁴And command thou the people, saying, Ye are to pass through the coast of your brethren the children of Esau, which dwell in Seir; and they shall be afraid of you: take ye good heed unto yourselves therefore:

⁵Meddle not with them; for I will not give you of their land, no, not so much as a foot breadth; because I have given mount Seir unto Esau for a possession.

⁶Ye shall buy meat of them for money, that ye may eat; and ye shall also buy water of them for money, that ye may drink.

⁷For the LORD thy God hath blessed thee in all the works of thy hand: he knoweth thy walking through this great wilderness: these forty years the LORD thy God hath been with thee; thou hast lacked nothing.

⁸And when we passed by from our brethren the children of Esau, which dwelt in Seir, through the way of the plain from Elath, and from Ezion-gaber, we turned and passed by the way of the wilderness of Moab.

⁹And the LORD said unto me, Distress not the Moabites, neither contend with them in battle: for I will not give thee of their land for a possession; because I have given Ar unto the children of Lot for a possession.

¹⁰The Emims dwelt therein in times past, a people great, and many, and tall, as the Anakims;

¹¹Which also were accounted giants, as the Anakims; but the Moabites called them Emims.

¹²The Horims also dwelt in Seir beforetime; but the children of Esau succeeded them, when they had destroyed them from before them, and dwelt in their stead;

as Israel did unto the land of his possession, which the LORD gave unto them.

¹³Now rise up, said I, and get you over the brook Zered. And we went over the brook Zered.

¹⁴And the space in which we came from Kadesh-barnea, until we were come over the brook Zered, was thirty and eight years; until all the generation of the men of war were wasted out from among the host, as the LORD sware unto them.

¹⁵For indeed the hand of the LORD was against them, to destroy them from among the host, until they were consumed.

¹⁶So it came to pass, when all the men of war were consumed and dead from among the people,

¹⁷That the LORD spake unto me, saying,

¹⁸Thou art to pass over through Ar, the coast of Moab, this day:

¹⁹And when thou comest nigh over against the children of Ammon, distress them not, nor meddle with them: for I will not give thee of the land of the children of Ammon any possession; because I have given it unto the children of Lot for a possession.

²⁰(That also was accounted a land of giants: giants dwelt therein in old time; and the Ammonites call them Zamzummims;

²¹A people great, and many, and tall, as the Anakims; but the LORD destroyed them before them; and they succeeded them, and dwelt in their stead:

²²As he did to the children of Esau, which dwelt in Seir, when he destroyed the Horims from before them; and they succeeded them, and dwelt in their stead even unto this day:

²³And the Avims which dwelt in Hazerim, even unto Azzah, the Caphtorims, which came forth out of Caphtor, destroyed them, and dwelt in their stead.)

²⁴Rise ye up, take your journey, and pass over the river Arnon: behold, I have given into thine hand Sihon the Amorite, king of Heshbon, and his land: begin to possess it, and contend with him in battle.

²⁵This day will I begin to put the dread of thee and the fear of thee upon the nations that are under the whole heaven, who shall hear report of thee, and shall tremble, and be in anguish because of thee.

²⁶And I sent messengers out of the wilderness of Kedemoth unto Sihon king of Heshbon with words of peace, saying,

²⁷Let me pass through thy land: I will go along by the high way, I will neither turn unto the right hand nor to the left.

²⁸Thou shalt sell me meat for money, that I may eat; and give me water for money, that I may drink: only I will pass through on my feet;

²⁹(As the children of Esau which dwell in Seir, and the Moabites which dwell in Ar, did unto me;) until I shall pass over Jordan into the land which the LORD our God giveth us.

³⁰But Sihon king of Heshbon would not let us pass by him: for the LORD thy God hardened his spirit, and made his heart obstinate, that he might deliver him into thy hand, as appeareth this day.

³¹And the LORD said unto me, Behold, I have begun to give Sihon and his land before thee: begin to possess, that thou mayest inherit his land.

³²Then Sihon came out against us, he and all his people, to fight at Jahaz.

³³And the LORD our God delivered him before us; and we smote him, and his sons, and all his people.

³⁴And we took all his cities at that time, and utterly destroyed the men, and the women, and the little ones, of every city, we left none to remain:

³⁵Only the cattle we took for a prey unto ourselves, and the spoil of the cities which we took.

³⁶From Aroer, which is by the brink of the river of Arnon, and from the city that is by the river, even unto Gilead, there was not one city too strong for us: the LORD our God delivered all unto us:

³⁷Only unto the land of the children of Ammon thou camest not, nor unto any place of the river Jabbok, nor unto the cities in the mountains, nor unto whatsoever the LORD our God forbad us.

CHAPTER 3

¹Then we turned, and went up the way to Bashan: and Og the king of Bashan came out against us, he and all his people, to battle at Edrei.

²And the LORD said unto me, Fear him not: for I will deliver him, and all his people, and his land, into thy hand; and thou shalt do unto him as thou didst unto Sihon king of the Amorites, which dwelt at Heshbon.

³So the LORD our God delivered into our hands Og also, the king of Bashan, and all his people: and we smote him until none was left to him remaining.

⁴And we took all his cities at that time, there was not a city which we took not from them, threescore cities, all the region of Argob, the kingdom of Og in Bashan.

⁵All these cities were fenced with high walls, gates, and bars; beside unwalled towns a great many.

⁶And we utterly destroyed them, as we did unto Sihon king of Heshbon, utterly destroying the men, women, and children, of every city.

⁷But all the cattle, and the spoil of the cities, we took for a prey to ourselves.

⁸And we took at that time out of the hand of the two kings of the Amorites the land that was on this side Jordan, from the river of Arnon unto mount Hermon;

⁹(Which Hermon the Sidonians call Sirion; and the Amorites call it Shenir;)

¹⁰All the cities of the plain, and all Gilead, and all Bashan, unto Salchah and Edrei, cities of the kingdom of Og in Bashan.

¹¹For only Og king of Bashan remained of the remnant of giants; behold his bedstead was a bedstead of iron; is it not in Rabbath of the children of Ammon? nine cubits was the length thereof, and four cubits the breadth of it, after the cubit of a man.

¹²And this land, which we possessed at that time, from Aroer, which is by the river Arnon, and half mount Gilead, and the cities thereof, gave I unto the Reubenites and to the Gadites.

¹³And the rest of Gilead, and all Bashan, being the kingdom of Og, gave I unto the half tribe of Manasseh; all the region of Argob, with all Bashan, which was called the land of giants.

¹⁴Jair the son of Manasseh took all the country of Argob unto the coasts of Geshuri and Maachathi; and called them after his own name, Bashan-Havoth-jair, unto this day.

¹⁵And I gave Gilead unto Machir.

¹⁶And unto the Reubenites and unto the Gadites I gave from Gilead even unto the river Arnon half the valley, and the border even unto the river Jabbok, which is the border of the children of Ammon;

¹⁷The plain also, and Jordan, and the coast thereof, from Chinnereth even unto the sea of the plain, even the salt sea, under Ashdoth-pisgah eastward.

¹⁸And I commanded you at that time, saying, The LORD your God hath given you this land to possess it: ye shall pass over armed before your brethren the children of Israel, all that are meet for the war.

¹⁹But your wives, and your little ones, and your cattle, (for I know that ye have much cattle,) shall abide in your cities which I have given you;

²⁰Until the LORD have given rest unto your brethren, as well as unto you, and until they also possess the

land which the LORD your God hath given them beyond Jordan: and then shall ye return every man unto his possession, which I have given you.

²¹And I commanded Joshua at that time, saying, Thine eyes have seen all that the LORD your God hath done unto these two kings: so shall the LORD do unto all the kingdoms whither thou passest.

²²Ye shall not fear them: for the LORD your God he shall fight for you.

²³And I besought the LORD at that time, saying,

²⁴O Lord GOD, thou hast begun to shew thy servant thy greatness, and thy mighty hand: for what God is there in heaven or in earth, that can do according to thy works, and according to thy might?

²⁵I pray thee, let me go over, and see the good land that is beyond Jordan, that goodly mountain, and Lebanon.

²⁶But the LORD was wroth with me for your sakes, and would not hear me: and the LORD said unto me, Let it suffice thee; speak no more unto me of this matter.

²⁷Get thee up into the top of Pisgah, and lift up thine eyes westward, and northward, and southward, and eastward, and behold it with thine eyes: for thou shalt not go over this Jordan.

²⁸But charge Joshua, and encourage him, and strengthen him: for he shall go over before this people, and he shall cause them to inherit the land which thou shalt see.

²⁹So we abode in the valley over against Beth-peor.

CHAPTER 4

¹Now therefore hearken, O Israel, unto the statutes and unto the judgments, which I teach you, for to do them, that ye may live, and go in and possess the land which the LORD God of your fathers giveth you.

²Ye shall not add unto the word which I command you, neither shall ye diminish ought from it, that ye may keep the commandments of the LORD your God which I command you.

³Your eyes have seen what the LORD did because of Baal-peor: for all the men that followed Baal-peor, the LORD thy God hath destroyed them from among you.

⁴But ye that did cleave unto the LORD your God are alive every one of you this day.

⁵Behold, I have taught you statutes and judgments, even as the LORD my God commanded me, that ye

should do so in the land whither ye go to possess it.

⁶Keep therefore and do them; for this is your wisdom and your understanding in the sight of the nations, which shall hear all these statutes, and say, Surely this great nation is a wise and understanding people.

⁷For what nation is there so great, who hath God so nigh unto them, as the LORD our God is in all things that we call upon him for?

⁸And what nation is there so great, that hath statutes and judgments so righteous as all this law, which I set before you this day?

⁹Only take heed to thyself, and keep thy soul diligently, lest thou forget the things which thine eyes have seen, and lest they depart from thy heart all the days of thy life: but teach them thy sons, and thy sons' sons;

¹⁰Specially the day that thou stoodest before the LORD thy God in Horeb, when the LORD said unto me, Gather me the people together, and I will make them hear my words, that they may learn to fear me all the days that they shall live upon the earth, and that they may teach their children.

¹¹And ye came near and stood under the mountain; and the mountain burned with fire unto the midst of heaven, with darkness, clouds, and thick darkness.

¹²And the LORD spake unto you out of the midst of the fire: ye heard the voice of the words, but saw no similitude; only ye heard a voice.

¹³And he declared unto you his covenant, which he commanded you to perform, even ten commandments; and he wrote them upon two tables of stone.

¹⁴And the LORD commanded me at that time to teach you statutes and judgments, that ye might do them in the land whither ye go over to possess it.

¹⁵Take ye therefore good heed unto yourselves; for ye saw no manner of similitude on the day that the LORD spake unto you in Horeb out of the midst of the fire:

¹⁶Lest ye corrupt yourselves, and make you a graven image, the similitude of any figure, the likeness of male or female,

¹⁷The likeness of any beast that is on the earth, the likeness of any winged fowl that flieth in the air,

¹⁸The likeness of any thing that creepeth on the ground, the likeness of any fish that is in the waters beneath the earth:

¹⁹And lest thou lift up thine eyes unto heaven, and when thou seest the sun, and the moon, and the stars, even all the host of heaven,

shouldest be driven to worship them, and serve them, which the LORD thy God hath divided unto all nations under the whole heaven.

²⁰But the LORD hath taken you, and brought you forth out of the iron furnace, even out of Egypt, to be unto him a people of inheritance, as ye are this day.

²¹Furthermore the LORD was angry with me for your sakes, and sware that I should not go over Jordan, and that I should not go in unto that good land, which the LORD thy God giveth thee for an inheritance:

²²But I must die in this land, I must not go over Jordan: but ye shall go over, and possess that good land.

²³Take heed unto yourselves, lest ye forget the covenant of the LORD your God, which he made with you, and make you a graven image, or the likeness of any thing, which the LORD thy God hath forbidden thee.

²⁴For the LORD thy God is a consuming fire, even a jealous God.

²⁵When thou shalt beget children, and children's children, and ye shall have remained long in the land, and shall corrupt yourselves, and make a graven image, or the likeness of any thing, and shall do evil in the sight of the LORD thy God, to provoke him to anger:

²⁶I call heaven and earth to witness against you this day, that ye shall soon utterly perish from off the land whereunto ye go over Jordan to possess it; ye shall not prolong your days upon it, but shall utterly be destroyed.

²⁷And the LORD shall scatter you among the nations, and ye shall be left few in number among the heathen, whither the LORD shall lead you.

²⁸And there ye shall serve gods, the work of men's hands, wood and stone, which neither see, nor hear, nor eat, nor smell.

²⁹But if from thence thou shalt seek the LORD thy God, thou shalt find him, if thou seek him with all thy heart and with all thy soul.

³⁰When thou art in tribulation, and all these things are come upon thee, even in the latter days, if thou turn to the LORD thy God, and shalt be obedient unto his voice;

³¹(For the LORD thy God is a merciful God;) he will not forsake thee, neither destroy thee, nor forget the covenant of thy fathers which he sware unto them.

³²For ask now of the days that are past, which were before thee, since the day that God created man upon the earth, and ask from the one side of heaven unto the other, whether there hath been any such thing

as this great thing is, or hath been heard like it?

³³Did ever people hear the voice of God speaking out of the midst of the fire, as thou hast heard, and live?

³⁴Or hath God assayed to go and take him a nation from the midst of another nation, by temptations, by signs, and by wonders, and by war, and by a mighty hand, and by a stretched out arm, and by great terrors, according to all that the LORD your God did for you in Egypt before your eyes?

³⁵Unto thee it was shewed, that thou mightest know that the LORD he is God; there is none else beside him.

³⁶Out of heaven he made thee to hear his voice, that he might instruct thee: and upon earth he shewed thee his great fire; and thou heardest his words out of the midst of the fire.

³⁷And because he loved thy fathers, therefore he chose their seed after them, and brought thee out in his sight with his mighty power out of Egypt;

³⁸To drive out nations from before thee greater and mightier than thou art, to bring thee in, to give thee their land for an inheritance, as it is this day.

³⁹Know therefore this day, and consider it in thine heart, that the LORD he is God in heaven above, and upon the earth beneath: there is none else.

⁴⁰Thou shalt keep therefore his statutes, and his commandments, which I command thee this day, that it may go well with thee, and with thy children after thee, and that thou mayest prolong thy days upon the earth, which the LORD thy God giveth thee, for ever.

⁴¹Then Moses severed three cities on this side Jordan toward the sunrising;

⁴²That the slayer might flee thither, which should kill his neighbour unawares, and hated him not in times past; and that fleeing unto one of these cities he might live:

⁴³Namely, Bezer in the wilderness, in the plain country, of the Reubenites; and Ramoth in Gilead, of the Gadites; and Golan in Bashan, of the Manassites.

⁴⁴And this is the law which Moses set before the children of Israel:

⁴⁵These are the testimonies, and the statutes, and the judgments, which Moses spake unto the children of Israel, after they came forth out of Egypt.

⁴⁶On this side Jordan, in the valley over against Beth-peor, in the land of Sihon king of the Amorites, who dwelt at Heshbon, whom Moses and the children of Israel smote,

after they were come forth out of Egypt:

⁴⁷And they possessed his land, and the land of Og king of Bashan, two kings of the Amorites, which were on this side Jordan toward the sunrising;

⁴⁸From Aroer, which is by the bank of the river Arnon, even unto mount Sion, which is Hermon,

⁴⁹And all the plain on this side Jordan eastward, even unto the sea of the plain, under the springs of Pisgah.

CHAPTER 5

¹And Moses called all Israel, and said unto them, Hear, O Israel, the statutes and judgments which I speak in your ears this day, that ye may learn them, and keep, and do them.

²The LORD our God made a covenant with us in Horeb.

³The LORD made not this covenant with our fathers, but with us, even us, who are all of us here alive this day.

⁴The LORD talked with you face to face in the mount out of the midst of the fire,

⁵(I stood between the LORD and you at that time, to shew you the word of the LORD: for ye were afraid by reason of the fire, and went not up into the mount;) saying,

⁶I am the LORD thy God, which brought thee out of the land of Egypt, from the house of bondage.

⁷Thou shalt have none other gods before me.

⁸Thou shalt not make thee any graven image, or any likeness of any thing that is in heaven above, or that is in the earth beneath, or that is in the waters beneath the earth:

⁹Thou shalt not bow down thyself unto them, nor serve them: for I the LORD thy God am a jealous God, visiting the iniquity of the fathers upon the children unto the third and fourth generation of them that hate me,

¹⁰And shewing mercy unto thousands of them that love me and keep my commandments.

¹¹Thou shalt not take the name of the LORD thy God in vain: for the LORD will not hold him guiltless that taketh his name in vain.

¹²Keep the sabbath day to sanctify it, as the LORD thy God hath commanded thee.

¹³Six days thou shalt labour, and do all thy work:

¹⁴But the seventh day is the sabbath of the LORD thy God: in it thou shalt not do any work, thou, nor thy son, nor thy daughter,

nor thy manservant, nor thy maidservant, nor thine ox, nor thine ass, nor any of thy cattle, nor thy stranger that is within thy gates; that thy manservant and thy maidservant may rest as well as thou.

¹⁵And remember that thou wast a servant in the land of Egypt, and that the LORD thy God brought thee out thence through a mighty hand and by a stretched out arm: therefore the LORD thy God commanded thee to keep the sabbath day.

¹⁶Honour thy father and thy mother, as the LORD thy God hath commanded thee; that thy days may be prolonged, and that it may go well with thee, in the land which the LORD thy God giveth thee.

¹⁷Thou shalt not kill.

¹⁸Neither shalt thou commit adultery.

¹⁹Neither shalt thou steal.

²⁰Neither shalt thou bear false witness against thy neighbour.

²¹Neither shalt thou desire thy neighbour's wife, neither shalt thou covet thy neighbour's house, his field, or his manservant, or his maidservant, his ox, or his ass, or any thing that is thy neighbour's.

²²These words the LORD spake unto all your assembly in the mount out of the midst of the fire, of the cloud, and of the thick darkness, with a great voice: and he added no more. And he wrote them in two tables of stone, and delivered them unto me.

²³And it came to pass, when ye heard the voice out of the midst of the darkness, (for the mountain did burn with fire,) that ye came near unto me, even all the heads of your tribes, and your elders;

²⁴And ye said, Behold, the LORD our God hath shewed us his glory and his greatness, and we have heard his voice out of the midst of the fire: we have seen this day that God doth talk with man, and he liveth.

²⁵Now therefore why should we die? for this great fire will consume us: if we hear the voice of the LORD our God any more, then we shall die.

²⁶For who is there of all flesh, that hath heard the voice of the living God speaking out of the midst of the fire, as we have, and lived?

²⁷Go thou near, and hear all that the LORD our God shall say: and speak thou unto us all that the LORD our God shall speak unto thee; and we will hear it, and do it.

²⁸And the LORD heard the voice of your words, when ye spake unto me; and the LORD said unto me, I have heard the voice of the words of this people, which they have

spoken unto thee: they have well said all that they have spoken.

²⁹O that there were such an heart in them, that they would fear me, and keep all my commandments always, that it might be well with them, and with their children for ever!

³⁰Go say to them, Get you into your tents again.

³¹But as for thee, stand thou here by me, and I will speak unto thee all the commandments, and the statutes, and the judgments, which thou shalt teach them, that they may do them in the land which I give them to possess it.

³²Ye shall observe to do therefore as the LORD your God hath commanded you: ye shall not turn aside to the right hand or to the left.

³³Ye shall walk in all the ways which the LORD your God hath commanded you, that ye may live, and that it may be well with you, and that ye may prolong your days in the land which ye shall possess.

CHAPTER 6

¹Now these are the commandments, the statutes, and the judgments, which the LORD your God commanded to teach you, that ye might do them in the land whither ye go to possess it:

²That thou mightest fear the LORD thy God, to keep all his statutes and his commandments, which I command thee, thou, and thy son, and thy son's son, all the days of thy life; and that thy days may be prolonged.

³Hear therefore, O Israel, and observe to do it; that it may be well with thee, and that ye may increase mightily, as the LORD God of thy fathers hath promised thee, in the land that floweth with milk and honey.

⁴Hear, O Israel: The LORD our God is one LORD:

⁵And thou shalt love the LORD thy God with all thine heart, and with all thy soul, and with all thy might.

⁶And these words, which I command thee this day, shall be in thine heart:

⁷And thou shalt teach them diligently unto thy children, and shalt talk of them when thou sittest in thine house, and when thou walkest by the way, and when thou liest down, and when thou risest up.

⁸And thou shalt bind them for a sign upon thine hand, and they shall be as frontlets between thine eyes.

⁹And thou shalt write them upon the posts of thy house, and on thy gates.

¹⁰And it shall be, when the LORD thy God shall have brought thee into the land which he sware unto thy fathers, to Abraham, to Isaac, and to Jacob, to give thee great and goodly cities, which thou buildedst not,

¹¹And houses full of all good things, which thou filledst not, and wells digged, which thou diggedst not, vineyards and olive trees, which thou plantedst not; when thou shalt have eaten and be full;

¹²Then beware lest thou forget the LORD, which brought thee forth out of the land of Egypt, from the house of bondage.

¹³Thou shalt fear the LORD thy God, and serve him, and shalt swear by his name.

¹⁴Ye shall not go after other gods, of the gods of the people which are round about you;

¹⁵(For the LORD thy God is a jealous God among you) lest the anger of the LORD thy God be kindled against thee, and destroy thee from off the face of the earth.

¹⁶Ye shall not tempt the LORD your God, as ye tempted him in Massah.

¹⁷Ye shall diligently keep the commandments of the LORD your God, and his testimonies, and his statutes, which he hath commanded thee.

¹⁸And thou shalt do that which is right and good in the sight of the LORD: that it may be well with thee, and that thou mayest go in and possess the good land which the LORD sware unto thy fathers.

¹⁹To cast out all thine enemies from before thee, as the LORD hath spoken.

²⁰And when thy son asketh thee in time to come, saying, What mean the testimonies, and the statutes, and the judgments, which the LORD our God hath commanded you?

²¹Then thou shalt say unto thy son, We were Pharaoh's bondmen in Egypt; and the LORD brought us out of Egypt with a mighty hand:

²²And the LORD shewed signs and wonders, great and sore, upon Egypt, upon Pharaoh, and upon all his household, before our eyes:

²³And he brought us out from thence, that he might bring us in, to give us the land which he sware unto our fathers.

²⁴And the LORD commanded us to do all these statutes, to fear the LORD our God, for our good always, that he might preserve us alive, as it is at this day.

²⁵And it shall be our righteousness, if we observe to do all these commandments before the LORD our God, as he hath commanded us.

CHAPTER 7

¹When the LORD thy God shall bring thee into the land whither thou goest to possess it, and hath cast out many nations before thee, the Hittites, and the Girgashites, and the Amorites, and the Canaanites, and the Perizzites, and the Hivites, and the Jebusites, seven nations greater and mightier than thou;

²And when the LORD thy God shall deliver them before thee; thou shalt smite them, and utterly destroy them; thou shalt make no covenant with them, nor shew mercy unto them:

³Neither shalt thou make marriages with them; thy daughter thou shalt not give unto his son, nor his daughter shalt thou take unto thy son.

⁴For they will turn away thy son from following me, that they may serve other gods: so will the anger of the LORD be kindled against you, and destroy thee suddenly.

⁵But thus shall ye deal with them; ye shall destroy their altars, and break down their images, and cut down their groves, and burn their graven images with fire.

⁶For thou art an holy people unto the LORD thy God: the LORD thy God hath chosen thee to be a special people unto himself, above all people that are upon the face of the earth.

⁷The LORD did not set his love upon you, nor choose you, because ye were more in number than any people; for ye were the fewest of all people:

⁸But because the LORD loved you, and because he would keep the oath which he had sworn unto your fathers, hath the LORD brought you out with a mighty hand, and redeemed you out of the house of bondmen, from the hand of Pharaoh king of Egypt.

⁹Know therefore that the LORD thy God, he is God, the faithful God, which keepeth covenant and mercy with them that love him and keep his commandments to a thousand generations;

¹⁰And repayeth them that hate him to their face, to destroy them: he will not be slack to him that hateth him, he will repay him to his face.

¹¹Thou shalt therefore keep the commandments, and the statutes, and the judgments, which I command thee this day, to do them.

¹²Wherefore it shall come to pass, if ye hearken to these judgments, and keep, and do them, that the LORD thy God shall keep unto thee the covenant and the mercy which he sware unto thy fathers:

¹³And he will love thee, and bless thee, and multiply thee: he will also bless the fruit of thy womb, and the fruit of thy land, thy corn, and thy wine, and thine oil, the increase of thy kine, and the flocks of thy sheep, in the land which he sware unto thy fathers to give thee.

¹⁴Thou shalt be blessed above all people: there shall not be male or female barren among you, or among your cattle.

¹⁵And the LORD will take away from thee all sickness, and will put none of the evil diseases of Egypt, which thou knowest, upon thee; but will lay them upon all them that hate thee.

¹⁶And thou shalt consume all the people which the LORD thy God shall deliver thee; thine eye shall have no pity upon them: neither shalt thou serve their gods; for that will be a snare unto thee.

¹⁷If thou shalt say in thine heart, These nations are more than I; how can I dispossess them?

¹⁸Thou shalt not be afraid of them: but shalt well remember what the LORD thy God did unto Pharaoh, and unto all Egypt;

¹⁹The great temptations which thine eyes saw, and the signs, and the wonders, and the mighty hand, and the stretched out arm, whereby the LORD thy God brought thee out: so shall the LORD thy God do unto all the people of whom thou art afraid.

²⁰Moreover the LORD thy God will send the hornet among them, until they that are left, and hide themselves from thee, be destroyed.

²¹Thou shalt not be affrighted at them: for the LORD thy God is among you, a mighty God and terrible.

²²And the LORD thy God will put out those nations before thee by little and little: thou mayest not consume them at once, lest the beasts of the field increase upon thee.

²³But the LORD thy God shall deliver them unto thee, and shall destroy them with a mighty destruction, until they be destroyed.

²⁴And he shall deliver their kings into thine hand, and thou shalt destroy their name from under heaven: there shall no man be able to stand before thee, until thou have destroyed them.

²⁵The graven images of their gods shall ye burn with fire: thou shalt not desire the silver or gold that is on them, nor take it unto thee, lest thou be snared therin: for it is an abomination to the LORD thy God.

²⁶Neither shalt thou bring an abomination into thine house, lest thou be a cursed thing like it: but

thou shalt utterly detest it, and thou shalt utterly abhor it; for it is a cursed thing.

CHAPTER 8

¹All the commandments which I command thee this day shall ye observe to do, that ye may live, and multiply, and go in and possess the land which the LORD sware unto your fathers.

²And thou shalt remember all the way which the LORD thy God led thee these forty years in the wilderness, to humble thee, and to prove thee, to know what was in thine heart, whether thou wouldest keep his commandments, or no.

³And he humbled thee, and suffered thee to hunger, and fed thee with manna, which thou knewest not, neither did thy fathers know; that he might make thee know that man doth not live by bread only, but by every word that proceedeth out of the mouth of the LORD doth man live.

⁴Thy raiment waxed not old upon thee, neither did thy foot swell, these forty years.

⁵Thou shalt also consider in thine heart, that, as a man chasteneth his son, so the LORD thy God chasteneth thee.

⁶Therefore thou shalt keep the commandments of the LORD thy God, to walk in his ways, and to fear him.

⁷For the LORD thy God bringeth thee into a good land, a land of brooks of water, of fountains and depths that spring out of valleys and hills;

⁸A land of wheat, and barley, and vines, and fig trees, and pomegranates; a land of oil olive, and honey;

⁹A land wherein thou shalt eat bread without scarceness, thou shalt not lack any thing in it; a land whose stones are iron, and out of whose hills thou mayest dig brass.

¹⁰When thou hast eaten and art full, then thou shalt bless the LORD thy God for the good land which he hath given thee.

¹¹Beware that thou forget not the LORD thy God, in not keeping his commandments, and his judgments, and his statutes, which I command thee this day:

¹²Lest when thou hast eaten and art full, and hast built goodly houses, and dwelt therein;

¹³And when thy herds and thy flocks multiply, and thy silver and thy gold is multiplied, and all that thou hast is multiplied;

¹⁴Then thine heart be lifted up, and thou forget the LORD thy God,

which brought thee forth out of the land of Egypt, from the house of bondage;

¹⁵Who led thee through that great and terrible wilderness, wherein were fiery serpents, and scorpions, and drought, where there was no water; who brought thee forth water out of the rock of flint;

¹⁶Who fed thee in the wilderness with manna, which thy fathers knew not, that he might humble thee, and that he might prove thee, to do thee good at thy latter end;

¹⁷And thou say in thine heart, My power and the might of mine hand hath gotten me this wealth.

¹⁸But thou shalt remember the LORD thy God: for it is he that giveth thee power to get wealth, that he may establish his covenant which he sware unto thy fathers, as it is this day.

¹⁹And it shall be, if thou do at all forget the LORD thy God, and walk after other gods, and serve them, and worship them, I testify against you this day that ye shall surely perish.

²⁰As the nations which the LORD destroyeth before your face, so shall ye perish; because ye would not be obedient unto the voice of the LORD your God.

CHAPTER 9

¹Hear, O Israel: Thou art to pass over Jordan this day, to go in to possess nations greater and mightier than thyself, cities great and fenced up to heaven,

²A people great and tall, the children of the Anakims, whom thou knowest, and of whom thou hast heard say, Who can stand before the children of Anak!

³Understand therefore this day, that the LORD thy God is he which goeth over before thee; as a consuming fire he shall destroy them, and he shall bring them down before thy face: so shalt thou drive them out, and destroy them quickly, as the LORD hath said unto thee.

⁴Speak not thou in thine heart, after that the LORD thy God hath cast them out from before thee, saying, For my righteousness the LORD hath brought me in to possess this land: but for the wickedness of these nations the LORD doth drive them out from before thee.

⁵Not for thy righteousness, or for the uprightness of thine heart, dost thou go to possess their land: but for the wickedness of these nations the LORD thy God doth drive them out from before thee, and that

he may perform the word which the LORD sware unto thy fathers, Abraham, Isaac, and Jacob.

⁶Understand therefore, that the LORD thy God giveth thee not this good land to possess it for thy righteousness; for thou art a stiffnecked people.

⁷Remember, and forget not, how thou provokedst the LORD thy God to wrath in the wilderness: from the day that thou didst depart out of the land of Egypt, until ye came unto this place, ye have been rebellious against the LORD.

⁸Also in Horeb ye provoked the LORD to wrath, so that the LORD was angry with you to have destroyed you.

⁹When I was gone up into the mount to receive the tables of stone, even the tables of the covenant which the LORD made with you, then I abode in the mount forty days and forty nights, I neither did eat bread nor drink water:

¹⁰And the LORD delivered unto me two tables of stone written with the finger of God; and on them was written according to all the words, which the LORD spake with you in the mount out of the midst of the fire in the day of the assembly.

¹¹And it came to pass at the end of forty days and forty nights, that the LORD gave me the two tables of stone, even the tables of the covenant.

¹²And the LORD said unto me, Arise, get thee down quickly from hence; for thy people which thou hast brought forth out of Egypt have corrupted themselves; they are quickly turned aside out of the way which I commanded them; they have made them a molten image.

¹³Furthermore the LORD spake unto me, saying, I have seen this people, and, behold, it is a stiffnecked people:

¹⁴Let me alone, that I may destroy them, and blot out their name from under heaven: and I will make of thee a nation mightier and greater than they.

¹⁵So I turned and came down from the mount, and the mount burned with fire: and the two tables of the covenant were in my two hands.

¹⁶And I looked, and, behold, ye had sinned against the LORD your God, and had made you a molten calf: ye had turned aside quickly out of the way which the LORD had commanded you.

¹⁷And I took the two tables, and cast them out of my two hands, and brake them before your eyes.

¹⁸And I fell down before the LORD, as at the first, forty days and forty nights: I did neither eat bread,

nor drink water, because of all your sins which ye sinned, in doing wickedly in the sight of the LORD, to provoke him to anger.

¹⁹For I was afraid of the anger and hot displeasure, wherewith the LORD was wroth against you to destroy you. But the LORD hearkened unto me at that time also.

²⁰And the LORD was very angry with Aaron to have destroyed him: and I prayed for Aaron also the same time.

²¹And I took your sin, the calf which ye had made, and burnt it with fire, and stamped it, and ground it very small, even until it was as small as dust: and I cast the dust thereof into the brook that descended out of the mount.

²²And at Taberah, and at Massah, and at Kibroth-hattaavah, ye provoked the LORD to wrath.

²³Likewise when the LORD sent you from Kadesh-barnea, saying, Go up and possess the land which I have given you; then ye rebelled against the commandment of the LORD your God, and ye believed him not, nor hearkened to his voice.

²⁴Ye have been rebellious against the LORD from the day that I knew you.

²⁵Thus I fell down before the LORD forty days and forty nights, as I fell down at the first; because the LORD had said he would destroy you.

²⁶I prayed therefore unto the LORD, and said, O Lord GOD, destroy not thy people and thine inheritance, which thou hast redeemed through thy greatness, which thou hast brought forth out of Egypt with a mighty hand.

²⁷Remember thy servants, Abraham, Isaac, and Jacob; look not unto the stubbornness of this people, nor to their wickedness, nor to their sin:

²⁸Lest the land whence thou broughtest us out say, Because the LORD was not able to bring them into the land which he promised them, and because he hated them, he hath brought them out to slay them in the wilderness.

²⁹Yet they are thy people and thine inheritance, which thou broughtest out by thy mighty power and by thy stretched out arm.

CHAPTER 10

¹At that time the LORD said unto me, Hew thee two tables of stone like unto the first, and come up unto me into the mount, and make thee an ark of wood.

²And I will write on the tables the words that were in the first tables which thou brakest, and thou shalt put them in the ark.

³And I made an ark of shittim wood, and hewed two tables of stone like unto the first, and went up into the mount, having the two tables in mine hand.

⁴And he wrote on the tables, according to the first writing, the ten commandments, which the LORD spake unto you in the mount out of the midst of the fire in the day of the assembly: and the LORD gave them unto me.

⁵And I turned myself and came down from the mount, and put the tables in the ark which I had made; and there they be, as the LORD commanded me.

⁶And the children of Israel took their journey from Beeroth of the children of Jaakan to Mosera: there Aaron died, and there he was buried; and Eleazar his son ministered in the priest's office in his stead.

⁷From thence they journeyed unto Gudgodah; and from Gudgodah to Jotbath, a land of rivers of waters.

⁸At that time the LORD separated the tribe of Levi, to bear the ark of the covenant of the LORD, to stand before the LORD to minister unto him, and to bless in his name, unto this day.

⁹Wherefore Levi hath no part nor inheritance with his brethren; the LORD is his inheritance, according as the LORD thy God promised him.

¹⁰And I stayed in the mount, according to the first time, forty days and forty nights; and the LORD hearkened unto me at that time also, and the LORD would not destroy thee.

¹¹And the LORD said unto me, Arise, take thy journey before the people, that they may go in and possess the land, which I sware unto their fathers to give unto them.

¹²And now, Israel, what doth the LORD thy God require of thee, but to fear the LORD thy God, to walk in all his ways, and to love him, and to serve the LORD thy God with all thy heart and with all thy soul,

¹³To keep the commandments of the LORD, and his statutes, which I command thee this day for thy good?

¹⁴Behold, the heaven and the heaven of heavens is the LORD's thy God, the earth also, with all that therein is.

¹⁵Only the LORD had a delight in thy fathers to love them, and he chose their seed after them, even you above all people, as it is this day.

¹⁶Circumcise therefore the foreskin of your heart, and be no more stiffnecked.

¹⁷For the LORD your God is God of gods, and Lord of lords, a great God, a mighty, and a terrible, which regardeth not persons, nor taketh reward:

¹⁸He doth execute the judgment of the fatherless and widow, and loveth the stranger, in giving him food and raiment.

¹⁹Love ye therefore the stranger: for ye were strangers in the land of Egypt.

²⁰Thou shalt fear the LORD thy God; him shalt thou serve, and to him shalt thou cleave, and swear by his name.

²¹He is thy praise, and he is thy God, that hath done for thee these great and terrible things, which thine eyes have seen.

²²Thy fathers went down into Egypt with threescore and ten persons; and now the LORD thy God hath made thee as the stars of heaven for multitude.

CHAPTER 11

¹Therefore thou shalt love the LORD thy God, and keep his charge, and his statutes, and his judgments, and his commandments, alway.

²And know ye this day: for I speak not with your children which have not known, and which have not seen the chastisement of the LORD your God, his greatness, his mighty hand, and his stretched out arm,

³And his miracles, and his acts, which he did in the midst of Egypt unto Pharaoh the king of Egypt, and unto all his land;

⁴And what he did unto the army of Egypt, unto their horses, and to their chariots; how he made the water of the Red sea to overflow them as they pursued after you, and how the LORD hath destroyed them unto this day;

⁵And what he did unto you in the wilderness, until ye came into this place;

⁶And what he did unto Dathan and Abiram, the sons of Eliab, the son of Reuben: how the earth opened her mouth, and swallowed them up, and their households, and their tents, and all the substance that was in their possession, in the midst of all Israel:

⁷But your eyes have seen all the great acts of the LORD which he did.

⁸Therefore shall ye keep all the commandments which I command you this day, that ye may be strong, and go in and possess the land, whither ye go to possess it;

⁹And that ye may prolong your days in the land, which the LORD

sware unto your fathers to give unto them and to their seed, a land that floweth with milk and honey.

¹⁰For the land, whither thou goest in to possess it, is not as the land of Egypt, from whence ye came out, where thou sowedst thy seed, and wateredst it with thy foot, as a garden of herbs:

¹¹But the land, whither ye go to possess it, is a land of hills and valleys, and drinketh water of the rain of heaven:

¹²A land which the LORD thy God careth for: the eyes of the LORD thy God are always upon it, from the beginning of the year even unto the end of the year.

¹³And it shall come to pass, if ye shall hearken diligently unto my commandments which I command you this day, to love the LORD your God, and to serve him with all your heart and with all your soul,

¹⁴That I will give you the rain of your land in his due season, the first rain and the latter rain, that thou mayest gather in thy corn, and thy wine, and thine oil.

¹⁵And I will send grass in thy fields for thy cattle, that thou mayest eat and be full.

¹⁶Take heed to yourselves, that your heart be not deceived, and ye turn aside, and serve other gods, and worship them;

¹⁷And then the LORD's wrath be kindled against you, and he shut up the heaven, that there be no rain, and that the land yield not her fruit; and lest ye perish quickly from off the good land which the LORD giveth you.

¹⁸Therefore shall ye lay up these my words in your heart and in your soul, and bind them for a sign upon your hand, that they may be as frontlets between your eyes.

¹⁹And ye shall teach them your children, speaking of them when thou sittest in thine house, and when thou walkest by the way, when thou liest down, and when thou risest up.

²⁰And thou shalt write them upon the door posts of thine house, and upon thy gates:

²¹That your days may be multiplied, and the days of your children, in the land which the LORD sware unto your fathers to give them, as the days of heaven upon the earth.

²²For if ye shall diligently keep all these commandments which I command you, to do them, to love the LORD your God, to walk in all his ways, and to cleave unto him;

²³Then will the LORD drive out all these nations from before you, and ye shall possess greater nations and mightier than yourselves.

²⁴Every place whereon the soles of your feet shall tread shall be yours: from the wilderness and Lebanon, from the river, the river Euphrates, even unto the uttermost sea shall your coast be.

²⁵There shall no man be able to stand before you: for the LORD your God shall lay the fear of you and the dread of you upon all the land that ye shall tread upon, as he hath said unto you.

²⁶Behold, I set before you this day a blessing and a curse;

²⁷A blessing, if ye obey the commandments of the LORD your God, which I command you this day:

²⁸And a curse, if ye will not obey the commandments of the LORD your God, but turn aside out of the way which I command you this day, to go after other gods, which ye have not known.

²⁹And it shall come to pass, when the LORD thy God hath brought thee in unto the land whither thou goest to possess it, that thou shalt put the blessing upon mount Gerizim, and the curse upon mount Ebal.

³⁰Are they not on the other side Jordan, by the way where the sun goeth down, in the land of the Canaanites, which dwell in the champaign over against Gilgal, beside the plains of Moreh?

³¹For ye shall pass over Jordan to go in to possess the land which the LORD your God giveth you, and ye shall possess it, and dwell therein.

³²And ye shall observe to do all the statutes and judgments which I set before you this day.

CHAPTER 12

¹These are the statutes and judgments, which ye shall observe to do in the land, which the LORD God of thy fathers giveth thee to possess it, all the days that ye live upon the earth.

²Ye shall utterly destroy all the places, wherein the nations which ye shall possess served their gods, upon the high mountains, and upon the hills, and under every green tree.

³And ye shall overthrow their altars, and break their pillars, and burn their groves with fire; and ye shall hew down the graven images of their gods, and destroy the names of them out of that place.

⁴Ye shall not do so unto the LORD your God.

⁵But unto the place which the LORD your God shall choose out of all your tribes to put his name there, even unto his habitation shall ye seek, and thither thou shalt come:

⁶And thither ye shall bring your burnt offerings, and your sacrifices, and your tithes, and heave offerings of your hand, and your vows, and your freewill offerings, and the firstlings of your herds and of your flocks:

⁷And there ye shall eat before the LORD your God, and ye shall rejoice in all that ye put your hand unto, ye and your households, wherein the LORD thy God hath blessed thee.

⁸Ye shall not do after all the things that we do here this day, every man whatsoever is right in his own eyes.

⁹For ye are not as yet come to the rest and to the inheritance, which the LORD your God giveth you.

¹⁰But when ye go over Jordan, and dwell in the land which the LORD your God giveth you to inherit, and when he giveth you rest from all your enemies round about, so that ye dwell in safety;

¹¹Then there shall be a place which the LORD your God shall choose to cause his name to dwell there; thither shall ye bring all that I command you; your burnt offerings, and your sacrifices, your tithes, and the heave offering of your hand, and all your choice vows which ye vow unto the LORD:

¹²And ye shall rejoice before the LORD your God, ye, and your sons, and your daughters, and your menservants, and your maidservants, and the Levite that is within your gates; forasmuch as he hath no part nor inheritance with you.

¹³Take heed to thyself that thou offer not thy burnt offerings in every place that thou seest:

¹⁴But in the place which the LORD shall choose in one of thy tribes, there thou shalt offer thy burnt offerings, and there thou shalt do all that I command thee.

¹⁵Notwithstanding thou mayest kill and eat flesh in all thy gates, whatsoever thy soul lusteth after, according to the blessing of the LORD thy God which he hath given thee: the unclean and the clean may eat thereof, as of the roebuck, and as of the hart.

¹⁶Only ye shall not eat the blood; ye shall pour it upon the earth as water.

¹⁷Thou mayest not eat within thy gates the tithe of thy corn, or of thy wine, or of thy oil, or the firstlings of thy herds or of thy flock, nor any of thy vows which thou vowest, nor thy freewill offerings, or heave offering of thine hand:

¹⁸But thou must eat them before the LORD thy God in the place which the LORD thy God shall choose, thou, and thy son, and thy

daughter, and thy manservant, and thy maidservant, and the Levite that is within thy gates: and thou shalt rejoice before the LORD thy God in all that thou puttest thine hands unto.

¹⁹Take heed to thyself that thou forsake not the Levite as long as thou livest upon the earth.

²⁰When the LORD thy God shall enlarge thy border, as he hath promised thee, and thou shalt say, I will eat flesh, because thy soul longeth to eat flesh; thou mayest eat flesh, whatsoever thy soul lusteth after.

²¹If the place which the LORD thy God hath chosen to put his name there be too far from thee, then thou shalt kill of thy herd and of thy flock, which the LORD hath given thee, as I have commanded thee, and thou shalt eat in thy gates whatsoever thy soul lusteth after.

²²Even as the roebuck and the hart is eaten, so thou shalt eat them: the unclean and the clean shall eat of them alike.

²³Only be sure that thou eat not the blood: for the blood is the life; and thou mayest not eat the life with the flesh.

²⁴Thou shalt not eat it; thou shalt pour it upon the earth as water.

²⁵Thou shalt not eat it; that it may go well with thee, and with thy children after thee, when thou shalt do that which is right in the sight of the LORD.

²⁶Only thy holy things which thou hast, and thy vows, thou shalt take, and go unto the place which the LORD shall choose:

²⁷And thou shalt offer thy burnt offerings, the flesh and the blood, upon the altar of the LORD thy God: and the blood of thy sacrifices shall be poured out upon the altar of the LORD thy God, and thou shalt eat the flesh.

²⁸Observe and hear all these words which I command thee, that it may go well with thee, and with thy children after thee for ever, when thou doest that which is good and right in the sight of the LORD thy God.

²⁹When the LORD thy God shall cut off the nations from before thee, whither thou goest to possess them, and thou succeedest them, and dwellest in their land;

³⁰Take heed to thyself that thou be not snared by following them, after that they be destroyed from before thee; and that thou enquire not after their gods, saying, How did these nations serve their gods? even so will I do likewise.

³¹Thou shalt not do so unto the LORD thy God: for every abomination to the LORD, which

he hateth, have they done unto their gods; for even their sons and their daughters they have burnt in the fire to their gods.

³²What thing soever I command you, observe to do it: thou shalt not add thereto, nor diminish from it.

CHAPTER 13

¹If there arise among you a prophet, or a dreamer of dreams, and giveth thee a sign or a wonder,

²And the sign or the wonder come to pass, whereof he spake unto thee, saying, Let us go after other gods, which thou hast not known, and let us serve them;

³Thou shalt not hearken unto the words of that prophet, or that dreamer of dreams: for the LORD your God proveth you, to know whether ye love the LORD your God with all your heart and with all your soul.

⁴Ye shall walk after the LORD your God, and fear him, and keep his commandments, and obey his voice, and ye shall serve him, and cleave unto him.

⁵And that prophet, or that dreamer of dreams, shall be put to death; because he hath spoken to turn you away from the LORD your God, which brought you out of the land of Egypt, and redeemed you out of the house of bondage, to thrust thee out of the way which the LORD thy God commanded thee to walk in. So shalt thou put the evil away from the midst of thee.

⁶If thy brother, the son of thy mother, or thy son, or thy daughter, or the wife of thy bosom, or thy friend, which is as thine own soul, entice thee secretly, saying, Let us go and serve other gods, which thou hast not known, thou, nor thy fathers;

⁷Namely, of the gods of the people which are round about you, nigh unto thee, or far off from thee, from the one end of the earth even unto the other end of the earth;

⁸Thou shalt not consent unto him, nor hearken unto him; neither shall thine eye pity him, neither shalt thou spare, neither shalt thou conceal him:

⁹But thou shalt surely kill him; thine hand shall be first upon him to put him to death, and afterwards the hand of all the people.

¹⁰And thou shalt stone him with stones, that he die; because he hath sought to thrust thee away from the LORD thy God, which brought thee out of the land of Egypt, from the house of bondage.

¹¹And all Israel shall hear, and fear, and shall do no more any such wickedness as this is among you.

¹²If thou shalt hear say in one of thy cities, which the LORD thy God hath given thee to dwell there, saying,

¹³Certain men, the children of Belial, are gone out from among you, and have withdrawn the inhabitants of their city, saying, Let us go and serve other gods, which ye have not known;

¹⁴Then shalt thou enquire, and make search, and ask diligently; and, behold, if it be truth, and the thing certain, that such abomination is wrought among you;

¹⁵Thou shalt surely smite the inhabitants of that city with the edge of the sword, destroying it utterly, and all that is therein, and the cattle thereof, with the edge of the sword.

¹⁶And thou shalt gather all the spoil of it into the midst of the street thereof, and shalt burn with fire the city, and all the spoil thereof every whit, for the LORD thy God: and it shall be an heap for ever; it shall not be built again.

¹⁷And there shall cleave nought of the cursed thing to thine hand: that the LORD may turn from the fierceness of his anger, and shew thee mercy, and have compassion upon thee, and multiply thee, as he hath sworn unto thy fathers;

¹⁸When thou shalt hearken to the voice of the LORD thy God, to keep all his commandments which I command thee this day, to do that which is right in the eyes of the LORD thy God.

CHAPTER 14

¹Ye are the children of the LORD your God: ye shall not cut yourselves, nor make any baldness between your eyes for the dead.

²For thou art an holy people unto the LORD thy God, and the LORD hath chosen thee to be a peculiar people unto himself, above all the nations that are upon the earth.

³Thou shalt not eat any abominable thing.

⁴These are the beasts which ye shall eat: the ox, the sheep, and the goat,

⁵The hart, and the roebuck, and the fallow deer, and the wild goat, and the pygarg, and the wild ox, and the chamois.

⁶And every beast that parteth the hoof, and cleaveth the cleft into two claws, and cheweth the cud among the beasts, that ye shall eat.

⁷Nevertheless these ye shall not eat of them that chew the cud, or of them that divide the cloven hoof; as the camel, and the hare, and the coney: for they chew the cud, but divide not the hoof; therefore they are unclean unto you.

⁸And the swine, because it divideth the hoof, yet cheweth not the cud, it is unclean unto you: ye shall not eat of their flesh, nor touch their dead carcase.

⁹These ye shall eat of all that are in the waters: all that have fins and scales shall ye eat: ¹⁰And whatsoever hath not fins and scales ye may not eat; it is unclean unto you.

¹¹Of all clean birds ye shall eat.

¹²But these are they of which ye shall not eat: the eagle, and the ossifrage, and the ospray,

¹³And the glede, and the kite, and the vulture after his kind,

¹⁴And every raven after his kind,

¹⁵And the owl, and the night hawk, and the cuckow, and the hawk after his kind,

¹⁶The little owl, and the great owl, and the swan,

¹⁷And the pelican, and the gier eagle, and the cormorant,

¹⁸And the stork, and the heron after her kind, and the lapwing, and the bat.

¹⁹And every creeping thing that flieth is unclean unto you: they shall not be eaten.

²⁰But of all clean fowls ye may eat.

²¹Ye shall not eat of anything that dieth of itself: thou shalt give it unto the stranger that is in thy gates, that he may eat it; or thou mayest sell it unto an alien: for thou art an holy people unto the LORD thy God. Thou shalt not seethe a kid in his mother's milk.

²²Thou shalt truly tithe all the increase of thy seed, that the field bringeth forth year by year.

²³And thou shalt eat before the LORD thy God, in the place which he shall choose to place his name there, the tithe of thy corn, of thy wine, and of thine oil, and the firstlings of thy herds and of thy flocks; that thou mayest learn to fear the LORD thy God always.

²⁴And if the way be too long for thee, so that thou art not able to carry it; or if the place be too far from thee, which the LORD thy God shall choose to set his name there, when the LORD thy God hath blessed thee:

²⁵Then shalt thou turn it into money, and bind up the money in thine hand, and shalt go unto the place which the LORD thy God shall choose:

²⁶And thou shalt bestow that money for whatsoever thy soul lusteth after, for oxen, or for sheep,

or for wine, or for strong drink, or for whatsoever thy soul desireth: and thou shalt eat there before the LORD thy God, and thou shalt rejoice, thou, and thine household,

27And the Levite that is within thy gates; thou shalt not forsake him; for he hath no part nor inheritance with thee.

28At the end of three years thou shalt bring forth all the tithe of thine increase the same year, and shalt lay it up within thy gates:

29And the Levite, (because he hath no part nor inheritance with thee,) and the stranger, and the fatherless, and the widow, which are within thy gates, shall come, and shall eat and be satisfied; that the LORD thy God may bless thee in all the work of thine hand which thou doest.

CHAPTER 15

1At the end of every seven years thou shalt make a release.

2And this is the manner of the release: Every creditor that lendeth ought unto his neighbour shall release it; he shall not exact it of his neighbour, or of his brother; because it is called the LORD's release.

3Of a foreigner thou mayest exact it again: but that which is thine with thy brother thine hand shall release;

4Save when there shall be no poor among you; for the LORD shall greatly bless thee in the land which the LORD thy God giveth thee for an inheritance to possess it:

5Only if thou carefully hearken unto the voice of the LORD thy God, to observe to do all these commandments which I command thee this day.

6For the LORD thy God blesseth thee, as he promised thee: and thou shalt lend unto many nations, but thou shalt not borrow; and thou shalt reign over many nations, but they shall not reign over thee.

7If there be among you a poor man of one of thy brethren within any of thy gates in thy land which the LORD thy God giveth thee, thou shalt not harden thine heart, nor shut thine hand from thy poor brother:

8But thou shalt open thine hand wide unto him, and shalt surely lend him sufficient for his need, in that which he wanteth.

9Beware that there be not a thought in thy wicked heart, saying, The seventh year, the year of release, is at hand; and thine eye be evil against thy poor brother, and thou givest him nought; and he cry unto the LORD against thee, and it be sin unto thee.

10 Thou shalt surely give him, and thine heart shall not be grieved when thou givest unto him: because that for this thing the LORD thy God shall bless thee in all thy works, and in all that thou puttest thine hand unto.

11 For the poor shall never cease out of the land: therefore I command thee, saying, Thou shalt open thine hand wide unto thy brother, to thy poor, and to thy needy, in thy land.

12 And if thy brother, an Hebrew man, or an Hebrew woman, be sold unto thee, and serve thee six years; then in the seventh year thou shalt let him go free from thee.

13 And when thou sendest him out free from thee, thou shalt not let him go away empty:

14 Thou shalt furnish him liberally out of thy flock, and out of thy floor, and out of thy winepress: of that wherewith the LORD thy God hath blessed thee thou shalt give unto him.

15 And thou shalt remember that thou wast a bondman in the land of Egypt, and the LORD thy God redeemed thee: therefore I command thee this thing to day.

16 And it shall be, if he say unto thee, I will not go away from thee; because he loveth thee and thine house, because he is well with thee;

17 Then thou shalt take an aul, and thrust it through his ear unto the door, and he shall be thy servant for ever. And also unto thy maidservant thou shalt do likewise.

18 It shall not seem hard unto thee, when thou sendest him away free from thee; for he hath been worth a double hired servant to thee, in serving thee six years: and the LORD thy God shall bless thee in all that thou doest.

19 All the firstling males that come of thy herd and of thy flock thou shalt sanctify unto the LORD thy God: thou shalt do no work with the firstling of thy bullock, nor shear the firstling of thy sheep.

20 Thou shalt eat it before the LORD thy God year by year in the place which the LORD shall choose, thou and thy household.

21 And if there be any blemish therein, as if it be lame, or blind, or have any ill blemish, thou shalt not sacrifice it unto the LORD thy God.

22 Thou shalt eat it within thy gates: the unclean and the clean person shall eat it alike, as the roebuck, and as the hart.

23 Only thou shalt not eat the blood thereof; thou shalt pour it upon the ground as water.

CHAPTER 16

¹Observe the month of Abib, and keep the passover unto the LORD thy God: for in the month of Abib the LORD thy God brought thee forth out of Egypt by night.

²Thou shalt therefore sacrifice the passover unto the LORD thy God, of the flock and the herd, in the place which the LORD shall choose to place his name there.

³Thou shalt eat no leavened bread with it; seven days shalt thou eat unleavened bread therewith, even the bread of affliction; for thou camest forth out of the land of Egypt in haste: that thou mayest remember the day when thou camest forth out of the land of Egypt all the days of thy life.

⁴And there shall be no leavened bread seen with thee in all thy coast seven days; neither shall there any thing of the flesh, which thou sacrificedst the first day at even, remain all night until the morning.

⁵Thou mayest not sacrifice the passover within any of thy gates, which the LORD thy God giveth thee:

⁶But at the place which the LORD thy God shall choose to place his name in, there thou shalt sacrifice the passover at even, at the going down of the sun, at the season that thou camest forth out of Egypt.

⁷And thou shalt roast and eat it in the place which the LORD thy God shall choose: and thou shalt turn in the morning, and go unto thy tents.

⁸Six days thou shalt eat unleavened bread: and on the seventh day shall be a solemn assembly to the LORD thy God: thou shalt do no work therein.

⁹Seven weeks shalt thou number unto thee: begin to number the seven weeks from such time as thou beginnest to put the sickle to the corn.

¹⁰And thou shalt keep the feast of weeks unto the LORD thy God with a tribute of a freewill offering of thine hand, which thou shalt give unto the LORD thy God, according as the LORD thy God hath blessed thee:

¹¹And thou shalt rejoice before the LORD thy God, thou, and thy son, and thy daughter, and thy manservant, and thy maidservant, and the Levite that is within thy gates, and the stranger, and the fatherless, and the widow, that are among you, in the place which the LORD thy God hath chosen to place his name there.

¹²And thou shalt remember that thou wast a bondman in Egypt: and thou shalt observe and do these statutes.

¹³Thou shalt observe the feast of tabernacles seven days, after that thou hast gathered in thy corn and thy wine:

¹⁴And thou shalt rejoice in thy feast, thou, and thy son, and thy daughter, and thy manservant, and thy maidservant, and the Levite, the stranger, and the fatherless, and the widow, that are within thy gates.

¹⁵Seven days shalt thou keep a solemn feast unto the LORD thy God in the place which the LORD shall choose: because the LORD thy God shall bless thee in all thine increase, and in all the works of thine hands, therefore thou shalt surely rejoice.

¹⁶Three times in a year shall all thy males appear before the LORD thy God in the place which he shall choose; in the feast of unleavened bread, and in the feast of weeks, and in the feast of tabernacles: and they shall not appear before the LORD empty:

¹⁷Every man shall give as he is able, according to the blessing of the LORD thy God which he hath given thee.

¹⁸Judges and officers shalt thou make thee in all thy gates, which the LORD thy God giveth thee, throughout thy tribes: and they shall judge the people with just judgment.

¹⁹Thou shalt not wrest judgment; thou shalt not respect persons, neither take a gift: for a gift doth blind the eyes of the wise, and pervert the words of the righteous.

²⁰That which is altogether just shalt thou follow, that thou mayest live, and inherit the land which the LORD thy God giveth thee.

²¹Thou shalt not plant thee a grove of any trees near unto the altar of the LORD thy God, which thou shalt make thee.

²²Neither shalt thou set thee up any image; which the LORD thy God hateth.

CHAPTER 17

¹Thou shalt not sacrifice unto the LORD thy God any bullock, or sheep, wherein is blemish, or any evilfavouredness: for that is an abomination unto the LORD thy God.

²If there be found among you, within any of thy gates which the LORD thy God giveth thee, man or woman, that hath wrought wickedness in the sight of the LORD thy God, in transgressing his covenant,

³And hath gone and served other gods, and worshipped them, either the sun, or moon, or any of the

host of heaven, which I have not commanded;

⁴And it be told thee, and thou hast heard of it, and enquired diligently, and, behold, it be true, and the thing certain, that such abomination is wrought in Israel:

⁵Then shalt thou bring forth that man or that woman, which have committed that wicked thing, unto thy gates, even that man or that woman, and shalt stone them with stones, till they die.

⁶At the mouth of two witnesses, or three witnesses, shall he that is worthy of death be put to death; but at the mouth of one witness he shall not be put to death.

⁷The hands of the witnesses shall be first upon him to put him to death, and afterward the hands of all the people. So thou shalt put the evil away from among you.

⁸If there arise a matter too hard for thee in judgment, between blood and blood, between plea and plea, and between stroke and stroke, being matters of controversy within thy gates: then shalt thou arise, and get thee up into the place which the LORD thy God shall choose;

⁹And thou shalt come unto the priests the Levites, and unto the judge that shall be in those days, and enquire; and they shall shew thee the sentence of judgment:

¹⁰And thou shalt do according to the sentence, which they of that place which the LORD shall choose shall shew thee; and thou shalt observe to do according to all that they inform thee:

¹¹According to the sentence of the law which they shall teach thee, and according to the judgment which they shall tell thee, thou shalt do: thou shalt not decline from the sentence which they shall shew thee, to the right hand, nor to the left.

¹²And the man that will do presumptuously, and will not hearken unto the priest that standeth to minister there before the LORD thy God, or unto the judge, even that man shall die: and thou shalt put away the evil from Israel.

¹³And all the people shall hear, and fear, and do no more presumptuously.

¹⁴When thou art come unto the land which the LORD thy God giveth thee, and shalt possess it, and shalt dwell therein, and shalt say, I will set a king over me, like as all the nations that are about me;

¹⁵Thou shalt in any wise set him king over thee, whom the LORD thy God shall choose: one from among thy brethren shalt thou set king over thee: thou mayest not set a stranger over thee, which is not thy brother.

16But he shall not multiply horses to himself, nor cause the people to return to Egypt, to the end that he should multiply horses: forasmuch as the LORD hath said unto you, Ye shall henceforth return no more that way.

17Neither shall he multiply wives to himself, that his heart turn not away: neither shall he greatly multiply to himself silver and gold.

18And it shall be, when he sitteth upon the throne of his kingdom, that he shall write him a copy of this law in a book out of that which is before the priests the Levites:

19And it shall be with him, and he shall read therein all the days of his life: that he may learn to fear the LORD his God, to keep all the words of this law and these statutes, to do them:

20That his heart be not lifted up above his brethren, and that he turn not aside from the commandment, to the right hand, or to the left: to the end that he may prolong his days in his kingdom, he, and his children, in the midst of Israel.

CHAPTER 18

1The priests the Levites, and all the tribe of Levi, shall have no part nor inheritance with Israel: they shall eat the offerings of the LORD made by fire, and his inheritance.

2Therefore shall they have no inheritance among their brethren: the LORD is their inheritance, as he hath said unto them.

3And this shall be the priest's due from the people, from them that offer a sacrifice, whether it be ox or sheep; and they shall give unto the priest the shoulder, and the two cheeks, and the maw.

4The firstfruit also of thy corn, of thy wine, and of thine oil, and the first of the fleece of thy sheep, shalt thou give him.

5For the LORD thy God hath chosen him out of all thy tribes, to stand to minister in the name of the LORD, him and his sons for ever.

6And if a Levite come from any of thy gates out of all Israel, where he sojourned, and come with all the desire of his mind unto the place which the LORD shall choose;

7Then he shall minister in the name of the LORD his God, as all his brethren the Levites do, which stand there before the LORD.

8They shall have like portions to eat, beside that which cometh of the sale of his patrimony.

9When thou art come into the land which the LORD thy God giveth thee, thou shalt not learn to do after the abominations of those nations.

¹⁰There shall not be found among you any one that maketh his son or his daughter to pass through the fire, or that useth divination, or an observer of times, or an enchanter, or a witch.

¹¹Or a charmer, or a consulter with familiar spirits, or a wizard, or a necromancer.

¹²For all that do these things are an abomination unto the LORD: and because of these abominations the LORD thy God doth drive them out from before thee.

¹³Thou shalt be perfect with the LORD thy God.

¹⁴For these nations, which thou shalt possess, hearkened unto observers of times, and unto diviners: but as for thee, the LORD thy God hath not suffered thee so to do.

¹⁵The LORD thy God will raise up unto thee a Prophet from the midst of thee, of thy brethren, like unto me; unto him ye shall hearken;

¹⁶According to all that thou desiredst of the LORD thy God in Horeb in the day of the assembly, saying, Let me not hear again the voice of the LORD my God, neither let me see this great fire any more, that I die not.

¹⁷And the LORD said unto me, They have well spoken that which they have spoken.

¹⁸I will raise them up a Prophet from among their brethren, like unto thee, and will put my words in his mouth; and he shall speak unto them all that I shall command him.

¹⁹And it shall come to pass, that whosoever will not hearken unto my words which he shall speak in my name, I will require it of him.

²⁰But the prophet, which shall presume to speak a word in my name, which I have not commanded him to speak, or that shall speak in the name of other gods, even that prophet shall die.

²¹And if thou say in thine heart, How shall we know the word which the LORD hath not spoken?

²²When a prophet speaketh in the name of the LORD, if the thing follow not, nor come to pass, that is the thing which the LORD hath not spoken, but the prophet hath spoken it presumptuously: thou shalt not be afraid of him.

CHAPTER 19

¹When the LORD thy God hath cut off the nations, whose land the LORD thy God giveth thee, and

thou succeedest them, and dwellest in their cities, and in their houses;

²Thou shalt separate three cities for thee in the midst of thy land, which the LORD thy God giveth thee to possess it.

³Thou shalt prepare thee a way, and divide the coasts of thy land, which the LORD thy God giveth thee to inherit, into three parts, that every slayer may flee thither.

⁴And this is the case of the slayer, which shall flee thither, that he may live: Whoso killeth his neighbour ignorantly, whom he hated not in time past;

⁵As when a man goeth into the wood with his neighbour to hew wood, and his hand fetcheth a stroke with the axe to cut down the tree, and the head slippeth from the helve, and lighteth upon his neighbour, that he die; he shall flee unto one of those cities, and live:

⁶Lest the avenger of the blood pursue the slayer, while his heart is hot, and overtake him, because the way is long, and slay him; whereas he was not worthy of death, inasmuch as he hated him not in time past.

⁷Wherefore I command thee, saying, Thou shalt separate three cities for thee.

⁸And if the LORD thy God enlarge thy coast, as he hath sworn unto thy fathers, and give thee all the land which he promised to give unto thy fathers;

⁹If thou shalt keep all these commandments to do them, which I command thee this day, to love the LORD thy God, and to walk ever in his ways; then shalt thou add three cities more for thee, beside these three:

¹⁰That innocent blood be not shed in thy land, which the LORD thy God giveth thee for an inheritance, and so blood be upon thee.

¹¹But if any man hate his neighbour, and lie in wait for him, and rise up against him, and smite him mortally that he die, and fleeth into one of these cities:

¹²Then the elders of his city shall send and fetch him thence, and deliver him into the hand of the avenger of blood, that he may die.

¹³Thine eye shall not pity him, but thou shalt put away the guilt of innocent blood from Israel, that it may go well with thee.

¹⁴Thou shalt not remove thy neighbour's landmark, which they of old time have set in thine inheritance, which thou shalt inherit in the land that the LORD thy God giveth thee to possess it.

¹⁵One witness shall not rise up against a man for any iniquity, or for any sin, in any sin that he sinneth: at the mouth of two witnesses, or at

the mouth of three witnesses, shall the matter be established.

¹⁶If a false witness rise up against any man to testify against him that which is wrong;

¹⁷Then both the men, between whom the controversy is, shall stand before the LORD, before the priests and the judges, which shall be in those days;

¹⁸And the judges shall make diligent inquisition: and, behold, if the witness be a false witness, and hath testified falsely against his brother;

¹⁹Then shall ye do unto him, as he had thought to have done unto his brother: so shalt thou put the evil away from among you.

²⁰And those which remain shall hear, and fear, and shall henceforth commit no more any such evil among you.

²¹And thine eye shall not pity; but life shall go for life, eye for eye, tooth for tooth, hand for hand, foot for foot.

CHAPTER 20

¹When thou goest out to battle against thine enemies, and seest horses, and chariots, and a people more than thou, be not afraid of them: for the LORD thy God is with thee, which brought thee up out of the land of Egypt.

²And it shall be, when ye are come nigh unto the battle, that the priest shall approach and speak unto the people,

³And shall say unto them, Hear, O Israel, ye approach this day unto battle against your enemies: let not your hearts faint, fear not, and do not tremble, neither be ye terrified because of them;

⁴For the LORD your God is he that goeth with you, to fight for you against your enemies, to save you.

⁵And the officers shall speak unto the people, saying, What man is there that hath built a new house, and hath not dedicated it? let him go and return to his house, lest he die in the battle, and another man dedicate it.

⁶And what man is he that hath planted a vineyard, and hath not yet eaten of it? let him also go and return unto his house, lest he die in the battle, and another man eat of it.

⁷And what man is there that hath betrothed a wife, and hath not taken her? let him go and return unto his house, lest he die in the battle, and another man take her.

⁸And the officers shall speak further unto the people, and they shall say, What man is there that is

fearful and fainthearted? let him go and return unto his house, lest his brethren's heart faint as well as his heart.

⁹And it shall be, when the officers have made an end of speaking unto the people that they shall make captains of the armies to lead the people.

¹⁰When thou comest nigh unto a city to fight against it, then proclaim peace unto it.

¹¹And it shall be, if it make thee answer of peace, and open unto thee, then it shall be, that all the people that is found therein shall be tributaries unto thee, and they shall serve thee.

¹²And if it will make no peace with thee, but will make war against thee, then thou shalt besiege it:

¹³And when the LORD thy God hath delivered it into thine hands, thou shalt smite every male thereof with the edge of the sword:

¹⁴But the women, and the little ones, and the cattle, and all that is in the city, even all the spoil thereof, shalt thou take unto thyself; and thou shalt eat the spoil of thine enemies, which the LORD thy God hath given thee.

¹⁵Thus shalt thou do unto all the cities which are very far off from thee, which are not of the cities of these nations.

¹⁶But of the cities of these people, which the LORD thy God doth give thee for an inheritance, thou shalt save alive nothing that breatheth:

¹⁷But thou shalt utterly destroy them; namely, the Hittites, and the Amorites, the Canaanites, and the Perizzites, the Hivites, and the Jebusites; as the LORD thy God hath commanded thee:

¹⁸That they teach you not to do after all their abominations, which they have done unto their gods; so should ye sin against the LORD your God.

¹⁹When thou shalt besiege a city a long time, in making war against it to take it, thou shalt not destroy the trees thereof by forcing an axe against them: for thou mayest eat of them, and thou shalt not cut them down (for the tree of the field is man's life) to employ them in the siege:

²⁰Only the trees which thou knowest that they be not trees for meat, thou shalt destroy and cut them down; and thou shalt build bulwarks against the city that maketh war with thee, until it be subdued.

Chapter 21

¹If one be found slain in the land which the LORD thy God giveth

thee to possess it, lying in the field, and it be not known who hath slain him:

²Then thy elders and thy judges shall come forth, and they shall measure unto the cities which are round about him that is slain:

³And it shall be, that the city which is next unto the slain man, even the elders of that city shall take an heifer, which hath not been wrought with, and which hath not drawn in the yoke;

⁴And the elders of that city shall bring down the heifer unto a rough valley, which is neither eared nor sown, and shall strike off the heifer's neck there in the valley:

⁵And the priests the sons of Levi shall come near; for them the LORD thy God hath chosen to minister unto him, and to bless in the name of the LORD, and by their word shall every controversy and every stroke be tried:

⁶And all the elders of that city, that are next unto the slain man, shall wash their hands over the heifer that is beheaded in the valley:

⁷And they shall answer and say, Our hands have not shed this blood, neither have our eyes seen it.

⁸Be merciful, O LORD, unto thy people Israel, whom thou hast redeemed, and lay not innocent blood unto thy people of Israel's

charge. And the blood shall be forgiven them.

⁹So shalt thou put away the guilt of innocent blood from among you, when thou shalt do that which is right in the sight of the LORD.

¹⁰When thou goest forth to war against thine enemies, and the LORD thy God hath delivered them into thine hands, and thou hast taken them captive,

¹¹And seest among the captives a beautiful woman, and hast a desire unto her, that thou wouldest have her to thy wife;

¹²Then thou shalt bring her home to thine house, and she shall shave her head, and pare her nails;

¹³And she shall put the raiment of her captivity from off her, and shall remain in thine house, and bewail her father and her mother a full month: and after that thou shalt go in unto her, and be her husband, and she shall be thy wife.

¹⁴And it shall be, if thou have no delight in her, then thou shalt let her go whither she will; but thou shalt not sell her at all for money, thou shalt not make merchandise of her, because thou hast humbled her.

¹⁵If a man have two wives, one beloved, and another hated, and they have born him children, both the beloved and the hated; and if

the firstborn son be hers that was hated:

¹⁶Then it shall be, when he maketh his sons to inherit that which he hath, that he may not make the son of the beloved firstborn before the son of the hated, which is indeed the firstborn:

¹⁷But he shall acknowledge the son of the hated for the firstborn, by giving him a double portion of all that he hath: for he is the beginning of his strength; the right of the firstborn is his.

¹⁸If a man have a stubborn and rebellious son, which will not obey the voice of his father, or the voice of his mother, and that, when they have chastened him, will not hearken unto them:

¹⁹Then shall his father and his mother lay hold on him, and bring him out unto the elders of his city, and unto the gate of his place;

²⁰And they shall say unto the elders of his city, This our son is stubborn and rebellious, he will not obey our voice; he is a glutton, and a drunkard.

²¹And all the men of his city shall stone him with stones, that he die: so shalt thou put evil away from among you; and all Israel shall hear, and fear.

²²And if a man have committed a sin worthy of death, and he be to be put to death, and thou hang him on a tree:

²³His body shall not remain all night upon the tree, but thou shalt in any wise bury him that day; (for he that is hanged is accursed of God;) that thy land be not defiled, which the LORD thy God giveth thee for an inheritance.

CHAPTER 22

¹Thou shalt not see thy brother's ox or his sheep go astray, and hide thyself from them: thou shalt in any case bring them again unto thy brother.

²And if thy brother be not nigh unto thee, or if thou know him not, then thou shalt bring it unto thine own house, and it shall be with thee until thy brother seek after it, and thou shalt restore it to him again.

³In like manner shalt thou do with his ass; and so shalt thou do with his raiment; and with all lost thing of thy brother's, which he hath lost, and thou hast found, shalt thou do likewise: thou mayest not hide thyself.

⁴Thou shalt not see thy brother's ass or his ox fall down by the way, and hide thyself from them: thou shalt surely help him to lift them up again.

⁵The woman shall not wear that which pertaineth unto a man, neither shall a man put on a woman's garment: for all that do so are abomination unto the LORD thy God.

⁶If a bird's nest chance to be before thee in the way in any tree, or on the ground, whether they be young ones, or eggs, and the dam sitting upon the young, or upon the eggs, thou shalt not take the dam with the young:

⁷But thou shalt in any wise let the dam go, and take the young to thee; that it may be well with thee, and that thou mayest prolong thy days.

⁸When thou buildest a new house, then thou shalt make a battlement for thy roof, that thou bring not blood upon thine house, if any man fall from thence.

⁹Thou shalt not sow thy vineyard with divers seeds: lest the fruit of thy seed which thou hast sown, and the fruit of thy vineyard, be defiled.

¹⁰Thou shalt not plow with an ox and an ass together.

¹¹Thou shalt not wear a garment of divers sorts, as of woollen and linen together.

¹²Thou shalt make thee fringes upon the four quarters of thy vesture, wherewith thou coverest thyself.

¹³If any man take a wife, and go in unto her, and hate her,

¹⁴And give occasions of speech against her, and bring up an evil name upon her, and say, I took this woman, and when I came to her, I found her not a maid:

¹⁵Then shall the father of the damsel, and her mother, take and bring forth the tokens of the damsel's virginity unto the elders of the city in the gate:

¹⁶And the damsel's father shall say unto the elders, I gave my daughter unto this man to wife, and he hateth her;

¹⁷And, lo, he hath given occasions of speech against her, saying, I found not thy daughter a maid; and yet these are the tokens of my daughter's virginity. And they shall spread the cloth before the elders of the city.

¹⁸And the elders of that city shall take that man and chastise him;

¹⁹And they shall amerce him in an hundred shekels of silver, and give them unto the father of the damsel, because he hath brought up an evil name upon a virgin of Israel: and she shall be his wife; he may not put her away all his days.

²⁰But if this thing be true, and the tokens of virginity be not found for the damsel:

²¹Then they shall bring out the damsel to the door of her father's

house, and the men of her city shall stone her with stones that she die: because she hath wrought folly in Israel, to play the whore in her father's house: so shalt thou put evil away from among you.

²²If a man be found lying with a woman married to an husband, then they shall both of them die, both the man that lay with the woman, and the woman: so shalt thou put away evil from Israel.

²³If a damsel that is a virgin be betrothed unto an husband, and a man find her in the city, and lie with her;

²⁴Then ye shall bring them both out unto the gate of that city, and ye shall stone them with stones that they die; the damsel, because she cried not, being in the city; and the man, because he hath humbled his neighbour's wife: so thou shalt put away evil from among you.

²⁵But if a man find a betrothed damsel in the field, and the man force her, and lie with her: then the man only that lay with her shall die.

²⁶But unto the damsel thou shalt do nothing; there is in the damsel no sin worthy of death: for as when a man riseth against his neighbour, and slayeth him, even so is this matter:

²⁷For he found her in the field, and the betrothed damsel cried, and there was none to save her.

²⁸If a man find a damsel that is a virgin, which is not betrothed, and lay hold on her, and lie with her, and they be found;

²⁹Then the man that lay with her shall give unto the damsel's father fifty shekels of silver, and she shall be his wife; because he hath humbled her, he may not put her away all his days.

³⁰A man shall not take his father's wife, nor discover his father's skirt.

CHAPTER 23

¹He that is wounded in the stones, or hath his privy member cut off, shall not enter into the congregation of the LORD.

²A bastard shall not enter into the congregation of the LORD; even to his tenth generation shall he not enter into the congregation of the LORD.

³An Ammonite or Moabite shall not enter into the congregation of the LORD; even to their tenth generation shall they not enter into the congregation of the LORD for ever:

⁴Because they met you not with bread and with water in the way, when ye came forth out of Egypt; and because they hired against thee

Balaam the son of Beor of Pethor of Mesopotamia, to curse thee.

⁵Nevertheless the LORD thy God would not hearken unto Balaam; but the LORD thy God turned the curse into a blessing unto thee, because the LORD thy God loved thee.

⁶Thou shalt not seek their peace nor their prosperity all thy days for ever.

⁷Thou shalt not abhor an Edomite; for he is thy brother: thou shalt not abhor an Egyptian; because thou wast a stranger in his land.

⁸The children that are begotten of them shall enter into the congregation of the LORD in their third generation.

⁹When the host goeth forth against thine enemies, then keep thee from every wicked thing.

¹⁰If there be among you any man, that is not clean by reason of uncleanness that chanceth him by night, then shall he go abroad out of the camp, he shall not come within the camp:

¹¹But it shall be, when evening cometh on, he shall wash himself with water: and when the sun is down, he shall come into the camp again.

¹²Thou shalt have a place also without the camp, whither thou shalt go forth abroad:

¹³And thou shalt have a paddle upon thy weapon; and it shall be, when thou wilt ease thyself abroad, thou shalt dig therewith, and shalt turn back and cover that which cometh from thee:

¹⁴For the LORD thy God walketh in the midst of thy camp, to deliver thee, and to give up thine enemies before thee; therefore shall thy camp be holy: that he see no unclean thing in thee, and turn away from thee.

¹⁵Thou shalt not deliver unto his master the servant which is escaped from his master unto thee:

¹⁶He shall dwell with thee, even among you, in that place which he shall choose in one of thy gates, where it liketh him best: thou shalt not oppress him.

¹⁷There shall be no whore of the daughters of Israel, nor a sodomite of the sons of Israel.

¹⁸Thou shalt not bring the hire of a whore, or the price of a dog, into the house of the LORD thy God for any vow: for even both these are abomination unto the LORD thy God.

¹⁹Thou shalt not lend upon usury to thy brother; usury of money, usury of victuals, usury of any thing that is lent upon usury:

²⁰Unto a stranger thou mayest lend upon usury; but unto thy brother thou shalt not lend upon usury: that the LORD thy God may bless thee in all that thou settest

thine hand to in the land whither thou goest to possess it.

²¹When thou shalt vow a vow unto the LORD thy God, thou shalt not slack to pay it: for the LORD thy God will surely require it of thee; and it would be sin in thee.

²²But if thou shalt forbear to vow, it shall be no sin in thee.

²³That which is gone out of thy lips thou shalt keep and perform; even a freewill offering, according as thou hast vowed unto the LORD thy God, which thou hast promised with thy mouth.

²⁴When thou comest into thy neighbour's vineyard, then thou mayest eat grapes thy fill at thine own pleasure; but thou shalt not put any in thy vessel.

²⁵When thou comest into the standing corn of thy neighbour, then thou mayest pluck the ears with thine hand; but thou shalt not move a sickle unto thy neighbour's standing corn.

CHAPTER 24

¹When a man hath taken a wife, and married her, and it come to pass that she find no favour in his eyes, because he hath found some uncleanness in her: then let him write her a bill of divorcement, and give it in her hand, and send her out of his house.

²And when she is departed out of his house, she may go and be another man's wife.

³And if the latter husband hate her, and write her a bill of divorcement, and giveth it in her hand, and sendeth her out of his house; or if the latter husband die, which took her to be his wife;

⁴Her former husband, which sent her away, may not take her again to be his wife, after that she is defiled; for that is abomination before the LORD: and thou shalt not cause the land to sin, which the LORD thy God giveth thee for an inheritance.

⁵When a man hath taken a new wife, he shall not go out to war, neither shall he be charged with any business: but he shall be free at home one year, and shall cheer up his wife which he hath taken.

⁶No man shall take the nether or the upper millstone to pledge: for he taketh a man's life to pledge.

⁷If a man be found stealing any of his brethren of the children of Israel, and maketh merchandise of him, or selleth him; then that thief shall die; and thou shalt put evil away from among you.

⁸Take heed in the plague of leprosy, that thou observe diligently,

and do according to all that the priests the Levites shall teach you: as I commanded them, so ye shall observe to do.

⁹Remember what the LORD thy God did unto Miriam by the way, after that ye were come forth out of Egypt.

¹⁰When thou dost lend thy brother any thing, thou shalt not go into his house to fetch his pledge.

¹¹Thou shalt stand abroad, and the man to whom thou dost lend shall bring out the pledge abroad unto thee.

¹²And if the man be poor, thou shalt not sleep with his pledge:

¹³In any case thou shalt deliver him the pledge again when the sun goeth down, that he may sleep in his own raiment, and bless thee: and it shall be righteousness unto thee before the LORD thy God.

¹⁴Thou shalt not oppress an hired servant that is poor and needy, whether he be of thy brethren, or of thy strangers that are in thy land within thy gates:

¹⁵At his day thou shalt give him his hire, neither shall the sun go down upon it; for he is poor, and setteth his heart upon it: lest he cry against thee unto the LORD, and it be sin unto thee.

¹⁶The fathers shall not be put to death for the children, neither shall the children be put to death for the fathers: every man shall be put to death for his own sin.

¹⁷Thou shalt not pervert the judgment of the stranger, nor of the fatherless; nor take a widow's raiment to pledge:

¹⁸But thou shalt remember that thou wast a bondman in Egypt, and the LORD thy God redeemed thee thence: therefore I command thee to do this thing.

¹⁹When thou cuttest down thine harvest in thy field, and hast forgot a sheaf in the field, thou shalt not go again to fetch it: it shall be for the stranger, for the fatherless, and for the widow: that the LORD thy God may bless thee in all the work of thine hands.

²⁰When thou beatest thine olive tree, thou shalt not go over the boughs again: it shall be for the stranger, for the fatherless, and for the widow.

²¹When thou gatherest the grapes of thy vineyard, thou shalt not glean it afterward: it shall be for the stranger, for the fatherless, and for the widow.

²²And thou shalt remember that thou wast a bondman in the land of Egypt: therefore I command thee to do this thing.

CHAPTER 25

¹If there be a controversy between men, and they come unto judgment, that the judges may judge them; then they shall justify the righteous, and condemn the wicked.

²And it shall be, if the wicked man be worthy to be beaten, that the judge shall cause him to lie down, and to be beaten before his face, according to his fault, by a certain number.

³Forty stripes he may give him, and not exceed: lest, if he should exceed, and beat him above these with many stripes, then thy brother should seem vile unto thee.

⁴Thou shalt not muzzle the ox when he treadeth out the corn.

⁵If brethren dwell together, and one of them die, and have no child, the wife of the dead shall not marry without unto a stranger: her husband's brother shall go in unto her, and take her to him to wife, and perform the duty of an husband's brother unto her.

⁶And it shall be, that the firstborn which she beareth shall succeed in the name of his brother which is dead, that his name be not put out of Israel.

⁷And if the man like not to take his brother's wife, then let his brother's wife go up to the gate unto the elders, and say, My husband's brother refuseth to raise up unto his brother a name in Israel, he will not perform the duty of my husband's brother.

⁸Then the elders of his city shall call him, and speak unto him: and if he stand to it, and say, I like not to take her;

⁹Then shall his brother's wife come unto him in the presence of the elders, and loose his shoe from off his foot, and spit in his face, and shall answer and say, So shall it be done unto that man that will not build up his brother's house.

¹⁰And his name shall be called in Israel, The house of him that hath his shoe loosed.

¹¹When men strive together one with another, and the wife of the one draweth near for to deliver her husband out of the hand of him that smiteth him, and putteth forth her hand, and taketh him by the secrets:

¹²Then thou shalt cut off her hand, thine eye shall not pity her.

¹³Thou shalt not have in thy bag divers weights, a great and a small.

¹⁴Thou shalt not have in thine house divers measures, a great and a small.

¹⁵But thou shalt have a perfect and just weight, a perfect and just

measure shalt thou have: that thy days may be lengthened in the land which the LORD thy God giveth thee.

¹⁶For all that do such things, and all that do unrighteously, are an abomination unto the LORD thy God.

¹⁷Remember what Amalek did unto thee by the way, when ye were come forth out of Egypt;

¹⁸How he met thee by the way, and smote the hindmost of thee, even all that were feeble behind thee, when thou wast faint and weary; and he feared not God.

¹⁹Therefore it shall be, when the LORD thy God hath given thee rest from all thine enemies round about, in the land which the LORD thy God giveth thee for an inheritance to possess it, that thou shalt blot out the remembrance of Amalek from under heaven; thou shalt not forget it.

CHAPTER 26

¹And it shall be, when thou art come in unto the land which the LORD thy God giveth thee for an inheritance, and possessest it, and dwellest therein;

²That thou shalt take of the first of all the fruit of the earth, which thou shalt bring of thy land that the LORD thy God giveth thee, and shalt put it in a basket, and shalt go unto the place which the LORD thy God shall choose to place his name there.

³And thou shalt go unto the priest that shall be in those days, and say unto him, I profess this day unto the LORD thy God, that I am come unto the country which the LORD sware unto our fathers for to give us.

⁴And the priest shall take the basket out of thine hand, and set it down before the altar of the LORD thy God.

⁵And thou shalt speak and say before the LORD thy God, A Syrian ready to perish was my father, and he went down into Egypt, and sojourned there with a few, and became there a nation, great, mighty, and populous:

⁶And the Egyptians evil entreated us, and afflicted us, and laid upon us hard bondage:

⁷And when we cried unto the LORD God of our fathers, the LORD heard our voice, and looked on our affliction, and our labour, and our oppression:

⁸And the LORD brought us forth out of Egypt with a mighty hand, and with an outstretched arm, and with great terribleness, and with signs, and with wonders:

9And he hath brought us into this place, and hath given us this land, even a land that floweth with milk and honey.

10And now, behold, I have brought the firstfruits of the land, which thou, O LORD, hast given me. And thou shalt set it before the LORD thy God, and worship before the LORD thy God:

11And thou shalt rejoice in every good thing which the LORD thy God hath given unto thee, and unto thine house, thou, and the Levite, and the stranger that is among you.

12When thou hast made an end of tithing all the tithes of thine increase the third year, which is the year of tithing, and hast given it unto the Levite, the stranger, the fatherless, and the widow, that they may eat within thy gates, and be filled;

13Then thou shalt say before the LORD thy God, I have brought away the hallowed things out of mine house, and also have given them unto the Levite, and unto the stranger, to the fatherless, and to the widow, according to all thy commandments which thou hast commanded me: I have not transgressed thy commandments, neither have I forgotten them.

14I have not eaten thereof in my mourning, neither have I taken away ought thereof for any unclean use, nor given ought thereof for the dead: but I have hearkened to the voice of the LORD my God, and have done according to all that thou hast commanded me.

15Look down from thy holy habitation, from heaven, and bless thy people Israel, and the land which thou hast given us, as thou swarest unto our fathers, a land that floweth with milk and honey.

16This day the LORD thy God hath commanded thee to do these statutes and judgments: thou shalt therefore keep and do them with all thine heart, and with all thy soul.

17Thou hast avouched the LORD this day to be thy God, and to walk in his ways, and to keep his statutes, and his commandments, and his judgments, and to hearken unto his voice:

18And the LORD hath avouched thee this day to be his peculiar people, as he hath promised thee, and that thou shouldest keep all his commandments;

19And to make thee high above all nations which he hath made, in praise, and in name, and in honour; and that thou mayest be an holy people unto the LORD thy God, as he hath spoken.

CHAPTER 27

¹And Moses with the elders of Israel commanded the people, saying, Keep all the commandments which I command you this day.

²And it shall be on the day when ye shall pass over Jordan unto the land which the LORD thy God giveth thee, that thou shalt set thee up great stones, and plaister them with plaister:

³And thou shalt write upon them all the words of this law, when thou art passed over, that thou mayest go in unto the land which the LORD thy God giveth thee, a land that floweth with milk and honey; as the LORD God of thy fathers hath promised thee.

⁴Therefore it shall be when ye be gone over Jordan, that ye shall set up these stones, which I command you this day, in mount Ebal, and thou shalt plaister them with plaister.

⁵And there shalt thou build an altar unto the LORD thy God, an altar of stones: thou shalt not lift up any iron tool upon them.

⁶Thou shalt build the altar of the LORD thy God of whole stones: and thou shalt offer burnt offerings thereon unto the LORD thy God:

⁷And thou shalt offer peace offerings, and shalt eat there, and rejoice before the LORD thy God.

⁸And thou shalt write upon the stones all the words of this law very plainly.

⁹And Moses and the priests the Levites spake unto all Israel, saying, Take heed, and hearken, O Israel; this day thou art become the people of the LORD thy God.

¹⁰Thou shalt therefore obey the voice of the LORD thy God, and do his commandments and his statutes, which I command thee this day.

¹¹And Moses charged the people the same day, saying,

¹²These shall stand upon mount Gerizim to bless the people, when ye are come over Jordan; Simeon, and Levi, and Judah, and Issachar, and Joseph, and Ben-jamin·

¹³And these shall stand upon mount Ebal to curse; Reuben, Gad, and Asher, and Zebulun, Dan, and Naphtali.

¹⁴And the Levites shall speak, and say unto all the men of Israel with a loud voice,

¹⁵Cursed be the man that maketh any graven or molten image, an abomination unto the LORD, the work of the hands of the craftsman, and putteth it in a secret place. And all the people shall answer and say, Amen.

¹⁶Cursed be he that setteth light by his father or his mother. And all the people shall say, Amen.

¹⁷Cursed be he that removeth his neighbour's landmark. And all the people shall say, Amen.

¹⁸Cursed be he that maketh the blind to wander out of the way. And all the people shall say, Amen.

¹⁹Cursed be he that perverteth the judgment of the stranger, fatherless, and widow. And all the people shall say, Amen.

²⁰Cursed be he that lieth with his father's wife; because he uncovereth his father's skirt. And all the people shall say, Amen.

²¹Cursed be he that lieth with any manner of beast. And all the people shall say, Amen.

²²Cursed be he that lieth with his sister, the daughter of his father, or the daughter of his mother. And all the people shall say, Amen.

²³Cursed be he that lieth with his mother in law. And all the people shall say, Amen.

²⁴Cursed be he that smiteth his neighbour secretly. And all the people shall say, Amen.

²⁵Cursed be he that taketh reward to slay an innocent person. And all the people shall say, Amen.

²⁶Cursed be he that confirmeth not all the words of this law to do them. And all the people shall say, Amen.

CHAPTER 28

¹And it shall come to pass, if thou shalt hearken diligently unto the voice of the LORD thy God, to observe and to do all his commandments which I command thee this day, that the LORD thy God will set thee on high above all nations of the earth:

²And all these blessings shall come on thee, and overtake thee, if thou shalt hearken unto the voice of the LORD thy God.

³Blessed shalt thou be in the city, and blessed shalt thou be in the field.

⁴Blessed shall be the fruit of thy body, and the fruit of thy ground, and the fruit of thy cattle, the increase of thy kine, and the flocks of thy sheep.

⁵Blessed shall be thy basket and thy store.

⁶Blessed shalt thou be when thou comest in, and blessed shalt thou be when thou goest out.

⁷The LORD shall cause thine enemies that rise up against thee to be smitten before thy face: they shall come out against thee one way, and flee before thee seven ways.

⁸The LORD shall command the blessing upon thee in thy storehouses, and in all that thou

settest thine hand unto; and he shall bless thee in the land which the LORD thy God giveth thee.

⁹The LORD shall establish thee an holy people unto himself, as he hath sworn unto thee, if thou shalt keep the commandments of the LORD thy God, and walk in his ways.

¹⁰And all people of the earth shall see that thou art called by the name of the LORD; and they shall be afraid of thee.

¹¹And the LORD shall make thee plenteous in goods, in the fruit of thy body, and in the fruit of thy cattle, and in the fruit of thy ground, in the land which the LORD sware unto thy fathers to give thee.

¹²The LORD shall open unto thee his good treasure, the heaven to give the rain unto thy land in his season, and to bless all the work of thine hand: and thou shalt lend unto many nations, and thou shalt not borrow.

¹³And the LORD shall make thee the head, and not the tail; and thou shalt be above only, and thou shalt not be beneath; if that thou hearken unto the commandments of the LORD thy God, which I command thee this day, to observe and to do them:

¹⁴And thou shalt not go aside from any of the words which I command thee this day, to the right hand, or to the left, to go after other gods to serve them.

¹⁵But it shall come to pass, if thou wilt not hearken unto the voice of the LORD thy God, to observe to do all his commandments and his statutes which I command thee this day; that all these curses shall come upon thee, and overtake thee:

¹⁶Cursed shalt thou be in the city, and cursed shalt thou be in the field.

¹⁷Cursed shall be thy basket and thy store.

¹⁸Cursed shall be the fruit of thy body, and the fruit of thy land, the increase of thy kine, and the flocks of thy sheep.

¹⁹Cursed shalt thou be when thou comest in, and cursed shalt thou be when thou goest out.

²⁰The LORD shall send upon thee cursing, vexation, and rebuke, in all that thou settest thine hand unto for to do, until thou be destroyed, and until thou perish quickly; because of the wickedness of thy doings, whereby thou hast forsaken me.

²¹The LORD shall make the pestilence cleave unto thee, until he have consumed thee from off the land, whither thou goest to possess it.

²²The LORD shall smite thee with a consumption, and with a fever, and with an inflammation, and with

an extreme burning, and with the sword, and with blasting, and with mildew; and they shall pursue thee until thou perish.

²³And thy heaven that is over thy head shall be brass, and the earth that is under thee shall be iron.

²⁴The LORD shall make the rain of thy land powder and dust: from heaven shall it come down upon thee, until thou be destroyed.

²⁵The LORD shall cause thee to be smitten before thine enemies: thou shalt go out one way against them, and flee seven ways before them: and shalt be removed into all the kingdoms of the earth.

²⁶And thy carcase shall be meat unto all fowls of the air, and unto the beasts of the earth, and no man shall fray them away.

²⁷The LORD will smite thee with the botch of Egypt, and with the emerods, and with the scab, and with the itch, whereof thou canst not be healed.

²⁸The LORD shall smite thee with madness, and blindness, and astonishment of heart:

²⁹And thou shalt grope at noonday, as the blind gropeth in darkness, and thou shalt not prosper in thy ways: and thou shalt be only oppressed and spoiled evermore, and no man shall save thee.

³⁰Thou shalt betroth a wife, and another man shall lie with her: thou shalt build an house, and thou shalt not dwell therein: thou shalt plant a vineyard, and shalt not gather the grapes thereof.

³¹Thine ox shall be slain before thine eyes, and thou shalt not eat thereof: thine ass shall be violently taken away from before thy face, and shall not be restored to thee: thy sheep shall be given unto thine enemies, and thou shalt have none to rescue them.

³²Thy sons and thy daughters shall be given unto another people, and thine eyes shall look, and fail with longing for them all the day long; and there shall be no might in thine hand.

³³The fruit of thy land, and all thy labours, shall a nation which thou knowest not eat up; and thou shalt be only oppressed and crushed alway:

³⁴So that thou shalt be mad for the sight of thine eyes which thou shalt see.

³⁵The LORD shall smite thee in the knees, and in the legs, with a sore botch that cannot be healed, from the sole of thy foot unto the top of thy head.

³⁶The LORD shall bring thee, and thy king which thou shalt set over thee, unto a nation which neither thou nor thy fathers have known;

and there shalt thou serve other gods, wood and stone.

³⁷And thou shalt become an astonishment, a proverb, and a byword, among all nations whither the LORD shall lead thee.

³⁸Thou shalt carry much seed out into the field, and shalt gather but little in; for the locust shall consume it.

³⁹Thou shalt plant vineyards, and dress them, but shalt neither drink of the wine, nor gather the grapes; for the worms shall eat them.

⁴⁰Thou shalt have olive trees throughout all thy coasts, but thou shalt not anoint thyself with the oil; for thine olive shall cast his fruit.

⁴¹Thou shalt beget sons and daughters, but thou shalt not enjoy them; for they shall go into captivity.

⁴²All thy trees and fruit of thy land shall the locust consume.

⁴³The stranger that is within thee shall get up above thee very high; and thou shalt come down very low.

⁴⁴He shall lend to thee, and thou shalt not lend to him: he shall be the head, and thou shalt be the tail.

⁴⁵Moreover all these curses shall come upon thee, and shall pursue thee, and overtake thee, till thou be destroyed; because thou hearkenedst not unto the voice of the LORD thy God, to keep his commandments and his statutes which he commanded thee:

⁴⁶And they shall be upon thee for a sign and for a wonder, and upon thy seed for ever.

⁴⁷Because thou servedst not the LORD thy God with joyfulness, and with gladness of heart, for the abundance of all things;

⁴⁸Therefore shalt thou serve thine enemies which the LORD shall send against thee, in hunger, and in thirst, and in nakedness, and in want of all things: and he shall put a yoke of iron upon thy neck, until he have destroyed thee.

⁴⁹The LORD shall bring a nation against thee from far, from the end of the earth, as swift as the eagle flieth; a nation whose tongue thou shalt not understand;

⁵⁰A nation of fierce countenance, which shall not regard the person of the old, nor shew favour to the young:

⁵¹And he shall eat the fruit of thy cattle, and the fruit of thy land, until thou be destroyed: which also shall not leave thee either corn, wine, or oil, or the increase of thy kine, or flocks of thy sheep, until he have destroyed thee.

⁵²And he shall besiege thee in all thy gates, until thy high and fenced walls come down, wherein thou trustedst, throughout all thy land: and he shall besiege thee in all thy gates throughout all thy land, which the LORD thy God hath given thee.

⁵³And thou shalt eat the fruit of thine own body, the flesh of thy sons and of thy daughters, which the LORD thy God hath given thee, in the siege, and in the straitness, wherewith thine enemies shall distress thee:

⁵⁴So that the man that is tender among you, and very delicate, his eye shall be evil toward his brother, and toward the wife of his bosom, and toward the remnant of his children which he shall leave:

⁵⁵So that he will not give to any of them of the flesh of his children whom he shall eat: because he hath nothing left him in the siege, and in the straitness, wherewith thine enemies shall distress thee in all thy gates.

⁵⁶The tender and delicate woman among you, which would not adventure to set the sole of her foot upon the ground for delicateness and tenderness, her eye shall be evil toward the husband of her bosom, and toward her son, and toward her daughter,

⁵⁷And toward her young one that cometh out from between her feet, and toward her children which she shall bear: for she shall eat them for want of all things secretly in the siege and straitness, wherewith thine enemy shall distress thee in thy gates.

⁵⁸If thou wilt not observe to do all the words of this law that are written in this book, that thou mayest fear this glorious and fearful name, THE LORD THY GOD;

⁵⁹Then the LORD will make thy plagues wonderful, and the plagues of thy seed, even great plagues, and of long continuance, and sore sicknesses, and of long continuance.

⁶⁰Moreover he will bring upon thee all the diseases of Egypt, which thou wast afraid of; and they shall cleave unto thee.

⁶¹Also every sickness, and every plague, which is not written in the book of this law, them will the LORD bring upon thee, until thou be destroyed.

⁶²And ye shall be left few in number, whereas ye were as the stars of heaven for multitude; because thou wouldest not obey the voice of the LORD thy God.

⁶³And it shall come to pass, that as the LORD rejoiced over you to do you good, and to multiply you; so the LORD will rejoice over you to destroy you, and to bring you to nought; and ye shall be plucked from off the land whither thou goest to possess it.

⁶⁴And the LORD shall scatter thee among all people, from the one end of the earth even unto the other; and there thou shalt serve

other gods, which neither thou nor thy fathers have known, even wood and stone.

⁶⁵And among these nations shalt thou find no ease, neither shall the sole of thy foot have rest: but the LORD shall give thee there a trembling heart, and failing of eyes, and sorrow of mind:

⁶⁶And thy life shall hang in doubt before thee; and thou shalt fear day and night, and shalt have none assurance of thy life:

⁶⁷In the morning thou shalt say, Would God it were even! and at even thou shalt say, Would God it were morning! for the fear of thine heart wherewith thou shalt fear, and for the sight of thine eyes which thou shalt see.

⁶⁸And the LORD shall bring thee into Egypt again with ships, by the way whereof I spake unto thee, Thou shalt see it no more again: and there ye shall be sold unto your enemies for bondmen and bondwomen, and no man shall buy you.

CHAPTER 29

¹These are the words of the covenant, which the LORD commanded Moses to make with the children of Israel in the land of Moab, beside the covenant which he made with them in Horeb.

²And Moses called unto all Israel, and said unto them, Ye have seen all that the LORD did before your eyes in the land of Egypt unto Pharaoh, and unto all his servants, and unto all his land;

³The great temptations which thine eyes have seen, the signs, and those great miracles:

⁴Yet the LORD hath not given you an heart to perceive, and eyes to see, and ears to hear, unto this day.

⁵And I have led you forty years in the wilderness: your clothes are not waxen old upon you, and thy shoe is not waxen old upon thy foot.

⁶Ye have not eaten bread, neither have ye drunk wine or strong drink: that ye might know that I am the LORD your God.

⁷And when ye came unto this place, Sihon the king of Heshbon, and Og the king of Bashan, came out against us unto battle, and we smote them:

⁸And we took their land, and gave it for an inheritance unto the Reubenites, and to the Gadites, and to the half tribe of Manasseh.

⁹Keep therefore the words of this covenant, and do them, that ye may prosper in all that ye do.

¹⁰Ye stand this day all of you before the LORD your God; your

captains of your tribes, your elders, and your officers, with all the men of Israel,

¹¹Your little ones, your wives, and thy stranger that is in thy camp, from the hewer of thy wood unto the drawer of thy water:

¹²That thou shouldest enter into covenant with the LORD thy God, and into his oath, which the LORD thy God maketh with thee this day:

¹³That he may establish thee to day for a people unto himself, and that he may be unto thee a God, as he hath said unto thee, and as he hath sworn unto thy fathers, to Abraham, to Isaac, and to Jacob.

¹⁴Neither with you only do I make this covenant and this oath;

¹⁵But with him that standeth here with us this day before the LORD our God, and also with him that is not here with us this day:

¹⁶(For ye know how we have dwelt in the land of Egypt; and how we came through the nations which ye passed by;

¹⁷And ye have seen their abominations, and their idols, wood and stone, silver and gold, which were among them:)

¹⁸Lest there should be among you man, or woman, or family, or tribe, whose heart turneth away this day from the LORD our God, to go and serve the gods of these nations; lest there should be among you a root that beareth gall and wormwood;

¹⁹And it come to pass, when he heareth the words of this curse, that he bless himself in his heart, saying, I shall have peace, though I walk in the imagination of mine heart, to add drunkenness to thirst:

²⁰The LORD will not spare him, but then the anger of the LORD and his jealousy shall smoke against that man, and all the curses that are written in this book shall lie upon him, and the LORD shall blot out his name from under heaven.

²¹And the LORD shall separate him unto evil out of all the tribes of Israel, according to all the curses of the covenant that are written in this book of the law:

²²So that the generation to come of your children that shall rise up after you, and the stranger that shall come from a far land, shall say, when they see the plagues of that land, and the sicknesses which the LORD hath laid upon it;

²³And that the whole land thereof is brimstone, and salt, and burning, that it is not sown, nor beareth, nor any grass groweth therein, like the overthrow of Sodom, and Gomorrah, Admah, and Zeboim, which the LORD overthrew in his anger, and in his wrath:

²⁴Even all nations shall say, Wherefore hath the LORD done thus unto this land? what meaneth the heat of this great anger?

²⁵Then men shall say, Because they have forsaken the covenant of the LORD God of their fathers, which he made with them when he brought them forth out of the land of Egypt:

²⁶For they went and served other gods, and worshipped them, gods whom they knew not, and whom he had not given unto them:

²⁷And the anger of the LORD was kindled against this land, to bring upon it all the curses that are written in this book:

²⁸And the LORD rooted them out of their land in anger, and in wrath, and in great indignation, and cast them into another land, as it is this day.

²⁹The secret things belong unto the LORD our God: but those things which are revealed belong unto us and to our children for ever, that we may do all the words of this law.

CHAPTER 30

¹And it shall come to pass, when all these things are come upon thee, the blessing and the curse, which I have set before thee, and thou shalt call them to mind among all the nations, whither the LORD thy God hath driven thee,

²And shalt return unto the LORD thy God, and shalt obey his voice according to all that I command thee this day, thou and thy children, with all thine heart, and with all thy soul;

³That then the LORD thy God will turn thy captivity, and have compassion upon thee, and will return and gather thee from all the nations, whither the LORD thy God hath scattered thee.

⁴If any of thine be driven out unto the outmost parts of heaven, from thence will the LORD thy God gather thee, and from thence will he fetch thee:

⁵And the LORD thy God will bring thee into the land which thy fathers possessed, and thou shalt possess it; and he will do thee good, and multiply thee above thy fathers.

⁶And the LORD thy God will circumcise thine heart, and the heart of thy seed, to love the LORD thy God with all thine heart, and with all thy soul, that thou mayest live.

⁷And the LORD thy God will put all these curses upon thine enemies, and on them that hate thee, which persecuted thee.

⁸And thou shalt return and obey the voice of the LORD, and do all his commandments which I command thee this day.

⁹And the LORD thy God will make thee plenteous in every work of thine hand, in the fruit of thy body, and in the fruit of thy cattle, and in the fruit of thy land, for good: for the LORD will again rejoice over thee for good, as he rejoiced over thy fathers:

¹⁰If thou shalt hearken unto the voice of the LORD thy God, to keep his commandments and his statutes which are written in this book of the law, and if thou turn unto the LORD thy God with all thine heart, and with all thy soul.

¹¹For this commandment which I command thee this day, it is not hidden from thee, neither is it far off.

¹²It is not in heaven, that thou shouldest say, Who shall go up for us to heaven, and bring it unto us, that we may hear it, and do it?

¹³Neither is it beyond the sea, that thou shouldest say, Who shall go over the sea for us, and bring it unto us, that we may hear it, and do it?

¹⁴But the word is very nigh unto thee, in thy mouth, and in thy heart, that thou mayest do it.

¹⁵See, I have set before thee this day life and good, and death and evil;

¹⁶In that I command thee this day to love the LORD thy God, to walk in his ways, and to keep his commandments and his statutes and his judgments, that thou mayest live and multiply: and the LORD thy God shall bless thee in the land whither thou goest to possess it.

¹⁷But if thine heart turn away, so that thou wilt not hear, but shalt be drawn away, and worship other gods, and serve them;

¹⁸I denounce unto you this day, that ye shall surely perish, and that ye shall not prolong your days upon the land, whither thou passest over Jordan to go to possess it.

¹⁹I call heaven and earth to record this day against you, that I have set before you life and death, blessing and cursing: therefore choose life, that both thou and thy seed may live.

²⁰That thou mayest love the LORD thy God, and that thou mayest obey his voice, and that thou mayest cleave unto him: for he is thy life, and the length of thy days: that thou mayest dwell in the land which the LORD sware unto thy fathers, to Abraham, to Isaac, and to Jacob, to give them.

CHAPTER 31

¹And Moses went and spake these words unto all Israel.

²And he said unto them, I am an hundred and twenty years old this day; I can no more go out and come in: also the LORD hath said unto me, Thou shalt not go over this Jordan.

³The LORD thy God, he will go over before thee, and he will destroy these nations from before thee, and thou shalt possess them: and Joshua, he shall go over before thee, as the LORD hath said.

⁴And the LORD shall do unto them as he did to Sihon and to Og, kings of the Amorites, and unto the land of them, whom he destroyed.

⁵And the LORD shall give them up before your face, that ye may do unto them according unto all the commandments which I have commanded you.

⁶Be strong and of a good courage, fear not, nor be afraid of them: for the LORD thy God, he it is that doth go with thee; he will not fail thee, nor forsake thee.

⁷And Moses called unto Joshua, and said unto him in the sight of all Israel, Be strong and of a good courage: for thou must go with this people unto the land which the LORD hath sworn unto their fathers to give them; and thou shalt cause them to inherit it.

⁸And the LORD, he it is that doth go before thee; he will be with thee, he will not fail thee, neither forsake thee: fear not, neither be dismayed.

⁹And Moses wrote this law, and delivered it unto the priests the sons of Levi, which bare the ark of the covenant of the LORD, and unto all the elders of Israel.

¹⁰And Moses commanded them, saying, At the end of every seven years, in the solemnity of the year of release, in the feast of tabernacles,

¹¹When all Israel is come to appear before the LORD thy God in the place which he shall choose, thou shalt read this law before all Israel in their hearing.

¹²Gather the people together, men and women, and children, and thy stranger that is within thy gates, that they may hear, and that they may learn, and fear the LORD your God, and observe to do all the words of this law:

¹³And that their children, which have not known any thing, may hear, and learn to fear the LORD your God, as long as ye live in the land whither ye go over Jordan to possess it.

¹⁴And the LORD said unto Moses, Behold, thy days approach

that thou must die: call Joshua, and present yourselves in the tabernacle of the congregation, that I may give him a charge. And Moses and Joshua went, and presented themselves in the tabernacle of the congregation.

¹⁵ And the LORD appeared in the tabernacle in a pillar of a cloud: and the pillar of the cloud stood over the door of the tabernacle.

¹⁶ And the LORD said unto Moses, Behold, thou shalt sleep with thy fathers; and this people will rise up, and go a whoring after the gods of the strangers of the land, whither they go to be among them, and will forsake me, and break my covenant which I have made with them.

¹⁷ Then my anger shall be kindled against them in that day, and I will forsake them, and I will hide my face from them, and they shall be devoured, and many evils and troubles shall befall them; so that they will say in that day, Are not these evils come upon us, because our God is not among us?

¹⁸ And I will surely hide my face in that day for all the evils which they shall have wrought, in that they are turned unto other gods.

¹⁹ Now therefore write ye this song for you, and teach it the children of Israel: put it in their mouths, that this song may be a witness for me against the children of Israel.

²⁰ For when I shall have brought them into the land which I sware unto their fathers, that floweth with milk and honey; and they shall have eaten and filled themselves, and waxen fat; then will they turn unto other gods, and serve them, and provoke me, and break my covenant.

²¹ And it shall come to pass, when many evils and troubles are befallen them, that this song shall testify against them as a witness; for it shall not be forgotten out of the mouths of their seed: for I know their imagination which they go about, even now, before I have brought them into the land which I sware.

²² Moses therefore wrote this song the same day, and taught it the children of Israel.

²³ And he gave Joshua the son of Nun a charge, and said, Be strong and of a good courage: for thou shalt bring the children of Israel into the land which I sware unto them: and I will be with thee.

²⁴ And it came to pass, when Moses had made an end of writing the words of this law in a book, until they were finished,

²⁵ That Moses commanded the Levites, which bare the ark of the covenant of the LORD, saying,

²⁶ Take this book of the law, and put it in the side of the ark of the covenant of the LORD your God,

that it may be there for a witness against thee.

²⁷For I know thy rebellion, and thy stiff neck: behold, while I am yet alive with you this day, ye have been rebellious against the LORD; and how much more after my death?

²⁸Gather unto me all the elders of your tribes, and your officers, that I may speak these words in their ears, and call heaven and earth to record against them.

²⁹For I know that after my death ye will utterly corrupt yourselves, and turn aside from the way which I have commanded you; and evil will befall you in the latter days; because ye will do evil in the sight of the LORD, to provoke him to anger through the work of your hands.

³⁰And Moses spake in the ears of all the congregation of Israel the words of this song, until they were ended.

CHAPTER 32

¹Give ear, O ye heavens, and I will speak; and hear, O earth, the words of my mouth.

²My doctrine shall drop as the rain, my speech shall distil as the dew, as the small rain upon the tender herb, and as the showers upon the grass:

³Because I will publish the name of the LORD: ascribe ye greatness unto our God.

⁴He is the Rock, his work is perfect: for all his ways are judgment: a God of truth and without iniquity, just and right is he.

⁵They have corrupted themselves, their spot is not the spot of his children: they are a perverse and crooked generation.

⁶Do ye thus requite the LORD, O foolish people and unwise? is not he thy father that hath bought thee? hath he not made thee, and established thee?

⁷Remember the days of old, consider the years of many generations: ask thy father, and he will shew thee; thy elders, and they will tell thee.

⁸When the Most High divided to the nations their inheritance, when he separated the sons of Adam, he set the bounds of the people according to the number of the children of Israel.

⁹For the LORD's portion is his people; Jacob is the lot of his inheritance.

¹⁰He found him in a desert land, and in the waste howling wilderness; he led him about, he instructed him, he kept him as the apple of his eye.

¹¹As an eagle stirreth up her nest, fluttereth over her young, spreadeth

abroad her wings, taketh them, beareth them on her wings:

¹²So the LORD alone did lead him, and there was no strange god with him.

¹³He made him ride on the high places of the earth, that he might eat the increase of the fields; and he made him to suck honey out of the rock, and oil out of the flinty rock;

¹⁴Butter of kine, and milk of sheep, with fat of lambs, and rams of the breed of Bashan, and goats, with the fat of kidneys of wheat; and thou didst drink the pure blood of the grape.

¹⁵But Jeshurun waxed fat, and kicked: thou art waxen fat, thou art grown thick, thou art covered with fatness; then he forsook God which made him, and lightly esteemed the Rock of his salvation.

¹⁶They provoked him to jealousy with strange gods, with abominations provoked they him to anger.

¹⁷They sacrificed unto devils, not to God; to gods whom they knew not, to new gods that came newly up, whom your fathers feared not.

¹⁸Of the Rock that begat thee thou art unmindful, and hast forgotten God that formed thee.

¹⁹And when the LORD saw it, he abhorred them, because of the provoking of his sons, and of his daughters.

²⁰And he said, I will hide my face from them, I will see what their end shall be: for they are a very froward generation, children in whom is no faith.

²¹They have moved me to jealousy with that which is not God; they have provoked me to anger with their vanities: and I will move them to jealousy with those which are not a people; I will provoke them to anger with a foolish nation.

²²For a fire is kindled in mine anger, and shall burn unto the lowest hell, and shall consume the earth with her increase, and set on fire the foundations of the mountains.

²³I will heap mischiefs upon them; I will spend mine arrows upon them.

²⁴They shall be burnt with hunger, and devoured with burning heat, and with bitter destruction: I will also send the teeth of beasts upon them, with the poison of serpents of the dust.

²⁵The sword without, and terror within, shall destroy both the young man and the virgin, the suckling also with the man of gray hairs.

²⁶I said, I would scatter them into corners, I would make the remembrance of them to cease from among men:

²⁷Were it not that I feared the wrath of the enemy, lest their adversaries should behave themselves strangely, and lest they should say, Our hand is high, and the LORD hath not done all this.

²⁸For they are a nation void of counsel, neither is there any understanding in them.

²⁹O that they were wise, that they understood this, that they would consider their latter end!

³⁰How should one chase a thousand, and two put ten thousand to flight, except their Rock had sold them, and the LORD had shut them up?

³¹For their rock is not as our Rock, even our enemies themselves being judges.

³²For their vine is of the vine of Sodom, and of the fields of Gomorrah: their grapes are grapes of gall, their clusters are bitter:

³³Their wine is the poison of dragons, and the cruel venom of asps.

³⁴Is not this laid up in store with me, and sealed up among my treasures?

³⁵To me belongeth vengeance and recompence; their foot shall slide in due time: for the day of their calamity is at hand, and the things that shall come upon them make haste.

³⁶For the LORD shall judge his people, and repent himself for his servants, when he seeth that their power is gone, and there is none shut up, or left.

³⁷And he shall say, Where are their gods, their rock in whom they trusted,

³⁸Which did eat the fat of their sacrifices, and drank the wine of their drink offerings? let them rise up and help you, and be your protection.

³⁹See now that I, even I, am he, and there is no god with me: I kill, and I make alive; I wound, and I heal: neither is there any that can deliver out of my hand.

⁴⁰For I lift up my hand to heaven, and say, I live for ever.

⁴¹If I whet my glittering sword, and mine hand take hold on judgment; I will render vengeance to mine enemies, and will reward them that hate me.

⁴²I will make mine arrows drunk with blood, and my sword shall devour flesh; and that with the blood of the slain and of the captives, from the beginning of revenges upon the enemy.

⁴³Rejoice, O ye nations, with his people: for he will avenge the blood of his servants, and will render vengeance to his adversaries, and will be merciful unto his land, and to his people.

⁴⁴And Moses came and spake all the words of this song in the ears of the people, he, and Hoshea the son of Nun.

⁴⁵And Moses made an end of speaking all these words to all Israel:

⁴⁶And he said unto them, Set your hearts unto all the words which I testify among you this day, which ye shall command your children to observe to do, all the words of this law.

⁴⁷For it is not a vain thing for you; because it is your life: and through this thing ye shall prolong your days in the land, whither ye go over Jordan to possess it.

⁴⁸And the LORD spake unto Moses that selfsame day, saying,

⁴⁹Get thee up into this mountain Abarim, unto mount Nebo, which is in the land of Moab, that is over against Jericho; and behold the land of Canaan, which I give unto the children of Israel for a possession:

⁵⁰And die in the mount whither thou goest up, and be gathered unto thy people; as Aaron thy brother died in mount Hor, and was gathered unto his people:

⁵¹Because ye trespassed against me among the children of Israel at the waters of Meribah-Kadesh, in the wilderness of Zin; because ye sanctified me not in the midst of the children of Israel.

⁵²Yet thou shalt see the land before thee; but thou shalt not go thither unto the land which I give the children of Israel.

CHAPTER 33

¹And this is the blessing, wherewith Moses the man of God blessed the children of Israel before his death.

²And he said, The LORD came from Sinai, and rose up from Seir unto them; he shined forth from mount Paran, and he came with ten thousands of saints: from his right hand went a fiery law for them.

³Yea, he loved the people; all his saints are in thy hand: and they sat down at thy feet; every one shall receive of thy words.

⁴Moses commanded us a law, even the inheritance of the congregation of Jacob.

⁵And he was king in Jeshurun, when the heads of the people and the tribes of Israel were gathered together.

⁶Let Reuben live, and not die; and let not his men be few.

⁷And this is the blessing of Judah: and he said, Hear, LORD, the voice of Judah, and bring him unto his people: let his hands be sufficient

for him; and be thou an help to him from his enemies.

⁸And of Levi he said, Let thy Thummim and thy Urim be with thy holy one, whom thou didst prove at Massah, and with whom thou didst strive at the waters of Meribah;

⁹Who said unto his father and to his mother, I have not seen him; neither did he acknowledge his brethren, nor knew his own children: for they have observed thy word, and kept thy covenant.

¹⁰They shall teach Jacob thy judgments, and Israel thy law: they shall put incense before thee, and whole burnt sacrifice upon thine altar.

¹¹Bless, LORD, his substance, and accept the work of his hands; smite through the loins of them that rise against him, and of them that hate him, that they rise not again.

¹²And of Ben-jamin he said, The beloved of the LORD shall dwell in safety by him; and the Lord shall cover him all the day long, and he shall dwell between his shoulders.

¹³And of Joseph he said, Blessed of the LORD be his land, for the precious things of heaven, for the dew, and for the deep that coucheth beneath,

¹⁴And for the precious fruits brought forth by the sun, and for the precious things put forth by the moon,

¹⁵And for the chief things of the ancient mountains, and for the precious things of the lasting hills,

¹⁶And for the precious things of the earth and fulness thereof, and for the good will of him that dwelt in the bush: let the blessing come upon the head of Joseph, and upon the top of the head of him that was separated from his brethren.

¹⁷His glory is like the firstling of his bullock, and his horns are like the horns of unicorns: with them he shall push the people together to the ends of the earth: and they are the ten thousands of Ephraim, and they are the thousands of Manasseh.

¹⁸And of Zebulun he said, Rejoice, Zebulun, in thy going out; and, Issachar, in thy tents.

¹⁹They shall call the people unto the mountain; there they shall offer sacrifices of righteousness: for they shall suck of the abundance of the seas, and of treasures hid in the sand.

²⁰And of Gad he said, Blessed be he that enlargeth Gad: he dwelleth as a lion, and teareth the arm with the crown of the head.

²¹And he provided the first part for himself, because there, in a portion of the lawgiver, was he seated; and he came with the heads of the people, he executed

the justice of the LORD, and his judgments with Israel.

²²And of Dan he said, Dan is a lion's whelp: he shall leap from Bashan.

²³And of Naphtali he said, O Naphtali, satisfied with favour, and full with the blessing of the LORD: possess thou the west and the south.

²⁴And of Asher he said, Let Asher be blessed with children; let him be acceptable to his brethren, and let him dip his foot in oil.

²⁵Thy shoes shall be iron and brass; and as thy days, so shall thy strength be.

²⁶There is none like unto the God of Jeshurun, who rideth upon the heaven in thy help, and in his excellency on the sky.

²⁷The eternal God is thy refuge, and underneath are the everlasting arms: and he shall thrust out the enemy from before thee; and shall say, Destroy them.

²⁸Israel then shall dwell in safety alone: the fountain of Jacob shall be upon a land of corn and wine; also his heavens shall drop down dew.

²⁹Happy art thou, O Israel: who is like unto thee, O people saved by the LORD, the shield of thy help, and who is the sword of thy excellency! and thine enemies shall be found liars unto thee; and thou shalt tread upon their high places.

CHAPTER 34

¹And Moses went up from the plains of Moab unto the mountain of Nebo, to the top of Pisgah, that is over against Jericho. And the LORD shewed him all the land of Gilead, unto Dan,

²And all Naphtali, and the land of Ephraim, and Manasseh, and all the land of Judah, unto the utmost sea,

³And the south, and the plain of the valley of Jericho, the city of palm trees, unto Zoar.

⁴And the LORD said unto him, This is the land which I sware unto Abraham, unto Isaac, and unto Jacob, saying, I will give it unto thy seed: I have caused thee to see it with thine eyes, but thou shalt not go over thither.

⁵So Moses the servant of the LORD died there in the land of Moab, according to the word of the LORD.

⁶And he buried him in a valley in the land of Moab, over against Beth-peor: but no man knoweth of his sepulchre unto this day.

⁷And Moses was an hundred and twenty years old when he died: his eye was not dim, nor his natural force abated.

⁸And the children of Israel wept for Moses in the plains of Moab

thirty days: so the days of weeping and mourning for Moses were ended.

⁹And Joshua the son of Nun was full of the spirit of wisdom; for Moses had laid his hands upon him: and the children of Israel hearkened unto him, and did as the LORD commanded Moses.

¹⁰And there arose not a prophet since in Israel like unto Moses, whom the LORD knew face to face,

¹¹In all the signs and the wonders, which the LORD sent him to do in the land of Egypt to Pharaoh, and to all his servants, and to all his land,

¹²And in all that mighty hand, and in all the great terror which Moses shewed in the sight of all Israel.